BEST OF THE JOURNALS IN
RHETORIC AND COMPOSITION

Best of the Journals in Rhetoric and Composition
SERIES EDITORS: STEVE PARKS, JESSICA PAUSZEK, KRISTI GIRDHARRY, AND CHARLES LESH

The Best of the Journals in Rhetoric and Composition series represents an attempt to foster a nationwide conversation—beginning with journal editors, but expanding to teachers, scholars and workers across the discipline of Rhetoric and Composition—to select essays that showcase the innovative and transformative work now being published in the field's journals. Representing both print and digital journals in the field, the essays in each edition represent a snapshot of the traditional and emergent conversations occurring in our field—from classroom practice to writing in global and digital contexts, from border rhetorics to social justice research. Together, the essays provide readers with a rich understanding of the present and future direction of the field.

Essays included in the series undergo a rigorous review process. First, all essays must have already crossed the threshold to be published in an academic journal in the field. Then, out of all the essays published by a journal, the editor can only select two essays. Next, the series editors create reading groups across the country. These groups feature full-time faculty, adjunct faculty, and graduate students who teach in a range of institutions. In this way, all the nominated essays are assessed and ranked for how they speak to the interests of all those who work in our field—a review process that is unique to the series. The series editors, plus one guest editor, then assemble a final selection of essays that have the strongest support from the reading groups for inclusion in a particular volume.

In this way, the Best of the Journals in Rhetoric and Composition series includes the only publications in the field that can truly claim to represent the collective insight of students, teachers, and scholars into the pressing issues of the current moment. For this reason, authors selected for inclusion are celebrated at their home institutions and journals actively seek recognition for their work. The series provides the broadest conception of scholarship in our field and so each volume can find a home in introductory graduate courses and advanced undergraduate courses everywhere.

BEST OF THE JOURNALS IN RHETORIC AND COMPOSITION 2019

Edited by Jessica Pauszek, Kristi Girdharry, Charles Lesh, David Blakesley, and Steve Parks

Parlor Press
Anderson, South Carolina
www.parlorpress.com

Parlor Press LLC, Anderson, South Carolina, USA

© 2020 by Parlor Press. Individual essays in this book have been reprinted with permission of the respective copyright owners.
All rights reserved.
Printed in the United States of America

S A N: 2 5 4 - 8 8 7 9

ISSN 2327-4778 (print)
ISSN 2327-4786 (online)

978-1-64317-064-0 (paperback)
(978-1-64317-065-7 (PDF)
(978-1-64317-066-4 (ePub)

1 2 3 4 5

Cover design by David Blakesley.
Printed on acid-free paper.

Parlor Press, LLC is an independent publisher of scholarly and trade titles in print and multimedia formats. This book is available in paper and digital formats from Parlor Press on the World Wide Web at http://www.parlorpress.com or through online and brick-and-mortar bookstores. For submission information or to find out about Parlor Press publications, write to Parlor Press, 3015 Brackenberry Drive, Anderson, South Carolina, 29621, or email editor@parlorpress.com.

Contents

Introduction *vii*
  Amber Simpson and Kristi Girdharry

Part I : Power and Politics

COMMUNITY LITERACY JOURNAL
  #StayWoke: The Language and Literacies of the #BlackLivesMatter Movement *3*
  Elaine Richardson and Alice Ragland

RHETORIC SOCIETY QUARTERLY
  "Tweet Me Your First Assaults": Writing Shame and the Rhetorical Work of #NotOkay *39*
  Shari J. Stenberg

LITERACY IN COMPOSITION STUDIES
  Toward a Theory and Pedagogy of Rhetorical Vulnerability *69*
  David Riche

Part II: Pedagogical Concerns and Meaningful Learning

JOURNAL OF TEACHING WRITING
  Activating the "Fund of Attention" to Empower Student Peer Review *98*
  Eileen Kogl Camfield, Lara Killick, and Ruth Lewis

PEDAGOGY
  "Real Research" or "Just for a Grade"? Ethnography, Ethics, and Engagement in the Undergraduate Writing Studies Classroom *122*
  Elizabeth G. Allan

WPA: WRITING PROGRAM ADMINISTRATION
  Inez in Transition: Using Case Study to Explore the Experiences of Underrepresented Students in First-Year Composition *161*
  Christina Saidy

Part III: Promoting Linguistic Diversity and Universal Access

TEACHING ENGLISH IN THE TWO-YEAR COLLEGE
A Critical Time for Reform: Empowering Interventions in a Precarious Landscape   *185*
  Anthony Warnke and Kirsten Higgins

RESEARCH IN THE TEACHING OF ENGLISH
Translanguaging, Coloniality, and English Classrooms: An Exploration of Two Bicoastal Urban Classrooms   *219*
  Cati V. de los Ríos and Kate Seltzer

WRITING CENTER JOURNAL
Unmaking Gringo-Centers   *251*
  Romeo García

JOURNAL OF BASIC WRITING
Cultivating Places and People at the Center: Cross-Pollinating Literacies on a Rural Campus   *285*
  Wendy Pfrenger

RHETORIC REVIEW
Integral Captions and Subtitles: Designing a Space for Embodied Rhetorics and Visual Access   *326*
  Janine Butler

Part IV: Innovative Research Methodologies

COLLEGE COMPOSITION AND COMMUNICATION
Writing in Social Worlds: An Argument for Researching Composing Processes   *353*
  Pamela Takayoshi

REFLECTIONS
Research as Care: A Shared Ownership Approach to Rhetorical Research in Trauma Communities   *386*
  Maria Novotny and John T. Gagnon

WRITING ON THE EDGE
Fieldwork with a Five-Year-Old: A Summative Report   *418*
  Kate Vieira

About the Authors   *433*

Introduction

Amber Simpson and Kristi Girdharry

In this collection, and in collections like it, we reconstruct a moment. In the time surrounding the original publication dates of these articles, we witnessed and bore witness to events that shook us personally and motivated us to act with our bodies and our pens. We marched after gun violence stole innocent lives at places like Marjory Stoneman Douglas High School in Parkland, Florida and the Tree of Life Synagogue in Pittsburgh, Pennsylvania. We listened to brave women who testified against their sexual abusers. We raged against children being torn from their families at the border.

Because of these collective experiences, it is no surprise that this edition includes discussions of vulnerability, of politics and power, of pedagogy and protest. It in, our colleagues show close attention to classrooms and communities by attending to how power and vulnerability are entwined and how that entwinement may be mobilized for the betterment of communities and classrooms. As you read through the selections, you will come across articles on pedagogy, diversity and access, cultural climates, political issues, and research methodologies. In our reconstruction of this historical moment by and through these exemplary texts, we also see the ways that the moment impacts us now—the ways that we are *still in* that moment. We hope that you will read these texts with that moment in mind.

Power and Politics

Several authors in this collection consider power and politics directly, namely in aims of making sense of the cultural and political moment. In "#StayWoke: The Language and Literacies of the #BlackLivesMatter Movement," Elaine Richardson and Alice Ragland examine "the language, literacies, communicative, and rhetorical practices of the Black Lives Matter movement" (30). By situating the rhetorical work of BLM within Black and African-American language traditions and histories, Richardson and Ragland examine how activists are "performing unapologetic Blackness, seeking to disrupt hegemonic race, gender, sexuality, class oppression, and other social inequalities for the greater good of all Black lives" (52). The rhetorical practices examined in this article are complex, multiple, and diverse, and Richardson and Ragland provide an urgent rhetorical reading and accounting of the force of BLM in digital and non-digital spaces.

In "'Tweet Me Your First Assaults': Writing Shame and the Rhetorical Work of #NotOkay," Shari J. Stenberg collected and analyzed tweets from the "#NotOkay" thread focusing on time periods right before and right after the election of Donald Trump to explore how women "write shame" a phrase that Stenberg pulls from Elspeth Probyn's "writing shame." Stenberg considers the tweets that erupted following the October 2016 release of the infamous Access Hollywood tapes (featuring a conversation with the then presidential candidate Donald Trump) and Kelly Oxford's subsequent invitation to "Tweet me your first assaults." Stenberg also explores the use of #NotOkay directly following the presidential election in November 2016. Notably, Stenberg explores how #NotOkay became a counterpublic, which "serve[d] as an invitational, collective space for survivors" as well "offer[ed] insight into the conditions that allow women to speak of shame and the rhetorical strategies that help to transform it."

In "Toward a Theory and Pedagogy of Rhetorical Vulnerability," David Riche draws on Richard Marback to discuss the ways we are exposed to the effects and affects of others through language. He explains the concepts of "rhetorical agency" and "rhetorical vulnerability" in detail in order to elucidate a pedagogical and theoretical approach toward rhetorical vulnerability. This approach requires rhetors to take responsibility for the potential violence of their communication, as we see in online trolling so ubiquitous today. The political moment we are in gives Riche exigence, which he takes advantage of in his text, but there is a clear application of this thinking beyond fake news and Twitter trolls, especially as communication continues (and perhaps increases) to take place online. Using a theoretical framework of rhetorical vulnerability, Riche offers a listening-based approach to feedback on student work.

Pedagogical Concerns and Meaningful Learning

Some selections in this collection take a closer look at pedagogical concerns and prioritize creating moments of meaningful learning for students that have the potential to impact writing beyond the classroom.

By prompting students to approach writing and research in a way that broadens their view of writing, these authors urge students to consider more distributed audiences and continuation of discourses.

In "Activating the 'Fund of Attention' to Empower Student Peer Review," Eileen Kogl Camfield, Lara Killick, and Ruth Lewis respond to the widespread dilemma of preparing students for effective peer review. They showcase their pilot study of their "Fund of Attention" model, which utilizes reader-based writing techniques wherein writers acknowledge that their readers' attention is finite. Students were asked to annotate texts to indicate moments in which their attention was held or lost. This model utilizes imagery as opposed to additional terms and writing techniques for students to remember and instead allows students to recognize rhetorical moments within their own writing. Camfield, Killick, and Lewis's Fund of Attention model has implications for teaching transfer across the curriculum, but it also more broadly asks writers to tend to the reciprocal relationship between writers and audiences.

Elizabeth G. Allan, too, asks students to develop a more nuanced view of writing projects in her text "'Real Research' or 'Just for a Grade'?" Allan presents a case study of an undergraduate writing class wherein she asks students to obtain IRB-approval for conducting microethnographies in an effort to have students see their work as "real" research rather than obligatory work for a class grade. Allan concludes by suggesting pedagogical moves to make research seem "real" for students and of benefit beyond themselves—to a field or community at large (including continuing ethical research methods, inviting community members to hear presentations, etc.). Allan's research has implications for making moments of significant learning for students and helping them to contribute to discourse communities.

Christina Saidy's "Inez in Transition" also addresses ways of facilitating meaningful learning for students. Her work addresses the complexities of transitioning from high school to college writing for Chicana undergraduate students. Saidy utilizes one student's writing as well as interviews and research memos to not only evaluate the complexities of this transition but also to bring insight into how WPAs can create programs that are more responsive to students' transitions into college. She concludes using the genre of a case-study as an educational tool to involve undergraduate students in graduate level research acts as an additional avenue for literacy sponsorship.

Promoting Linguistic Diversity and Universal Access

Other texts in this collection emphasize the importance of linguistic diversity and universal access in academic and non-academic spaces. These selections show a growing trend in Rhetoric and Composition towards attention to diversity in languaging and modes of composing. Language diversity has been a topic of conversation for some decades, and these texts aim to continue the work that needs to be done.

In "A Critical Time for Reform," Anthony Warnke and Kirsten Higgins consider the impact that institutional reform has on writing teachers and the tension that often arises out of these calls for reform. Through an analysis of instructors' self-reported experiences, the authors identify both resistance and enthusiasm from instructors who may be implicated in an institutional reform. In response to their findings, the authors propose a "critical reform" approach to writing program reform within the two-year college. To illustrate their aspirations for what they call "critical reformers," Warnke and Higgins present scenarios which illustrate four components to their framework which can be used as tools for those facing writing program reform: dialoguing between the national and the local, separating agency from autonom, rethinking a "deficit mindset", and maintaining values while embracing flexibility.

While Warnke and Higgins do not specifically consider reform related to translanguaging, many calls for institutional and curricular reforms do address language diversity. Academic conversations around language diversity and access have resulted in interrogating biases and ideally changing approaches to teaching. Critical to this conversation is "Translanguaging, Coloniality, and English Classrooms: An Exploration of Two Bicoastal Urban Classrooms" by Cati V. de los Ríos and Kate Seltzer. This article examines translanguaging and translanguaging pedagogy through year-long ethnographic studies of two urban English classrooms, one in New York and one in Los Angeles. The authors identify moments in which students used translanguaging as resistance to colonial ideologies as well as moments where instructors employed translanguaging pedagogy "to leverage their students' bilingualism through student-centered, culturally sustaining curricula" (69).

Romeo García's "Unmaking Gringo-Centers" examines the antiracist work and agendas of writing centers by pointing to a problematic white-black paradigm that has emerged in the field's discussion and interrogation of race. García argues that progressive politics in writing center work has often worked within an exclusionary framework; to address this, García asks teachers to truly listen to the needs of all bodies who enter our writing spaces and. Specifically, García speaks to the presence of Mexican Americans, both local and global, in academic and non-academic spaces, and discusses the need to account for Mexican American students within writing center conversations on race and power.

Wendy Pfrenger's "Cultivating Places and People at the Center: Cross-Pollinating Literacies on a Rural Campus" expands notions of who a "basic writer" is by emphasizing overlapping identities among writing consultants and their students in a writing center on a rural, regional campus in an Appalachian county of Ohio. As Pfrenger shows, writing consultants who grew up and still participate in the community are able to translate literacy tasks by setting them in a place-based literacy context. Such interactions sustain both writing consultant and student in their academic aspirations across divides of deepening poverty and widening opportunity gaps. Pfrenger highlights an appreciation for the value of community-based literacy practices and shows the rural-cultural leverage of place that a writing center can potentialize with positive identity impacts for writing consultants and basic writers alike.

Janine Butler's "Integral Captions and Subtitles: Designing a Space for Embodied Rhetorics and Visual Access" also considers matters of access. In this piece, Butler presents the rhetorical value of integral captions and integral subtitles, as opposed to traditional methods of cautioning which place the words on the bottom of the screen, separate from the overall multimodal experience, and serve exclusively to deliver the text visually. She presents five criteria for integral captions and subtitles which create an embodied multimodal experience.

RESEARCH METHODOLOGIES

Finally, selected texts also attended to innovative and conscientious approaches to research and methodology. These authors consider patterns of research in Rhetoric and Composition as well as what it means to research ethically and with a sense of self.

Pamela Takayoshi calls for a field-focused retrospective in "Writing in Social Worlds: An Argument for Researching Composing Processes." Takayoshi argues that writing process research went out of fashion at a moment of immense change to composing, namely the rise of digital writing technologies. Takayoshi's calls for researchers to return to a particular type of process research is an important one, especially in the age of continuing (and rising) use of digital technologies for writing.

In "Research as Care: A Shared Ownership Approach to Rhetorical Research in Trauma Communities," Maria Novotny and John T. Gagnon offer a methodological toolkit for trauma-related research to reduce participant risk. This framework draws from indigenous and feminist perspectives centered on the concept of "shared ownership." Both authors share narratives of how each of their ethnographic, trauma-related research projects raised critical questions about their responsibility to participants in their studies. Novotny and Gagnon's research as care framework offers five pillars to help other researchers more effectively navigate similar territory in their own work.

Lastly, Kate Vieira's "Fieldwork with a Five-Year-Old: A Summative Report" offers a deeply personal look into her research identity, or, as we come to find, the multiple identities that form, challenge, and complement her research on the writing of immigrants in Latvia. Drawing from the foreignness of the country with the intimacy of motherhood, Vieira utilizes the genre of a research report that simultaneously distances her from the subject matter while drawing readers more closely into the nuances of why and how we do such work.

Taken together, the texts showcased in this collection have the potential to move us to action. These pieces can inspire us to learn from this political moment to attend in positive ways to issues of power, improve our teaching, curate more inclusive spaces, and pursue our research ethically.

NEW FOR 2019

The editors of this collection are committed to showcasing the exciting scholarship coming from across the field's journals in order to provide a current snapshot of exigent themes, trends, and ideas within

Rhetoric and Composition. Furthermore, in order to emphasize the collection as a resource for courses and professional development opportunities, we have collected additional materials from the authors that you will find placed alongside each article: a reflection on the origin of the piece, a discussion of research methods, findings, and/or pedagogical impacts for the author, and discussion questions for readers and reading groups. By including these materials, we hope to facilitate critical engagement with the works so that researchers and students alike might be emboldened to enter these conversations.

We have also developed a digital version of this collection—though hard copies are still available through Parlor Press—in order to make this as cost effective as possible for students and faculty members who would benefit from understanding the field in this particular moment but who may not have access to all of the journals represented here. We will continue to build our digital resources with items like author interviews and classroom activities, and we look forward to the creative ways students, instructors, and administrators will take up this collection in their own contexts.

A Note on the Selection Process

The fourteen articles selected for this volume represent important scholarship from journals in our field. Each selection was first nominated by the current editor(s) of the journal. From these nominations, graduate students, dual credit high school instructors, and faculty of all ranks from a range of institutions read and ranked each article according to the following criteria:

- Article demonstrates a broad sense of the discipline, demonstrating the ability to explain how its specific focus in a sub-disciplinary area addresses broader concerns in the field.
- Article makes original contributions to the field, expanding or rearticulating central premises.
- Article is written in a style which, while based in the discipline, attempts to engage with a wider audience or concerns a wider audience.

Based on the recommendations from reading groups, the editors selected the final list of essays. We hope that this selection illustrates the richness and diversity of our field and the possibilities that emerge when we are given the chance to read across journals and publishing platforms.

We are very grateful to all of the associate editors who organized and participated in reading groups that helped choose the selected essays. We are also grateful to our assistant editors who took the time to diligently read and discuss the nominated articles and offer their insights. We proudly list them here:

Associate Editors

Emily Artiano, University of Southern California
Amy Carleton, Massachusetts Institute of Technology
Erin Costello Wecker, University of Montana
Kristen Getchell, Babson College
Abbie Levesque, Northeastern University
Michelle Niestepski, Lasell College
Megan Opperman, Texas A&M University – Commerce
Sadie Shorr-Parks, Shepherd University
Kevin G. Smith, University of Virginia

Assistant Editors

Emerson College
Stephen Shane

Framingham State University
Colleen Coyne

Lasell College
Gregory Cass
Sara Large
Annie Ou

Northeastern University
Cara Marta Messina
Greg Zuch

Northern Essex Community College
Patricia Portanova
Shepherd University
Yildiz Nuredinoski
Brian Santana

Christy Wenger

Syracuse University
Vincent Portillo

Texas A&M University—Commerce
Dylan Hevron
Nabiha El Khatib
John G. Gibbons
Jennifer Goldston
Daniel Jones
Marzieh Keshavarz
Brian McShane
Keri Rowback
Ana E. Saenz

University of Massachusetts—Boston
Matthew Davis

University of Providence
Gavin Hurley

University of Southern California
Stephanie Bower
Brent D. Chappelow
Rochelle Gold
Cory Elizabeth Nelson
Alisa Sánchez
Atia Sattar

University of Virginia
Kiera Allison
Devin Jude Donovan
Jon D'Errico
Keith Driver
Eva Höenigess
Eva Latterner
Marcus Meade
Sarah O'Brien
Indu Ohri
S. Fain Riopelle
Kate Stephenson

Washington State University – Tri-Cities
Patty Wilde

Finally, we would like to thank Steve Parks and Dave Blakesley for their support and guidance throughout this project as we build on the vision for *Best Of* that they have continued to develop for the past ten years.

Best of the Journals
Rhetoric and Composition

COMMUNITY LITERACY JOURNAL

Community Literacy Journal is on the Web at http://www.communityliteracy.org/

The *Community Literacy Journal* is an interdisciplinary journal that publishes both scholarly work that contributes to theories, methodologies, and research agendas and work by literacy workers, practitioners, and community literacy program staff. We are especially committed to presenting work done in collaboration between academics and community members, organizers, activists, teachers, and artists

#StayWoke: The Language and Literacies of the #BlackLivesMatter Movement[1]

This important study pays attention to the communication practices of the #BlackLivesMatter and Hip Hop generation in its extension of Black and African American language traditions and prior liberation movements in their unapologetic performance of Black chants, Black grammar, phonology, vocabulary, Black fashion and music, to die-ins, hands-up, and the technologization of the movement through social media, Black Twitter, hashtags, and memes. Richardson and Ragland analyze how language and literacies of the Black Lives Matter movement represent diverse identities within Black community, vernacular associated with various economic and educational classes, diaspora, culturally rooted, Hip Hop generations, cis-gendered women, men, as well as LGBTQ and gender non-conforming. In their sweeping analysis, Ragland and Richardson make the argument that the languages and literacies of BLM promote the value of all Black lives.

---

1. *Community Literacy Journal*, vol 12, no. 2. © 2018 Community Literacy Journal

#StayWoke: The Language and Literacies of the #BlackLivesMatter Movement

Elaine Richardson and Alice Ragland

Abstract

This paper examines the language, literacies, communicative, and rhetorical practices of the Black Lives Matter (BLM) movement. The work pays attention to the communication practices of the BLM and Hip Hop generation in its extension of Black and African American language traditions and prior liberation movements in their unapologetic performance of Black chants, Black grammar, phonology, vocabulary, Black fashion and music, to die-ins, hands-up, and the technologization of the movement through social media, Black Twitter, hashtags, and memes. The language and literacies of the Black Lives Matter movement represent diverse identities within Black community, vernacular associated with various economic and educational classes, diaspora, culturally rooted, Hip Hop generations, cis-gendered women, men, as well as LGBTQ and gender non-conforming. In this way, the language and literacies of BLM promote the value of ALL Black lives.

Introduction and Context

Twelve-year-old Tamir Rice was playing by himself under the pavilion in an empty park behind his house in Cleveland, Ohio on November 22, 2014. Minutes after a 911 caller reported that there was someone in the park with a gun that might be fake, two police officers pulled up in a squad car within two feet of the child. One of the officers jumped out of the car within two seconds of arrival and shot Tamir. Tamir Rice's lifeless, bloody body lay outside on the ground for several hours. Neither of the officers bothered to give him medical attention or to call an ambulance. When Tamir's sister ran to the park to see what happened, she was tackled by the officers (Taylor, 14). Not only did the officers involved not serve a single day in jail for the killing of the child, but the case was never even brought to trial.

There is countless historical precedence for such a phenomenon. Wilderson explains that *Black* and *slave* were synonyms for *anti-human*, "a position against which humanity establishes, maintains, and renews its coherence, its corporeal integrity…" (11). This lack of sanctity for Black life is a text against which Black people have lived throughout the various eras of the Black experience. Tamir Rice's killing has been compared to that of Emmitt Till in the popular imagination, in order to historicize the devaluation of Black life. Both youths were seen as threatening adult men who caused their own murders. Though the details of each killing differed, the end result was the same: our criminal justice system provided justice for neither the family of Mamie Till nor the family of Samaria Rice. Parallels between the 20th Century white-based state-sanctioned lynching of Black people and today's state-sanctioned police brutality and killing of Black people include lack of empathy, further objectification, and rationalization of disenfranchisement. Another parallel is Black people's "[development of] traditions to affirm themselves in the midst of both physical and institutionalized violence" (Mitchell).

Fig. 1. The Reel Network, *Is Tamir Rice the New Emmett Till*, 31 December 2015, http://thereelnetwork.net/is-tamir-rice-the-new-emmett-till/

Ta-Nehisi Coates, in *Between the World and Me*, explains to his son the current and haunting truth of the disposability of Black life in the United States of America:

> I write to you in your fifteenth year. I am writing you because this was the year you saw Eric Garner choked to death for selling cigarettes; because you know now that Renisha McBride was shot for seeking help, that John Crawford was shot down for browsing in a department store. And you have seen men in uniform drive by and murder Tamir Rice, a twelve-year-old child whom they were oath-bound to protect. And you have seen men in the same uniforms pummel Marlene Pinnock, someone's grandmother, on the side of a road. And you know now, if you did not before that the police departments of your country have been endowed with the authority to destroy your body. It does not matter if the destruction is the result of an unfortunate overreaction. It does not matter if it originates in a misunderstanding. It does not matter if the destruction springs from a foolish policy… The destroyers will rarely be held accountable. Mostly they will receive pensions. And destruction is merely the superlative form of a dominion whose prerogatives include friskings, detainings, beatings, and humiliations. All of this is common to black people. And all of this is old for black people. No one is held responsible. (9)

In the above passage, Coates has captured the contemporary and continuing saga of Black people in this country. Unwarranted violence against the Black body, such as the state-sanctioned killings of Michael Brown, Tamir Rice, Timothy Russell, Malissa Williams, Tanisha Anderson, John Crawford, Aiyana Stanley-Jones, and innumerable others, is a manifestation of the culture of systemic white supremacy. The treatment of the victims' bodies, such as leaving Michael Brown's corpse to lie in the street for hours without calling for medical attention, as well as the judicial system's continual failure to punish the uniformed and vigilante killers of Black people, is evidence that in the eyes of the oppressor, Black still equals not fully human.

The denial of full Black humanity is precisely what the Black Lives Matter movement challenges:

> It goes beyond the narrow nationalism that can be prevalent within Black communities, which merely call on Black people to love Black, live Black and buy Black, keeping straight cis Black men in the front of the movement while our sisters, queer and trans and disabled folk take up roles in the background or not at all.
>
> Black Lives Matter affirms the lives of Black queer and trans folks, disabled folks, black-undocumented folks, folks with records, women and all Black lives along the gender spectrum. It centers those that have been marginalized within Black liberation movements. It is a tactic to (re)build the Black liberation movement (Source: "Black Lives Matter—About")

The phrase "Black Lives Matter" is subversive in and of itself, as it challenges the institutional, political, and societal practices, and all of the ways the state is complicit in depriving Black people of their humanity, their culture, their lives. The Black Lives Matter movement consists of BLM chapters around the world and is also allied with other social and racial justice organizations addressing human rights and social inequality in and beyond the domains of labor rights, environmental justice, food security, immigration, prison abolition, and education. The Black Lives Matter movement centers Black humanity and Black people's determination to represent their own realities, to value themselves on and in their own terms. Thus, BLM expands upon Black language traditions and creates its own semiotic system and literacy practices to signify pride, resilience, and affirmation of all Black humanity.

Through its examination of the language, literacies, communicative, and rhetorical practices of the Black Lives Matter movement, this article focuses upon the movement's discursive impetus to affirm all segments of Black humanity and to disrupt the intersectional effects of white supremacist capitalist patriarchal logics, which sustain hegemonic normativity of anti-Blackness, cis-gendered heterosexuality, racialized sexualities, criminalization of economically impoverished and otherwise disenfranchised Black people. This effort to create social change can be discerned through the (re)production, circulation, and performance of unapologetic Black language and literacy traditions across diverse domains of Black community employing performative communication of chants, Black styles and music, enactment of die-ins, hands-up, Black brunch, Black grammar, phonology, vocabulary, and the technologization of the movement through social media, Black Twitter, hashtags, and memes.

The Language of #BlackLivesMatter

The language of the Black Lives Matter movement is rooted in and expands upon Black and African American language traditions. Smitherman's definition of African American Language (AAL) underscores language forms and how those forms reflect shared experience, Black solidarity, and identity:

> Black or African American Language (BL/AAL) is a style of speaking [mostly] English words with Black flava—with [AfroAmericanized] semantic, grammatical, pronunciation, and rhetorical patterns. AAL comes out of the experience of U.S. slave descendants. This shared experience has resulted in common speaking styles, systematic patterns of grammar, and common language practices in the Black community. Language is a tie that binds. It provides solidarity with your community and gives you a sense of personal identity. AAL served to bind the enslaved together, melding diverse African ethnic groups into one community. Ancient elements of African speech were transformed into a new language forged in the crucible of enslavement, U.S. style apartheid, and the Black struggle to survive and thrive in the face of dominating and oppressive whiteness. (3)

Rickford and Rickford alert us to the significance of Black slang and Black vocabulary. Although Black slang—as opposed to Black vocabulary—varies from region to region, every African American can be said to speak some form of Black Talk. Spoken Soul terms often represent the daily experience of life in the skin we speak (94). Although AAL words can be identified as (mostly) European American Language (EAL), it is the way the words are used and their nuanced meanings that make them distinctly Black (Smitherman, "Chain Remain the Same" 8). Concurrently, Spears explains that distinctive Blackness suffuses the utterance. Beyond the word level, distinctive Black language usage is communicated through Black stylistic devices such as "prosodic semantics" and "metadiscursive principles," which emanate from an alternate worldview, contextually and historically relevant situations, and experiences that produce the ideologically potent discursive field for the Black speaker ("Theorizing African American Women's Language" 77-78). This is evident in the ways that a phrase such as "stay woke" has a particular Black meaning, of which more will be discussed later in this article.

Black language comes out of Black experience. "The Black Experience is a narrative of resistance, of an on-going struggle to be free, perhaps the motive force in African American history" (Smitherman, "Introduction to Ebonics" 34). The language of BLM is similar to previous Black movements such as Black Arts, Civil Rights, Black Power, and current Hip Hop generations in that they "speak the language of the people" (Smitherman, "Black Talk" 37). In so doing, this language is "rooted in the Black oral tradition of tonal semantics, narrativizing, signification/signifying, the dozens/playing the dozens, [AfroAmericanized] syntax, and other communicative practices. The oral tradition itself is rooted in the surviving African tradition of 'Nommo,' and the power of the word in human life" (Smitherman, "Black Talk" 4).

The Literacies of #BlackLivesMatter

The power of the word underscores the Black Lives Matter movement as Black literacies in motion. New literacies theorists understand literacy as socio-culturally situated. "Literacies are social practices: ways of reading and writing and using [...] texts that are bound up in social processes which locate individual action within social and cultural processes" (Martin-Jones and Jones 4-5). As opposed to dominant [imperialist white supremacist capitalist patriarchal][1] literacy practices, which are understood as a neutral "set of isolated skills divorced from social context, politics, culture, and power" (Richardson 9), Black literacies are based in the lived experiences of Black people and center the ways in which power and oppression operate in those experiences. "African American literacies include vernacular resistance arts and cultural productions that are created to carve out free spaces in oppressive locations such as the classroom, the streets, or the airwaves to name a few" (Richardson 18).

The literacy practices of the Black Lives Matter movement are both new and rooted in Black protest literacies of the past. Kynard states that Black student protest literacies

> [...] have been part of a historical trajectory that have included practices that encompass: visual and musical aesthetics and conversations with other people of color; reading and writing outside of class based on racial, class-inflected politics not offered in classrooms; rhetorics that are crafted for community

organizing and cultural programming... contemporary critiques of the social institutions that create barriers and oppressive relations for people of color. (66)

Building on African American literacies scholarship, Kynard locates a Black literacies protest tradition led by students at Historically Black Colleges and Universities (HBCUs) from the 1920s through the 1960s, wherein Black students enact and embody an education and literacy tradition relevant to the sustainment, survival, and honoring of Black lives (25-66). In this tradition, Black students build on the counter values, ideologies and practices of their formerly enslaved ancestors. These vernacular insurrections redefine what it means to be literate in the interests of Black people. In this tradition Black people circulate their own culturally specific modes of literacy learning and values. Literacy is something people do, not something they have or do not have, or sets of skills according to hegemonic literacy, or what Pritchard calls "literacy normativity" (24). Pritchard's theorization of Black Queer literacies[2] helps us to see literacy normativity as "uses of literacy that inflict harm," uses of literacy that drain people of emotional—and other—resources that they need to advance their individual and collective best interests (24). Literacy normativity ideologies control who is defined as normal, and control what is considered to be literate, appropriate, and moral. Falling outside of state-sanctioned autonomous ideologies of literacy and morality implicate people as deviant. Pritchard helps us to see that "[f]or both literacy and racialized sexualities and genders, when you are already labeled as being outside of ... normality" (as Black people are), you are a target (16).

Though today's generation builds on prior language, cultural foundations, and movements, the Black Lives Matter Hip Hop generation is shaping freedom in their own terms, sounds, and likeness. Cohen asserts:

> In their chants at demonstrations, spoken word to hype the crowd, or just their aesthetic, one can see and hear the influences of hip hop on this generation of protestors and activists. Hip hop is not just a genre of music to them; it is lifestyle, it is their theme song, and it tells the story of their politics, their degradation, and their rising up. As this new queered configuration of young activists declares "This is what democracy looks like," they are also reclaiming and democratizing hip hop and asserting "This is what my hip hop looks and sounds like."

And as they revitalize and remix movement politics, they are also finding new ways to help hip hop evolve and inspire. (289)

Remixing of movement politics and language can recall common Black diasporic and Pan-African cultural discourse practices, performances, referents, and ways of being that can also cut across intersectional boundaries between United States Blacks. Performances of Black language and literacies display Black people's negotiation and deciphering of public transcripts in order to protect and advance Black life (Richardson 35). Black "performative literacies include embodied ways of knowing, communicating, and meaning making" (Muhammad and Haddix 315). In the following section, we offer examples of performative literacies in the form of chants, wearing T-Shirts, Black brunch, die-ins, hands-up, and other performance of unapologetic Blackness.

Performative Literacies of Black Lives Matter: Chants

Through chants, Black Lives Matter protesters perform distinctive Black language practices that seek to dismantle systemic oppression and affirm Black life. For example, consider the following chant, in which one of this essay's authors has regularly partaken:

Chant down Babylon
Black people are da bomb
We ready, we comin
We ready, we comin

This chant creatively and strategically employs various aspects of Black language. First off, it revisits the Black musical tradition of earlier Black artists/rhetors as it samples "Chant down Babylon," a Bob Marley reggae song that references "Babylon" (Smitherman, "Chain Remain the Same," 15). According to Edmonds, Babylon references people and institutions carrying out the objectives of colonialism and its legacies, which have oppressed African peoples since the seventeenth century (23). And as defined by Cassidy and LePage, in *The Dictionary of Jamaican English,* Babylon is a "biblical allusion often made by the Rastafari, hence, from their point of view, non-believers, white men" (17). Thus, the language in this chant is influenced by Black diaspora speech, not just within the United States. This diasporic phenomenon is captured by the superordinate term coined by Robert

Williams and incorporated into the Conference on College Composition and Communication's Statement on Ebonics:

> ...Black language forms ... derive from common historical, social, cultural, and material conditions. ... [Ebonics] refers to language forms such as African American Language, Jamaican Creole, Gullah Creole, West African Pidgin English, and Haitian Creole, as well as Afro-Euro language varieties spoken in European countries. The term was created ... to identify the various languages created by Africans forced to adapt to colonization and enslavement. (Conference on College Composition and Communication (CCCC), Language Policy Committee)

The chant describes Black people with the Black slang term *da bomb* that means "superb, outstanding, excellent" (Smitherman, *Word from the Mother* 27). Further, *da* exhibits Black phonology, where what might be realized as a *th* sound in the initial position of a word in other varieties of English is sonically rendered as *d* sound. The form, zero copula, which is a common and distinctive Black grammatical pattern is exemplified in "we ready, we comin" (Rickford and Rickford, 114). With this form, Black Lives Matter demonstrators express the condition that the movement is a force in perpetual forward motion. Standardized English ("we are ready, we are coming") does not capture this dual truth as succinctly. Other Black pronunciation patterns such as word final consonant cluster simplification in words such as *comin* add to the flow, contour and sonic vibration of the movement for freedom (Rickford and Rickford, 150).

The following chant is another example of the use of African American language:

> *Why are you in riot gear?*
> *We don't see no riot here!*

This chant includes a double negative ("we don't see no"), which is not grammatically distinctive in and of itself to Black language, as it occurs in other English vernaculars, yet the Black bodies themselves, taking up (white) space, performing and embodying the soul-filled rhythmic vocality of the chants, emit and envision critical Black freedom sounds (Rickford and Rickford, 123).

Fig. 2. Jonathan Backman, A Single Photo From Baton Rouge That's Hard to Forget, The Atlantic, 10 July 2016, https://www.theatlantic.com/notes/2016/07/a-single-photo-that-captures-race-and-policing-in-america/490664/

We next emphasize performance and style through signifying practices. Gee's discussion of semiotics is helpful as he underscores sets of "practices that recruit one or more modalities (e.g. oral or written language, images, equations, symbols, sounds, gestures, graphics, artifacts) to communicate distinctive types of meanings" (18).

Literacies of #BlackLivesMatter: Wearing T-Shirts

Wearing T-shirts with messages pertaining to BLM is a sign that conveys meaning. This practice is an important visual communicative aspect of the movement. Whether in an organized mass protest or in one's everyday life, Black people (and others seeking to show up for racial justice) can be spotted wearing T-shirts that read "Black Lives Matter," "Hands Up, Don't Shoot," "I Can't Breathe," names of historical freedom fighters, and other messages that affirm Black life.

Fig. 3. Facebook post from Roots Collective, December 29, 2015: https://www.facebook.com/ThaRootsCollective/photosa.778774428845864.1073741828.774442379279069/1019815881408383/?type=3&theater

The words that appear on the shirts have a way of disturbing the peace of people who are trying to ignore or erase the issue of systemic racism. Public displays of movement paraphernalia work to put the issue of state violence against Black bodies in the faces of all passersby.

On December 8th, 2014, Lebron James, Kyrie Irving, and several Brooklyn Nets players wore T-shirts that read "I CAN'T BREATHE" in recognition of Eric Garner, a Black man choked to death by a police officer for selling cigarettes. A controversy ensued from the fact that these NBA athletes chose to use their platform to make a statement about the senseless theft of Black life. This is an example of movement slogans and discourses being brought into unexpected, white ideologically controlled space. Whether the predominantly white audiences agreed with the athletes or not, they were forced to think about the world from a Black person's perspective, or at the very least the athletes confronted them. As characteristic of the boldness of this movement, the NBA players perform fictive kinship for Eric Garner (or represent for his humanity) by wearing "I CAN'T BREATHE" shirts. Implicated in the semiotic and symbolic field is the meaning that killing Eric Garner is killing me (the collective I of Black men, even wealthy NBA playing Black men).

Fig. 4. Robert Deutsch, *LeBron James, Kyrie Irving and Nets players wear 'I can't breathe' shirts before Cavs game,* USA Today, 8 December 2014, http://ftw.usatoday.com/2014/12/kyrie-irving-i-cant-breathe-t-shirt-before-cavaliers-eric-garner-lebron-james

Similarly, the Black woman in Fig. 5 represents for Eric Garner and a collective Black community, as Kimberle Crenshaw and the African American Policy Forum indicate in the "Why We Can't Wait" letter to President Obama and the My Brother's Keeper (males only) Initiative: "[G]irls and women of color suffer, struggle and succeed with the men and boys in their lives. Only together will our collective well-being improve" (online).

Fig. 5. Patrick Scott Barnes, *Black Lives Matter Orlando 12 I Can't Breathe T-Shirt*, Orlando Culture Shock, 11 December 2014, https://orlandocultureshock.wordpress.com/2014/12/11/protestors-stages-die-in-at-downtown-orlandos-amway-center/black-lives-matter-orlando-12-i-cant-breathe-t-shirt/

Similarly, #Fuck12 T-shirts (Fig. 6) highlight a slang phrase that means fuck the police and the anti-Black establishment. The phrase was also incorporated into a popular rap song, "(Trust God) Fuck 12" by Gucci Mane and Rich Homie Quan in 2013. This lyric evinces residue of the traditional African worldview shared by non-westernized Africans, wherein "there is fundamental unity between the spiritual and the material aspects of existence," though the spiritual is prioritized (Smitherman, *Talkin and Testifyin* 75).

Fig. 6: Post from @Pot_Lord on Twitter, 19 May, 2014 https://twitter.com/PotLord/status/468513016774803457

Literacies of #BlackLivesMatter: Black Brunch

The sacredness of Black life is also put on display by Black brunch performances. Black brunch is an activity in which BLM activists protest the killing of Black people at the hands of police by disrupting brunch spots in affluent white neighborhoods. As such, activists enter these spaces and read off names of the Black dead, in order to upset the comfort, indifference and privileged lives of the predominantly white patrons "who had expected nothing more than a Bloody Mary and an overpriced eggs Benedict."[3] The message is white silence is violence.

Fig. 7. A sign from a "Black Lives Matter" protest march in Rochester, Minnesota. Rose Colored Photo, *Confronting Brunch,* Truthout, 26 April 2015, http://www.truth-out.org/opinion/item/30427-black-lives-matter-wage-slaves-labor-and-brunch

Writing about organizing the largest march she had planned at that point, in the wake of the acquittal of George Zimmerman for killing seventeen year-old Trayvon Martin, co-founder of Black Lives Matter, Patrisse Khan-Cullors, explains the message that seemingly disconnected white people, who were shopping and brunching on Rodeo Drive and Beverly Hills, needed to hear about the realities of living while Black:

> I say that they, those who come for brunch, have to confront the police presence today but that this is our everyday. I say that we were not born to bury our children, we were born to love and nurture them just like they were, and because of this, finally we had to acknowledge that in fact this is what we had been forced to do and we had been forced to do it for too long, centuries too long. We say that those children, now our dead, now our Ancestors, are calling to us, Trayvon is calling to us and asking that we remember so that we at last make the change that deserves to be made, that has to be made. I ask the people who are lunching, perhaps spending more on a single lunch than many of us spend to feed our families for an entire week, to remember the dead and to remember that once they

Fig. 8., Jeremy Allen, "Die-In at the Diag: Hundreds of U-M students, community members protest police killings," 10 December 2014: http://www.mlive.com/news/ann-arbor/index.ssf/2014/12/die-in_at_the_diag_hundreds_of.html

Die-ins are a widely used communicative strategy in the Black Lives Matter movement, wherein people present their bodies as dead. This is intended to disrupt the flow of traffic and to draw attention to the fact that too many Black people are dying at the hands of aggressive state violence and systemic racism. Die-ins have occurred in shopping malls, in university buildings, in busy intersections, in and near political buildings. Historian Robert Widell explains, to BBC News, that during the AIDS epidemic of the 1980s die-ins began. Die-ins were also done by cyclists in London to bring awareness to road safety, and against Dow Chemical, an Olympic sponsor. Specifically, related to the Black protest tradition, Widell says

> …black people [wading] into the water of whites-only beaches, along with sit-ins and teach-ins, were popular when public spaces were segregated by Jim Crow laws. The idea is to create an image that makes an impression. This kind of publicity forces the country to deal with the violence that faces African-Americans….

Additionally, protestors putting their hands up (a symbol for surrender intended to notify police officers not to shoot) is a protest practice that visually represents the protest phrase "hands up, don't shoot." This gesture is often accompanied by the chant, "Hands up, don't shoot!" The hands-up gesture is a widely recognized symbol used to raise awareness that many Black people have been shot by police even when they had their hands up.

Fig. 9. Scott Olson, *Hands Up, Don't Shoot,* Vox, 13 August 2014, https://www.vox.com/2014/8/13/5998591/hands-up-dont-shoot-photos-ferguson-michael-brown

Die-ins and the hands up gesture are widely known symbols of resistance. They are easily noticeable in photos shared via social media, and they have successfully raised awareness about unchecked police violence. Other ways to communicate Black humanity and resist oppression include unapologetic Black cultural expressions such as dancing, flaunting natural hair, and taking up space as a Black person.

Literacies of #BlackLivesMatter: Black Performance and Style

At the 2016 Superbowl, superstar Beyoncé and her dancers performed these and other unapologetic Black rhetorical, communicative, signifying language and gestural practices. Beyoncé's "Formation" performance was Braggadocio-full. Smitherman explains Braggadocio as a practice rendered "with clever rhymes, puns, culturally toned experiences and references from a fresh and new perspective" (Smitherman, "Chain Remain the Same," 12):

> I see it, I want it, I stunt, yellow bone it...
> I grind til I own it...
> I just might be a Black Bill Gates in the making
> I slay

Beyoncé's lyrics do not necessarily align with Black revolutionary consciousness suggested by iconographic aspects of her performance (Ward, 147). However, her use of Hip Hop slang and powerful referents evince the swag of an emcee (in older terms a toast-teller):

> [Beyoncé] is powerful, all-knowing, omnipotent hero, able to overcome all odds. In this way, [she] personifies the self-empowerment dreams of [her] Black audience and symbolizes for them triumph and accomplishment against the odds. (Smitherman, "Chain Remain the Same," 13)

For example, she "stunt, yellow bone it, grind," and "slay." In other words, she "shows off and shows out." As a light complexioned woman—she "yellow bone it," (which also includes a play on the word *bone*, meaning she is a supreme lovemaker). She "grind" or works hard (also pun on lovemaking), and she "slay," meaning she cannot be outdone in nothing (she is so good, double negative needed)! According to Holliday in *Word: The Online Journal on African American English*, Beyoncé uses *slay* 36 times in under five minutes. The lyrics also underscored Black African cultural features, such as "baby hair," "afros," "Negro nose," while the performers were clad in powerfully symbolic Black panther-inspired outfits, shaking and moving with Black woman-power in formation.

Fig. 10. http://ew.com/article/2016/02/08/beyonce-super-bowl-black-panther/

These Black cultural practices are part of the literacies of the Black diaspora. As Kynard argues, literacy is something that you do, not something that you have or do not have (32).

Use of Black language and communication style is a pivotal aspect of Black performance culture and movement discourse. Arguably, one of the most significant phrases (also expressed as a hashtag) is "stay woke." It has become a common phrase among young, Black, conscious people. The phrase means to remain aware of what is going on around you and in society, more specifically, to remain politically aware, or conscious. Also, it doesn't just mean now or today; it means "stay woke" all the time. *Woke* is an African American Language word, related to the *awake* occurring in many types of English. *Awake* can be defined as "to come out of the state of sleep; to cease to sleep; awaken to arise or spring into existence or rouse from sleep; and wake to be or remain awake; to keep oneself, or be kept, awake" ("Awake"). "I'm awake," the predicate adjective, means to be out of the state of sleep. The Black word *woke*, in referring specifically to a political consciousness type of being awake, is an excellent example of how Black people develop African American Language by imbuing it with concepts needing to be expressed efficiently—in one word. As a matter of fact, *stay* is also a word first developed by AAL speakers and that is now spreading beyond the Black community. The *stay* in "stay woke" has the meaning of all the time. It's a different word from *stay*, as in "She stay [reside] at grandma's house [sometimes]" (Spears, 168). It's the same *stay* as that in "stay awake" in other English varieties. Standardized varieties of English use *awake* instead of *woke* as the predicate adjective form (or part) of the verb, as in the following:

(be) awake e.g. "I'm awake."
(vernacular) AAL/Black (Lives Matter) "woke"
(be) woke e.g. "I'm woke."

It should be noted that there is a lot of variation with the verb *awake* and related verbs such as *wake*, *wake up*, etc. AAL speakers have taken the form *woke* and given it a special twist in meaning, bringing in the idea of political consciousness. Over time, *woke* has become its own word, so to speak: people who use *awake*, as in "stay awake," also use *woke* in the political sense of the word. The words have diverged in meaning.

The Hip Hop soul artist Erykah Badu's usage of "stay woke" is cited, on the *Know Your Meme* website, as one of the first public attestations (see below). It is well known that Erykah Badu was a practitioner of Five

Percenter Islam (Miyakawa, *Five Percenter Rap* 63). Five Percent Hip Hop artists have a tradition of bringing their teachings of Black nationalist consciousness and solidarity, empowerment through knowledge of self, and awareness of the workings of social inequality and racism to the masses through their music. For example, Five Percent rappers, Brand Nubian (specifically Grand Puba), in their 1990 song, "Wake Up" warn the eighty-five percent that the "The [white] devil's a conniver" (Miyakawa "The Duty of the Civilized Is to Civilize the Uncivilized" 175).

According to the website *Know Your Meme*,

> Stay Woke, derived from the phrase 'stay awake," is an internet slang term often used to demonstrate the need for awareness of an issue, particularly those relating to social justice or the Black Lives Matter movement. The term is also used ironically in a similar manner to Wake Up, Sheeple. Origin-The first instance of the use of stay woke is unknown. One of the first instances of public use was in the chorus to Erykah Badu's 2008 song "Master Teachers" from the album *New Amerykah Part 1: The 4th World War*.

The phrase was first defined on *Urban Dictionary* on August 19, 2014, where the definer linked it directly to the 2014 Ferguson Riots.

> Deriving from "stay awake," is to keep informed of the shitstorm going on around you in times of turmoil and conflict, specifically on occasions when the media is being heavily filtered-such as the events in Ferguson Missouri in August 2014. (https://www.urbandictionary.com/define.php?term=stay%20woke)

The hashtag #staywoke is in wide use on Twitter, Tumblr, and Instagram, where it has more than 128,000 associated posts. In the summer of 2015, programmers Darius Kazemi and Courtney Stanton built a Twitter bot called @StayWokeBot, intended to automate replies to those who might need more education about racism in society. On January 5th, 2016, MTV declared that *woke* was a new slang term for the new year, but many commenters noted that the term was not new ("Stay Woke"). Charles Pulliam-Moore discusses how #staywoke went from Black activist watchword to internet slang.

Actor and activist, Jesse Williams, executive produced a documentary about Black Lives Matter entitled "StayWoke: The Black Lives Matter Movement." In an interview in the *HuffPost* written by Lilly Workneh entitled "Jesse Williams Wants You to Stay Woke in New Film on Black Lives Matter," Workneh uncovers Williams' passion for social transformation:

> One of the first steps to being "woke" is understanding the depth of these dangerous myths and how societal constructs impede on the lives of marginalized people. In one poignant moment in the documentary, Williams says "no matter what we do, we're late"—it's a striking comment that stresses the requirement for resolution and represents the urgent need to get woke, stay woke and better the state of black lives.

Another significant phrase reflecting Black experience and expressions of freedom that has been utilized in BLM protest is "we gon be alright." The phrase was popularized by rapper Kendrick Lamar's song, "Alright," and it is chanted vigorously in many protests. It is also used as a hashtag, #WeGonBeAlright, and can be found in tweets that speak of Black struggle. *Gon* is often described as a reduced form of *gonna* or "going to" in AAL. "We gon" is one of the most Black of AAL syntax patterns as it reflects a higher rate of zero copula[4] than other Black patterned phrases where zero copula can occur (in noun phrases) [He a teacher], (in adjective phrases) [She happy] (Rickford and Rickford, 116). Adding to a Black diasporic perspective, linguists such as Rickford have convincing research which suggests the creole roots of "African American Vernacular English" (AAVE) as this feature of Black language is similar to creole and Englishes of the world such as Barbados, Jamaica, Guyana, Hawaii, and Liberia (Rickford and Rickford, 116; Spears, "Pidgeons/Creoles in African American Language, 8").

So far, we have emphasized the context of Black language and Black literacies and their development with regard to the experiences of Black people, and some of their cultural priorities and properties with regard to the Black Lives Matter movement in this current historical moment. We have emphasized how people give language meaning, structure, and value. In this sense, language, written, spoken, or otherwise signified, is not universal. It is always under construction and contested. It is always connected to context and discourse. We will turn now to usages of Black language and literacies in new media platforms to disrupt assault on Black lives.

The "New" Literacies of #BlackLivesMatter

The Black Lives Matter movement extends the Black protest literacies that Kynard mentions through use of Black Twitter and other online and offline modalities. Hashtags, memes, videos, and other social media practices are all important aspects of the movement's new literacies.

Khan-Cullors recounts that the origins of "#BlackLivesMatter" emerged from commiserating with her friend and comrade, Alicia Garza, on Facebook after the announcement of George Zimmerman's acquittal for the killing of the Black teenager, Trayvon Martin, in Sanford, Florida:

> ... [Alicia] writes these words
>
> Btw stop saying that we are not surprised. That's a damn shame in itself. I continue to be surprised at how little Black lives matter. And I will continue that. Stop giving up on black life. black people, I will NEVER give up on us. NEVER. (180)

Khan-Cullors responds with "#BlackLivesMatter" (180). With the help of Opal Tometi, the three Black queer women social activists began mobilizing by "creating Tumblr pages, influencing other social media outlets, and placing posters in local California businesses in order to spread news about ... #BlackLivesMatter..." (Ince, Rojas and Davis, 1819). Though police killings of unarmed Black people continued and BLM became more pronounced in the public discourse, the killing of Black teenager, Michael Brown, in Ferguson, Missouri, on August 9, 2014, propelled the #BlackLivesMatter moniker into discursive prominence "as a cry for racial justice" (Ince, Rojas and Davis 1819).

Tate thinks the current Hip Hop generation can thank BLM and Black Twitter for the communication revolution. The Rap music industry is no longer Black folks' CNN (Tate). The Nielson Report aligns with Tate's observation:

> Technology and social media is transforming and elevating the way in which African-Americans use their mobile devices. African-Americans are the second-largest multicultural group with regard to smartphone ownership, with 91% of Blacks owning smartphones (compared to 94% of Asian Americans, and 90% of Hispanics). The use of social media for community-based activism brought national awareness to issues affecting the Black community, and African-Americans, especially

Millennials, are leading the charge to bring about institutional change. The #BlackLivesMatter, #BankBlack, and #OscarsSoWhite social media movements, all of which sparked national conversations, are just three viral examples of how savvy applications of social media and technology are increasingly able to focus national attention on issues of social, civic and political importance. (4)

The language of Black Twitter is common to Black folks. Use of so-called mainstream United States English or codeswitching is not required and outsiders who can't get the references need to build community and background knowledge to successfully participate. McDonald observes:

> [...] Perhaps the most significant contribution of Black Twitter is that it increases visibility of black people online, and in doing so, dismantles the idea that white is standard and everything else is "other." It's a radical demand for acceptance by simply existing — or sometimes dominating — in a space and being yourself, without apology or explanation.

New Literacies: Hashtags

Perhaps one of the most important new literacies of the Black Lives Matter movement is its use of hashtags. Hashtags are words and phrases used on social media, particularly Twitter, that have a pound (#) symbol in front. Hashtags make it possible to create a digital footprint or catalogue messages of the same subject matter from various social media users. They have been used to organize people, to generate conversations, and to raise awareness of issues. For example, a search of #BlackLivesMatter on Twitter will yield any and all tweets that have used the hashtag, allowing for a quick means of viewing of Twitter conversations related to the topic. Hashtags are generally catchy, concise, and straightforward. Hashtags are also used in event names, for example "#SayHerNameVigil" or "#BlackLivesMatterRally." Hashtags get to the point and with accompanying video can illustrate the need for constant vigilance of state-sanctioned violence and anti-Blackness, as can be seen in a fairly recent tweet (Fig. 11).

Hashtags have also been used to illuminate intersectionality within the Black Lives Matter movement. For example, in order to bring awareness to the fact that Black women and girls are also victims of state violence, the hashtag #SayHerName has been widely used. #SayHerName was created by Dr. Kimberle Crenshaw and the African American Policy Forum (AAPF). #SayHerName in its creation of a community focused around a more specific issue within BLM represents an example of distributed framing (Ince, Rojas and Davis, 1827). #SayHerName tweets are usually accompanied by the names and media coverage of women and girls whose lives have been taken by law enforcement, including Sandra Bland, Rekia Boyd, Tanisha Anderson, Aiyana Stanley-Jones, and many many others whose stories are often disregarded. #BlackGirlsMatter is also a related hashtag that grew out of the work of Kimberle Crenshaw and her associates. #BlackGirlsMatter and #BlackWomenMatter are used to illuminate ways that Black women and girls experience gendered racism, subordination, and criminalization in American institutions by various types of violence (discursive and physical) by state-sanctioned and naturalized systems and policies that go unquestioned and unchallenged. The consequences of which deeply influence Black women and girls' life outcomes and power to control their futures.

Lindsey's "Herstory: A Brief and Painful History of State Violence Against Black Women and Girls" offers a powerful condensed rendering of this situation as it pertains to Black women and girls:

> Beyond calling the names of black women and girls, understanding a history of anti-black racial violence which includes all black people irrespective of gender renders the deeply disturbing arrest and suspicious death of Sandra Bland less anomalous. The stories of Bland as well as the other black women found dead in police custody in July 2015 and the black women and girls killed by police officers over the past 30 years profoundly illustrate the reality of anti-black state and state sanctioned violence. Ranging in age from seven to 93, black female victims of police violence fit within a painful legacy of black women and girls victimized by state and state-sanctioned terror. (15)

The Pew study observed that Black women's use of Twitter exceeds that of other demographic groups.[5] Sherri Williams highlights particular ways that Black feminists use Twitter to generate movement. She writes:

> Black feminists' use of hashtag activism is a unique fusion of social justice, technology, and citizen journalism. It should

serve as a fertile ground for emerging news for journalists, a point of connection for white feminists, and a ripe area of study for academics. Twitter is often a site of resistance where black feminists challenge violence committed against women of color and they leverage the power of Black Twitter to bring attention and justice to women who rarely receive either (343).

Fig. 11. A tweet from @SHXT_WZRD posted on August 18 2017.

The hashtag #AllBlackLivesMatter has also been important in acknowledging intersectionality of the movement. Black queer and trans people, Black working class and poor people, undocumented Black people, and

Black people with disabilities, are typically rendered invisible in the dominant discourse, and even in the Black community, while the experiences of straight, male, cisgender, able-bodied and middle-class Black people are privileged. The hashtag #AllBlackLivesMatter is a way of distributing the idea that all Black life is sacred regardless of income, sexual orientation, gender, age, (formerly) incarcerated, or (dis)ability.

BLMChicago
@BLMChi

Join us at 47th & the Dan Ryan for the vigil! #SayHerName #JessicaHampton #AlexisStubbs #BlackGirlsMatter #BlackLivesMatter

Kofi Ademola and 8 others
6/23/17, 7:30 PM from CTA - 47th

Fig. 12. @BLMChi, Twitter, 23 June 2017

Fig.13. @DMVBlackLives, Twitter, 4 April 2017.

As reported by Rankin in *Colorlines.com*,[6] since 2010 the National Coalition of Anti-Violence database began keeping track of transgender murders. Of the trans and gender non-conforming Americans murdered between 2010 and 2016, seventy-five percent were Black women. The 2015 publication, "Meaningful Work: Transgender Experiences in the Sex Trade," reports on the National Transgender Discrimination Survey (NTDS), conducted between 2008-2009, which documented the experiences of over 6400 transgender adults. Because of discrimination and racism, many transgender individuals do sex work as a way to avoid homelessness and non-employment. "Black and Black Multiracial NTDS respondents had the highest rate of sex trade participation overall (39.9%), followed by those who identified as Hispanic or Latino/a (33.2%) [p.4]." Trans and gender non-conforming people of color experienced disproportionate rates of incarceration and interaction with police. "People of color were more than twice as likely (46.8%) than their white counterparts (18.3%) to report being "arrested for being trans" (5). Similarly, 58.8% of people of color and 35.2% of respondents reported being sent to jail/prison "for any reason" (5). Pritchard, following Cohen, admonishes that because of "the complexity of racial formations of gender and sexuality that, in their nonheteronormative heterosexuality," more privileged racialized heterosexuals are yet queered (Pritchard, 23). It behooves queered groups to work across diverse intersectional identities to build coalition for collective empowerment. This is the goal of Black Lives Matter activism.

Memes

Memes are thought-provoking (and sometimes entertaining) images that are spread via social media. Throughout the course of the Black Lives Matter movement, they have been utilized to raise awareness of the state's violent and unjust treatment of Black people. For example, one popular and non-entertaining meme that has been shared on Twitter and Instagram has a picture of Dylann Roof, the white male mass-murderer, being peacefully arrested by police after killing nine Black parishioners (including an elderly woman) at a bible study at Mother Emmanuel African Methodist Episcopal Church in Charleston, South Carolina in 2015. Next to Roof's photo is a picture of Eric Garner, a Black male, being pinned to the ground by several officers and suffocated in a debilitating chokehold, which resulted in his death.

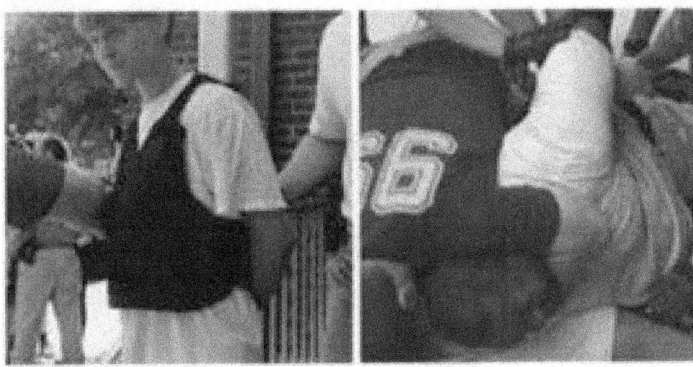

Fig. 14. *Charleston Church Shooting in Memes*, Grasshopper, 20 June 2015, https://grasshoppernews.wordpress.com/2015/06/20/charleston-church-shooting-in-memes/

In another meme, the same picture (Fig. 15) of the Charleston shooter's peaceful arrest is placed next to a picture of a Black teenaged girl in a swimsuit being violently attacked and pinned down by a white police officer during a pool party.

These memes contrast the brutal treatment that Black people are subjected to by the racist law enforcement and criminal justice system with the favorable treatment that white people are shown. The juxtaposition of these images not only exposes police brutality against Black bodies, but it highlights the racism of a corrupt system that devalues Black life while protecting and serving white life. Memes are easy to access, to understand, and they spread critical discourse and critical consciousness via social media, and they are used to mobilize against injustice during this current moment of the Black Lives Matter movement.

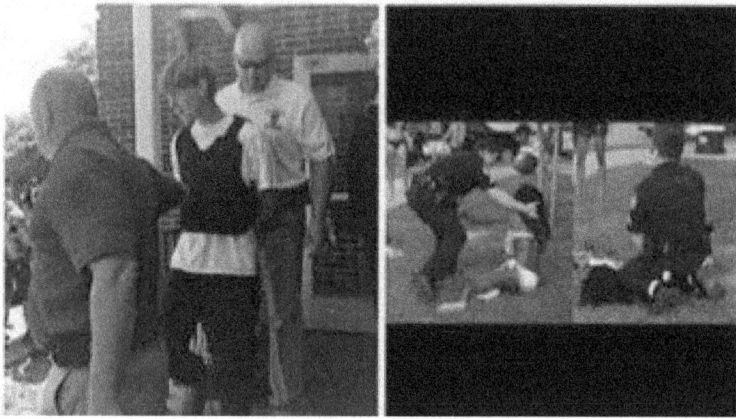

Fig. 15. *All bad,* Imgur, 18 June 2015, http://imgur.com/2FmvdHV

Conclusion

This article has sought to survey, codify, and trace a sampling of the language and literacy practices of the Black Lives Matter movement, and its productive communicative approach in mobilizing masses to confront racial injustice. The aesthetics—sonic, kinesthetic, and visual—contribute to power-knowledge with the aim of liberation of Black people throughout the U.S. and the Black diaspora. Through the purposeful use of Black language, communicative practices, and new literacies, young Black people are challenging racism, police brutality, and social inequality, while fighting for effective alliances. In so doing, they are performing unapologetic Blackness, seeking to disrupt hegemonic race, gender, sexuality, class oppression, and other social inequities for the greater good of all Black lives. The movement's use of social media and popular culture has resulted in heightened consciousness among many Black youth, encouraging them to stand against state-sanctioned violence against Black people. By making it clear that people will not stand for the continued assault on Black life, the

Black Lives Matter movement has asserted that all lives will matter when *all Black lives matter.*

Notes

1. "Understanding Patriarchy" http://imaginenoborders.org/pdf/zines/UnderstandingPatriarchy.pdf
2. Also see Pritchard 22 for further discussion of Black queer literacies.
3. http://www.truth-out.org/opinion/item/30427-black-lives-matter-wage-slaves-labor-and-brunch
4. Zero copula-the joining of subject and predicate without use of the verb 'to be'.
5. http://www.pewinternet.org/2014/01/06/african-americans-and-technology-use/
6. https://www.colorlines.com/articles/new-database-tracks-deaths-transgender-homicide-victims

Works Cited

African American Policy Forum. "Why We Can't Wait." *AAPF*, 2014, http://www.aapf.org/recent/2014/06/woc-letter-mbk

"Awake." *Merriam-Webster.com*, https://www.merriam-webster.com/dictionary/awake

"Black Lives Matter—About." *Black Lives Matter*, https://blacklivesmatter.com/about/

Cassidy, Frederic and LePage, Robert B. *Dictionary of Jamaican English*. 2nd ed., University of the West Indies Press, 2002.

Coates, Ta-Nehisi. *Between the World and Me*. Spiegel and Grau, 2015.

Cohen, Cathy J. "When Will Black Lives Matter?: Neoliberalism, Democracy, and the Queering of American Activism in the Post-Obama Era." *The Hip Hop and Obama Reader*, edited by Gosa, Travis and Nielson, Erik, Oxford UP, 2015, pp. 280-290.

Conference on College Composition and Communication (CCCC), Language Policy Committee "Statement on Ebonics." *NCTE*, May 2016, www.ncte.org/cccc/resources/positions/ebonics

Edmonds, Ennis B. "Dread "I" In-a Babylon: Ideological Resistance and Cultural Revitalization." *The Rastafari Reader: Chanting Down Babylon*, edited by Murrell, Nathaniel et al., Temple UP, 1998.

Fitzgerald, Erin, et al. *Meaningful Work: Transgender Experiences in the Sex Trade*. National Center for Transgender Equality, 2015.

Garza, Alicia. "A Herstory of the #BlackLivesMatter Movement." *The Feminist Wire,* October 7 2014, http://www.thefeministwire.com/2014/10/blacklivesmatter-2/.

Gee, James Paul. *What Video Games Have to Teach Us About Learning and Literacy.* Routledge, 2003.

Holliday, Nicole. "Beyonce's "Formation" and AAE in the Celebration of Blackness." *Word: Online Journal on African American English,* 2016, https://africanamericanenglish.com

Ince, Jelani, Rojas, Fabio, and Davis, Clayton A. "The Social Media Response to Black Lives Matter: How Twitter Users Interact with Black Lives Matter Through Hashtag Use." *Ethnic & Racial Studies,* vol. 40, no. 11, 2017, pp. 1814-1830.

Khan-Cullors, Patrisse. and Bandele, Asha. *When They Call You A Terrorist: A Black Lives Matter Memoir. Foreword by Angela Davis.* St. Martin's Press, 2018.

Kynard, Carmen. "'Before I'll Be a Slave, I'll Be Buried in My Grave'" Black Student Protest as Discursive Challenge and Social Turn in Nineteenth-and-Twentieth Century Literacies." *Vernacular Insurrections: Race, Black Protest, and the New Century in Composition –Literacy Studies.* SUNY Press, 2013.

Lindsey, Treva. "Race in the U.S.: Herstory: A Brief and Painful History of State Violence against Black Women and Girls." *Al Jazeera,* 7 February 2016, http://www.aljazeera.com/indepth/features/2015/09/race-herstory-150904052450065.html

Luxun, Micha. "When Did Die-ins Become a Form of Protest?" *Magazine Monitor,* BBC News Magazine, 9 December 2014, http://www.bbc.com/news/blogs-magazine-monitor-30402637

Martin-Jones, Marilyn and Jones, Kathryn. *Multilingual Literacies: Reading and Writing Different Worlds.* John Benjamins, 2000.

McDonald, Soraya Nadia. "Black Twitter-A Virtual Community Ready to Hashtag Out a Virtual Response to Cultural Issues." *Washington Post,* 20 January 2014, https://www.washingtonpost.com/lifestyle/style/black-Twitter-a-virtual-community-ready-to-hashtag-out-a-response-to-cultural-issues/2014/01/20/41ddacf6-7ec5-11e3-9556-4a4bf7bcbd84_story.html?utm_term=.36ba6ab32d9b

Mitchell, Koritha. "What I Learned about Police Brutality Videos from Studying Images of Lynchings." *Vox,* 28 July 2016, https://www.vox.com/2016/7/28/12241082/police-brutality-lynchings-self-care

Miyakawa, Felicia. "'The Duty of the Civilized is to Civilize the Uncivilized'": Tropes of Black Nationalism in the Messages of Five Percent Rappers." *Understanding African American Rhetoric: Classical Origins to Contemporary Innovations,* edited by Jackson, Ronald A. and Richardson, Elaine B., Routledge, 2003, pp. 171-185.

Miyakawa, Felicia. *Five Percenter Rap: God Hop's Music, Message, and Black Muslim Mission.* Indiana UP, 2005.

Muhammad, Gholnecsar and Haddix, Marcelle. "Centering Black Girls' Literacies: A Review of the Literature on Multiple Ways of Knowing of Black Girls." *English Education*, vol. 48, no. 4, July 2016, pp. 299-336.

Nielsen Report. "Young Connected and Black: African American Millenials are Driving Social Change and Leading Digital Advancement." *Nielsen*, 016, http://www.nielsen.com/us/en/insights/reports/2016/young-connected-and-black.html

Pritchard, Eric Darnell. *Fashioning Lives: Black Queers and the Politics of Literacy*. Carbondale, IL, Southern Illinois UP, 2017.

Pulliam-Moore, Charles. "How 'Woke Went from Black Activist Watchword to Teen Internet Slang," *Splinter*, 8 January 2016, https://splinternews.com/how-woke-went-from-black-activist-watchword-to-teen-int-1793853989

Rankin, Kenrya. "New Database Tracks Deaths of Transgender Homicide Victims." *Colorlines*, December 2016, https://www.colorlines.com/articles/new-database-tracks-deaths-transgender-homicide-victims

Richardson, Elaine B. *African American Literacies*. New York & London: Routledge, 2003.

Rickford, John R. and Rickford, Russell J. *Spoken Soul: The Story of Black English*. Wiley, 2000.

Smitherman, Geneva. *Black Talk: Words and Phrases from the Hood to the Amen Corner*. Boston & New York: Houghton Mifflin Company, 1994.

—. "Chain Remain the Same: Communicative Practices in the Hip Hop Nation." *Journal of Black Studies*, vol. 28, no. 1, 1997, pp. 3-29.

—. "Introduction to Ebonics." *Talkin that Talk: Language, Culture and Education in African America*. New York & London: Routledge, 2000.

—. *Talkin and Testifyin: The Language of Black America*. 1977. Detroit: Wayne State UP, 1986.

—. *Word from the Mother: Language and African Americans*. New York & London: Routledge, 2006.

Spears, Arthur K. "Pidgins/Creoles and African American English." *The Handbook of Pidgin and Creole Studies*, edited by Silvia Kouwenberg and John Victor Singler, Wiley-Blackwell Pub., 2008, pp. 512-542.

—. "Unstressed *Been*: Past and Present in African American English." *American Speech*, vol. 92, no. 2, 2017, pp.151-75.

"Stay Woke" knowyourmeme.com/memes/stay-woke

"Stay Woke" https://www.urbandictionary.com/define.php?term=stay%20woke

Tate, Greg. "How #BlackLivesMatter Changed Hip-Hop and R&B in 2015." *Rolling Stone*, 16 December 2015, http://www.rollingstone.com/music/news/how-blacklivesmatter-changed-hip-hop-and-r-b-in-2015-20151216

Taylor, Keeanga-Yamahtta. *From #BlackLivesMatter to Black Liberation*. Haymarket Books, 2016.

Wilderson III, Frank B. *Red, White, and Black: Cinema and the Structure of US Antagonisms.* Duke UP, 2010.

Ward, Mako Fitts. "Close Up: Beyoncé: Media and Cultural Icon. Queen Bey and the New Niggeratti: Ethics of Individualism in the Appropriation of Black Radicalism." *Black Camera*, vol. 9, no.1, 2017, pp. 146-153.

Williams, Robert. L., editor. *Ebonics: The True Language of Black Folks.* Institute of Black Studies, 1975.

Williams, Sherri. "Digital Defense: Black Feminists Resist Violence with Hashtag Activism." *Feminist Media Studies*, vol. 15, no. 2, 2015, pp. 341-344.

Workneh, Lilly. "Jesse Williams Wants You to 'Stay Woke' in New Film on Black Lives Matter." *HuffPost,* Huffington Post, 16 May 2016, https://www.huffingtonpost.com/entry/jesse-williams-stay-woke-documentary-black-lives-matter_us_5739516ee4b077d4d6f3688a

Supplemental Material

Part I: Reflection on the Origins of the Article

This piece originated as a final paper when Alice took an African American Language and Literacies Course with Dr. E. Alice has been active in the #BlackLivesMatter Movement and was encouraged by Dr. E. to do a project that documented and delved into the language practices of the chants, freedom songs, and memes that she frequently saw and heard in the various protests, die-ins, and organizing workshops that she took part in. The project was also inspired by a drive to bring light to the purposes and necessity of the #BlackLivesMatter movement as Black lives continue to be devalued and subjected to gratuitous violence.

Part II: Description of Research Methods, Findings, and/or Pedagogical Impact

The project used content analysis rooted in Black language studies to examine tweets, memes, chants, die-ins, and other language and literacy practices that have been popular in the #BlackLivesMatter movement. Although many of these language practices are dismissed by mainstream society as illegitimate, broken and/or substandard English, we found that the language practices used in the #BlackLivesMatter movement are rooted in a deep history of African Diaspora struggle and have linguistic and social roots that span centuries or longer. Supporters and organizers of the movement creatively used new media and Black literacies as a form of resistance to systemic oppression. They used social media such as memes, hashtags, videos, and Twitter, and as a primary mode of communication in the struggle against anti-Black violence. Movement supporters embraced T-shirts with protest messages and participated in die-ins to disrupt the taken-for-granted dominance and violence against Black bodies. The study also found that the language and literacy practices of the #BlackLivesMatter movement reflect an embrace of Blackness as opposed to attempting to separate from it. Whereas some Black social movements have involved attempts to prove that Black people are worthy of freedom by centering respectability politics, the #BlackLivesMatter movement has unapologetically advocated for all Black lives—including poor, women, queer, etc.—to be valued.

Part III: Discussion Questions

1. How do the language and literacy practices of the #BlackLivesMatter movement reflect the diversity of Black people and experiences?

2. How do you define anti-Blackness? What makes anti-Blackness a distinct form of racism?

3. What can you do (now and in the future) to ensure a future in which all Black lives are valued? How can you interrupt social structures that perpetuate anti-Black violence?

RHETORIC SOCIETY QUARTERLY

> *RSQ* is on the Web at https://associationdatabase.com/aws/RSA/pt/sp/rsq

Rhetoric Society Quarterly is the official publication of the Rhetoric Society of America. It publishes original scholarship in the interdisciplinary field of rhetoric studies for a readership including scholars from the U.S., Canada, and a few other countries. The journal currently has an acceptance rate of 10-12%. Our authors and readers come from departments of English, Communications, Rhetoric and Writing Studies, and other disciplines. The major methods employed by *RSQ* authors are historical, theoretical, and critical including visual rhetoric studies; less often, we publish work from ethnography, pedagogy, writing studies, media studies (music/film/sound/social media), digital rhetoric, and literary criticism with an emphasis on rhetorical issues. *RSQ* is committed to publishing work by and about diverse rhetorical agents. We welcome scholarship drawn from a wide spectrum of knowledge and experience including considerations of differences in race, gender, sexuality, social class, ethnicity, religion, age, ability, and species.

"Tweet Me Your First Assaults": Writing Shame and the Rhetorical Work of #NotOkay

Stenberg's article is a timely study of the role that social media played in sparking and sustaining the #NotOkay response to the Access Hollywood Trump tape. Stenberg argues that, collectively, this hashtag "serves as an invitational space for women to rewrite assault-related shame; revises the locus of shame from the individual to the culture that shames; and generates calls to transform this emotional and rhetorical sphere." The article exemplifies how rhetorical scholars can contribute to broader discussions surrounding the most pressing issues of our time. Whereas Stenberg focuses rhetorical scrutiny on the present, Frank and Park draw our attention to the Cold War and specifically to the involvement of Robert T. Oliver, a professor of speech at Penn State, in the administration of Syngman Rhee, the first president of South Korea. As Frank and Park explain in their abstract: "Our essay fills a gap in our understanding of nation building through mythic rhetoric in the global Cold War, contributes to our disciplinary history with its focus on Oliver's role in Rhee's symbolic efforts, and offers a judgment of the mythic rhetoric crafted by the Rhee-Oliver collaboration." In addition to the fascinating transnational subject matter, Frank and Park's essay is notable for being the product of a transnational collaboration between a scholar based in the US and a scholar based in South Korea.

"Tweet Me Your First Assaults": Writing Shame and the Rhetorical Work of #NotOkay

Shari J. Stenberg

This essay features a study of the #NotOkay Twitter thread, which arose as a response to the Access Hollywood Trump tape and comprises thousands of tweets by women who describe their first experience of sexual assault. I analyze this hashtag as an act of what Elspeth Probyn calls "writing shame." I first trace the cultural habitus of emotion around sexual assault and harassment, which teaches survivors to internalize shame and normalizes assault. I then examine how #NotOkay contributors—both before and after the election—participate in writing shame, a practice that does the following rhetorical work: serves as an invitational space for women to rewrite assault-related shame; revises the locus of shame from the individual to the culture that shames; and generates calls to transform this emotional and rhetorical sphere.

On October 7, 2016, one month before the presidential election, *The Washington Post* released a now infamous recording of Donald Trump boasting about his sexual prowess.[1] In an interview with Billy Bush of *Access Hollywood*, Trump explained that his celebrity status gives him license to sexually assault women. "When you're a star, they let you do it. You can do anything," he bragged. "Grab 'em by the pussy. You can do anything."

Trump's words, amplified in the context of his presidential run, are markers of rape culture, a term coined in the 1970s that has resurfaced due to increased awareness of sexual assault. Within rape culture, sexual abuse is normalized and trivialized, a characteristic aptly reflected in Trump's defense of his words as mere "locker room banter." Since "boys will be boys," rape culture places the responsibility of avoid-

---

1. *Rhetoric Society Quarterly*, vol. 48, no. 2 © 2018 The Rhetoric Society of America. DOI: https://doi.org/10.1080/02773945.2017.1402126

ing sexual assault on women. And when they are not able to avoid it, women are blamed or disbelieved. They are shamed. Often, this shame manifests in silence.

Following the Trump tape, however, the response was different; this moment sparked an outpouring of sexual assault stories. Just after the story broke, Kelly Oxford, a bestselling author and social media figure, used Twitter to invite women to tweet her their first assaults. She issued the invitation on Friday, October 7. By Monday Oxford had received more than twenty-seven million responses, many using the hashtag #NotOkay. *New York Times* writer Amanda Taub declared the public outrage over Trump's remarks a "silver lining" to the incident. The tape, she argues, "appears to have prompted the kind of change in public consciousness that usually takes decades." Citing the widespread indignation and deluge of women's stories of sexual assault, Taub's sources deemed it a moment of "transformation" regarding both views of sexual assault and costs for speaking out. Along with the public condemnation of Trump's disregard for women came the hope that the public would hear the outcry of sexual assault survivors and reject a candidate who demeaned women. As *Slate* writer Michelle Goldberg observed, "At times, the election can feel like a referendum on whether we as a nation trust women."

For those watching the election as a gauge of the nation's stance on sexual assault, the results were devastating. This sentiment was covered in numerous national media outlets, with psychologists expressing fear that women would be deterred from speaking out or taking legal action against perpetrators (Welch). Sue Varma, a psychiatry MD, made this statement to a CBS reporter: "people will feel [a] greater sense of shame, [be] less likely to come forward, and feel belittled and invalided" (Welch).

Shame is certainly connected to sexual assault disclosure and willingness to seek prosecution (see DeCou et al.). But shame, as established by psychologist Silvan S. Tomkins, is also a response to an interest disrupted (Sedgwick and Frank). Those who held an abiding interest in seeing a public rejection of the demeaning views of women (not to mention Muslims; immigrants; lesbian, gay, bisexual, transgender, and queer [LGBTQ] folk; and people of color) likely felt that interest disrupted by the election results. In addition to disrupting interest, shame marks a break in connection, signaling unbelonging or isolation. As Catherine Olive-Marie Fox describes the emotion, "[shame courses] through my veins signaling an interest being severed: you are not like us, you do not belong here" (351). Indeed, the election results drew boundaries around what, and who, belongs, and what stories do or do not matter, in the public sphere.

But this is not the end of the story, because as Elspeth Probyn argues in *Blush: Faces of Shame*, shame reminds us "with urgency" what we value and desire (x). We feel the heat of shame when "our interest has been interfered with *but not canceled out*" (15, emphasis added). Melissa V. Harris-Perry, for instance, argues that at the same time shame leads subjects to view themselves as malignant, "black women's attempts to escape or manage shame are part of what motivates their politics" (109). Shame, then, is both a political emotion and a rhetorical exigency. Even further, feminist and queer scholars contend that shame may become a site of revisionary work.

In this essay, I focus on how women write shame, a phrase I borrow from Probyn, in order to realign themselves with a disrupted interest, commitment, or connection. Writing shame, Probyn contends, is an "ethical practice" (131) that allows us to be its "impassioned witness" (148). This act moves beyond a view of shame as "merely a personal affliction" to instead articulate it as a collision of "mind, body, place and history" (148). In this essay, I consider the rhetorical work of writing shame by sexual assault survivors as part of the Twitter hashtag #NotOkay. Because this movement was touted as evidence of a "change in public consciousness" with regard to sexual assault, I became particularly interested in this thread's rhetorical approaches and functions both before and after Trump won the presidential election.

To set the scene for this analysis, I begin with an overview of shame as a social emotion, demonstrating why and how it is often treated as feminized and deemed unworthy of attention. I then describe the emotional habitus (Gould) that shaped the rhetorical scene around sexual assault disclosure both before and after the election. Building on Bourdieu, Deborah B. Gould defines an emotional habitus as an "implicit pedagogy about what to feel and how to express one's feeling about self and society" (233). After describing my methodology and the ethical considerations of the study, I move to analyze how the women write shame when they tweet to #NotOkay, which I contend functions rhetorically in four ways: (1) it fosters an invitational sphere that allows women's shame related to sexual assault to be rewritten; (2) it denaturalizes and critiques rape culture; (3) it highlights the emotional habitus that perpetuates it; and (4) it generates calls for action. Based on my findings, I argue that writing shame is an invitational (Foss and Griffin), critical, and generative rhetorical act. Writing shame is a way to restore the interest that shame disrupts and the connection that shame severs.

The Cultural Role of Shame

Contemporary scholars agree that shame arises when a break in social connection is made or threatened, whether real or imagined (Konstan; Lewis; Scheff). Since shame involves even a "slight threat to a bond," Thomas J. Scheff suggests that it is "present or anticipated in virtually any social interaction" (256). While shame is a universal part of the human curriculum of emotion, it has historically been assigned to particular subjects, namely women, people of color, the LGBTQ community, and disabled people.

In the West, in particular, shame is often viewed as a lesser partner, or a precursor, to the preferred emotion: guilt. This conception is illuminated in Sigmund Freud's claim to have witnessed little evidence of shame in himself or male colleagues; instead, he found shame in his interactions with female patients and therefore came to view shame as the emotion of "children, women, and savages" (Scheff 251). Freud categorized guilt, in contrast, as an adult, male emotion. Guilt is often tied to a state of individualism, allowing the "morally autonomous self of the modern man [sic]" (Konstan 1031) to realign himself with his own values. Since shame is associated with the judgment of others, it is regarded as a lower emotional state than guilt, which is connected to one's own moral principles. Until recently, shame has remained largely ignored even in psychology, deemed a state of socialization passed through by children (Konstan; Scheff). To address this gap, it is helpful to turn to feminist and queer studies for articulations of shame as social and as constitutive of identity, thereby challenging shame's concealment and individuation.

One such articulation comes from Eve Kosofsky Sedgwick, who contends that a subject's life history is a record shaped in part by shame's occurrence; while shame's presence is fleeting, like the arrival of a free radical that damages a cell, it institutes "far more durable, structural changes in one's relational and interpretive strategies toward both self and others" (59). Experienced at the level of the individual, both emotionally and physiologically—through blushing, bowing the head, or folding in on oneself—what triggers shame and how (and for whom) it is deployed are closely tied to social location and social context. So while all humans experience shame, some subjects face repetitive shaming, relentless breaks in connection, and resultant social isolation. That is, in the economy of emotion, where emotion is dynamic and relational (Micciche), shame "sticks" to particular subjects, who have been shamed over and over—overtly or implicitly—leading to what Sara Ahmed names "the accumulation of affective value" (92).

The accumulation of shame is particularly significant for marginalized groups (women, LGBTQ folk, people of color, people with disabilities) who have been repeatedly marked—through language, legislation, social exclusions—as inherently shameful. W.E.B. Du Bois said being black in America means living with a "constant awareness that others view one as a problem" (Harris-Perry 109). "This observation," Harris-Perry writes, "captures shame as a defining element of African-American life" (109). To be part of a group, in this case, is to be deemed shameful; shame becomes part of how one learns to experience her identity, learns how to feel about herself.

For my purposes here, I am interested in how women are schooled by the strictures of shame. This dynamic was first made visible in Helen Block Lewis's 1971 *Shame and Guilt in Neurosis*. Lewis's analysis of hundreds of therapy session transcripts led her to discern that shame is an inherently social emotion that emerges from seeing oneself through the scrutinizing gaze of the other (real or internalized). Because women are taught to be more attuned to the needs and opinions of others, she argues, they are also more shame-prone; they are more susceptible to the consequences of a broken social tie, or of failing to meet societal ideals. As feminist scholar Jennifer C. Manion observes, women "tend to organize their personal sense of self around feelings of shame," perpetually negotiating the potential consequences of failing others' expectations (24). Because societal expectations for women are often conflicting, opportunities for shame abound.

The female body, in particular, is a target of group shaming; deemed sexualized and excessive, it serves as a "critical locus for discourses and representations that link femininity with shame" (Johnson and Moran 10). In the introduction to their collection *The Female Face of Shame*, Erica L. Johnson and Patricia Moran observe that around the globe, women's bodies are viewed as a liability, and therefore clothed and covered in "intricate and culturally freighted modes" (10); at the same time, of course, they are objectified and presented for male pleasure. And when the female body does not measure up to cultural standards of beauty, women who do not presumably discipline and control their bodies are shamed. To be read as a female body, then, is to risk being shamed, made invisible or hyper-visible to an objectifying, disciplinary gaze. This shaming is doubly loaded for women of color, who are read, and indeed, valued, according to white standards of beauty.

Shame is particularly "sticky" in relation to bodies of sexual assault survivors, due to the pervasive trope of victim-blaming in our culture. Women are blamed for what they wore, for their body language, for alcohol they may have consumed. They are shamed for being marked as sexual. And survivor shame is part of what prohibits disclosure. As Taub observes, "pervasive shame and stigma" has made silence the "rational choice" for survivors. Shame threatens to break a connection, to disrupt an interest, and when survivors are blamed for the crime, or subjected to humiliating and invasive interrogation, the threat of being disbelieved or blamed interferes with an interest in sharing one's story, let alone pressing charges.

While the prevalent role shame plays in cultural dynamics would seem to lend it visibility, in fact, the opposite is true. Because shame is deemed a shame*ful* emotion, it is often experienced overtly on an affective level but cognitively unacknowledged. Lewis finds that this results in women's experience of depression, as unacknowledged shame is turned back on the self. In shame, Lewis finds, "hostility against the self is experienced in the passive mode" (41).

For survivors of sexual assault, shame and depression are also dangerous partners. A 2016 study by Christopher DeCou et al. was the first to examine the relationship between negative social reactions, mediated by shame, and disclosure of sexual assault. Of 207 undergraduate women who had been sexually assaulted, 55% who disclosed their assault experienced victim-blaming reactions (4). Only two participants indicated they experienced no negative response to their disclosure. Most survivors—88.4% of the sample—described experiencing assault-related shame (4). The researchers further found that assault-related shame "significantly mediated the relationship between negative reactions to disclosure and symptoms of depression" (4). Internalized shame that prevents disclosure is also dangerous, leading to higher rates of "clinically significant" post-traumatic stress disorder (6). This study, then, illuminates the cultural and rhetorical climate that shapes how and whether survivors give voice to their experiences, demonstrating the salient role shame plays in interfering with disclosure and agency.

But this is not the inevitable path. Feminist and queer scholars make the important case that shame can also function as a potential site of transformation, serving as an exigency for rhetorical work. Ahmed reminds us that the origin of the word "shame" is the Indo-European verb "to cover" (104). Shame compels us to cover what is exposed, through a lowered face or averted gaze, at the same time "shame exposes that which has been covered (it un-covers)" (104). To illustrate, Ahmed uses Tomkins's example of the child whose interest is disrupted, but not annihilated, by the witness to her shame. "While the child may be ashamed before another, she or he may also be excited by that very other, such that the child may peep and look at another through the hands that cover the face" (Tomkins, paraphrased in Ahmed 105). It is this peeping that interests me—what happens when we allow ourselves to look through shame? What might shame reveal? Often, shame arises because one has failed, or refused, to adhere to a societal expectation; the "other" in this case is an internalized witness shaped by cultural norms and strictures. Here, peering through shame allows us to see what gives rise to it in the first place. This seeing may then serve as an avenue to uncover a particular cultural apparatus of shaming.

Ahmed describes shame as restorative "only when the shamed other can 'show' that its failure to measure up to a social ideal is temporary" (107). Restoration, here, indicates reestablishment and accommodation of social norms. Social structures are restored but not the subject who has been shamed. I would argue that revealing and *writing shame* works in the opposite manner, to restore the subject and resist the social structure. When shame is an affective response to one's "failure" to abide by cultural scripts, writing shame may enable one to probe "failure" as, in Judith Halberstam's words, "a way of refusing to acquiesce to dominant logics of power and disciplines" (88). Failure, Halberstam argues, "recognizes that alternatives are embedded already in the dominant and that power is never total or consistent" (88). In what follows, I examine the act of writing shame in the thread #NotOkay as a vehicle used for women to peer through, make visible, and critique the shaming messages associated with sexual assault.

"Tweet Me Your Sexual Assaults": Methodology and Ethical Considerations

To study women's rhetorical use of the thread before the election and after Trump's victory, I collected tweets from October 7–14, the week following Oxford's invitation, and November 9–16, 2016, the week after the election. The latter collection produced 1,398 tweets. To work with equal sample sizes, I randomly sampled 1,400 texts from the October group, taken from a pool of 39,084. Not only did this give me two sets of roughly equal size, but the data group was small enough that I could conduct a close analysis of the language use in the tweets.

To study the rhetorical work of this thread, I employed a coding method informed by Johnny Saldana's two-cycle process. In this first cycle, I used "process coding," which locates action in the data and uses gerunds as descriptors. Saldana deems this an appropriate method for coding action, interaction, and/or emotion in response to a situation or problem. In the first cycle of coding, my codes included phrases describing assault; commenting on ubiquity of assault; praising/supporting the women in a thread; naming rape culture; describing emotion; calling for action; describing others' response to assault disclosure; and, critiquing the media response to the Trump tape.

In the second round of coding, I developed a thematic organization of my first set of codes using "theoretical coding," wherein all categories "become systemically linked with the central or core category" (Saldana 163). More specially, I organized each theme in relationship to the larger category of "writing shame." These themes identify the particular strategies that constitute the rhetorical work of writing shame in the #NotOkay thread. They comprise the following: (1) inviting other voices and stories; (2) naming characteristics and enactments of rape culture; (3) revealing the emotional habitus that surrounds sexual assault; and (4) calling for collective rhetorical action. Within each of these categories, I conducted a more granular study of language use, coding descriptors of emotion as well as references to rape culture.[2]

Analyzing a Twitter thread like #NotOkay, where women share sensitive information, raises complicated ethical issues. On one hand, participants have chosen to make their stories public on the Twitter platform. On the other, they have not consented to be part of a study

---

2. To quantify word repetition, I used the program AntConc.

or to publicize their tweets in another context. Consulting with the Association of Internet Researchers's 2010 recommendations for ethical decision making, and following Rosemary Clark's approach in "'Hope in a Hashtag': The Discursive Activism in #WhyIStayed," I decided to replace thread contributors' Twitter handles with pseudonyms and to change 1–3 words in the tweet, so that the meaning is preserved but the tweet cannot be traced back to its writer.[3]

Because the post-election #NotOkay tweets were much more diffuse in focus than the first set, I first offer a close analysis of the October 7–14 texts to examine how they write shame. I then describe how this thread expanded in reach and focus postelection to examine how Trump's victory shaped the rhetorical work of the hashtag.

An Invitation to Disclose: Restoring Connection

If, as Taub claims, shame makes silence the "rational choice" for survivors, what allowed women, in this case, to make a different choice? What allows one to write shame? In analyzing the rhetorical conditions preceding the thread, Oxford's call, and the torrent of tweets that followed, I would argue that the first condition of writing shame was Oxford's kairotic invitation. Kelly Oxford's tweet both invited other voices and offered her own experience: "Women: tweet me your first assaults. they aren't just stats. I'll go first: Old man on city bus grabs my 'pussy' and smiles at me, I'm 12." In 111 characters, Oxford's tweet packs rhetorical punch. By calling for a "first assault," Oxford implicitly argues that for many women, assault history is multiple, thereby underscoring the pervasiveness of the problem. Further, her depiction of the incident, where a man in a public space "grabs my 'pussy' and smiles at me" mirrors Trump's language and disposition of entitlement. Recall Trump's brag to Billy Bush: "You know, I'm automatically attracted to beautiful—I just start kissing them. It's like a magnet. Just kiss. I don't even wait. And when you're a star, they let you do it. You can do anything." In describing the smile that accompanies the old man's words, Oxford surfaces the emotional habitus of rape culture, whereby a man, in a public setting, can control a female's body, without fear of reprimand. His smile shows he is in control, or perhaps, like Trump, just having fun. Fear is hers alone. But what

---

3. One exception is Kelly Oxford, whose tweets and name I have left unchanged, as she is a public figure.

makes Oxford's invitation most powerful, I contend, is that it does not require women to persuade anyone that the incident occurred. Her request cuts through the shaming mechanism of denial and doubt that is typically lodged against the victim to say, instead: you will be believed; I want to hear your story.

In their oft-cited article, "Beyond Persuasion: A Proposal for Invitational Rhetoric," Sonja K. Foss and Cindy L. Griffin forward invitational rhetoric, which is rooted in feminist understanding, as an offering to an audience rather than masculinist persuasion and control over an audience. While I would argue that persuasion and invitation need not be positioned as dualistic, Foss and Griffin's articulation of invitational rhetoric nevertheless offers a useful theoretical lens for the work of writing shame. For instance, they contend that one of the primary forms of invitational rhetoric is that of offering. The offering, or the sharing of one's story, functions first and foremost to articulate a viewpoint, rather than to convince or persuade the audience of that viewpoint. They write, "a story is not told as a means of supporting or achieving some other end but as an end in itself" (7). To value the story for its own sake is particularly crucial in the case of sharing assault stories, because of the way shaming practices work to silence them.

Importantly, the women responding to Oxford were not required to convince others of the validity of their stories, to supply evidence, to defend themselves: demands that typically accompany sexual assault disclosure. Instead, they were invited to share in a thread that would listen. As Foss and Griffin contend, "[invitational rhetoric] involves not only the offering of the rhetor's perspective but the creation of an atmosphere in which audience members' perspectives can be offered" (10). Foss and Griffin go on to contend that this kind of atmosphere is only possible if the rhetors' safety, value, and freedom are secured. I would contend that online, as in face-to-face relations, there is never a guarantee of any of these conditions. However, as thousands of tweets followed Oxford's original post, it became clear that despite the culture that fostered the need for this thread, this hashtag sponsored disclosure in the face of shame and fear. Nowhere in the sample I studied did I see anyone doubt another's story. Instead, one story seemed to beget another, and another, and another, until it became a roaring outcry. As @Kam tweets, "@kellyoxford Thank you for making us 1 collective voice … that's truly been heard. For many it is the scariest thing we've ever done. #NotOkay." Whereas shame breaks a connection, Oxford's invitation restored and sponsored mutuality.

In fact, a frequent repetition of voices offers encouragement and care to the women sharing stories. More prevalent than trolls—which, in my October sample, numbered only five—are the messages women describe as having internalized, which require them to move through shame and self-censorship in order to post. In this space, that journey is often met with encouragement from a stranger, as in this example:

> Kelly oxford Verified account @kellyoxford 8 Oct 2016 I am in such horrendous shock and yet so proud of the women sharing their assaults. #NotOkay trending in US. Not our shame anymore (October 8, 2016)

> @puccinigirlnyc @kellyoxford I've spent the last 20 min. thinking I should delete my #NotOkay tweets so people don't think I'm damaged (@nycgirl, October 8, 2016)

> @nycgirl @kellyoxford you are strong. Please know this. Your sharing helps me too #NotOkay (ava37, October 9, 2016)

Such examples demonstrate a rhetorical mutuality on this thread that changes the dominant dynamics of sexual assault disclosure, which require evidence not only of the crime but that one did not "bring it upon herself." Of course, the aim of this thread is not to prosecute the perpetrator through a criminal or legal process. The purpose is rather to claim agency in a climate of shame. "Sexual assault is a universal truth for women. You are not alone," offers @lucil, underscoring the utter pervasiveness of the problem and striving to unite women. While shame isolates, this thread fosters connection.

This is not to say, however, that writing shame is only invitational. In reviewing the tweets from the week of October 8, it became clear that as woman after woman added her story, the collective story—"the one massive voice"—contributed to a larger argument about the social nature of shame. As Thomas Scheff contends, the "taboo on shame" functions as a way of "upholding the status quo in the emotional/relational world" (258). Acknowledged shame, on the other hand, "could be the glue that holds relationships and societies together" (258). Oxford's invitational rhetoric spurred a site for connection of millions of voices to acknowledge, and to write through, shame. In so doing,

#NotOkay allowed a powerful collective voice to emerge, which makes a persuasive case about sexual assault, and its accompanying shame, as a social problem. The exigency was underscored by national coverage from outlets (CNN; *Glamour; NPR*; and *The Washington Post*). Even further, many of the tweets articulated the conditions that give rise to shame and that perpetuate the silence of sexual assault survivors. I turn, next, to examining this facet of the thread's rhetorical work.

Illuminating a Culture that Shames

Probyn contends that writing shame "provides an *argument* against considering expressions of shame as merely a personal affliction"; shame is not a personal feeling, she explains, but an "explosion of mind, body, place, and history" (148, emphasis added). The majority of the tweets that comprise the #NotOkay thread offer individual stories of brief but harrowing incidents of assault; as a collective, they make a clear argument that neither the act, nor the shame that enshrouds its survivors, are indivi-dual experiences. Woven among these stories are tweets that illuminate the conditions that normalize sexual assault and the emotional habitus that enforces silence. In what follows, I highlight a set of tweets that articulates sexual assault as a normalized part of being female and calls attention to the power dynamics that give rise to these condi-tions. Woven together with the accounts of violation, these tweets create a powerful argument about the ubiquity of assault and the conditions that allow it. They write shame as a cultural, shared phenomenon in order to seek transformation.

One rhetorical function of these tweets is to explicitly unearth sexual assault as culturally pervasive and normalized. As @chardy tweets, "LockerRoomTalk explains why every woman I know has been raped or sexually assaulted, including me." The repetition of "every woman I know" is resounding in this thread, both explicitly stated, and of course, vividly demonstrated. Writes @red57, "I bet if I asked any woman if she was ever sexually assaulted or harassed in some way? Every. Single. One. Would say yes." Adds @kbyrd, "I have untold stories. I suspect nearly every woman does & That Must & is Will Change." "Every woman I know has a story like this," tweets @kenda. Offered alongside the thousands of stories, these tweets serve as commentators, arguing that these incidents are not "personal afflictions" but evidence of a toxic public culture for women. "And what's more," @sarahart tweets, "that's the POINT of the question right? Your first, because we KNOW it won't likely be your last." The ubiquity of assaults is confirmed by @KatPowell: "For a lot of us, it's like asking what happened the first time you brushed your teeth or put on your pajamas."

Also punctuating the stories are tweets that explicitly name rape culture. In my sample of 1,400 tweets, rape culture was named nineteen times. Although only a small percentage of the overall sample, these tweets work in dialogue with the stories to name the culture that allows and silences such experiences. Paulo Freire reminds us that "to exist, humanly, is to name the world, to change it. Once named, the world in its turn reappears to its namers as a problem and requires of them a new naming" (76). This overt naming shifts the shame from the individuals who experienced assault and places it on a culture that denies women agency over their bodies. As @shine89 writes, "9,700,000 stores of sexual violence have been shared on Twitter. This is rape culture."

Indeed, several of these contributors use their tweets to simply acknowledge that rape culture is "real" and rape culture "exists." These tweets serve as a challenge to cultural messages like that of Caroline Kitchens, who, in a *TIME* magazine opinion piece, equates rape culture theory to a kind of hysteria that "poison[s] the minds of young women and lead[s] to hostile environments for innocent males." Women, according to this logic, are imagining or exaggerating the cultural messages they experience. In contrast, the #NotOkay contributors make the workings of rape culture explicit, showing that the poison is not inside them but in cultural workings that normalize rape and sexual harassment. As @yourebrave tweets, "Anyone who questions rape culture should read this #NotOkay thread. It's happening to our sisters, cousins, friends, girlfriends and MUST STOP."

Women's internalization of this toxic culture, in fact, is a form of shaming and is one of the costs of naturalizing rape culture and assigning blame to assault survivors. Harris-Perry uses field dependence theory to describe this experience for African-American women. In one study, subjects were placed in a room that was tilted as much as 35 degrees and then asked to align themselves vertically (29): "Some individuals assume the room must be correct, so they adapt themselves to it, while others can detect that the room itself is askew. When we feel ashamed, we assume the room is straight and that the self is off-kilter. Shame urges us to internalize the crooked room" (105). In the #NotOkay thread, women describe experiencing a tilted reality ascribed as a personal affliction, not a cultural misalignment. They reveal rape culture as a crooked room.

This revelation is evident in tweets in which women describe being told that their experience of assault or harassment is part of "being a woman." @phillip-brown writes, "Next was groping by the boy babysitting my little brother and me. My mother said it was part of growing up. #NotOkay." Referring to Trump's claim that "when you're a star, they let you do it," @berkeley tweets, "I've had strangers 'grab my pussy' without asking. They weren't even stars! I guess that's just being a woman in a public space. #NotOkay." "My best male friends constantly objectified me & I normalized it bc that's what I thought being the only girl meant. #NotOkay," offers @JPont. Similarly, @ramazz writes, "#NotOkay Being sexually assaulted by your boyfriend for 6 months and thinking this is what I do as a female. This is intimacy." These texts highlight the "room" as skewed, showing how women and men learn roles and attitudes that allow assault to be normalized. If they are troubled, they are told they need to adjust their thinking and feelings. This requirement is underscored by @cflora: "#NotOkay 17yrs old..at work. Told my boss, a female Doctor. She said to me, That's how men are. He stayed. I quit."

Another way tweets in this category illuminate such conditions is by naming the power dynamics that result in excusing men and disbelieving women. In a tweet that received 179 "likes," @Harris-Jay writes, "I wish Hillary would say that not only Trump's behavior toward women but her husbands was wrong. That was #NotOkay either." Other tweets mention Bill Cosby and Brock Turner, a former Stanford student who was sentenced to a mere six months in prison, of which he served only three, after raping an unconscious woman at a party. Writes @TMandy, "Trump's words are locker room talk just like Brock Turner was 'just a good kid having some fun.'" Here, contributors link to a visible cultural pattern of men in power being excused for sexual assault. Contributor @leadla calls out Eric Trump for explaining that "locker room talk" sometimes happens when "alpha personalities are in the same presence" (Keneally). She writes, "You know where it's common, Eric? Among men who commit assault. #NotAnExcuse #NotOkay." By revealing a cultural repetition of excusing male abuse of power, the contributors refuse to allow further normalization of the problem.

Another subtheme in this category reveals women's experience of being disbelieved and silenced. Writing through this silence illuminates it as a cultural problem. Writes @lolea, "A LOT of #men #trump supporters r bashing women cuz we never told. We don't tell cuz ppl don't believe us! #cops #family #friends #NotOkay." As many tweets highlight, this propensity to disbelieve and silence survivors is learned as much in the family as in larger cultural messages. "My abuse at age 7 was reported to the police. Years later, my parents continue to ignore my questions about it," offers @gicody.

Still other tweets in this category point to the shaming mechanism of blaming the survivor for the assault by not punishing the perpetrator. In many cases, these lessons are learned as girls and reinforced by authority figures. @diamond explains, "5, creepy relative grabs, gropes, and kisses me. I glare and wipe it off. Mother slaps me/makes me say sorry to him. #NotOkay." For others, it surfaces with adolescence; a developing woman's body invites harassment. Tweets @sjol, "#NotOkay in 6th grade, boys began to grope me in the halls. Told once-was ignored and dismissed by the principal." A similar story is narrated by @julhope: "#NotOkay 11, two senior boys grope and harass me on school bus. Driver punished me, Made me sit in the front seat all year for being bad." And finally, tweets in this category reveal the conflation of sexual intimacy and sexual assault that too often occurs in our culture: @edred writes, "My first sexual experience in high school, not my choice. My classmates shamed me for it and I had to transfer. #NotOkay."

Together, the stories and the commentary make visible the toxic conditions that give rise to and normalize these incidents and depict the shame women experience as a result. I turn next to show how this thread illuminates the emotional cost of rape culture, making intelligible emotions that are usually squelched.

REVEALING THE EMOTIONAL HABITUS

In her article "Going Public—in a Disabling Discourse" Linda Flower complicates the notion of "going public" in a sphere that valorizes "critical rationality" (109). She draws on Habermas's normative vision of the public sphere to underscore that the "power, the glory, and the trademark" of its reigning discourse requires a disinterested "critical rationality" that excludes the private and, I would add, the emotional, realm (109). Articulations of emotion are often devalued and disregarded in the public sphere, rather than treated as inseparable from reason. As a result, cultural apparatuses of emotion are hidden from public view—or shamed into hiding. This dynamic is evident in then-vice presidential nominee Mike Pence's response to First Lady Michelle Obama's speech addressing the Trump tapes. In her speech, Obama describes her emotional response to Trump's words as part of her condemnation of them: "I can't believe that I'm saying that a candidate for president of the United States has bragged about sexually assaulting women. And I have to tell you that I can't stop thinking about this. It has shaken me to my core in a way that I couldn't have predicted." She proceeds to name the emotional ramifications women experience in the face of words that shame:

> It is cruel. It's frightening. And the truth is, it hurts. It hurts. It's like that sick, sinking feeling you get when you're walking down the street minding your own business and some guy yells out vulgar words about your body.
>
> … Maybe we've grown accustomed to swallowing these emotions and staying quiet, because we've seen that people often won't take our word over his. Or maybe we don't want to believe that there are still people out there who think so little of us as women. Too many are treating this as just another day's headline, as if our outrage is overblown or unwarranted, as if this is normal, just politics as usual.

Pence's response to Obama's speech proves her point. "I have a lot of respect for the first lady and the job she has done for the American people over the last seven and a half years," he said. "But I don't understand *the basis of her claim*" (qtd. in Nelson et al., emphasis added). He goes on to insist that although regrettable, it was "just talk" (Nelson et al.). Consequently, her response seems unreasonable, because, he says, Trump did not act on his comments. His comments suggest that her emotioned response is not intelligible, has no basis, in the public sphere.

Meanwhile, *The Washington Post* hailed this speech as "epic" and "remarkable," deeming it one of the most powerful speeches delivered during the Hillary Clinton campaign. Columnist Chris Cillizza describes the speech as a "moment in which she crystallized the feelings of many women in the wake of the Trump tape. She was outraged, yes, but also hurt—for herself and for women more broadly. And she expressed all of those emotions in ways you rarely see any politician (or private citizen do)—particularly one as well known as Obama." Contributors to the #NotOkay thread agreed, responding with gratitude and passion for Obama's words. Writes @newspring, "Thank you, @FLOTUS! I needed your words today. I woke up in a political despair today & you reminded all of us, this is #NotOkay." Tweets @hilaryk, "Getting my newsletter out at work, but had @Flotus in my earbuds and I wanted to stand at my desk and start shouting! #NotOkay." Indeed, in a harrowing thread depicting thousands of sexual assault stories, these are among the few representing celebration and relief. Michelle Obama's act of melding an emotioned response to the rebuking of a cultural problem highlights the emotional habitus; reveals the ramifications for women; and invites other women to do the same.

While it is impossible to determine whether this is causal, my sample showed that tweets articulating emotional descriptors (i.e., shame, sick, exhausted, overwhelmed, etc.) began to emerge on the date after Obama's speech. The most frequently occurring emotional descriptor was "shame," which occurred twenty-one times, followed by "my fault," which occurred eighteen times. "Sad" was mentioned thirteen times and "sick" seven times. In reference to the #NotOkay hashtag itself, "heartbreaking" was used sixteen times. "Angry" was used just once. At the same time, the declaration of #NotOkay that accompanies each tweet articulates a righteous anger that simultaneously makes an argument: these acts, this culture, and the emotions survivors are taught to bear are unacceptable.

By articulating the emotions that accompany sexual assault and harassment, this thread reveals an emotional habitus that gains its power through concealment. As Gould argues, in order to understand and respond to an emotional habitus, we need to ask how feelings are produced, how power dynamics are "exercised through and reproduced in our feelings," and how society's prevalent feelings and taken-for-granted understandings and norms constitute and discipline its members (228). The act of writing shame involves answering these questions.

As I suggest above, many of the tweets either mention shame directly or depict the self as lacking worth, bad, or wrong—in need of cover. "#NotOkay is hiding myself as an adult behind hats, oversized clothes & bare face to avoid drawing attention from men in public" tweets @morgic. Ahmed describes this turning away as part of the physicality of experiencing shame. Shame involves the "de-forming and re-forming of bodily and social spaces, as bodies 'turn away' from others who witness the shame," she writes (103). Because of the cultural denial of sexual assault and silencing of its survivors, women learn to attribute their pain to their own embodied selves, which they then seek to cover and disguise.

Writes @fleur, "Hiding behind glasses, wearing baggy clothes, avoiding people....what did you try? #NotOkay." This tweet is striking because she describes the concealment that she has sought, while at the same time she uses direct address—"what did you try?"—to connect with, rather than to turn away from, others. The "you" she addresses here is not the judgmental other (likely both internalized and real) that has disciplined her feelings and prompted her to hide. It is an audience she assumes shares an experience, whom she then invites into conversation.

Texts in this category also highlight the emotional habitus surrounding sexual assault by naming the Trump tapes as a "trigger." #NotOkay contributors describe how Trump's lewd and entitled remarks about women resurfaced emotional pain from past abuse or trauma. Explains @sunrae, "Never in a thousand years would I have imagined my ptsd triggered repeatedly by a election, but here we are. #NotOkay." Addressing the First Lady, @bimlla tweets, "@FLOTUS I recognize your outrage as my own. I also can't stop thinking about it. His comments triggered millions of women. #NotOkay." Writes @Rokslam, "I'm a sexual assault survivor too, triggered and sickened by Trump and his predatory ways. #NotOkay." Demonstrating the impact of Trump's comments, during the weekend after the Trump tape's release, the Rape, Abuse and Incest National Network saw a 33% increase in calls to its hotline for support, and its web traffic rose by 45% (Goldberg). Some #NotOkay contributors named the feed itself as triggering. For my purposes here, though, I want to underscore that naming the Trump tapes as triggering reveals the emotional weight survivors bear, a weight that is not usually discussed in the public sphere.

Part of what makes tapes, and the discourse around them, triggering is that so much of the discourse reinforces the "crooked room" for survivors. In writing about Trump's triggering effect for *Slate*, columnist Michelle Goldberg explains that Trump's denial of this moment's gravity combined with his blaming of the women who came forward as victims of harassment by him,[4] resurface a larger pattern of abusers who "crowd out their victims' sense of reality." To elucidate the dynamic further, she quotes trauma therapist Kristin Seslar, "In conversation and arguments with this person who is so able to change reality or deny reality and shift blame and responsibility, the victim ends up doubting [herself], getting really confused, feeling really unstable." That is to say, the survivor learns to feel, to believe, herself as an *unreliable witness* to her own experience. This emotion of shame and "it's my fault" is reinforced again and again through acts of victim blaming, a justice system that puts survivors on trial, and in a culture that normalizes objectification of and violence against women. *Los Angeles Times* columnist Robin Mather aptly summarizes the situation as "a form of emotional terrorism employed against women and children."

The final emotion I want to address, repeated in tweets that use "sad" or "heartbreaking," is that of grief. In all cases, the sadness is a response to the epidemic of sexual assault revealed by the thread. "I shouldn't be surprised by this, but it still breaks my heart #NotOkay," tweets @G_Ruban. "Reading this thread is completely heartbreaking. i think about my own assaults and hurt for every woman that has been through it. #NotOkay," writes @allyemma. Because the pain of sexual assault and harassment survivors is privatized, the need for grieving is not recognized. In discussing what she calls a "queer politics of grief," Ahmed asserts that those whose losses are not publicly acknowledged need "space and time to grieve," and to be recognized as the "subject rather than the object of grief" (161). While she is focused on loss of loved ones for the gay community after 9/11, her call for recognition of grief that is culturally denied seems helpful in analyzing the #NotOkay thread. Here, women write their sadness into being; they mark these stories as worthy of the time and space of grief, and they grieve a culture that allows this to happen, over and over, most often to women and children.

By highlighting a collective shaming that survivors face, this thread makes legible how power dynamics are "exercised through and repro-

---

4. In a campaign rally, Trump denied the claims of one woman, saying, "Take a look, you take a look. Look at her, look at her words, you tell me what you think. I don't think so," indicating she was not attractive enough to merit his advances (Lim).

duced in our feelings" (Gould 228) and how these norms discipline and shame women to be silent. In describing the emotions that circulate through and around the experience of assault, women write with, and through, the shame in order, ultimately, to name these dynamics as "not okay." There is transformative power in revealing what is violently concealed. There is also transformative power in women bearing witness to one another's testimonies, to see that one is not alone in the experience or in the feelings that accompany it. In "Shame and the Future of Feminism," Jill Locke argues that it is "the availabilty of a meaningful sphere of action" or a "radical counterpublic"[5] that may undercut the power of shame and allow an "alternative world" to be visible (156). In this thread, women witness thousands of stories of sexual assault; they reveal and complicate the shame that women are taught to feel as a result; and they create a counterpublic in which members insist, "this is *not okay*."

The Aftermath: Calls for Action against a Trump Presidency

I turn now to briefly analyze themes within the 1,398 tweets that surfaced between November 9 and November 16, the week following the 2016 election, on the #NotOkay thread. I sought to discover what the thread might reveal about the emotional habitus following the election, whether its work of writing shame prior to November 8 would be undone, and whether (and how) its rhetorical effects might continue to reverberate.

In fact, I found that after the election, the thread ceased to serve as a site to post assault stories and instead became a place for people to respond to the election and to call for action. The subject of sexual violation, however, remained prominent, with fifty-six mentions of assault; twenty of harassment; eleven of abuse; and eight of rape. Additionally, misogyny is mentioned thirty-eight times and sexism/sexist twenty-two. Many tweets underscore the devastating effect of Trump's win for those who have suffered assault, harassment, or abuse. Tweets @cross5, "This isn't just horrific, it is an atrocity. Asking women to

---

5. For another study of a feminist counterpublic surfacing on Twitter, see Jackson and Banaszczyk's "Digital Standpoints: Debating Gendered Violence and Racial Exclusions in the Feminist Counterpublic," which features #YesAllWomen and #YesAllWhiteWomen.

accept him as POTUS is more abuse #notmypresident #NotOkay." "Heartbroken for the brave women who shared their sexual assault stories, only to have sexual predator elected to White House. #NotOkay," writes @atinsects.

The work of writing shame in relation to sexual assault continues, however, through mentions of a video project inspired by #NotOkay. Film reporter, writer, and producer Alicia Malone followed #NotOkay with "The Girls on Film are #NotOkay," a three part depiction of women in the film industry sharing stories of sexual assault, abuse, and harassment. The video is mentioned in forty tweets, demonstrating a continued commitment to making stories of assault survivors audible.

While the October sample is marked by shame and sadness, the emotional tenor of the November sample is much more varied. "Sad" surfaces twenty-five times, but the eighteen references to shame are directed outward at voters, the country, or Trump, rather than inward, as in the October sample. Writes @shelive, "Fellow white women, this is highly shameful. We betrayed ourselves and enabled, celebrated an abuser. #NotOkay." Tweets @MsGood, "#Trump supporters who share any of his racist, sexist or homophobic views should be deeply ashamed! #NotOkay." "It is a sad day in US when citizens feel this kind of shame for a chosen leader. #NotOkay," offers @NoCon. In this thread, shame is transported from the bodies of assault survivors to a body politic of citizens who voted for Trump. As such, it can be seen, critiqued, and challenged.

In the days following the election, the #NotOkay thread also expanded its scope to condemn not only sexual assault but also racism, homophobia, and Islamophobia. Rascism/racist is mentioned sixty-seven times, in reference both to election results and to reports that Trump would appoint Steve Bannon to his Cabinet. The thread also decries the hate acts that surfaced after the election, including demeaning and violent threats to Melania Trump. If there is any overarching emotion mentioned, it is defiance. #Notmypresident is the most commonly used hashtag (aside from #NotOkay), evoked 238 times.

Sedgwick contends that while shame cannot be excised like a toxic part of one's identity, the forms taken by shame "are available for the work of metamorphosis, reframing, refiguration, transformation" (60). In the November sample, we see the work of writing shame transformed into calls for action, and the action items widened to defy acts of hate more broadly. While the week following the election was emotionally fraught and marked with high levels of uncertainty, the seeds of activism are visible in the #NotOkay thread. The Women's March on Washington was already in the works, and Kelly Oxford's November 12 tweet, "In October I asked if we could all share our stories of sexual assault. #notokay was born. Can you march on Washington JAN 21 with me?" was retweeted 683 times and received 3,415 likes—the highest number of any tweet in this thread. In addition to mentions of the march, contributors began to advocate for Grab Your Wallet, a campaign that surfaced after the Trump tapes were released, encouraging consumers to avoid retailers that carry Trump products.

While there is clearly much despair evident in the November sample, there is also a swelling of righteous anger. The word angry surface five times, furious three, and offended twice; more than through emotional descriptors, however, anger manifests in pleas for action. As Gould observes, the emotional habitus affects which political acts seem possible for marginalized subjects, and whether these calls pull toward social conformity or confrontation (224). Writes @mari34, "This is no time for unity, it is time for confrontation. This is worth fighting for. #President Trump #NotOkay." In response to someone telling her to "pump the breaks," @A4babies writes, "have you ever experienced a sexual assault? I will not hit the breaks, I will fight back #NotOkay." Other tweets follow a similar tack:

> be angry, rage against this, speak despite quivering voice, be compassionate & loving #TrumpHate #overcome #fight #NotOkay"(@Ninedoors, November 9, 2016)

> This is NOT going to be our new world under Trump. We must refuse to back down! #LoveTrumpsHate #NotOkay (@balane, November 15, 2016)

> In addition to solidarity with immigrants, minorities & Muslims, I'm protesting today because it's something I can DO to say #NotOkay (@bailih, November 12, 2016).

If writing shame is an ethical act (Probyn), its rhetorical purview, at least in this thread, begins with the self and moves to cultural mechanisms of shaming that dehumanize and disregard others. In an October 10 *New York Times* article on Trump's "locker room talk," Julie Oppenheimer, who shared her assault stories, is quoted as saying, "I've never really thought about these moments cumulatively before.

In part, because they seem so 'small' compared to what many have experienced—not worthy of consideration. That's because all of us already live in Trump's world, where these behaviors are commonplace" (Mahler). Rather than returning to silence after posting their #NotOkay stories, women were prompted to act after the election, writing from their own shame to offer ways to protest and to resist what has become commonplace. This is shame transformed.

Conclusion: Lessons from #NotOkay

While Trump's comments to *Access Hollywood* occurred 11 years before the election, his administration's approach to sexual assault vis-à-vis Title IX signals a continued disregard for survivors. In September 2017, Education Secretary Betsy DeVos rescinded the Obama era Title IX guidance, now allowing universities to require a higher burden of proof, and thus, providing more protection for the accused.

This undermining of sexual assault survivors' ethos will undoubtedly reverberate on campuses across the nation and shape broader public conversations about sexual assault. This public discourse, in turn, influences the emotional habitus that surrounds sexual assault, teaching survivors that should they publicly disclose, they will not be believed. In short, the Trump administration's public actions and statements function to shame survivors.

For this reason, counterpublics like the #NotOkay movement are all the more crucial in this political moment. Not only do they serve as an invitational, collective space for survivors, but they also offer insight into the conditions that allow women to speak of shame and the rhetorical strategies that help to transform it.

Those of us who study, teach, and practice rhetoric can build on this important work, seeking to illuminate how rhetorical agency is enmeshed not only in social, historical, and political structures but also *emotional* systems. Doing so means challenging the enduring presumption of a rational, sovereign rhetorical agent and acknowledging the rhetor as a thinking, feeling, embodied subject. Building on this work also involves analyzing the tactics used by counterpublics to challenge the normative emotional habitus. What does it mean to speak into a culture that shames? How do counterpublics—from the Women's March to Black Lives Matter—do rhetorical work that allows for connections to be made, shame to be disrupted, and transformation to occur?

This attention to the interface of rhetorical action and the emotional habitus in which it occurs will not only lead to deeper, more nuanced rhetorical analysis and engagement, but it will also serve to expand our "vocabularies of emotion" (Worsham) so that we may unearth the workings of shame that disproportionately affect marginalized groups. Perhaps most importantly, attending to shame as part of the rhetorical scene helps us—and our students—see how rhetors work with and transform shame into powerful narratives, testimonies, and activism. This witnessing, in turn, gives us all access to new available means of persuasion.

Acknowledgments

I am indebted to Zach Beare for his support and wisdom through many iterations of this project and for our ongoing conversations about the importance of making abject emotions visible. I also thank Debbie Minter, Chris Gallagher, two anonymous reviewers, and editor Susan Jarratt for fueling forward movement of this piece. Justin Collier captured the Twitter sample for this study; I am grateful for his assistance.

Works Cited

Ahmed, Sara. *The Cultural Politics of Emotion*. New York: Routledge, 2015. Print.

Cillizza, Chris. "Michelle Obama's Speech on Donald Trump Was Remarkable." *The Washington Post*. 13 Oct. 2016. Web. 26 Sept. 2017.

Clark, Rosemary. ""Hope in a Hashtag": The Discursive Activism of #WhyIStayed." *Feminist Media Studies* 16.5 (2016): 788–804. Print.

Decou, Christopher R., Trevor T. Cole, Shannon M. Lynch, Maria M. Wong, and Kathleen C. Matthews. "Assault-Related Shame Mediates the Association between Negative Social Reactions to Disclosure of Sexual Assault and Psychological Distress." *Psychological Trauma: Theory, Research, Practice, and Policy* 9.2 (2017): 166–72. Web. 26 Sept. 2017.

Flower, Linda. "Going Public—In a Disabling Discourse." *The Public Work of Rhetoric: Citizen-Scholars and Civic Engagement*. Ed. John Ackerman and David Coogan. Columbia: U of South Carolina, 2013. 104–18. Print.

Foss, Sonja K., and Cindy L. Griffin. "Beyond Persuasion: A Proposal for an Invitational Rhetoric." *Communication Monographs* 62.1 (1995): 2–18. Web. 26 Sept. 2017.

Fox, Catherine Olive-Marie. "Toward a Queerly Classed Analysis of Shame: Attunement to Bodies in English Studies." *College English* 76.4 (2014): 337–56. Print.

Freire, Paulo. *Pedagogy of the Oppressed*. New York: Continuum, 2000. Print.

Goldberg, Michelle. "Donald Trump Is a Human Trigger." *Slate Magazine*. N. pag. 18 Oct. 2016. Web. 26 Sept. 2017.

Gould, Deborah B. "The Shame of Gay Pride in Early AIDS Activism." *Gay Shame*. Ed. David M. Halperin and Valerie Traub. Chicago: U of Chicago P, 2009. 221–55. Print.

Halberstam, Judith. *The Queer Art of Failure*. Durham: Duke UP, 2011. Print.

Harris-Perry, Melissa V. *Sister Citizen: Shame, Stereotypes, and Black Women in America*. New Haven: Yale UP, 2013. Print.

Jackson, Sarah J., and Sonia Banaszczyk. "Digital Standpoints: Debating Gendered Violence and Racial Exclusions in the Feminist Counterpublic." *Journal of Communication Inquiry* 40.4 (2016): 391–407. Print.

Johnson, Erica L., and Patricia Moran. *The Female Face of Shame*. Bloomington: Indiana UP, 2013. Print.

Keneally, Meghan. "Eric Trump Says 'Alpha Personalities' Sometimes Engage in 'Locker Room Talk.'" *ABC News*. 11 Oct. 2016. Web. 26 Sept. 2017.

Kitchens, Caroline. "It's Time to End 'Rape Culture' Hysteria." *Time*. 20 Mar. 2014. Web. 26 Sept. 2017.

Konstan, David. "Shame in Ancient Greece." *Social Research* 70.4 (2003): 1031–60. Print. Lewis, Helen Block. *Shame and Guilt in Neurosis*. New York: International Universities, 1974. Print.

Lim, Naomi. "Donald Trump on Accuser: 'Take a Look at Her … I Don't Think So.'" *CNN.com*. 13 Oct. 2016. Web. 26 Sept. 2017.

Locke, Jill. "Shame and the Future of Feminism." *Hypatia* 22.4 (2007): 146–62. Web. 26 Sept. 2017.

Mahler, Jonathan. "For Many Women, Trump's 'Locker Room Talk' Brings Memories of Abuse." *The New York Times*. 10 Oct. 2016. Web. 26 Sept. 2017.

Manion, Jennifer C. "Girls Blush, Sometimes: Gender, Moral Agency, and the Problem of Shame." *Hypatia* 18.3 (2003): 21–41. Web. 26 Sept. 2017.

Mather, Robin. "For Survivors of Sexual Abuse, the Presidential Campaign Is a Giant Trigger." *Los Angeles Times*. 14 Oct. 2016. Web. 27 Nov. 2017.

Micciche, Laura R. *Doing Emotion: Rhetoric, Writing, Teaching*. Portsmouth: Boynton/Cook, 2007. Print.

Nelson, Louis, Nolan D. McCaskill, Richard Gowan, Zia Weise, Bill Scher, and David McKean. "Pence: 'I Don't Understand the Basis' of Michelle Obama's Claims." *Politico*. N. pag. 14 Oct. 2016. Web. 27 Nov. 2017.

Probyn, Elspeth. *Blush: Faces of Shame*. Minneapolis: U of Minnesota, 2005. Print.

Saldana, Johnny. *The Coding Manual for Qualitative Researchers*. Los Angeles: SAGE, 2015. Print.

Scheff, Thomas J. "Shame in Self and Society." *Symbolic Interaction* 26.2 (2003): 239–62. Print. Sedgwick, Eve Kosofsky. "Shame, Theatricality, and Queer Performativity: Henry James's *The Art of the Novel*." *Gay Shame*. Ed. David M. Halperin and Valerie Traub. Chicago: U of Chicago P, 2009. 49–62. Print.

Sedgwick, Eve Kosofsky, and Adam Frank, eds. *Shame and Its Sisters: A Silvan Tompkins Reader*. Durham, NC: Duke UP, 1995. Print.

Taub, Amanda. "Trump Recording Narrows Divide on Sexual Assault." *New York Times*. N.pag. 22 Oct. 2016. Web. 26 Sept. 2017.

Tomkins, Silvan S. *Affect, Imagery, Consciousness: The Negative Affects. Volume 2*. New York: Springer, 1963. Print.

"TRANSCRIPT: Michelle Obama's Speech On Donald Trump's Alleged Treatment Of Women." *NPR*. 13 Oct. 2016. Web. 26 Sept. 2017.

Welch, Ashley. "Sexual Assault Survivors Struggle to Cope with Trump Election." *CBS News*. N. pag. 17 Nov. 2016. Web. 26 Sept. 2017.

Worsham, Lynn. "Pedagogic Violence and the Schooling of Emotion." *JAC* 18.2 (1998): 213–45. Print.

Supplemental Material

Part I: Reflection on the Origins of the Article

On the night of the 2016 Presidential election, I watched with cautious optimism as the newscasters began to shade their maps with red and blue. I believed we were on the cusp of electing our country's first female president. Friends wrote me throughout the day, expressing emotion from gratitude to awe about seeing a woman's name on the ballot. This was a sign, many of us believed, that as a country, our boundaries around belonging were shifting. It wouldn't change everything, of course, but the election of Hillary Clinton would serve as a vehement objection to the names she had been called, to the disciplining of her body and emotions, to the times she had been interrupted (she, and so many women). It would provide a defiant "no" to condoning sexual assault as "locker room talk" and to the idea that women are objects for men to judge and score. This, I admit, was foremost on my mind. Just weeks before the election, a *New York Times* article contended that Trump's boasting about sexual assault "appears to have prompted the kind of change in public consciousness that usually takes decades" (Taub). Citing the widespread outrage and outpouring of women's stories of sexual assault, sources interviewed deemed it a moment of "transformation" regarding both views of sexual assault and costs for speaking out. Clinton's election, I reasoned, would confirm that this was so.

We all know what happened next. And when the map's saturation in red made a Clinton victory impossible, I didn't, at first, feel sadness or anger. Heat crawled up my face. I felt shame.

Despite having immersed myself in shame research for the last several years, I was initially perplexed by this response. Upon further reflection, however, I began to understand why shame surfaced. Psychologist Silvan Tomkins names shame as a response to an interest disrupted. My deep and abiding interest in seeing the derogatory and disturbing views of women (not to mention Muslims, immigrants, and people of color) publicly rejected was disrupted by the election results. In addition to marking an interference of interest, shame represents a break from connection. In her 2014 *College English* essay "Toward a Queerly Classed Analysis of Shame: Attunement to Bodies in English Studies" Catherine Olive-Marie Fox powerfully describes shame's effects: "[shame courses] through my veins signaling an interest being severed: you are not like us, you do not belong here" (351). This is how shame feels—like isolation or unbelonging.

In search of connection, I wanted to understand how other women were navigating this cultural and political moment, and I became particularly interested in the women who, upon release of the Access Hollywood tape, defiantly and publicly stated, #NotOkay. Even more, I wondered what happened to the thread after Trump's election; what were women doing with their emotion? This is how the study began.

Part II: Description of Research Methods, Findings, and/or Pedagogical Impact

I have long been interested in emotion as a site of pedagogy—in the notion that we learn not only through cognition but also through emotion. The concept of the emotional habitus I feature in this piece, drawn from Deborah B. Gould (who is informed by Bourdieu), is also helpful pedagogically: the emotional habitus is "an implicit pedagogy about what to feel and how to express one's feeling about self and society." Using this concept in class, I prompt my students to mine their experiences for how they *learned to feel* about an issue, a concept, or even themselves. As we study the rhetorical contexts that surround sexual assault, we can examine the emotional habitus that shapes public and private responses. What cultural messages teach us to "feel" that harassment is mere "locker room talk"? How do women learn to feel that they are at fault, even if they "know" better, when assault occurs? What are the costs for speaking up, and what kind of emotional labor is required in doing so?

This work extends to larger cultural messages about emotions, too, as we explore what the range of acceptable emotions we are allowed to express and in what contexts. Who is regaled and who is punished for expressing particular feelings? How is the emotional habitus experienced differently depending on one's social location? Last semester, in my Intro to Women's and Gender Studies class, my students and I had a dynamic conversation about tennis player Serena Williams, who was penalized for showing anger during the 2018 U.S. Open final. We grappled with these questions: What messages have you heard about anger and gender? What does it mean for a woman to show anger? How is displaying anger even more fraught for a black woman? One of my students shared that as a black woman, she finds that no matter her expression or body language, white people read her as angry. So, in our predominantly white institution, she finds herself monitoring her speech, behavior, and facial expressions to try to control this reading by others; the labor to ensure the comfort of white people falls on her.

The #NotOkay movement shows us, however, that there are possibilities for disrupting the emotional habitus, as we see shame transformed into connection and action. In a historical moment marked by social activism, from Black Lives Matter to Pipeline Protests, we can also consider how counterpublics disrupt shaming practices. How does the formation of counterpublics allow for connection to be made, for shame to be disrupted, and for transformation to occur? How does an invitation to share an experience squelched or denied by dominant pedagogies allow for possibilities of new, transformative rhetorical work?

The concepts I worked with in this article, then, have helped me to sponsor what Lynn Worsham calls a "vocabulary of emotion," so that my students and I can attend more closely to how rhetorical situation is enmeshed not only in social, historical, political structures, but also *emotional* systems.

Part III: Discussion Questions

1. Melissa V. Harris-Perry argues that shame both leads black women to view themselves as malignant and is part of what motivates their politics (109). In this way, shame may serve as a political emotion and a rhetorical exigency. Can you think of other examples when abject emotions, like shame or anger, become an exigence for rhetorical or political work?

2. Since the emergence of #NotOkay, we have seen a proliferation of hashtag movements, from #MeToo to #NeverAgain. What do you see as the rhetorical possibilities and limitations of hashtag movements? How do we measure the success of a hashtag movement? For whom?

3. In their study of shame as a barrier to sexual assault disclosure, DeCou et al. contend that we need to revise reporting procedures so that they address assault-related shame, a change that may increase reporting among undergraduate women (6). What aspects of the reporting process on your own campus might contribute to the emotional habitus around reporting? What would be required to acknowledge and alter the emotional habitus that fosters assault-related shame on college campuses?

LITERACY IN COMPOSITION STUDIES

Literacy in Composition Studies is on the Web at http://licsjournal.org

Literacy in Composition Studies is a refereed open access online journal sponsoring scholarly activity at the nexus of Literacy and Composition Studies. With *literacy* and *composition* as our keywords we denote practices that are deeply context-bound and always ideological and recognize the institutional, disciplinary, and historical contexts surrounding the range of writing courses offered at the college level. Literacy is often a metaphor for the ability to navigate systems, cultures, and situations. At its heart, literacy is linked to interpretation—to reading the social environment and engaging and remaking that environment through communication. Orienting a Composition Studies journal around literacy prompts us to analyze the connections and disconnections among writing, reading and interpretation, inviting us to examine the ways in which literacy constitutes writer, context, and act.

Toward a Theory and Pedagogy of Rhetorical Vulnerability[1]

David Riche's "Toward a Theory and Pedagogy of Rhetorical Vulnerability" was also published in the *LiCS* special issue "Literacy, Democracy, and Fake News." We nominated this piece because in it Riche offers a new approach to teaching rhetoric in response to the changing rhetorical landscape. Focusing on examples of public trolling on Twitter and fake news stories, including the Pizzagate controversy, Riche examines how discussing fake news and trolling rhetoric with students can help them understand "something fundamental about how we experience rhetoric" (93). According to Riche, it's no longer sufficient to teach students how to critically evaluate sources; instead, we have to help students recognize how rhetorical actions can and do "manage" people's vulnerabilities. Teaching students to recognize the linkages between rhetoric and vulnerability is crucial because, in Riche's words, "fake news stories do not simply work to deceive audiences; they also work to disturb audiences, subvert trust, and disrupt critical literacies before we are even aware of such rhetorical effects" (92).

---

1. *Literacy in Composition Studies*, vol. 5, no. 2 © 2017 by David Riche. Creative Commons Attribution 3.0 License.

Toward a Theory and Pedagogy of Rhetorical Vulnerability

David Riche

This article responds to the proliferation of fake news in today's media by considering how a rhetorical theory and pedagogy more deeply grounded in a rethinking of vulnerability might help us as rhetoricians and writing scholars to address fake news as more than just dis-informative rhetoric. In the first part, I bring together scholarship from within and outside of rhetoric and writing studies in order to frame vulnerability as a fundamental component of all rhetorical encounters. In the second part, I propose the use of trolling rhetoric as an object of analysis that may help students better understand how deceptive and disruptive genres of discourse (including, but not limited to, fake news) may, in the process of trying to exploit our rhetorical vulnerability, actually call attention to this crucial aspect of rhetorical encounters.

The question of what speech has made asks at least two things: what account can we give of language's capacity for effecting change, and at the same time, what account can we give of ourselves as manipulators of language's capacity for effecting change?
—Richard Marback, *Managing Vulnerability* (16)

On more than one occasion during my time as a graduate student, I had the experience of passing through a section of campus known as Free Speech Alley within earshot of a local church group as they publicly vilified the stereotypical sources of modern America's moral disintegration, including unwed mothers, godless liberals, Muslims, and homosexuals. As a self-identified gay man born and raised in southern Louisiana, I was not unaccustomed to hearing such rhetoric in public spaces, though these encounters always left me wondering what the most optimal manner of response would be. Once or twice, I considered joining the throng of students and civilians who inevitably gathered to hear about the perils of sin and the wrath of God, if for no other reason than to acknowledge their rhetorical address. I imagined myself more than once confronting these speakers face to face, refuting their self-righteous polemics with a well-reasoned, well-researched argument, the kind I push my students to prefer in my writing courses. Instead, I made a habit of changing my route whenever this group appeared on campus, drowning out their diatribes by humming to myself. Still, even while I did my best to avoid their direct address, I always felt a creeping anxiety as I passed them, imagining that one of them might see me, see through me, and shout, "Where're you going, faggot?"

I begin with this anecdote in order to foreground one of the key concepts underwriting my current theory of rhetoric and writing pedagogies. Ever since my first encounter with these demonstrators, I have been intrigued not only by their rhetorical strategies, but also by the ways in which their rhetorical practices make me feel *vulnerable*, acutely aware of how I am precariously exposed to the words and actions of those around me. From the moment I entered into the proximity of their protests, I was provoked (*pro-vocare*; literally, "called forth") into making a decision about how to respond to that address. Beyond that moment, even if I chose to ignore them, I could not avoid *responding* to them in one form or another. As rhetorician Diane Davis puts it, "You might whip out your Blackberry or plug into your iPod or feign sleep or complete absorption in your magazine, iPad, or Nintendo DS, but the active refusal to be responsive is a response and so no longer simple indifference" (*Inessential Solidarity* 11). In other words, my decision to ignore these demonstrators was already a response to their rhetoric, and an attempt to manage my vulnerability within that scene of address. What's more, the provocation of that decision, the calling forth to respond even if that response turned out to be a diversion, was partly a reminder that my existence as a rhetorical being necessitates my existence as a vulnerable being, someone whose life is contingent, perpetually exposed, and always subject to the effects of language (among countless other factors).

By "rhetorical being," I do not simply mean that I am able to affect others through language, a capacity that we might call *rhetorical agency*; I also mean that I am constantly exposed to the effects/ affects of others, a capacity that I will tentatively call *rhetorical vulnerability*. As Richard Marback notes, the "question of what speech [or any other form of rhetoric] has made" demands a two-fold answer: one accounting for the ways in which we effect change through language, and one accounting for the conditions that allow language to affect us so deeply (*Managing Vulnerability* 16). The first account has been the subject of numerous commentaries concerning the nature of rhetorical agency (see, for example, Geisler; Turnbull, "Rhetorical"; Greene; Lundberg and Gunn; Campbell; Wallace and Alexander; and Cooper). The second account—of language's capacity for creating change— cannot be fully addressed without provoking us, calling us forth, into further reflection on our own capacity to be moved by language, our rhetorical vulnerability.

Here, I attempt to respond to this aforementioned provocation by considering how a rhetorical theory and pedagogy more deeply grounded in a rethinking of vulnerability might help us as rhetoricians and writing scholars to address the proliferation of fake news and trolling in our public discourse. In the first part, I bring together a range of scholarly voices from within and outside of rhetoric and writing studies in order to move towards a fuller theory of rhetorical vulnerability. In the second part, I propose the use of trolling rhetoric as an object of analysis that may help students better understand how deceptive and disruptive genres of discourse (including, but not limited to, fake news) may, in the process of trying to exploit our rhetorical vulnerability, actually call attention to something fundamental about rhetoric.

Toward a Theory of Rhetorical Vulnerability

As both a term and a concept, vulnerability typically is not framed in a positive light. Rather, the term is more commonly used to describe an unfortunate exposure to the threat of subjugation and injury, which should be avoided or mitigated whenever possible. These typically negative connotations can be attributed to a wide range of factors, including culturally learned presumptions and linguistic associations. After all, vulnerability is derived from *vulnus*, the Latin word for "wound" ("Vulnerable"). However, in recent years, scholars from many different fields have begun to question this conventional wisdom by reimagining vulnerability not just as a position of precarious exposure, but also as a basic condition for social connection, political existence, ethical engagement, and even rhetorical responsiveness.

Outside of rhetorical studies, vulnerability has become a complex and ever-growing discourse of its own. Political theorists like Judith Butler, legal scholars like Martha Albertson Fineman, and ethical philosophers like Alasdair MacIntyre, William Connolly, and Erinn Gilson (among others) have composed a wide range of texts exploring vulnerability as an ethical relation, a political position, a concept for critical theory, and so on. One recurring theme that has emerged from this scholarship is the notion that vulnerability is simultaneously (1) a *predisposition* to being affected by others that is mutually experienced by all, including humans and nonhumans, and (2) a precarious *position* that is uniquely experienced by each of us based on an ever-changing configuration of external forces, contingencies, and interdependencies. Judith Butler makes this distinction in her 2010 book *Frames of War* when she introduces the interrelated terms "precariousness" and "precarity":

> Lives are by definition *precarious*: they can be expunged at will or by accident; their persistence is in no sense guaranteed. In some sense, this is a feature of all life, and there is no thinking of life that is not precarious.... *Precarity* designates that politically induced condition in which certain populations suffer from failing social and economic networks of support and become differentially exposed to injury, violence, and death. (25; emphasis added)

In other words, while all lives are precarious by virtue of simply being alive and broadly dependent upon forces beyond one's control, each life's exposure to harm can be exacerbated by "failing networks of support," leading to differentiated experiences of vulnerability. Ultimately, Butler's terms help to highlight the fact that while all of us experience vulnerability, none of us experience it in *exactly* the same ways. Her distinction here is helpful; however, her terms also run the risk of implying an inevitable link between vulnerability and harm.

This negative yet persistent perception is one that scholars like Erinn Gilson have been working to challenge, most often by emphasizing vulnerability's priority as a fundamental openness that foregrounds our ethical engagements with the world (42). To be sure, Gilson readily acknowledges the commonly perceived negatives that underscore vulnerability. She writes that the "experience of vulnerability presents us with the reality of fallibility, mutability, unpredictability and uncontrollability," elaborating,

> We are affected by forces outside our control, the effects of which we can neither fully know nor fully control. Thus, ex-

periences of vulnerability can also prompt fear, defensiveness, avoidance, and disavowal. Where the ability to predict and control is valued, the inability to do so is perceived as a failing and thus to be avoided at all costs. Hence, we are often ill at ease with vulnerability because it is a form of exposure to that with which we are unfamiliar or uncomfortable. (3-4)

Importantly, Gilson does not reject the aforementioned link between vulnerability and harm, but she works to expand the concept by strongly emphasizing the idea that vulnerability entails far more than an inevitable exposure to injury. "Vulnerability is regarded as definitive of life," she writes, "a condition that links humans to nonhuman animals, and an experience that roots us in the corporeality of our existence. [...] Thus, vulnerability is a topic of concern...because it is a fundamental part of the human condition ..." (4).

Within rhetoric and writing studies more specifically, an increasingly explicit concern for vulnerability has been developing along similar lines. To be fair, this attentiveness to vulnerability is not a particularly recent development. After all, Socrates's condemnation of rhetoric in Plato's *Gorgias* stems at least in part from his suspicions about how easily people can be fooled into believing false character and acting on untruths (455a-460e). Similarly, as Brooke Rollins has argued, one of the oldest texts in the rhetorical tradition, Gorgias's *Encomium of Helen*, simultaneously elaborates on and exploits vulnerability insofar as it treats persuasion as a kind of force, both in the body of the text, when Helen is characterized as being unable to resist the power of speech, and in the performance of the text, when Gorgias concludes the speech by calling attention to his own attempt at persuasion (8-21). Rhetoric is troublesome, then, not merely because it can be deceitful, but also because it can be compelling, exerting a kind of force on audiences that cannot be easily detected, avoided, or diverted.

In more contemporary commentaries, this link between rhetoric and force has often been coupled with arguments about the distinction (or lack thereof) between rhetoric and violence. On the one hand, some rhetoricians have argued that rhetoric provides a counterpoint to violence, a method for engaging people and enacting change that does not run the risk of injury for audiences. For example, George Kennedy links rhetoric to vulnerability by suggesting that rhetorical practices emerged from an instinct to survive and control, which could be done "by direct action—force, threats, bribes, for example" or "by the use of 'signs'" (*A New History* 3). Similarly, Wayne Booth suggests that "the effort at genuine, deep listening [or listening-rhetoric] has fewest successes when violence and war are at stake," thus implying that "good" rhetoric is most successful when separated from violence (150).

On the other hand, a number of rhetoricians, including feminist rhetoricians, have argued that rhetoric (in its traditional, masculine, agonistic form) enacts a kind of coercive violence upon others. Sally Miller Gearhart, for example, makes this case in her 1979 article "The Womanization of Rhetoric" when she asserts that "any intent to persuade is an act of violence" insofar as it attempts to coerce rather than communicate (195). She further describes students of modern rhetoric as "weapon specialists who are skilled in emotional maneuvers" and "expert in intellectual logistics" (197). Sonja K. Foss and Cindy L. Griffin echo Gearhart's characterization, writing that any "act of changing others not only establishes the power of the rhetor over others but also devalues the lives and perspectives of those others" (3). They further suggest that the distinction between rhetorical and physical force is unsustainable: "Although these discursive strategies allow more choice to the audience than do the supposedly more heavy-handed strategies of physical coercion, they still infringe on others' rights to believe as they choose and to act in ways they believe are best for them" (3). Challenging this coercive power of persuasion, Foss and Griffin propose what they call "invitational rhetoric," defined as "an invitation to understanding as a means to create a relationship rooted in equality, immanent value, and self-determination" (5). Implicit in both of these critiques of rhetoric is a concern for how vulnerability is managed by rhetors. As Rollins observes, Gearhart's "weapon specialists" are able to exert their persuasive force from a "safe distance," thereby "encroaching on the space of the other without ever endangering the self " (542). Similarly, Foss and Griffin argue that persuasion "can constitute a kind of trespassing on the personal integrity of others" (3). Their critiques thus characterize rhetors as strategists who attack others from guarded positions, exploiting vulnerabilities and imposing themselves upon available audiences.

However, while debates about the deceptive, exploitative, and violent powers of rhetoric continue (for very good reasons), recent scholarship has begun to expand what it means (or what it *could* mean) to be vulnerable to rhetoric. Richard Marback, for example, has noted that our "aversion to deception, to being led astray, to giving in, can and does motivate us to commit some of our energies to defending ourselves against empty words and deceitful representations" ("A Meditation" 2). Importantly, although our vulnerability to rhetorical effects is not something we are always conscious of, rhetorical training may help us to enhance our awareness of others' appeals (2). This awareness, however, is not contiguous with becoming *invulnerable* to rhetorical effects. If it were possible to completely guard ourselves against the influence of others, we would become *a-rhetorical* beings, immune to the address of others.

This idea—that "none of us are so self-sufficient that rhetoric is without persuasive power"— describes what Marback calls "strong versions" of rhetoric, which presume that all rhetoric is underscored by vulnerability (3). "Recognizing our interdependence through our appeals to each other," he writes, "compels us to accept that rhetoric leads us beyond ourselves to experiences, feelings, ideas, sensations, and thoughts we can embrace as our own and that we could never have had alone" (3). Rhetoric, in this view, always involves a prior exposure to appeals and constraints, a giving of ourselves to others, or a kind of dispossession. Marback explains:

> Rhetoric is a given; people cannot have relationships or communicate with each other except through their aspirations to appeal to, influence, inspire, or persuade each other. The rhetor who appeals to and has influence over an audience by virtue of awareness and preparation and strategy is at the same time influenced by an audience's awarenesses, expectations, preferences, and responses. The nature and extent of the rhetor's influence does not blind an audience. Instead, both audience and rhetor are made aware of the contingencies of being and knowing through their participation together in rhetorical activity. (3)

However, while strong versions of rhetoric accept the reality of vulnerability, they do not necessarily see anything "good" in it. Marback explains that while "mere rhetoric is grounded in a blatant fear of the devious rhetor preying on an audience's vulnerability, strong rhetoric responds to fear of audience susceptibility with the guarantee of a rhetor's good intentions and an audience's shared responsibility for meaningfulness and valuation" ("A Meditation" 4). Thus, vulnerability is rendered as an openness that is ironically unwelcome, a condition of exposure that prompts us to want some reassurance. This aversion subsequently inflects our concepts in the field, including our notions of agency and efficacy. Marback writes that both mere rhetoric and strong rhetoric "share a commitment to rhetorical efficacy as a kind of strength defined in terms of a capacity to avert the self-pity and self-loathing that come from being duped" (5). So, when we realize our rhetorical efficacy, we also minimize our rhetorical vulnerability, which is framed as primarily *negative* potential.

To counter this perception, Marback proposes a rethinking of vulnerability's positive potential. This is not to say that he advocates gullibility; rather, he suggests that if vulnerability is central to rhetoric, then we as rhetoricians and writing scholars should consider how we might manage it otherwise. And we have good reason for doing so:

> What we gain in acknowledging and accepting our vulnerability to the appeals of others is an awareness of ourselves in our responsiveness to others. If we are aware of our responsiveness to others, we are aware of ourselves as being affected by them; we are aware at some level and in some sense of the irresistible power of their persuasiveness. Such awareness cannot but sensitize us to the subtleties and gradations of our vulnerabilities. (10-11)

Marback furthers this argument in his most recent book on post-apartheid rhetoric, in which he describes how the management of vulnerability is a basic condition for rhetorical processes of democratic deliberation. "If we are to take part in deliberations," he writes, "we must at least accept the prospects of acquiescence, compromise, and defeat" (*Managing Vulnerability* 131). He goes on to argue that acknowledging our rhetorical vulnerability "involves more than resigning ourselves to the limits of our rhetorical capacities. While everyone at one time or another will experience disappointment with deliberation, we constrain our participation if we cynically conclude that disappointment is inevitable as the price to be paid for hope in a common good" (131). In other words, rhetorical deliberations demand something from us; they require us to risk ourselves and our ambitions in pursuit of a common good. Although these risks may result in disappointments, they are essential if we hope for deliberations to achieve anything other than perpetuating conflicts and complaints.

Marback's vision of vulnerability as a fundamental condition for rhetoric intersects productively with the recent work of Diane Davis. In *Inessential Solidarity: Rhetoric and Foreigner Relations*, Davis takes up the philosophy of Emmanuel Levinas in order to propose a vision of rhetoric that begins with vulnerability rather than argumentation or communication. Davis challenges rhetoricians to consider how all of us are made available to rhetoric before means and meanings are made available to us. She explains:

> If rhetorical practices work by managing to have an effect on others, then an always prior openness to the other's affection is its first requirement: the "art" of rhetoric can be effective only among affectable existents, who are by definition something other than distinct individuals or self-determining agents, and whose relations necessarily precede and exceed symbolic intervention. (3)

Importantly, this concept of vulnerability is not just an abstraction for rhetorical theorists. In a more recent essay on "Creaturely Rhetorics" (2011), Davis applies this theory to rhetorical studies' burgeoning interest in animals by responding to George Kennedy's assertion that "rhetoric is a form of energy," which is "prior in biological evolution and prior psychologically in any specific instance" ("A Hoot" 4). Davis contends that what Kennedy's argument misses is "an always prior rhetoricity, and affect*ability* or persuad*ability* that is due not to any creature's specific genetic makeup but to corporality more generally, to the *exposedness* of corporeal existence" (89, emphasis in original). She explains further:

> Your material incarnation is the site of a passivity more ancient than the active/passive dichotomy. It's the condition for your exposure, susceptibility, vulnerability, and therefore for your *responsivity*. Responsibility (response-ability) begins not with a subject who recognizes itself but with "proximity," in Levinas's terminology, immediate (as in nonmediated) contact and responsivity.... (90)

Rhetorical vulnerability, then, is not simply a matter of cognitive uptake. Rather, it is rooted in our embodiment, our affective lives, and our material connections to the world around us, which closes in on us and at the same time keeps us open. "There is no representational power," Davis writes, "that could catch up to this immediate 'touch,' this primordial persuasive appeal," and so rhetoric arises not simply as a strategy for making and sharing meaning, but as "an underivable provocation ['calling forth'], an imperative to respond," even at a very physical level (90). Whatever capacity we have for effecting change in our environments through language is thus grounded in this fundamental rhetorical vulnerability that goes beyond active-passive, thinking-unthinking, and human-animal binaries.

It seems to me that this more expansive understanding of vulnerability as a basic condition of mutual, material, and managed exposure offers a great deal to the study of rhetoric, writing, and literacy. After all, what purpose would communication or persuasion serve in a world where we could fully inoculate ourselves against the effects of language? Similarly, what purpose would rhetorical awareness serve in a world where we are all vulnerable to the same appeals in exactly the same ways at all times? How can we study the uses and effects of rhetoric in our world without first presuming that others are (or can become more) affect-able? If, as Aristotle famously put it, rhetoric describes "the faculty of observing in any given case the available means of persuasion," then we should acknowledge from the beginning that rhetoric is premised upon an always prior *availability*, not only of means, but also of rhetors, audiences, and others (1.2.1). Furthermore, if our ability to function within rhetorical situations is dependent upon the availability of means, minds, and bodies, then how can we imagine the possibility of rhetorical agency without the prior necessity of rhetorical vulnerability?

Importantly, this concern for rhetorical vulnerability is not something that is implied or expressed only in the pages of rhetorical scholarship. Insofar as rhetoric is dependent upon an exposure to persuasive and communicative action, this concern is already deeply embedded within all rhetorical practices. To assess the opportunities and constraints of any given rhetorical situation is in part to gauge the ways in which all participants within that situation (including interlocutors, audiences, and even bystanders) are vulnerable to both verbal and nonverbal forces and influences. For example, a rhetor who is interested in persuading an audience or prompting social action must be attuned to that audience's shared and diverse vulnerabilities, the ways in which they can be moved through language. At the same time, the rhetor must also be aware of her own vulnerabilities, including the basic risk of failing to achieve a desired goal given the uncertainties of the situation. A well-trained rhetor must therefore ask, "What actions or appeals will generate the responses that I am hoping for? How receptive would my audience be to such actions or appeals? How can I make them more receptive to persuasion? What risks would my actions entail, and are they worth it?" In this way, the concern for vulnerability is not just something that rhetoricians think about; it is also something that rhetors think through, something that readers and writers face whenever they compose or encounter texts, something that precedes all communicative action. There is, in other words, a necessary concern for vulnerability at the heart of rhetorical studies; without this concern, the entire enterprise of rhetoric would become little more than a series of rote exercises in disengaged discourse.

Toward a Pedagogy of Rhetorical Vulnerability

If we acknowledge the fundamental role that vulnerability plays in all of our rhetorical interactions, then it is not a far stretch to perceive how it already influences our writing and literacy pedagogies. Like all communicative actions, writing means attempting to affect others in some way, even if that effect is the expression of one's thoughts or emotions. What's more, writing, like any rhetorical move, involves taking risks; this mentality is one that our students are probably already familiar with, even if they do not realize it. As Alexander Reid notes, any student who stresses about an essay grade practices a form of risk-management, "a set of pre-established procedures that all students can follow to compose passable essays" and "minimize risk" (191-2). Reid goes on to suggest that these strategies of risk-management reflect rhetoric more broadly: "We employ rhetoric to maximize our chances of achieving some purpose and to minimize the likelihood of negative consequences. At the same time, we recognize an inescapable relationship between risk and reward" (192). What Reid describes as risk-management might also be framed in terms of what Richard Marback calls "rhetoric's functioning as a management of vulnerability," though the vulnerabilities that Marback describes go far beyond writing assessment (*Managing Vulnerability* 22). Still, when students present their writing to an audience, whether the instructor, a peer group, or a public, they are taking a kind of calculated risk, hoping to achieve a desired outcome. At the same time, they are exposing themselves to an encounter in which they have little (if any) control, whether or not their writing is deeply personal or strictly academic.

What I mean to suggest here is that much of what we do as writing and literacy instructors *already* involves the management of rhetorical vulnerabilities. That being said, I would also contend that by bringing a fuller and more reflective awareness of rhetorical vulnerability into our classrooms, we might prompt compelling discussions with our students about what it means to be affected by the communicative actions of others. These discussions are particularly opportune today given the ongoing proliferation of fake news stories in our public discourse, stories that frequently prey on audiences' vulnerabilities both through their outrageous rhetoric and through their subversion of trust in sources. To help our students engage more mindfully with fake news media today, I argue that we must teach them not only how to evaluate the integrity of sources, but also how to recognize "rhetoric's functioning as a management of vulnerability," including their own rhetorical vulnerability (*Managing Vulnerability* 22). Both of these outcomes are vital, in my opinion, because fake news stories do not simply work to deceive audiences; they also work disturb audiences, subvert trust, and disrupt critical literacies before we are even aware of such rhetorical effects.

To help students develop a fuller understanding of rhetorical vulnerability as both a concept and a reality, I have begun using the rhetoric of trolling as a topic of discussion in my classes. Anyone who has ever read the comments section on a blog or YouTube video has probably encountered trolling rhetoric in some form. In modern parlance, the term "troll" typically refers to two very different but comparable activities: (1) the practice of fishing by dragging a baited lure behind a boat and waiting for a bite, and (2) the practice of posting distracting or inflammatory comments to an online community, such as a forum or blog, in order to provoke a response (Herring et al. 372). The origins of online trolling can be traced back to Usenet forums, where trolling played out as what Judith Donath calls "a game about identity deception" (43). Herring, Job-Sluder, Scheckler, and Barab describe this game as such:

> The troller tries to write something deceptive, but not blatantly so, in order to attract the maximum number of responses. [...] In the context of Usenet...a highly successful troll is one that is cross-posted to, and responded to on, many different

newsgroups, thereby disrupting multiple groups with a minimum expenditure of effort. (372-3)

Herring, Job-Sluder, Scheckler, and Barab offer three valuable criteria for identifying trolling messages in online forums: (1) "Messages from a sender who appears outwardly sincere"; (2) "[m]essages designed to attract predictable responses or flames"; and (3) "[m]essages that waste a group's time by provoking futile argument" (375). These messages are thus crafted as a kind of discursive bait, dropped strategically into the sea of information. For trolls, the rhetorical aim is to lure vulnerable media-users into exposing their naiveté or sensitivity, thereby disrupting the flow of communication, subverting trust among networked interlocutors, and sometimes going so far as to induce outrage or actual harm.

However, digital culture has evolved significantly since the early days of Usenet, and with that evolution, the term "trolling" has become more, not less, ambiguous. Take, for example, a small sampling of news articles published since Donald Trump's election in November 2016: Andrew Marantz's *New Yorker* article "Is Trump Trolling the White House Press Corps?"; Robinson Meyer's *Atlantic* article "Trump's Solar-Powered Border Wall is More Than a Troll"; John Cassidy's *New Yorker* article "Donald Trump Will Go Down in History as the Troll-in-Chief." I could go on, but there's only so much time. As Libby C. Watson, writing for the tech news website *Select All* in 2015, humorously puts it, "you could be forgiven for thinking that *trolling* is a synonym for 'doing something on the internet'" (para. 1). While trolling's semantic ambiguity has not gotten any better over the last few years, Matt Sautman, writing for *The Artifice* in April 2017, has provided a more scholarly interpretation of trolling by arguing that "the history of trolling is a history of rhetoric" (para. 1). Sautman notes that trolling rhetoric is not limited to digital spaces; in fact, it may be as old as the rhetorical tradition itself. He suggests, for example:

> Based on how Plato depicts Socrates within [the *Gorgias*], having him outwit and shut down both Gorgias and his pupils, what the reader encounters is not a discussion amongst conversation partners contributing their thoughts equally and productively, but a fairly one-sided discussion where Socrates sets a series of verbal and logical traps to make his opposition incapable of responding in a reasonable fashion. (para. 10)

Whether or not Plato's Socrates practices a kind of trolling rhetoric is debatable, of course, but the link between trolling rhetoric and traditional rhetoric that Sautman teases out is an important one because, in my opinion, it raises the possibility that trolling exposes something fundamental about how we experience rhetoric, something that might make trolling not only a genre of rhetoric but also a method of exposing (while, sadly, exploiting) our rhetorical vulnerability.

To better explain what I mean, consider a recent case of public trolling with political consequences. On February 3, 2013, the same day that Super Bowl XLVII drew national media attention (along with millions of viewers), Todd Kincannon, former executive director of the Republican Party of South Carolina, posted the following comment to his personal Twitter account (@ToddKincannon): "This Super Bowl sucks more dick than adult Trayvon Martin would have for drug money." This inflammatory comment, with its explicitly racist and homophobic overtones, was not a hoax, as Kincannon himself admitted after the tweet went viral. More disturbingly, it was not an isolated incident but one of a series of tweets that Kincannon posted during and after the Super Bowl. Many of these tweets expressed similar sentiments. For example, in response to another Twitter user (@coreybking), Kincannon replied: "Hey what's the difference between Trayvon Martin and a dead baby? They're both dead, but Pepsi doesn't taste like Trayvon." Not all of Kincannon's tweets included references to Trayvon Martin, but several were racially charged. For example, in response to the power failure that blacked out half of the New Orleans Superdome shortly after the beginning of the game's second half, Kincannon tweeted: "It hasn't been this dark in the Superdome since all those poors occupied it after Hurricane Katrina."

As one might expect, public outrage and condemnation quickly followed on the heels of Kincannon's tweets, with numerous responses posted and circulated on social media networks. Given the controversial nature of the incident, responses ranged from whole-hearted support (Todd: "that's why I like you Todd, balls of pure steel") to shock (Caplan: "Did you really go after a murdered teenager? Why go there? Do you have kids, if so, then why would you hurt parents this way?") to criticism (XXX: "Right to free speech isn't a right to speak without criticism or being called out for racism") to retaliatory insult (Dawn: "Really? You're going to go after a 17yr old murder victim—have fun on that fast train to hell you destined for!"). Some even questioned the authenticity of Kincannon's account, with one respondent (XXX) replying, "I'm really hoping this is a troll account." The day after the incident, news outlets picked up the story, and Kincannon was invited to respond to the backlash via phone on *HuffPost Live*. When asked to explain why he would post something so insensitive knowing that it would spark public outrage and political controversy, Kincannon replied:

> One of the things I like to do on Twitter is, I'll tweet something that's inflammatory or borderline crazy sounding, just for fun. And I enjoy watching people go nuts. And one of the best things about it is that if you say something that's borderline offensive, or that is offensive, the people that attack you and say just the awfulest [sic] things about you, they do the very thing that they accuse you of. [...] I guess you could call it kind of *high-profile trolling*, but it definitely worked. ("Todd Kincannon," italics mine)

By describing his actions as a "kind of high-profile trolling," Kincannon showed that the uses of trolling today extend beyond games of online deception and provocation. In contrast to what we normally perceive as the goals of civic rhetoric, Kincannon used his words to "get a rise" out of his audience and garner as much attention as he could. If this was indeed his rhetorical aim, then it seems rather obvious that he succeeded, at least within the increasingly small window of time afforded him by the nonstop news cycles.

It is tempting at this point to focus on the motives that inspire trolling rhetors to use these tactics. That desire is understandable; however, the reality is that there are as many motives behind trolling rhetoric as there are active trolling rhetors today, and the expanding usage of the term only complicates the search for a central motive. Therefore, in order to describe trolling rhetoric without focusing on characteristic motives, it may be helpful for us to focus instead on the characteristic effects of trolling. For my purposes here, I want to recognize two main effects of trolling rhetoric: (1) disrupting the flow of information and communication, and (2) garnering as much attention as possible for as long as possible. Securing the uptake of a trolling message can be done either by generating a temporary façade of integrity and credibility or by provoking audiences into reacting intensely and emotionally. Either tactic, when successful, leads to a disruption of discourse that distracts or incites audiences while also interfering with the application of reflective and critical literacies. Case in point: through his tweets, Kincannon worked to intensify his audience's emotional reactions while also setting himself up as an easy target for destructive criticism. Furthermore, if the trolling rhetor is savvy, the trolling message can then perpetuate itself by exploiting economies of attention, such as Kincannon's appearance on *HuffPost Live* (Lanham). Ultimately, what distinguishes trolling from other rhetorical genres is that it is not (or not primarily, at least) a *meaning making* activity. Instead of drawing audiences into a shared system of signification, identification, and deliberation, trolling rhetoric works primarily to provoke responses and claims attention for as long as it can. The quality of the response is generally less important (if at all) to the success of a trolling message than the gesture of response itself.

So what can we learn from trolling rhetoric if its goals do not necessarily align with the rhetorical goals that we generally *want* our students to prioritize, such as informed argument or democratic deliberation? I argue that what makes trolling rhetoric worth discussing with students is the way in which it provokes us, "calls us forth," into an awareness of (1) our fundamental rhetorical vulnerability and (2) how that vulnerability can be managed or exploited. While trolling rhetoric may be more disruptive than productive, the fact that it is disruptive *by design* while still achieving a rhetorical effect suggests that rhetoric in general may have less to do with meaning making *per se* and more to do with understanding and managing our vulnerabilities to rhetorical forces. This is *not* to say that rhetoric plays no part in meaning making, but it does acknowledge the possibility that rhetoric is not limited to what John Muckelbauer calls the "apparatus of signification" ("Rhetoric, Asignification" 239). Muckelbauer explains this point by separating the "communicative" (or "signifying") operation of language from what he calls its "persuasive" (or "asignifying") operation:

> An act of communication…endeavors to reproduce, as accurately as possible, the proposition in the mind of its audience. Hence, communication responds to the preexisting proposition as if that proposition were primarily a meaning, as if it were, above all, an identifiable content that can be reproduced. […] An act of persuasion, on the other hand, is not primarily a signifying operation…Rather than attempting to identically reproduce the proposition as a meaning in the mind of its au-

dience, persuasive rhetoric attempts to make the proposition compelling, to give it a certain force. (*The Future* 17)

Persuasion as an asignifying operation is thus "interested in provoking the proposition's effects rather than facilitating its understanding" (18). Or, to put it another way, persuasion focuses on "what the proposition *does*" rather than "what the proposition *is*" (18, emphasis in original). Muckelbauer is careful to point out that communication and persuasion are not completely separate from one another; in fact, they often coincide. "But the fact that these two dimensions exist in close proximity," he writes, "does not indicate that they are the same" ("Rhetoric, Asignification" 239). Thus, if we are to understand trolling as a rhetorical genre, it may require us to acknowledge that despite rhetoric's "proximity" to meaning making activities, its foremost concern is with the application of forces and the production of effects (239). It may also require us to acknowledge that, insofar as rhetoric deals with such forces and effects, it must also deal with our vulnerability to those forces and effects. As Nathan Stormer observes in his study of language and violence, "The capacity to impose derives from the capacity to be affected" (188). So, even if trolling rhetors do not set out to facilitate understanding, they nonetheless reveal, through their disruptions, how rhetoric is premised upon both an awareness of and a managing of rhetorical vulnerability.

But what does this have to do with the proliferation of fake news today? Quite a bit, I would argue. Although fake news is problematic partly because it is fake and dis-informative, I would contend that it is also problematic because it exploits our rhetorical vulnerability in much the same way as trolling rhetoric. Given the ever-expanding marketing powers of the Internet as well as the increasingly enclosed media bubbles we now find ourselves occupying, fake news outlets are capable of managing our rhetorical vulnerabilities in ways that turn the game of trolling rhetoric into the business of trolling rhetoric. Consider, for example, the case of the *Denver Guardian*. On November 5, 2016, a fake news website called the *Denver Guardian* published an article with the headline "FBI Agent Suspected in Hillary Email Leaks Found Dead in Apparent Murder-Suicide" (Lubbers). Although the website has since been deleted, screenshots and news reports have preserved elements of the original article, which delivers a fictional account of an FBI agent who shot his own wife, set his house on fire, and then shot himself after being implicated in the leak of emails from

Hillary Clinton's private email server (Mikkelson). Despite its claims, the *Denver Guardian* was neither "Denver's oldest news source" nor a credible source of information; in fact, as revealed by the *Denver Post*, the address given for the website's newsroom was actually a parking lot in Denver, and the image attached to the story originated from a Flickr account (Lubbers).

Nonetheless, the article spread on Facebook like wildfire to the extent that, according to *NPR* and the *Denver Post*, it generated around half a million shares, or "100 shares per minute" at times (Sydell; Lubbers). Reporter Hannah Ritchie, writing for *CNBC.com*, even listed the story as one of the "biggest fake news stories of 2016," along with the likes of the Pizzagate conspiracy. It is perhaps unsurprising why a story like this would have generated such a reaction. The article, which played into a longstanding narrative about Hillary Clinton's supposed criminal activities and exploited the contentiousness of the 2016 presidential campaign, was a powerful combination of trolling rhetoric and disinformation, one specifically designed to provoke those already suspicious of Hillary Clinton into reacting with unblinking outrage. In fact, one screenshot of the story as it appeared on Facebook, which is still hosted by the *Denver Post,* includes a response post that describes Hillary Clinton as "that murdering witch!!" (Lubbers). To be sure, both the article and the *Denver Guardian* have been thoroughly discredited at this point; however, I would argue that efforts to discredit the story have addressed only its dis-informative (signifying) elements, not its trolling (asignifying) elements. In other words, what mattered was not the credibility of the story, since it needed only to exploit an existing right-wing narrative about the Clinton campaign. What mattered was the outraged reaction that the story generated and the attention it garnered, including the attention of mainstream news outlets who felt compelled to publicly refute the story.

Interestingly enough, the *Denver Guardian* was one of several fake news outlets that *NPR* linked to Jestin Coler, a registered Democrat who claims that he started producing fake news in order to "'infiltrate the echo chambers of the alt-right, publish blatantly or fictional stories and then be able to publicly denounce those stories and point out the fact that they were fiction…'" (Sydell). In other words, Coler hoped to use fake news stories, including the story about the fictional FBI agent, as a means of educating his readers about their susceptibility to rhetoric. However, given the prominence of fake news today, it would seem that his plan backfired, though Coler has nonetheless made thousands of dollars each month in ad revenue through his combination of fake news and trolling rhetoric (Sydell).

To counter this dangerous combination, I contend that we cannot simply focus on teaching our students to distrust sources until proven trustworthy (though those lessons *are* still important); we must also help our students come into a fuller awareness of what trolling rhetors have long recognized: that we are rhetorically vulnerable beings, that we can never not be rhetorically vulnerable and responsive, and that our rhetorical vulnerability can be managed and exploited for better and, unfortunately, for worse.

Toward a Conclusion

For now, my approach to trolling rhetoric and fake news in the classroom has focused primarily on using the genres as topics of discussion and in-class analysis with students. While I am still experimenting with specific lessons, I have found it helpful to have students compare readings on traditional rhetorical theory with more recent readings on how to compose trolling messages. Consider, for example, how one dated but useful web guide to trolling explains the "design issues" that a trolling rhetor must take into account:

> The experienced troller spends time carefully choosing the right subject and delivering it to the right newsgroup. With trolls, delivery is just as important as the subject. Start the troll in a reasonable and erudite manner. You have to engage your readers' interest and draw them in. Never give too much away at the start—although a brief abstract with hints of what's to come can work wonders. Construct your troll in a manner to make it readable. Use short paragraphs and lots of white space. Keep line length below eighty characters. Use a liberal amount of emphasis and even the occasional illustration. A good rule of thumb is that as your troll becomes more and more ludicrous put extra effort into the presentation.... Let confusion and chaos be your goal. (Spumante)

Several parallels with the rhetorical tradition are already evident in these guidelines. The anonymous author's emphasis on "choosing the right subject" and "delivering it to the right newsgroup" bridges two of the five classical canons of rhetoric: invention and delivery. Although the author is focusing here on online trolling, these bridges (and the trolls living beneath them) are noticeable in political trolling as well; if "delivery is just as important as the subject," it is little wonder why the combination of Trayvon Martin, social media, and the Super Bowl would have proven so opportune for Todd Kincannon. Similarly, the anonymous author's insistence that the trolling rhetor must choose the right subject ("right" being a relative term) echoes Aristotle's system for selecting effective *topoi* to suit the rhetorical situation. Finally, mentions of "manner" (from "reasonable," "erudite," and "readable" to increasingly "ludicrous") link trolling to the canons of arrangement and style, with the principle of decorum largely subverted. These parallels suggest that, as difficult as it may be to admit, modern-day trolling is built upon the same principles as the rhetorical tradition more broadly.

That being said, some of my students have pointed out that trolling rhetoric differs from civic rhetoric in terms of its exploitation of *ethos* and *pathos* (i.e., deception and provocation) as well as its subversion of *logos* (i.e., disinformation). In contrast to Aristotle, who stresses the importance of treating *ethos*, *pathos*, and *logos* in balanced measure, trolling rhetors express little interest in advancing deliberation through balanced appeals. If anything, trolling rhetors design their appeals to create imbalances, interfering with the critical literacies that make civic rhetoric possible. In doing so, they achieve their goals of gaining attention and disrupting communicative exchanges. Thus, although trolling rhetors exercise many of the same principles that form the core of the rhetorical tradition rehearsed by academics, they apply those principles to ends that would likely have Aristotle and Cicero turning in their graves. These comparisons have proven useful in my own writing courses as a way to complicate the concept of rhetoric for my students. On the one hand, rhetoric certainly carries the potential for harm and exploitation, as trolling rhetoric makes clear. But on the other hand, the vulnerability that trolling rhetoric relies upon is not unique to its purposes; instead, trolling rhetoric exposes vulnerability as a definitive and fundamental component of *all* rhetorical encounters.

Of course, a fuller pedagogy of rhetorical vulnerability cannot depend on discussions alone. To help students further expand their awareness of rhetorical vulnerability, I have also turned to contemporary work on listening and attunement for inspiration, such as the work of Krista Ratcliffe and Lisbeth Lipari, which I believe offers teachers of rhetoric and writing a powerful and potentially transformative vision of what it means to think about and with vulnerability. Christian Smith, for example, has drawn upon the work of Arthur Zajonc and Christy I. Wenger to propose "contemplative listening," an approach to rhetorical and literacy education that integrates mindfulness "by inviting students to sit in silence before reading aloud a mutual text together—going from student to student until the text is finished and, again, sitting in silence" (82). "Such practices," Smith writes, "can work to expose cultural logics without an immediate identification with them. In that moment between, that aporetic pause, is an invitation to practice listening" (82).

Part of what strikes me about these listening-based approaches is that they also invite students to develop an awareness of rhetorical vulnerability. In fact, listening-based pedagogies are particularly well aligned to this task because through listening, we experience rhetoric not only cognitively but also materially. As Lipari has persuasively pointed out, the act of listening means that "our bodies vibrate with the sound waves pulsing toward and then through us. [...] Listening may or may not compel you to wiggle your hips or bounce your head, but the waves of sound are nevertheless moving you" (31). When we listen, we consequently open ourselves up to the world around us so that it may affect us intellectually, emotionally, and bodily. At the same time, we are reminded of our embeddedness in a larger web of social relations, contingencies, and interdependencies. As a pedagogical method, then, listening can be another way for us to help our students become more fully aware of how rhetorical vulnerabilities are exposed and managed, both in our classrooms and in our public discourse saturated with fake news.

Inspired by these listening-based approaches, I have shifted from providing purely written feedback on students' projects to conferencing with each of my students individually on a regular basis. During each conference, I read, watch, and/or listen to the student's work in real time while the student observes me. In doing so, I encourage the student to pay attention to my bodily cues, such as when I raise my eyebrows or nod affirmatively. Initially, I began doing this as a way to help students learn how to read body language; but over time, I have realized that this process also helps students better perceive how an audience might *experience*, or be *affected by*, their texts. More than once, I have had a student in my office ask me, "Why were you squinting your eyes when you read that paragraph?" or "What was that head-shaking about earlier?" When students ask me these questions, I take time to reflect on my encounter with their text and explain how I physically and mentally processed their work in the moment. This generally leads to a productive discussion about how I was affected by the student's text more broadly and whether or not that effect aligned with the student's stated intentions. In retrospect, I find that this method ironically but positively contrasts with my encounters with the church group during my grad school years. Whereas that group made me feel the need to guard myself and maintain a "safe distance" from their rhetorical address, my conference-based approach compels me to make myself more available to my students while actively reflecting on what my reactions mean. Currently, I am working to develop a method for integrating this approach into peer response, though that is still a work in progress.

I must note before finishing that as we move towards a fuller theory and pedagogy of rhetorical vulnerability, we cannot deny the potential for exploitation and harm that comes with it. Fake news and trolling rhetoric are just two examples of how our openness to rhetorical effects can be tragically mismanaged, as the Pizzagate incident and the shooting at a Congressional baseball game have sadly demonstrated. However, as scholars have pointed out, this potential does not have to be what defines our discussions of vulnerability, especially not when so much of what we already do requires us to be affected by others. This brings me back once more to the protesters in Free Speech Alley I mentioned earlier. On the one hand, those protesters made me feel unwelcome on my own campus and exposed to their rhetoric in ways that still disturb me. However, those protesters also (inadvertently or otherwise) provoked me, called me forth, into an awareness of how my experience of rhetoric is also an experience of being vulnerable. Furthermore, they continue to remind me as both a rhetorician and a writing teacher that this abiding concern for vulnerability exposes something at the heart of what I do, something at the heart of the rhetorical tradition itself, whether I make a habit of acknowledging it or simply continue humming to myself.

WORKS CITED

Aristotle. *On Rhetoric: A Theory of Civic Discourse.* 2nd ed. Trans. George A. Kennedy. New York: Oxford UP, 2007. Print.

Booth, Wayne C. *The Rhetoric of Rhetoric: The Quest for Effective Communication.* Malden: Blackwell Publishing, 2004. Print.

Butler, Judith. *Frames of War: When Is Life Grievable?* Brooklyn: Verso, 2009. Print. Campbell, Karlyn Kohrs. "Agency: Promiscuous and Protean." *Communication and Critical / Cultural Studies* 2.1 (2005): 1-19. Print.

Caplan, Debbie (DebbieCaplanPR). "@ToddKincannon Did you really go after a murdered teenager? Why go there? Do you have kids, if so, then why would you hurt parents this way?" 3 Feb. 2013, 7:05 p.m. Tweet.

Cassidy, John. "Donald Trump Will Go Down in History as the Troll-in-Chief." *The New Yorker.* The New Yorker, 29 June 2017. Web. 30 June 2017.

Connolly, William E. *The Fragility of Things: Self-Organizing Processes, Neoliberal Fantasies, and Democratic Activism.* Durham: Duke UP, 2013. Print.

Cooper, Marilyn M. "Rhetorical Agency as Emergent and Enacted." *College Composition and Communication* 62.3 (2011): 420-49. Print.

Davis, Diane. "Creaturely Rhetorics." *Philosophy and Rhetoric* 44.1 (2011): 88-94. Print.

---. *Inessential Solidarity: Rhetoric and Foreigner Relations.* Pittsburgh: U of Pittsburgh P, 2010. Print.

Dawn Catherine (DAWNCATHERINE). "@ToddKincannon Really? You're going to go after a 17yr old murder victim – have fun on that fast train to hell you're destined for!" 3 Feb. 2013, 11:52 p.m. Tweet.

Donath, Judith S. "Identity and Deception in the Virtual Community." *Communities in Cyberspace.* Ed. Marc A. Smith and Peter Kollock. New York: Routledge, 1999. 27-58. Print. Fineman, Martha Alberston. "The Vulnerable Subject: Anchoring Equality in the Human Condition." *Yale Journal of Law & Feminism* 20.1 (2008): 1-23. Print.

---. "The Vulnerable Subject and the Responsive State." *Emory Law Journal* 60 (2010): 251-75. Print. Foss, Sonja K., and Cindy L. Griffin. "Beyond Persuasion: A Proposal for an Invitational Rhetoric." *Communication Monographs* 62 (1995): 2-18. Print.

Gearhart, Sally Miller. "The Womanization of Rhetoric." *Women's Studies International Quarterly* 2.2 (1979): 195-201. Print.

Geisler, Cheryl. "How Ought We to Understand the Concept of Rhetorical Agency? Report from the ARS." *Rhetoric Society Quarterly* 34.3 (2004): 9-17. Print.

Gilson, Erinn C. *The Ethics of Vulnerability: A Feminist Analysis of Social Life and Practice.* New York: Routledge, 2014. Print.

Gorgias. *Encomium of Helen*. Trans. George Kennedy. *The Rhetorical Tradition: Readings from Classical Times to the Present*. 2nd ed. Ed. Patricia Bizzell and Bruce Herzberg. Boston: Bedford/St. Martin's, 2000. 44-46. Print.

Greene, Ronald Walter. "Rhetoric and Capitalism: Rhetorical Agency as Communicative Labor." *Philosophy and Rhetoric* 37.3 (2004): 188-206. Print.

Herring, Susan, Kirk Job-Sluder, Rebecca Scheckler, and Sasha Barab. "Searching for Safety Online: Managing 'Trolling' in a Feminist Forum." *The Information Society* 18 (2002): 371-84. Print.

Kennedy, George A. "A Hoot in the Dark: The Evolution of General Rhetoric." *Philosophy and Rhetoric* 25.1 (1992): 1-21. Print.

---. *A New History of Classical Rhetoric*. Princeton: Princeton UP, 1994. Print.

Kincannon, Todd (ToddKincannon). "@coreybking Hey what's the difference between Trayvon Martin and a dead baby? They're both dead, but Pepsi doesn't taste like Trayvon." 4 Feb. 2013, 1:57 p.m. Tweet.

---. "It hasn't been this dark in the Superdome since all those poors occupied it during Hurricane Katrina." 3 Feb. 2013, 6:49 p.m. Tweet.

---. "This Super Bowl sucks more dick than adult Trayvon Martin would have for drug money." 3 Feb. 2013, 6:09 p.m. Tweet.

Lanham, Richard A. *The Economics of Attention: Style and Substance in the Age of Information*. Chicago: U of Chicago P, 2006. Print.

Lipari, Lisbeth. *Listening, Thinking, Being: Toward an Ethics of Attunement*. University Park: Pennsylvania State UP, 2014. Print.

Lubbers, Eric. "There Is No Such Thing as the *Denver Guardian*, Despite that Facebook Post You Saw." *The Denver Post*. The Denver Post, 7 Nov. 2016. Web. 26 Sept. 2017.

Lundberg, Christian, and Loshua Gunn. "'Ouija Board, Are There Any Communications?' Agency, Ontotheology, and the Death of the Humanist Subject, or, Continuing the ARS Conversation." *Rhetoric Society Quarterly* 35.4 (2005): 83-105. Print.

MacIntyre, Alasdair. *Dependent Rational Animals: Why Human Beings Need the Virtues*. Chicago: Open Court, 1999.

Marantz, Andrew. "Is Trump Trolling the White House Press Corps?" *The New Yorker*. The New Yorker, 20 March 2017. Web. 25 June 2017.

Marback, Richard C. *Managing Vulnerability: South Africa's Struggle for a Democratic Rhetoric.*
Columbia: U of South Carolina P, 2012. Print.

---. "A Meditation on Vulnerability in Rhetoric." *Rhetoric Review* 29.1 (2010): 1-13. Print.

Meyer, Robinson. "Trump's Solar-Powered Border Wall is More Than a Troll." *The Atlantic*. Atlantic Media Company, 7 June 2017. Web. 25 June 2017.

Mikkelson, David. "FALSE: FBI Agent Suspected in Hillary Email Leaks Found Dead in Apparent Murder-Suicide." *Snopes.com*. Snopes.com, 5 Nov. 2016. Web. 26 Sept. 2017.

Muckelbauer, John. *The Future of Invention: Rhetoric, Postmodernism, and the Problem of Change*. Albany: SUNY P, 2008. Print.

---. "Rhetoric, Asignification, and the Other: A Response to Diane Davis." *Philosophy and Rhetoric* 40.2 (2007): 238-47. Print.

Plato. *Gorgias*. Trans. Donald J. Zeyl. *Plato: Complete Works*. Ed. John M. Cooper and D. S. Hutchinson. Indianapolis: Hackett Publishing, 1997. 791-869. Print.

Ratcliffe, Krista. *Rhetorical Listening: Identification, Gender, Whiteness*. Carbondale: Southern Illinois UP, 2005. Print.

Reid, Alexander. "The Activity of Writing: Affinity and Affect in Composition." *First-Year Composition: From Theory to Practice*. Ed. Deborah Coxwell-Teague and Ronald F. Lunsford. Anderson: Parlor P, 2014. 184-210. Print.

Ritchie, Hannah. "Read All About It: The Biggest Fake News Stories of 2016." *CNBC*. CNBC, 30 Dec. 2016. Web. 26 Sept. 2017.

Rollins, Brooke. "Persuasion's Ethical Force: Levinas, Gorgias, and the Rhetorical Address." *JAC* 29.3 (2009): 539-59. Print.

Sautman, Matt. "The Art of Trolling: A Philosophical History of Rhetoric." *The Artifice*. N.p., April 2017. Web. 25 June 2017.

Smith, Christian. "Contemplative Listening, Contemplative Literacy." *LiCS* 5.1 (2017): 81-4. Web. 25 June 2017.

Spumante, Steve. "Trolling the Web: A Guide." *Urban75 Magazine*. Urban75, n.d. Web. 2 April 2014.

Stormer, Nathan. "On the Origins of Violence and Language." *Quarterly Journal of Speech* 99.2 (2013): 182-90. Print.

Sydell, Laura. "We Tracked Down a Fake-News Creator in The Suburbs. Here's What We Learned." *NPR*. NPR, 23 Nov. 2016. Web. 26 Sept. 2017.

Todd, Derrick (Derricktodd). "@ToddKincannon that's why I like you Todd, balls of pure steel." 3 Feb. 2013, 6:16 p.m. Tweet.

"Todd Kincannon Defends Trayvon Martin Tweet." *HuffPost Live*. The Huffington Post, 4 Feb. 2013. Web. 7 Feb. 2013.

Turnbull, Nick. "Rhetorical Agency as a Property of Questioning." *Philosophy and Rhetoric* 37.3 (2004): 207-22. Print.

"Vulnerable, adj." *OED Online*. Oxford University Press, 2000. Web. 1 Feb. 2012.

Wallace, David L., and Jonathan Alexander. "Queer Rhetorical Agency: Questioning Narratives of Heteronormativity." *JAC* 29.4 (2009): 793-819. Print.

Watson, Libby C. "It's Time to Reclaim Trolling." *Select All*. New York Media, n.p., 2 Nov. 2015. Web. 25 June 2017.

XXX (hjaybee). "@ToddKincannon <--- I'm really hoping this is a troll account." 4 Feb. 2013, 7:11 a.m. Tweet.

---. "@Spritely2315 @ToddKincannon Right to free speech isn't a right to speak without criticism or being called out for racism." 4 Feb. 2013, 7:16 a.m. Tweet.

Supplemental Material

Part I: Reflection on the Origin of the Article

Shortly after completing my comprehensive exams in graduate school, I realized that I still had not come to terms with rhetoric. To be sure, I had read and written about key texts in the rhetorical tradition, analyzed a wide range of artifacts, and experimented with several different approaches to rhetorical pedagogy in my first-year writing courses. However, I still found myself struggling to define rhetoric in a way that reflected my felt experiences of it. I knew from my readings that the definition of rhetoric was a topic of longstanding and ongoing debate in the field. Is rhetoric a form of violence or a counterpoint to violence? Is it meant to win arguments, or is it meant to structure conversations? Do rhetoric, persuasion, communication, and argument refer to the same idea? I wrestled with these questions for months.

A close friend of mine, Cat Godbold, took note of my frustration and invited me to have a conversation-plus-brainstorming-session over lunch. Shortly after we sat down with our sandwiches, she took out her smartphone. "I just want you to talk about your ideas," she told me. "I'll take notes on my phone. Just say what comes to your mind. Make connections as you go, or don't. It's up to you. I'll just listen and write. Then I'll tell you what I'm hearing."

So I talked, and Cat patiently listened. For the next thirty minutes, I ran through a string of ideas and artifacts that seemed to have nothing in common save for my own desire to make them cohere. When I ran out of things to say, Cat put down her phone and offered a few keywords based on what she had heard. "What do you mean by 'vulnerability,'" she asked me. "You kept coming back to that term, so it seems important to you."

I didn't even realize that I had repeated the term until she showed me the typed notes on her phone. We proceeded to have a conversation in which I tried to unpack what the term "vulnerability" meant to me in the context of rhetoric. I told her the story of my experience walking through Free Speech Alley, listening to the hate-filled rhetoric of a local anti-gay church group. She advised me to write about it. That was when this article really began to take shape, though it would not become a full-fledged article for quite some time.

Part II: Description of Research Methods, Findings, and/or Pedagogical Impact

Once I realized that vulnerability would be central to my understanding of rhetoric, I began to gather as many sources as I could find on the concept. Philosophy and legal studies proved to be rich discourses for the study of vulnerability. In particular, scholars like Martha Albertson Fineman, Judith Butler, and Erinn Gilson challenged me to reimagine vulnerability not only as a position of exposure to harm but also as an always prior condition of material, political, and ethical life. Similarly, within rhetoric and composition studies, Richard Marback's Managing Vulnerability and Diane Davis's Inessential Solidarity (among many other texts) helped me focus my attention on the always prior conditions of affectability that make rhetoric possible in the first place.

In the midst of this research, I repeatedly asked myself how I could integrate this working theory of rhetorical vulnerability into a classroom context. How could I help my students learn not only how to argue effectively but also how to be more aware of the conditions that make arguments possible, including rhetorical vulnerability? I returned again and again to that conversation that Cat and I had over sandwiches, reflecting on the vulnerability that that kind act of listening demanded from each of us. These reflections eventually led me to the study of listening in the context of rhetoric, and this research had the result of completely changing the way I provide feedback on student writing. I decided that instead of relying primarily on marginal comments and emails to communicate feedback to my students, I would instead make time to conference with each student for twenty minutes following each major assignment. During these conferences, the student and I would read their work in real time, allowing both of us to actively listen to the text and to each other. To this day, I continue to provide feedback in this way.

My initial goal during these conferences was to help my students develop a greater awareness of how our interactions, including our responses to textual artifacts, require us to be materially and rhetorically available to one another. But these conferences also had another effect, one that I have just begun to notice. When I listen to my students today, I frequently find myself asking them to define the term "argument," often as justification for their choices on an assignment. In some cases, the student will struggle to produce a definition, though they have a felt sense of it. But in other cases, the student will articulate a working theory of rhetoric, one that is informed by our discussions of classical rhetoric, Burkean rhetoric, invitational rhetoric, and even trolling rhetoric. When a student proposes a definition, I do my best to listen and take notes, followed by a conversation about their key terms. It strikes me as a bit ironic that my pedagogy has come full circle from where this article began. Then again, perhaps it isn't ironic at all.

Part III: Discussion Questions

1. The author argues that rhetorical vulnerability is an always prior condition for rhetoric, without which "the entire enterprise of rhetoric would become little more than a series of rote exercises in disengaged discourse." Do you agree with this claim? What are some other conditions that make rhetoric and/or arguments possible?

2. The author argues that "much of what we do as writing and literacy instructors already involves the management of rhetorical vulnerabilities" (emphasis in original). In what ways do we as rhetoric and writing teachers already manage rhetorical vulnerabilities in our classrooms? In what ways could we? In what ways should we not?

3. The author argues that we as rhetoric and writing teachers need to help our students recognize that "we are rhetorically vulnerable beings, that we can never not be rhetorically vulnerable and responsive, and that our rhetorical vulnerability can be managed and exploited for better and, unfortunately, for worse." What strategies can we use to enhance our students' awareness of rhetorical vulnerability, in our classrooms and in our assignments?

JOURNAL OF TEACHING WRITING

Journal of Teaching Writing is on the Web at http://journals.iupui.edu/index.php/teachingwriting

Now in its thirty-seventh year of publication, the *Journal of Teaching Writing* (JTW) is devoted to the teaching of writing at all academic levels, from pre-school to university, and in all subject areas of the curriculum. Our mission is to publish refereed articles that address the practices and theories that bear on our knowledge of how people learn and communicate through writing. Also, an important part of our mission is to demystify the editorial review process for our contributors and to model the teaching of writing as a process of reflection and revision. Back issues can be downloaded free at http://journals.iupui.edu/index.php/teachingwriting.

Activating the "Fund of Attention" to Empower Student Peer Review[1]

After introducing the model, we describe its powerful impact on our students and on ourselves as educators. In so doing, Eileen Kogl Camfield, Lara Killick, and Ruth Lewis offer a contribution to the literature concerning faculty and student experience of peer review, especially in the context of WID and/or faculty new to writing instruction.

---

1. *Journal of Teaching Writing*, vol. 33 no 1 © 2018 by Eileen Kogl Camfield, Lara Killick, and Ruth Lewis.

Activating the "Fund of Attention" to Empower Student Peer Review

Eileen Kogl Camfield, Lara Killick, and Ruth Lewis

While often vaunted for its utility in improving student writing, peer review does not always live up to its promise. Put another way, it poses operational challenges when faculty and students feel unprepared or unequal to effectively engage the process. This challenge is especially fraught for faculty in the disciplines who may lack a sense of efficacy about teaching writing. This article tells the story of the relationship forged between a director of university writing programs and two sociology professors at a mid-sized, private university as we collectively developed and deployed a new model for student peer review—the 'Fund of Attention'—that subsequently blossomed into a philosophy for pedagogy and curriculum development.

Remember the fabled straw that broke the camel's back? For faculty in the disciplines, teaching writing might feel like just such a straw. While some universities have robust cohorts of dedicated composition teachers, others, like our own, primarily rely on discipline-based faculty to embed writing instruction in their courses. With specific regards to the latter, writing program administrators commonly extol the myriad benefits of incorporating peer review (peer feedback or peer response) in the classroom, claiming peer feedback helps catch problems with student writing before they hit the instructor's desk. Peer review is believed to help students become more self-regulated learners who are motivated to write multiple drafts, implying the time spent grading student papers will be lessened (Nichol and MacFarlane-Dick 201). However, many who use peer review are left deeply unsatisfied because this promise remains largely unmet. As many in the composition community attest (Wirtz 5), peer review makes good theoretical sense, but as we will explore in this article, it poses operational challenges when faculty and students outside that community feel unprepared or unequal to the task. Thus, it often falls to writing program administrators to help empower writing instructor classroom-based proficiency and efficacy through targeted faculty development.

This teaching narrative tells the story of the relationship forged between the director of university writing programs and two sociology professors at a mid-sized, private university as we collectively developed and deployed a simple-but-effective model for student peer review. After introducing the "Fund of Attention" (FofA) model, we draw on pilot data and personal reflections to describe its impact on our students and ourselves as educators. Our primary intention here is to describe the conditions from which FofA emerged and examine our pilot experiences using the model. However, given our transformative experiences, we conclude by recommending further inquiry and empirical assessments of FofA's efficacy and capacity for translation across diverse faculty-student relationships. In so doing, we seek to open conversations about the potential of FofA to blossom into a broader philosophy for pedagogy and curriculum development, especially in the context of writing in the disciplines (WID) and faculty new to writing instruction.

The Promise and Perils of Peer Review: A (Very) Brief Overview

Proponents of peer review affirm that it helps students practice their critical analysis skills, widens their sense of audience, builds an active learning space, and bolsters classroom community. They often assert that this pedagogical technique allows students to learn from the intellectual and stylistic choices of others and that this experience provides long-term benefits when students find themselves working collaboratively in their professions. Years of research underpins and extends these claims. Evidence suggests student peer review is as good as teacher feedback (Topping 262). Indeed, it may be better, especially for ESL learners: A responsive "real" audience lets the reader know if their message was effective, allows students to maintain possession of their texts, and offers a higher density of feedback (Rollinson 25). Research shows it benefits the reviewer as much as (if not more than) the writer (Lundstrom and Baker 38). Moreover, benefits are not merely concrete or skill-focused. If "meaning is a social construct negotiated by writer and reader through the medium of text" (Nystrand 78), nothing could be more conducive to meaning-making than peer review. Moreover, participation in a social composing process "helps students learn firsthand the communal nature and intellectual excitement of writing" (Holt 391). This is "politically important" as a social negotiation in which a writer "finds his or her identity" (Holt 392). It might also have psychological benefits by helping students overcome the alienation felt when writing does not have a clear audience (Gere 10). Together, these sociocultural aspects of peer review can facilitate student acculturation into the collegiate world, so vital to student success (Bruffee 9).

Despite its potential benefits, a great deal of scholarly attention has been paid to the problems of peer review. Root sources of student and faculty dissatisfaction stem from a lack of reviewer mindfulness that is expressed in hastily written feedback and exacerbated by reductionistic checklist evaluation forms (Holt 384). More profoundly, the student-reviewer identity is ill-defined and unclear. According to Kay Halasek, if students see themselves as proxy for the teacher, the role is inauthentic and they lack a sense of authority. So, they focus on low-hanging fruit and discrete elements of a student's paper, thus distancing themselves from their own expertise and perspective. They don't respond as *readers*. Alternatively, if they see themselves as friends, their role is uncritical. Either identity orientation causes students to ignore or discount their peers' responses. Faculty complaints range from the poor quality of student reviewer responses to the failure of peer review to improve students' final papers (Brammer and Rees 71). Therefore, it does not save instructor time (Brammer and Rees 72). Moreover, students are dissatisfied. Literature identifies grievances that run the gamut of frustration: review was too uncritical or cursory, reviewers fail to honor the author's intentions, reviewers feel intimidated or overwhelmed, reviewers are too critical, and reviewers are not the professor (Brammer and Rees 71; Holt 384). Hence, many scholars have called for reform and more careful instructor management of the peer review process. This article documents our experiences in responding to these calls.

Inspiration from Desperation: The Collaborative Development of FofA

Our collaborative journey began with a deceptively simple question late in spring 2015: *"Can you lead a workshop for my students to help them elevate their writing?"* As director of university writing programs (DUWP), first author Eileen Camfield is accustomed to such pleas. Sometimes they amount to wishes for wands that magically organize students' thoughts into coherent arguments or requests for silver bullets to eliminate all grammatical errors. However, this question felt a bit different, in part because Camfield knew how deeply committed this professor, co-author Lara Killick, was to her teaching and her students. She did not just want Camfield to fix her students' writing problems; she wanted to know how to address them herself. Both Killick and Ruth Lewis, two sociology professors, considered themselves committed-but-inexperienced writing teachers, teachers, identities borne out of shared frustration with the quality of student writing, a sincere desire to help students improve their fundamental writing skills, and personal imposter syndrome about teaching writing. Both were at a loss about how to develop their students' skills, as well as how to develop their own efficacy and identity as writing instructors. This sense of bewilderment stemmed not only from a lack of formal training in writing pedagogy but also from the intuitive (rather than intentional) cultivation of their own writing skills.

In both Killick's and Lewis's undergraduate experiences, they rarely received formative feedback from professors during the writing process, and the limited summative feedback they did receive centered on mechanical aspects of writing with only brief annotations regarding the ideas presented. Rarely (if at all) did they receive comments on the clarity of thesis statements, the effectiveness of transitions, or use of supporting evidence. Thus, they were neither formally trained in writing composition, nor did they have any modeling of effective writing pedagogy. During their Ph.D. processes, Killick and Lewis started to develop an implicit sense of "good writing" through more regular and deeper engagement with a range of literature in their field. They also began to fully appreciate the value of revising their work through the drafting process. They regularly submitted drafts to their doctoral supervisors for critique, and comments were often both detailed and critical in nature, with explicit attention paid to the persuasiveness of their arguments and their emerging voices as academics. While this feedback certainly advanced the quality of their writing, they also found the intensity and isolation of the experience had a profoundly negative impact on their emotional engagement with the writing process. They felt their confidence as writers diminish and the onset of a deep-rooted imposter syndrome regarding their supposed identities as expert writers. In addition, they were immersed in a graduate student culture that involved regular discussions about writing anxiety and dissertation horror stories. Rarely did either encounter other Ph.D. students who expressed satisfaction in the quality of their work, pleasure in the writing process, or optimism about their future as academics. In short, for Killick and Lewis, while their Ph.D. experiences culminated in a more secure sense of their disciplinary expertise, they found their emerging identities as writing instructors far more fragile.

Thus, Killick found herself in Camfield's office in a state of complete disillusionment, utterly lost regarding solutions and seeking help for problems she couldn't even articulate. Despite scaffolding the capstone assignment across the whole semester, Killick feared if she did not change her approach, the final peer review session was going to be a complete waste of class time. The old-school "review your peer's paper and give them feedback to help them improve" simply had not been producing the desired effect. Camfield's experience leading the campus interdisciplinary writing program made her aware of just how common this dilemma is. Many are caught at a crossroads of dissatisfaction with student writing performance and with a sense of helplessness regarding what to do about it. Such helplessness was revealed when Camfield asked Killick what she meant by "elevate" her students' writing. Killick's reply was an anguished: *"I don't know; make it sound better; make it sound like they are writing at the college-level."* Sadly, Killick's efforts to help students with their writing were further impeded by a departmental culture that did not foster that kind of pedagogical support.

Killick's request for writing "elevation" immediately brought to mind a traditional class workshop on diction, but Camfield feared a stand-alone training session would be inadequate and ineffective. Moreover, after talking with Killick about what she had observed in her students' papers, it became clear that they needed more global help. In essence, the students needed to better understand their roles as readers and writers. They needed a simple but comprehensive framework through which they could develop a sense of audience for their ideas and come to align their tone and language accordingly. In other words, they needed a metaphor to guide their writing practice.

The Development of FofA: Basic Principles

Camfield reflected on the fact that the multi-valent dimensions of writing and complex terminology—from "discourse community," to "thesis," to "genre," to "stance," to "subordination," to "dangling modifier" (the list goes on)—often seemed to inhibit student writer and inexperienced writing teacher agencies by mystifying the writing process. The authors believed they needed to strip all that away in order to empower students to engage in the work of writing. By activating their willingness to get their hands dirty (or to learn by doing without fear of harsh judgment), they could get on with the work of improvement. All this is not to claim that what follows sprang into independent being without context. The values and ideas about writing embedded below are grounded in the works of composition scholars like Donald Murray, Peter Elbow, and Linda Flower who see writing as process-oriented, situated and context-dependent, and emerging from writers who are aware of their readers. More specifically, the model aligns with Richard Lanham's dictum: "When you are revising, the scarcest resource is human attention," which views all sentences as "attention economies" (21). Writing teachers are formally trained in such ideas and develop appropriate pedagogical strategies. Camfield hoped the Fund of Attention (FofA) model would provide WID teachers a simple shorthand for the composition teacher's expertise. To further this end, she believed students and WID teachers alike might benefit from a visual metaphor, rather than more words, to describe the writing process (see Figure 1).

FofA highlights the interdependent relationship between the processes of reading and writing. It acknowledges that the primary purpose of writing is to communicate ideas from a writer to a reader. Therefore, as we explain it, for a writer the worst possible thing is for your reader to fall asleep in the middle of your conversation: Writers need to keep the reader's attention. All readers are human beings who have a finite fund of attention; they eventually get hungry, sleepy, or thirsty. The trick for a writer is to hold that attention as long as possible. There are certain moves writers can make that fill the fund of attention; other moves deplete the fund. Rather than exposing students to these moves via direct instruction, FofA starts from a position whereby the students identify what moves them.

In Written Communication: The writer makes strategic stylistic choices to engage the reader's attention and advance shared understanding.

- **Strategic stylistic choices** refer to the writer's control of language (e.g., grammar, spelling, clarity, usage, diction, organization) to serve the writer's purpose (to inform, persuade, subvert, champion, etc.).

- **Engaging the reader's attention** refers to the writer's awareness of context (e.g., genre conventions) and audience (e.g., readers' interests and expectations).

- **Advancing shared understanding** refers to the degree to which the writer communicates new ideas or sheds new light on previously familiar ideas.

Figure 1: Fund of Attention, handout provided to students.

Students were introduced to the concept of reader-based writing through an introductory in-class workshop that could be adapted to various class lengths and sizes. The workshop briefly introduced the model and encouraged student reflection on the process of writing for an audience. Students were provided a sample essay and asked to read through and mark a plus (+) each time they felt a coin drop into their metaphoric "fund of attention," noting the *exact* location in the essay where the author had done something to pique their interest. Conversely, they marked a minus (-) at each spot where they felt their funds deplete. Those were the *only* marks they could write on the paper. Once done, each student created two columns at the end of the paper, one for pluses and one for minuses, in which themes were described in bullet points. They were not to merely list errors. Instead, they were each required to analyze and synthesize to create categories. For example, the list for pluses might have included general themes like: really interesting ideas, clear thesis and topic sentences, compelling evidence, effective paragraph lengths, and active verbs. The list for minuses might have included: a hard-to-follow sequence, logic problems, unsubstantiated claims, distracting diction, and unnecessary repetition. Next, students met with others in small groups and shared their personal lists. Through this discussion they engaged in further synthesis to develop a list of the top five activation-depletion moves appearing in the writing—always framing their observations by describing the impact on the reader (e.g., *"As a reader, I was confused by the abrupt shift in topic in the second paragraph."*). Along with honing analytical skills, another objective with this approach was to de-emphasize punitive judgment and develop a sense of writing as a shared experience.

The initial level of positive student engagement exceeded our expectations, raised our hopes, and led to the decision to more formally investigate the effects of the FofA model—particularly as they related to peer review. Could it convey the interactive essentials of written communication so effectively as to potentially revolutionize how student peer review is usually conducted? Our first step towards answering this question took the form of a pilot study spanning two semesters (academic year 2015-16) and eight courses within Lewis's and Killick's respective departments.

Unleashing the "Fund of Attention": Pilot

FofA was deployed in a total of eight classes across the pilot period: four lower-division, three upper-division, and one graduate class with a total of 174 students (M=21.75, range = 12-26). Each class had been classified writing-intensive by their departments, suggesting a history of substantive writing assignments within the coursework. Both Lewis's and Killick's delivery of FofA included the introductory workshop conducted by Camfield followed by intentional in-class peer review sessions. However, the specific delivery mechanisms varied between the two sociology professors.

Introductory FofA workshops: Both professors started by asking Camfield to host the introductory workshop early in the semester, well in advance of embarking on their writing assignments. While Lewis asked Camfield to run a workshop with one of her classes, she did not ask Camfield to do so for her other class, instead delivering the workshop herself. Conversely, Killick asked Camfield to run both FofA workshops in her fall classes. Previously, Camfield and Killick observed some reticence amongst students to share their past peer review experiences and to express challenges interpreting her assignment guidelines and expectations. Interested to see whether this was a product of Killick's presence in the room, we agreed that Killick would not attend the workshops. Camfield noticed a different learning climate emerging. Students appeared to feel more relaxed—less under the microscope, less worried about "saying the wrong thing" and more open to identifying deficiencies in Killick's assignment guidelines/writing expectations. Since these are all desired student behaviors, Killick remained absent from the spring workshops.

In-class peer review: Similarly, both instructors scheduled whole class periods for peer review prior to submission of major writing assignments, allowing students time to meaningfully reflect on the feedback they had received from their peers, and use it to revise their work, if desired. Lewis's in-class peer review sessions involved students working in small groups of three or four to read and annotate each other's work one paper at a time, allowing 15-20 minutes to collaborate in providing constructive FofA feedback to each student. As students in these two lower-division classes ranged from freshmen to seniors, working in small groups (rather than pairs) allowed the opportunity for those less confident providing feedback to their peers to work collaboratively with others. Comparatively, students in Killick's classes completed an online FofA review of each other's papers three days prior to the in-class session. Reviewers were randomly assigned, and their feedback was returned to the student author immediately by Canvas (the campus learning management system). This gave the students an opportunity to give/receive one round of FofA feedback before the in-class session during which additional readers provided reviews. In her graduate level class, Killick also responded to her students' work using FofA, intentionally using the same procedure described above;

the rationale was threefold. It enabled her to provide content/style formative feedback and, more significantly, did so by modeling FofA for her graduate students. In addition, she made this pedagogical move to flatten the hierarchy between herself (as the expert) and her students (as the novices). This seemed particularly pertinent in developing a supportive graduate student-faculty mentor relationship.

STUDENT RESPONSE: FALL PILOT SEMESTER

Pre-FofA experiences of peer review were recorded via a short in-class survey at the start of Killick's FofA introductory workshops (n=32). Questions addressed previous participation in, and perceived value of, peer review. The data revealed that while 100% of the students had participated in peer review in previous classes, only 28% (n=9) reported some positive experiences. Conversely, all thirty-two students reported negative experiences. The most common were that peer review was *"just a grammar check,"* reviewers are *"too nice,"* reviewers *"took over the paper,"* reviewers are afraid to critique papers that *"seem really good,"* reviewers get *"overwhelmed"* by papers that appear really weak, reviewers *"fail to catch all of the errors,"* responses are not thorough enough, reviewers *"cover the page with red ink,"* and the *"only opinion we care about is the professor's anyway."* These collective grievances mirrored those identified in the literature (Brammer and Rees 71; Holt 384).

At the end of the semester, after completing the FofA workshop and two rounds of FofA peer review (one online and one in-class), the fall pilot cohort responded to the following prompt as part of their capstone assignment: *"Reflect on your developing writing skills. Do you think your writing skills have improved over the course of this semester? Why/why not?"* Open coding was employed to identify raw data points related to student experiences of, and attitudes towards, FofA as an alternative strategy for peer review. This open coding was followed by a round of axial coding to categorize emergent themes in the raw data (Corbin and Strauss).

Two preliminary themes emerged from the coding: 1) FofA's perceived contribution to improved student writing and 2) its similar impact on student writing efficacy. Articulated here using the students' own words to honor their agency and to emphasize some demographics, one senior credited FofA with her renewed *"passion in writing again* which is something I lost recently." One junior reflected that *"keeping a steady flow and not depleting the fund of attention"* were two of his core takeaways from the class. In addition, two student populations who normally experience difficulty with collegiate writing were also quick to praise FofA. One non-traditional student felt that his *"writing skills have improved immensely ... and that is exciting for me,"* while his ESL classmate commented that *"as an international student, I was struggling with writing papers and to be honest, I just never really liked writing. But this class ... I actually enjoyed researching and writing about my stance on the given topic."* These student responses, combined with Camfield's and Killick's own personal reflections and collective discussions throughout the semester, furthered their interest in FofA's potential as a pedagogical tool.

Student Response: Spring Pilot Semester

As in the fall, data were gathered via a pre-workshop survey to establish the spring pilot cohort previous experiences and attitudes towards peer review. Almost identical trends were observed, with 100% of the students having experienced peer review in prior classes and these experiences being primarily negative. This cohort described peer review as *"a waste of time"* and *"not at all helpful."* Yet by the mid-semester, survey data (n=39) presented far more positive student attitudes towards peer review. The overwhelming majority of the class (95%) considered FofA useful/very useful in their endeavors towards improved writing skills. FofA was assessed to be *"a fairly simple way for us to edit other people's papers"* and *"much more useful than the peer review [I] am used to, where people just fix grammar mistakes and only occasionally comment on the actual content."* Camfield also noted student responses during the initial workshop were more reader-based, complex, and nuanced after their exposure to FofA, revealing a more profound grasp of what makes writing effective.

Additional post-FofA reflection data was generated through the capstone assignments (n=45). Students were again asked to respond to the following prompt: *"Reflect on your developing writing skills. Do you think your writing skills have improved over the course of this semester? Why/why not?"* The qualitative coding drew attention to the impact of several specific characteristics of the model. One student reflected:

> [FofA] is extremely beneficial, not only to the audience, because it makes the reader pay more attention to the content of the paper he/she is reading, but also to the author of the paper because it gives both positive and negative feedback to work on.

Such comments suggest FofA prompts students to consider the symbiotic relationship *between* the reader and writer. They acknowledged that as writers they *"sometimes forget about retaining my reader's attention ... as [they] can get bogged down by details and other things"* and *"find FofA useful because it is interesting to see where the reader's attention was intrigued and where [they] needed to work on how information was presented."*

Furthermore, they observed that *"unlike other techniques, FofA allows me to see what I am struggling with as well as my strengths."* The provision of *"specific positive feedback in addition to negative feedback"* served to *"boost my confidence,"* make it *"easier to see/distinguish between where I need improvement and where I don't,"* and gave *"me an indicator from a reader-perspective that I was losing their attention."* The ability of FofA to give *"feedback without cluttering it with comments that I may or may not use"* was also valued. It also enabled students to identify *"what I had to change in my writing overall instead of at specific points that peer reviewers point out."* In these ways FofA may help instructors realize the promise of peer review by "giv[ing] students something to say and push[ing] them toward a more complicated cognitive perspective" (Holt 388).

Emerging Outcomes: Recommendations for Future Lines of Inquiry

While the primary intention of this article was to provide a narrative of FofA's development and to introduce readers to its potential and practice, our pilot experiences also highlight the need for intentional assessment and further development of the model. To this end, we have identified four potential lines of inquiry as a platform for future empirical analysis: the assessment of FofA's capacity to 1) develop student writing skills, 2) cultivate positive writer-reader student identity, 3) cultivate positive writing instructor identity and enhance pedagogy, and 4) transfer across diverse curriculums and student cohorts.

Student Skill Development: In addition to the themes identified previously, students described FofA's impact beyond its effectiveness as a peer review technique. One hundred percent of the spring pilot cohort identified at least one new writing behavior they attributed to FofA. These included, but were not limited to, putting more thought into writing, increased time outlining and planning essays, producing multiple drafts, and spending more time reviewing drafts. These behaviors align with effective writing practices identified in composition literature, and the changes appear to have been intrinsically motivated. This potentially could result in the self-regulation David Nichol and Debra MacFarlane-Dick describe (201). What is unknown is the longevity of these new behaviors. Moreover, to what extent are *all* students able to extrapolate from reader feedback and develop specific plans of action? It is one thing to know that you lost your reader's attention but quite another to know what to do about it. For some writers, awareness might be enough, but for others (especially those with less-developed basic skills) follow-up direct instruction may still be required. Determining the form and point of instructor intervention should be explored.

In addition to developing students' writing skills, FofA's simple, holistic, and egalitarian view of the reading-writing-thinking process enabled faculty to hone students' critical reading skills and to better structure class discussion. For instance, Lewis implemented FofA as a core criterion for critiquing assigned course reading in one of her upper-division classes focused on developing skills in literature review. Each week, students submitted reading responses intended to help them formalize their thoughts about the assigned reading prior to class discussion. Students were provided with prompt questions encouraging them to critique both the content *and* style of the assigned article. With regard to the latter, students were asked to apply the FofA model, and in each class discussion students were then asked to identify points where their fund of attention was either replenished or depleted. Lewis's primary aim was to build familiarity with the notion of a fund of attention through critique of "distant other's" work, prior to critiquing the work of known peers and ultimately using the concept as a tool to self-evaluate; however, she was surprised to discover how effectively the model seemed to facilitate the development of critical reading skills. Future work could explore, in particular, if this new area of FofA application benefits at-risk students who are least familiar with academic conventions or who read at a below-college level. More generally, does using the FofA frame better integrate reading and writing as synergistic skills in students' minds?

Cultivating Positive Writer-Reader Identities: FofA appears to cultivate a multifaceted student identity—as writers and as readers—by developing self-efficacy and by honoring student agency. As noted in our preliminary data, FofA offers opportunities for students to experience success with their writing—all those plus marks, notations far removed from the traditional "red pen of death." Such positive experiences are not mere feel-good moments. When their writing is praised, students' writing anxiety drops and their levels of motivation to write rise (Daiker 156), creating mastery experiences associated with writing self-efficacy (Pajares 140). Thus, FofA may also operate as a harm prevention—or at least, reduction—strategy, depending on students' previous writing experiences.

Along with writing self-efficacy, FofA appears to build student agentic identity in two ways. First, the very structure of the approach aligns "teaching and assessment with a set of student-focused values" (Broad 14) and emphasizes the students' rights to their own words, showing "why new choices would positively change their texts, and ... the potential for development implicit in their own writing" (Sommers 115), as opposed to focusing on error. Composition scholars call for reviewers, most especially writing teachers, to "replace idiosyncratic models of how writing *ought* to appear" with "less authoritarian concern for how student texts make us respond as readers and whether those responses are congruent with the writer's intentions or not" (Brannon and Knoblauch 122). FofA responds to this call with particular sensitivity to the fact that:

> Writing comments is a dubious and difficult enterprise. ... [T]he things ... least likely to waste our time or to cause harm [are] ... to read what [students] write with good attention and respect; to show them that we understand what they have written—even the parts where they had trouble getting their meaning across. ... Surely what writers need most is the experience of being heard and a chance for dialogue. (Elbow 200-01)

Certainly, during the pilot, instructors observed livelier student interactions using FofA peer review than with previous structures for providing feedback—more curiosity from writers and more thoughtful analysis from readers. Additional process reflection could help inform how FofA develops student dialogue, which in turn could improve procedures.

Some important structural changes have already occurred based off feedback from other FofA users. Instead of the "pot of coins" image (see Figure 1), one humanities instructor suggested a treasure chest might be a better metaphor in that not everything that goes into or out of a reader's fund of attention is of equal weight or value: A few comma errors might be worth the loss of a small copper coin, whereas a flawed thesis statement could be equivalent to a missing golden chalice. This more nuanced framing appears to have removed student concerns about the quantity of comments in either the "plus" or "minus" columns and re-focused them on the qualities of those observations, thus adding another layer of critical thinking to their identities as writers. Future use of FofA in new contexts with different student populations may reveal other structural ways the model could evolve to expand student writer-reader identity.

Second, FofA may build student agency by clearly defining roles. Peer review practitioners are told students need coaching (Min 306), clear procedures, and training (Rollinson 26). FofA's insistence on authentic, jargon-free language and its uncomplicated protocols attempts to demystify the reading-writing-responding process. In so doing, we believe it offers a method for alleviating reviewer identity-imposter problems where students may feel pressured to perform as proxy for the instructor. FofA attempts to firmly establish the reviewer's identity as a *reader*. This clarification of their role seems to empower voice, ensuring all reviewers have something to say. It also may force reviewers to fully engage with the text, not only by marking pluses and minuses but through the second layer of theme-generation analysis—a complex cognitive process indeed. The *writer* is also encouraged to actively participate in similar complex cognitive processes, determining which in-text marks apply to the reader's various themes and aligning stylistic choices accordingly. FofA appears to prime the capacity to do so effectively by increasing writers' awarenesses of themselves as readers and vice versa. Consequently, both reviewer and author agency are not only honored but required. Framed another way, FofA invites students to engage in precisely the kind of collaborative work identified as a "politically important" social negotiation in which a writer "finds his or her identity" (Holt 392), overcoming the alienation felt when writing does not have a clear audience (Gere 10). Thus, understanding more about FofA's effect on student identity through self-efficacy and agency is promising ground for future investigation. Specifically, although we have an intuitive sense it develops positive writing identities, is this borne out empirically? Is there variation in which students gain the most from this model (e.g., across disciplines, class standing, GPA, English learners, etc.)? Are there any unintended consequences (e.g., where FofA may be damaging to student writing identities)?

Cultivating Positive Writing Instructor Identity and Enhancing Pedagogy: Our experiences suggest that student reviewers may not be the only beneficiaries of FofA; faculty also stand to gain. For the two sociology professors described in this article, FofA revolutionized their approach to peer review and transformed their entire pedagogical mindset. Its first impact was to minimize Killick's and Lewis's impostor syndrome around teaching writing. As with students using traditional peer review protocols, Killick and Lewis often felt inauthentic and lacking a sense of authority when expected to perform as proxy for composition teachers. Similar to its value for students, FofA provided them with uncomplicated protocols, accessible language, and the simple role of "reader responding to writing." Further, because FofA acknowledges the difficulties of writing and the needs of readers, Killick and Lewis also found it generated mutual empathy between instructor and student. FofA appeared to soften the arbitrary boundaries between traditional notions of novice and expert to create a safer, more democratic learning space for more honest dialogue. This boundary softening was underscored by having the DUWP conduct initial workshops in the Writing Center, which both ensured students had effective instruction on how to operationalize FofA and created a space in which students felt empowered to critique assignment guidelines before they were due. During the subsequent debriefs, faculty were then able to hear student concerns and proactively adjust their pedagogical strategies accordingly. Thus, this identity shift helped the instructors close the assessment loop. Future work could investigate the role of FofA as an antidote to faculty imposter syndrome about teaching writing in the disciplines—including the impact of openness to assessment, changes in pedagogy, and the added value of students feeling heard by responsive instructors. To what degree are these separable outcomes, or if not, how are they inter-related?

Furthermore, FofA assisted faculty in the meaningful engagement with standard student learning outcomes. Listing "improving student writing" on a course syllabus is commonplace, but for Killick merely identifying writing as a desirable skill was not effective at actually attaining the outcome. Introducing FofA to the curriculum necessitated two macro changes to the design of the class: 1) the establishment of explicit, measurable student-learning outcomes connected to student writing and 2) the integration of FofA principles into curriculum and assessment tools. With regard to the latter, Killick increased the frequency of all FofA peer review activities and provided more structured guidance via FofA worksheets tailored to each stage of the cumulative assignment. In addition, she revised all assignment rubrics to explicitly reflect the increased emphasis on writing skills *and* the FofA model. For example, her rubrics contained evaluative criteria such as *"The author's positions were clear and logically presented," "The author used credible and compelling evidence to support positions,"* and *"The reader's fund of attention was enhanced more than it was depleted."* The impact of such changes in assessment represents a further avenue for inquiry.

Closing Thoughts: FofA Across the Curriculum

In conclusion, we hope to connect FofA to the teaching for transfer (TFT) movement in composition study. TFT postulates that when students learn to draw on prior knowledge and to link key concepts under a self-determined guiding framework, they develop identities as writers that allow them to move to "new contexts, where through 'retrieval and application' ... they can write anew" (Yancey, Robertson, and Taczak 137). If this is so, then FofA might serve as just such a framework for transfer across the curriculum. As discussed, our work suggests that by simplifying responding to writing as a process described in students' own terms and grounded in their experiences as readers, FofA appears to build student agency. In so doing, might it also help build the kind of writerly identities associated with skill transfer? As this article has indicated, such transfer may not apply only to students. WID faculty also need to transfer their writing pedagogy skills from one class to the next. FofA seems to offer a framework to do so. At our own institution, we have already witnessed the model begin to permeate myriad contexts. Promising work has already begun testing FofA in science and humanities classes to explore whether FofA operates effectively across other disciplinary lines and serves diverse student constituencies equally well. The need for ongoing research in this area is paramount.

Further, we are particularly interested in examining the transfer of FofA beyond its role as a peer review tool for non-specialists. In serving as a shorthand for composition theory and in providing a coherent framework for writing pedagogy, FofA is providing our university a collective language, building writing-center-based relationships across disciplines, and strengthening stakeholders' senses of shared purpose. The model has become the foundation for faculty development in our first-year seminar program, functions as the training tool for writing mentors in the Student Writing Center, and has informed the definition of and rubric for our institutional learning outcome for written communication. As such it has been presented at our regional accrediting agency's Academic Renewal Conference where it was well-received as an alternative assessment approach. It seems possible that FofA could offer a philosophical framework for an integrated writing curriculum and pedagogy development. We invite our readers to help us explore this new terrain.

Works Cited

Brammer, Charlotte, and Mary Rees. "Peer Review from the Students' Perspective: Invaluable or Invalid?" *Composition Studies*, vol. 35, no. 2, 2007, pp. 71-85.

Brannon, Lil, and C. H. Knoblauch. "On Students' Right to Their Own Texts: A Model of Teacher Response." *A Sourcebook for Responding to Student Writing*, edited by Richard Straub. Hampton Press, 1999, pp. 117-28.

Broad, Bob. *What We Really Value: Beyond Rubrics in Teaching and Assessing Writing*. Utah State UP, 2003.

Bruffee, Kenneth. *Collaborative Learning: Higher Education, Interdependence, and the Authority of Knowledge*. 2nd ed. Johns Hopkins UP, 1999.

Corbin, Julliet, and Anselm Strauss. *Basics of Qualitative Research: Techniques and Procedures for Developing Grounded Theory*. 3rd ed. Sage, 2008.

Daiker, Donald A. "Learning to Praise." *A Sourcebook for Responding to Student Writing*, edited by Richard Straub. Hampton Press, 1999, pp.153-63.

Elbow, Peter. "Options for Responding to Student Writing." *A Sourcebook for Responding to Student Writing*, edited by Richard Straub. Hampton Press, 1999, pp. 196-202.

Gere, Anne Ruggles. *Writing Groups: History, Theory, and Implications*. Southern Illinois UP, 1987.

Halasek, Kay. "Interrogating Peer Response as 'Proxy:' Reframing and Reimagining Peer Review as Connected Practice." Conference on College Composition and Communication, Houston, TX. 7 April 2016. Concurrent Session.

Holt, Mara. "The Value of Written Peer Criticism." *College Composition and Communication*, vol. 43, no. 3, 1992, pp. 384-92.

Lanham, Richard. *Revising Prose*. 5th ed. Pearson, 2007.

Lundstrom, Kristi, and Wendy Baker. "To Give Is Better Than to Receive: The Benefits of Peer Review to the Reviewer's Own Writing." *Journal of Second Language Writing*, vol. 18, no. 1, 2009, pp. 30-43.

Min, Hui-Tzu, "Training Student to Become Successful Peer Reviewers." *System,* vol. 33, no. 2, 2005, pp. 293-308.

Nichol, David, and Debra MacFarlane-Dick. "Formative Assessment and Self-Regulated Learning: A Model and Seven Principles of Good Feedback Practice." *Studies in Higher Education*, vol. 31, no. 2, 2006, pp. 199-218.

Nystrand, Martin. "A Social-Interactive Model of Writing." *Written Communication*, vol. 6, no. 1, 1989, pp. 66-85.

Pajares, Frank. "Self-Efficacy Beliefs, Motivation, and Achievement in Writing: A Review of the Literature." *Reading & Writing Quarterly*, vol. 19, no. 2, 2003, pp. 139-58.

Rollinson, Paul. "Using Peer Feedback in the ESL Writing Class." *ELT Journal*, vol. 59, no. 1, 2005, pp. 23-29.

Sommers, Nancy. "Responding to Student Writing." *A Sourcebook for Responding to Student Writing*, edited by Richard Straub. Hampton Press, 1999, pp. 107-15.

Topping, Keith. "Peer Assessment Between Students in Colleges and Universities." *Review of Educational Research*, vol. 68, no. 3, 1998, pp. 249-76.

Wirtz, Jason. "Writing Courses Live and Die by the Quality of Peer Review." *Collaborative Learning and Writing: Essays on Using Small Groups in Teaching English and Composition*, edited by Kathleen Hunzer, McFarland Press, 2012, pp. 5-16.

Yancey, Kathleen Blake, Liane Robertson, and Kara Taczak. *Writing Across Contexts: Transfer, Composition, and Sites of Writing*. Utah State UP, 2014.

SUPPLEMENTAL MATERIAL

Part I: Reflection on the Origins of the Article

Our article describes the origins of our piece as "inspiration from desperation," telling the anecdote of sociology professor Dr. Killick approaching Writing Program Director Dr. Camfield for help improving her students' writing. We subsequently identify Killick and Lewis as experts in their disciplinary fields but suffering from a kind of "imposter syndrome" when it came to teaching writing. What the article does not describe is the larger context that enabled Killick to approach Camfield in the first place.

When Camfield first became Director of Writing Programs at the University of the Pacific and took the lead on faculty development for writing in the disciplines (WiD), she did what many others do: offer one-off workshops on general topics, such as thesis development. Unfortunately, these were poorly attended. What did attract faculty were pedagogy seminars designed for those teaching the first-year writing course. These seminars were spaces where faculty could receive practical teaching ideas for immediate application. They also developed camaraderie and a strong sense of shared purpose. This made Camfield wonder how she might create other kinds of faculty cohorts. During her investigation, she discovered the Carnegie Foundation's concept of Networked Improvement Communities (NICs). These groups draw individuals together who might otherwise be siloed in their home institutions or departments in the service of a common purpose—in this case, improving writing instruction in the disciplines. NICs are theory-based and solution-focused, perfect for driving real change in a developing WiD program.

Thus, in fall of 2014, Camfield invited eight faculty members to join Writing in the Disciplines Networked Improvement Communities, or "WiD-NICs." Initially, there were three groups of two-three faculty members from different departments in the humanities, sciences, or social sciences. Killick was amongst the social sciences group. In these communities, faculty had the opportunity to talk about their struggles with student writing and their aspirations for what they hoped it could be. Camfield provided concrete suggestions for how to achieve those outcomes. These ranged from things like crafting clearer prompts, offering more low-stakes assignments to help students feel better about taking intellectual risks, and scaffolding assignments more effectively. Fall semester was spent developing new curriculum; spring semester was spent delivering the revised class and developing strategies for "course correction" during monthly NIC meetings. Faculty with similar concerns became *networked* across departments and could build solutions through a recursive process. Perhaps more important was the *community* forged within the groups. Participation in the WiD-NICs developed Killick's trust in Camfield to the extent that she was empowered to express her deeply vulnerable sentiment that she was failing her students. She knew she had not just an expert in her corner but an ally and an advocate. This experience speaks profoundly to the importance of relationship-building in faculty development. Done well, a small group can attract larger membership – our initial group of 8 has grown to 34 faculty members from 21 disciplines – and can put effective writing on the institutional map.

Part II: Description of Research Methods, Findings, and/or Pedagogical Impact

It's now been 4 years since Killick[1] walked into Camfield's office. The collaborative journey described in this article has had a profound impact on Killick's pedagogy. For Killick, the Fund of Attention (FofA), initially designed as a tool for peer review, has evolved into a much broader philosophical framework and has re-imagined her role in facilitating student-writing success. In preparing to write these remarks, Killick returned to early iterations of her course syllabi as a baseline. This was an illuminating exercise. The position of writing development in her teaching goals was patently clear: there was no position. The syllabi did not contain explicit written communication learning outcomes. Rather, writing skill development was simply one competency among many in which students would become "more proficient." On reflection, this cursory course objective demonstrated her past belief that writing improvements would "magically" occur through the traditional feedback process she had seen modelled previously.

When such improvements were modest and/or unequally distributed across the class, Killick began to utilize a classroom-based peer writing mentor as the primary source of direct feedback and direction for students seeking help with writing skills. She would encourage students to initiate this assistance and would also refer students to him who needed "extra" help. While well-intentioned, this strategy may have served to increase writing-related anxiety and present "good writing" as a destination rather than a process. Furthermore, it reinforced a problematic remediation message, since negative feedback drove students to seek help. It became evident that, while helpful in many ways, outsourcing writing support *exclusively* to such 1-on-1 interactions was

---

1. Note: Since writing the article, Dr. Lewis has taken up a research position that does not involve classroom-based teaching.

doing little to facilitate long-term writing development or transferable writing skills.

Through the collaboration with Camfield, Killick recognized that system-level change rather than direct individual interventions was needed in order to support student writing development. It was here that FofA moved beyond a pedagogical tool towards a more cogent philosophical framework. Encouraged by the positive impact of the introductory FofA workshops and subsequent peer review sessions, Killick began to apply the core principles of FofA to her broader pedagogical practice. Killick moved written communication from its peripheral position in her course objectives to an explicit and prominent SLO. This simple revision to her syllabi increased the visibility of writing development as a central goal of her classes and signaled an increased value attached to writing. But, simply paying lip service to "writing development" was not sufficient. She embedded a specific FofA scoring item in the rubrics for both the weekly writing assignments and the more substantive paper submitted towards the end of the semester. She also changed the way she talked about writing to her students, emphasizing writing as crosscutting skill, important in professional life regardless of career field. To reinforce this message, she moved away from assigning "traditional" papers. Instead, writing tasks emphasize authorial voice as it aligns with purpose.

For Camfield, the impact of this experience has revolutionized her approach to faculty development by erasing an artificial distinction in her mind that somehow faculty needs were different from undergraduate student needs. Through developing the faculty learning community that spawned the FofA technique (amongst other pedagogical innovations), Camfield came to recognize the degree to which faculty can be isolated and thrive within a connected group. Like undergraduates, faculty can experience imposter syndrome, wither under harsh judgement, and need to be meaningfully supported. To this latter end, now Camfield better recognizes the importance of validating faculty work, of *gently* suggesting alternative practice, and of offering herself as a model for writing pedagogy. Thus, her calendar is now full of demonstration workshops. The FofA experience has also validated her impulse to strip away alienating jargon from composition work and instead to radicalize writing instruction by questioning traditional formulae. As faculty design new assignments, she asks "what kind of writing would students like to produce and would you actually *enjoy* reading?" Thus, she better activates faculty agency and student voice. Finally, this experience has influenced her scholarship, for example encouraging her to explore the impact of shame in academic culture and to call for academic empathy.

Part III: Discussion Questions

1. How was your identity shaped as a writer and a teacher of writing? What role models did/do you have?

2. Do the experiences of the authors resonate with your experiences in supporting student writers, perhaps particularly during peer review?

3. In what ways does the "Fund of Attention" align with your teaching philosophy and how might you incorporate it into your practice?

4. How might the "Fund of Attention" impact your students' identities as writers and their writing self-efficacy?

5. What adaptations to the model and applications of "Fund of Attention" could be made for special student populations (e.g., graduate students, English-language learners, etc.)?

PEDAGOGY

Pedagogy is on the Web at
http://pedagogy.dukejournals.org/

Pedagogy is a journal dealing exclusively with pedagogical issues. *Pedagogy* is intended as a forum for critical reflection and as a site for spirited and informed debate from a multiplicity of positions and perspectives. It strives to reverse the longstanding marginalization of teaching and the scholarship produced around it and instead to assert the centrality of teaching to our work as scholars and professionals.

"Real Research" or "Just for a Grade"? Ethnography, Ethics, and Engagement in the Undergraduate Writing Studies Classroom[1]

Elizabeth G. Allan's "'Real Research' or 'Just for a Grade'? Ethnography, Ethics, and Engagement in the Undergraduate Writing Studies Classroom" (issue 18.2) is based on teacher research conducted in an ethnography course in a writing studies department. This ethnographic case study demonstrates the pedagogical benefits of institutional review board–approved, collaborative student research projects. Implementing an experiential learning approach to teaching undergraduate research also revealed that students' perceptions of what counts as "real" research are more complex than previous studies have indicated.

---

1. *Pedagogy*, vol. 18, no. 2 © 2018 by Duke University Press.

"Real Research" or "Just for a Grade"? Ethnography, Ethics, and Engagement in the Undergraduate Writing Studies Classroom

Elizabeth G. Allan

Based on teacher research conducted in an ethnography course in a writing studies department, this ethnographic case study demonstrates the pedagogical benefits of institutional review board–approved, collaborative student research projects. Implementing an experiential learning approach to teaching undergraduate research also revealed that students' perceptions of what counts as "real" research are more complex than previous studies have indicated.

Everything depends on the quality of the experience which is had.

—John Dewey

Introduction

Setting the Scene

From the back corner of the classroom, Mary's voice broke the silence: "Do we have to go through the IRB if we have no intention of publishing?"[1] I held my breath. The guest speaker, a research ethics specialist, responded that a classroom activity is just a paper for a grade; it's not really research. Silently, I raised the counterarguments: Are all classroom activities simply graded learning experiences? What counts as publishing? Can't students conduct authentic human subjects research in an undergraduate course?

Later, I reminded the students that the central project of this course was to apply ethnographic research to address issues that affect our community. The course goals included not only learning about cultural diversity by reading ethnographies but also learning how to design and conduct collaborative ethnographic research projects (see appendix A). The students would submit proposals to our university's institutional review board, even if the outcome was that the institutional review board (IRB) classified those projects as "not research" under the common rule definition.[2] Then, if the student researchers chose to submit their work to research fairs, conferences, or undergraduate journals, they could disseminate their findings beyond our classroom.

During the first few weeks of the course, we had studied the ethnographic research methods used in writing studies, education, and related fields. We had analyzed experienced researchers' published accounts of the ethical issues they had faced, and we had critiqued publicly available examples of undergraduate research on YouTube—some of which demonstrated questionable ethical practices. The students had completed the required online modules of Collaborative Institutional Training Initiative (CITI) training for human subjects research and had consulted disciplinary guidelines for ethical research practices (American Anthropological Association 2004; Conference on College Composition and Communication 2003). Now, they were preparing to conduct their own small-scale ethnographic studies that could potentially help others understand teaching and learning practices from new perspectives—their own as well as those of their study participants.

Considering the Role of the IRB in Undergraduate Research

Within the last decade, writing studies scholars (a term I use inclusively to refer to composition and rhetoric, English studies, and related fields) have promoted undergraduate research that reaches beyond the traditional research paper assignment. As our pedagogical practices have expanded to include primary research, the advantages of undergraduate research experiences have been widely reported (Downs and Wardle 2004, 2010; Cavanagh 2010; Collins et al. 2010; Grobman and Kinkead 2010; Hersh, Hiro, and Asarnow 2011; Hunter 2012; Purdy and Walker 2013). IRB review for undergraduate research has long been accepted as both ethically and pedagogically important in other fields, such as psychology (e.g., Kallgren and Tauber 1996). In writing studies coursework, however, the role—if any—of IRB review for undergraduate research is still a contested issue.

Because IRB regulations were originally developed in response to unethical medical research practices, the language of ethical review, even for social and behavioral research, is often medically inflected. As researchers and as teachers of research, we need to look beyond the obvious issue that IRB applications may contain questions like "Will the research involve pregnant women or fetuses?" One undergraduate student who had written an IRB application in another course recalled that this question prompted the class catchphrase "Fetuses don't write." True enough. However, this nonmedical research focus does not mean that writing studies research is risk-free and therefore does not require ethical review.

Some educators view IRBs as an obstacle to minimal-risk, classroom-based research conducted by students (Downs and Wardle 2010). Others advocate for the pedagogical value of ethical reviews of undergraduate research, claiming that students view their research as "real" *because* it has been reviewed by an IRB (Kallgren and Tauber 1996). Another popular position is that, when their findings are disseminated beyond the classroom to a wider audience, students regard their research as "real" (Hersh, Hiro, and Asarnow 2011; Cavanagh 2010; Downs and Wardle 2010; Hunter 2012). My student researchers' experiences demonstrate that students' perception of what counts as "real" undergraduate research is more complex.

Overview of the Case Study

I conducted a teacher research study in an undergraduate ethnography course offered by the writing studies department. This course fulfills elective requirements for writing studies majors and upper-level general education requirements for students in other disciplines. Initially, my goal was to document my approach to teaching collaborative, IRB-approved qualitative research at the undergraduate level from both my own and my students' perspectives. Would conducting original ethnographic research be a valuable learning experience? Would the frustrations of getting the student researchers' studies reviewed by the IRB be worth the time and effort it would take? To answer these questions, I invited the students to add their voices to the scholarly conversation on best practices for undergraduate research in the areas of student engagement, research ethics, and curricula that feature "microethnographies," which "report on the culture of a single classroom, the single learner, and even the single learning event" (Bishop 1999: 13). We used Ethnography of the University Initiative (EUI) projects, like those described by Gina Hunter (2012), as models.

In the sections that follow, I first identify the pedagogical theories that framed my study. Then, I briefly review several models of undergraduate research and explain how they inform and differ from my approach to teaching the ethnography course. Next, I describe my own ethnographic research process. Ethnographers value open-ended questions rather than hypotheses that can be tested by experimental research. Ethnographic writing also has a strong narrative tradition that foregrounds participants' voices. Therefore, I present the results thematically, showing how the undergraduate research experiences yielded pedagogical benefits. I tell the story of how the student researchers expanded their definition of what counts as research, how they became more aware of research ethics, and how they engaged— or did not engage—with hands-on learning. Within each section, I reveal the messy, recursive process that led to each finding, and I analyze key examples by comparing them with other researchers' conclusions. As the narrative unfolds, I trace the path through the data that led to an unanticipated finding: the student researcher's stance in describing and reporting the study's findings is the key factor that, from the students' perspective, distinguished undergraduate research "just for a grade" from "real research." I conclude by considering how educators can create undergraduate learning experiences that foster student engagement through ethically reviewed human subjects research.

Learning through Experience

As a qualitative researcher and a writing instructor, I argue that there is no substitute for learning by doing. Drawing on John Dewey's ([1938] 1997) theory of experiential learning, as well as approaches to writing pedagogy that emphasize collaboration and scaffolding (e.g., Lee and Smagorinsky 2000), I developed the course so that a combination of professional modeling, peer collaboration, and hands-on practice activities would support a firsthand experience with ethnography. In the "continuous spiral" of Dewey's experiential learning model, "the educator's responsibility" is to set up a problem-based learning situation that "grows out of the conditions of the experience," "is within the range of the capacity of students," "arouses in the learner an active quest for information and for production of new ideas," and "become[s] the ground for further experiences in which new problems are presented" ([1938] 1997: 79). With this theory of learning in mind,

I reasoned that if my students were going to *learn about* ethnography, then my responsibility was to help them to *do* an authentic, albeit scaled-down, ethnography. Requiring IRB review for undergraduate student projects was a pedagogical risk. If approval took too long or was denied, the foundation of my course would crumble. I was confident that we would succeed, but like any research project, this pedagogical plan included the possibility of failure. I expected that both the students and I would need to learn from our mistakes.

Writing studies research often investigates how people develop rhetorical skill and acquire an awareness of disciplinary expectations. Seen through this lens, the IRB review process is a high-stakes rhetorical act that both shapes and relies upon the researcher's ethos. It requires the researcher to craft a well-supported argument to persuade the audience of IRB reviewers that the study conforms to commonly held values of the academic community. As Will Banks and Michelle Eble (2007: 42) argue, our research "requires us to think rhetorically about risk and benefit and to make arguments about the social value of our work." The IRB review process exposes theoretical differences that mark the boundaries of disciplinary cultures. To negotiate these differences, researchers and IRBs need to state explicitly—and sometimes challenge—the assumptions they each hold. Failure to do so can interfere with their ability to communicate effectively with one another (Kramer, Miller, and Communri 2009). One of my pedagogical goals was to create an engaging, collaborative learning experience that would guide undergraduate students through the complex process of writing rhetorically effective IRB applications. Then, I hoped, these novice student researchers would conduct ethically sound, authentic ethnographic research—not just write a paper for a grade.

Pedagogical Approaches to Undergraduate Research

The "writing about writing" model of first-year composition (Downs and Wardle 2004) may mark the beginning of our disciplinary discussion of authentic undergraduate research. As Doug Downs and Elizabeth Wardle (2010) observe, "A library research paper, for all its hope of having the writer reach a new insight, is not learning based on discovery new to *other* inquirers" (177); rather, it is "recitative research" (184) that too often only requires "regurgitation of sources to 'take a stand'" (177). James Purdy and Joyce Walker (2013: 23) found that, in the instructional materials they analyzed, "the idea of introductory university students as 'knowledge makers' and active practitioners of research activities is markedly absent." However, Downs and Wardle (2010: 174) maintain that even first-year students can produce "genuine, contributive research" that has pedagogical benefits. The role of the IRB in this form of student research is complicated by local institutional policies. Downs and Wardle (2010) list the IRB as one of the "impediments to contributive first-year research" (183) and note that "teachers at some institutions will need to consider arrangements for IRB approval of undergraduate, course-based human-subjects research" (187). For example, some IRBs and writing programs have negotiated local policies whereby individual teachers or departmental committees oversee research ethics for undergraduate projects (e.g., Rogers 2010). At my own institution, neither the IRB nor the first-year writing program advocates subjecting first-year students' introduction to primary research (via informational interviews, field observations, or peer questionnaires) to IRB review, and institutional policies preclude the IRB from delegating formal ethical review to others. However, bypassing the IRB may call into question the authenticity of students' research contributions, especially in writing studies programs that build on Downs and Wardle's model to introduce disciplinary research methods in more advanced undergraduate coursework.

My approach to teaching ethnography is consistent with both Downs and Wardle's contributive model and the type of research promoted by the Council on Undergraduate Research (2011). Its model of research is considered "genuine research" and is "*distinct from the ubiquitous research paper*" because it "involves students as apprentices, collaborators, or independent scholars in critical investigations using fieldwork and discipline-specific methodologies under the sponsorship of faculty mentors" (Grobman and Kinkead 2010: ix). Such undergraduate research experiences often take the form of independent study projects, honors college theses, or summer enrichment activities (e.g., research assistantships in a faculty research lab) in science, technology, engineering, and math (STEM) disciplines, psychology, and the human sciences (Collins et al. 2010). Ruben Mancha and Carol Yoder (2014: 38) note that "research in the social sciences and humanities often does not entail laboratory work" and that undergraduate research in these fields "has not been as widely embraced as in the [STEM] sciences because of the nature of the research itself, which is typically non-collaborative." Recently, several promising examples of undergraduate research in the humanities and social sciences have been presented in *CUR Quarterly*: a faculty-student collaboration in archival research (Conliffe 2014); a course-based, mixed methods study using oral histories (Murray 2014); and practicum-based action research studies for preservice teachers (Manak and Young 2014; Slobodzian and Pancsofar 2014; Szecsi 2015). Unlike these examples of CUR research, my pedagogical model emphasizes student-led research teams (groups of two to four) conducting microethnographies in the context of an upper-level writing studies course.

My model also differs from other approaches that have been used to teach undergraduate research in the growing number of writing studies programs. For example, Deaver Traywick (2010: 52) asserts that, in writing studies, "RCR [responsible conduct of research] instruction for undergraduate researchers has not been formalized at a disciplinary level. Research ethics may be taught in some composition methodology courses, but students often do not encounter these courses until graduate school." Faculty who mentor undergraduate researchers may be expected to provide individualized, project-specific RCR instruction. However, Traywick claims that thorough RCR instruction is "certainly impossible" (69) under these conditions. Faculty who want to include undergraduate student research projects in their courses often struggle to fit adequate RCR instruction into the curriculum. For example, Jacquelyn Rogers (2010) describes an undergraduate research methods practicum that introduces students to both quantitative and qualitative writing studies research. Rogers's students conduct individual studies that undergo an "abridged" (81) departmental review process, in accordance with local policies. One drawback to this approach is that these projects "*cannot* be published," although students "committed from the outset to seeking publication" could submit their proposals to the university's IRB (89). Another drawback is that the diversity of individual projects, especially in large classes, can be difficult to manage (88). Faculty may avoid teaching research-based courses because "accompanying even a small group of students through individual research projects is time consuming and unpredictable" (Hunter 2012: 40).

In the EUI model, Hunter provides a "preapproved protocol" (2012: 25) for ethnographic student research before the semester begins. Although Hunter's anthropology course "privilege[s] standard ethnographic methods, the students' [actual] data collection techniques emerge from their areas of substantive concern" (26). Not all IRBs allow such methodological flexibility, however. In contrast to these models, my approach to teaching undergraduate qualitative research limits the number of projects by requiring collaborative research teams and embeds instruction in research ethics, including the IRB review process, in a writing studies course that focuses solely on ethnography.

The Ethnographic Teacher Research Process

The Institutional Context

The student researchers in my study attend a midwestern doctoral research university that serves over sixteen thousand undergraduates. Demographically, the student population is more economically and ethnically mixed than racially diverse, and 60 percent of the undergraduate population is female. The university prides itself on creating opportunities for undergraduate research, particularly in STEM disciplines (e.g., summer research experiences in faculty-led labs) and the honors college program (e.g., thesis projects supervised by faculty mentors).

The Course and the Students

The ethnography course draws a large number of education students because it fulfills the language arts certification program's general education writing intensive course requirement. Twenty-four students (sixteen females, eight males) participated (see appendix B): twelve of the twenty-two students who were enrolled in the first-semester section (cohort A); twelve of the seventeen students who were enrolled in the second-semester section (cohort B). In their reflective essays and interviews, several students commented that they did not know what ethnography was when they signed up for the course. Since the informed consent process took place early in the semester, some students may not have participated because they felt uncertain about what the course would entail. However, the informed consent records show that no one joined or withdrew from the study after the second week of classes.

The Study Design

I chose an ethnographic approach for my teacher research because it is a "recursive, collaborative, and explicitly change-based endeavor" (Nickoson 2012: 110) and because it aligns with the type of research that students enrolled in the course could be expected to conduct when they become professionals. For example, Carolyn Frank (1999: 1) argues that preservice teachers need to develop "an ethnographic perspective" of classroom cultures. I also wanted to apply this perspective to understand undergraduate research experiences from the students' point of view and to improve my own and possibly others' teaching practices.

As an ethnographer, I began with broad research questions, expecting that more refined questions would emerge as I analyzed the data. The initial questions guiding my research were as follows: (1) What are novice undergraduate student researchers' perceptions of the benefits and challenges of conducting IRB-approved, small-scale, collaborative ethnographic research projects? (2) Do undergraduate students' perceptions of research shift in response to their experiences as student researchers? (3) Based on their experiences in the course, what recommendations would undergraduate student researchers make to improve teaching and learning practices in qualitative research pedagogy at the undergraduate level?

To create a "firewall between the roles of teacher and researcher" (Brydon-Miller and Greenwood 2006: 125), I designed the study so that I would not know who had chosen to participate until after the course had ended. Signed informed consent forms were collected and securely stored by a third party and were not released to me until after grades had been submitted. At any point in the semester, students could visit the department office and review their consent form in order to join, withdraw from, or change their level of participation in the study without my knowledge. Both participating and nonparticipating students completed the same required assignments for the course: written and multimodal texts composed in response to in-class activities and formal assignments, as well as individual and collaborative student presentations that were video recorded for instructor review. The study was divided into two data collection phases. Students who agreed to participate in phase 1 allowed me to analyze the work they had produced for the course. This coursework includes conceptual drawings and ethnographic maps, field notes, IRB proposals, ethnographic reports, multimodal presentations, and reflective essays. After the semester ended, I analyzed the phase 1 data using pseudonyms in place of participants' names. Phase 2 involved a thirty-minute stimulated recall interview after the semester had ended.[3] Phase 2 participants reviewed their informed consent forms to confirm their level of participation at the beginning of the interview session. Interviews were video recorded, unless the participant preferred that I use audio recording or written notes.

The interviews opened with questions about the types and importance of research practiced in the student's major/profession, the typical college research assignment, the student's definition of research, whether that definition had shifted since high school or since taking the ethnography course, and their prior research experiences. During the stimulated recall portion of the interview, I showed students

- participants' conceptual drawings of research (without names);
- a video clip of their own ethnographic mapping presentation, based on their first fieldwork assignment;
- their own field notes from an in-class assignment and from the research project;
- the handout from the IRB presentation on research ethics by a guest speaker;
- the instructions for the research project (see appendix C) and their own report; and
- their own reflective essay and anonymous excerpts from other participants' reflections.

When reviewing these materials, students described what they remembered about their approach to the microethnography research project assignment, including their research study design; what stood out to them as they looked back at their work; what they might do differently if they could do it again; which activities were most/least helpful to them; what it was like to work as a part of a student research team; and whether what they had learned had been or would be useful in another course or in their career. Students also reflected on the IRB review process, whether they had encountered any ethical dilemmas in their research, whether they thought it was important for student researchers to submit research proposals to the IRB, and what they would change about the IRB process if they could. Finally, I asked students what advice they would give to future undergraduate student researchers taking the course.

The Data Analysis Process

Mary Sheridan (2012: 79) argues that "ethnographers need to disclose in the final written document their positionality and the decisions they make. Such practices not only allow readers to understand what and how conclusions were made but also expose the messiness of these research stages." I used the constant-comparative method to analyze the data (O'Connor, Netting, and Thomas 2008; Sheridan 2012). Using a grounded-theory approach, I wrote analytical memos based on my own participant-observation field notes while the first section of the course was in session.[4] Since I could not know which (if any) students in the first section had consented to participate until the semester had ended, I did not begin formally coding data from cohort A participants until I was teaching the second section. The first round of coding focused on students' definitions of research, experiences with research, and attitudes toward research. During the phase 2 interviews, students responded to my preliminary findings, including the emerging theme of students' perspectives on what counts as "real" research.

Initially, I anticipated that the difference between those who viewed their research as "real" and those who saw it merely as classroom activity for a grade might be explained by the student researchers' definitions of research, their attitudes toward the IRB review process, or their awareness of research ethics—especially an understanding of the risks that might actually befall their participants. However, as Rebecca Moore Howard (2014, 79) explains, "Coding pushes the researcher away from confirmation bias, beyond grasping at bright shiny objects in an impressionistic reading of text. . . .

It facilitates unexpected insights." The codes *real research* and *just for a grade* are grounded in the participants' own language, as demonstrated in the sections that follow. Once the interviews were completed, I reexamined all of the data systematically to test preliminary findings. Additional coding categories included *typical college research, research instruction, research ethics, researcher identity,*[5] *research in specific fields, collaboration, engagement,* and *research-related writing.* By examining the relationships among these coded categories, I explored the pedagogical benefits of IRB-reviewed undergraduate research experiences, described below. More importantly, I discovered that the stance students adopted when they articulated the actual or potential benefits of the study in their reports, reflections, and interviews correlated with whether they considered their studies "real" research or "practice" research assignments "just for a grade."

"What Is Research?": Expanding Definitions and Shifting Attitudes

On the first day of class, I asked students to draw their definition of research. I used this informal conceptual drawing technique to elicit students' initial perceptions of key ideas that they would encounter during the semester. I collected the first-day drawings and displayed them again during the last class meeting, asking students to reflect on whether or not their learning experiences in the course had altered their views. In the phase 2 interviews, I asked students to describe any patterns they noticed in participants' drawings.

Books/libraries and computers were the two most commonly depicted features, with both appearing together in just over half of the drawings (eleven of twenty).[6] Seven of the drawings included a researcher, but only three of those drawings showed the researcher interacting with another person. These interactions were usually interpreted as interviews, although Lucy, an education major, read them as "brainstorming topics for a research paper." Other drawings depicted solitary researchers reading, thinking, or using scientific equipment. In addition to the three interview scenes, three other drawings showed a digital recorder, a list labeled "Interview Questions," and a person saying "Blah blah," which may have signified either an interview or a presentation. Question marks, light bulbs, brains, and clocks appeared as details alongside the more prominent features of books and computers in many of the drawings. These initial conceptual drawings aligned with students' verbal descriptions of the typical research assignment. Samuel was surprised by the number of drawings that featured books: "I feel like I can tell which ones are Elementary Ed because they look like the kind of projects that you would have for a class for that [major]." Sheila, an education major, drew what phase 2 participants agreed was an apt representation of the typical college research assignment: a library building, a computer, an index card, and a written document (see appendix D).

This narrow view of research as the retrieval and re-presentation of written texts, Purdy and Walker (2013: 30) argue, leads students to "believe that academic projects can be created only through linear, step-based processes and through the use of certain kinds of acceptable resources," and to "develop the stunningly inaccurate notion that academic knowledge is actually made primarily in these ways and through these processes." Consequently, "the concept of knowledge making as an act engaged in by professionals through practices such as creating experiments, conducting ethnographies, or visiting archives is deemphasized, and the idea of students as engaged in such knowledge-making is even further deemphasized" (25). Students need to develop "a sense of the ways that disciplines actually make knowledge through messy, complicated, thoughtful interactions with research materials and a whole range of activities that move well beyond the library and the resources that can be found there" (30). We would expect, then, that students who had actually engaged in disciplinary research would have a more complete picture of what counts as research.

Nevertheless, the six students who reported having had primary research experiences prior to taking the ethnography course did not necessarily represent those experiences in their drawings. These students had used interviews and surveys in anthropology, communication, or first-year writing classes. Interestingly, as Samuel's comment on the research definition drawings suggests, none of these students were education majors. Nicole, who had archeological field research experience, drew a face half-hidden behind an open book surrounded by question marks. She included a label pointing to the person's "frown of contemplation," and in place of a book title she wrote, "Could also be a computer." In her interview, Nicole reflected that it was "kind of shameful" that she had neglected to include interviewing in her visual definition, since she had conducted interview-based research in her anthropology classes. Even students who had had previous experience with the IRB felt, upon reflection, that their drawings were limited. Samuel drew a light bulb connected by lines to a microscope, computer, and interview scene to depict scientific, secondary, and qualitative research. He later described these features as "really typical signs" and "research-y paraphernalia." Cory drew an IRB application, audio recorder, and computer. He reflected that he had included only physical artifacts used to conduct research; both the researcher and the participants were "completely absent." Although Nicole, Samuel, and Cory had each learned about qualitative research from previous course-related experiences, they all recognized that their first-day drawings revealed lingering assumptions that limited their definitions of research.

Three of the drawings stood out as being unusual: Lisa's circular process diagram surrounding a huge question mark, Ken's drawing of a stylized bear, and Richard's drawing of New York City's Times Square. All three students explained their drawings during the interviews. Lisa stated that she had drawn a diagram to illustrate that "everything leads back into that question that you originally had or that comes from what you're learning." Ken had drawn a totem animal that an anthropologist might analyze as a cultural artifact. Richard explained that his drawing represented fieldwork: his first encounter with an unfamiliar culture and his realization that he "was not the center of the universe." These students' drawings represented their experiences with research as a learning process, as opposed to the drawings that objectified knowledge as a product of research.

When I designed the ethnography course, I anticipated that a firsthand research experience would have the pedagogical value of broadening students' definitions of research. Dewey ([1938] 1997: 87) argues that "experiences in order to be educative must lead out into an expanding world of subject-matter"; such experiences are possible only when the educator "has a long look ahead" and views each learning experience as "a moving force in influencing what future experiences will be." Based on this theory of experiential learning, the contrast between the students' initial visual definitions of research and their reflections suggests that their experiences with ethnography positively impacted their perceptions of research.

In cohort A, ten of the twelve participating students stated that their definition of research had expanded as a result of their experiences as student researchers, and the remaining two expressed an increased appreciation for the work that goes into research. As Danielle put it, "Before this course, I thought there was one, and only one, way to conduct research." Echoing Downs and Wardle's (2010) description of recitative research, Lisa commented that the pattern of "typical research paper" drawings "comes from our limited experience with research. We've always done research as 'Read an article and write about it.' I feel like that is just regurgitating someone else's interpretation." In cohort B, seven of the twelve participating students reported that their definition of research had expanded as a result of the ethnography course. Of the remaining five, Cory stated that his understanding of primary research had been shaped by his experiences in previous writing and rhetoric courses, and four students who were not interviewed did not address the question in their reflections. Hannah commented that before taking the ethnography course, she "wouldn't have considered talking to someone or [to] my peers research" because that was "not valid to use in a paper." Ken noted that even though he had written a proposal for a survey study as an assignment for a sociology research methods course, he had not actually conducted the study. Ken stated that the ethnography project had "definitely expanded" his view of research and had "highlighted the ability of ethnographic research to have far-reaching implications."

Conducting their own microethnographies was pedagogically valuable from the standpoint of extending many of the students' views of what counts as research. Yet their reflections on the first-day drawings did not explain why some students regarded their projects as an assignment for a grade while others considered their projects to be "real" research. For example, Ned drew one of the less typical definitions—an explorer with a telescope—but he did not describe his own explorations of teaching practices as "real" research. In contrast, Samuel characterized the project he and Brian had done as "real research," but he noted that it "came at a cost of extreme time consumption early in the semester" as they worked to obtain IRB approval.

"Frustration and Elation": Research Ethics and Navigating the IRB

By requiring IRB review, I had a pedagogical goal of emphasizing that external perspectives on ethical issues are crucial to ethnographic research design. I expected that my students would learn about research ethics through participating in the IRB review process, just as they would learn about research methods through hands-on experience as student researchers. Michael Kramer, Vernon Miller, and Suraj Commuri (2009: 498) argue, "Researchers who frame IRB compliance as a necessary evil or counterproductive to research goals convey a very different socialization message to students than researchers who portray IRB relationships as productive." Knowing that the ethical review process would take time, I planned a more traditional unit that involved reading and responding to published ethnographies in the middle of the semester, after the research teams' microethnography proposals had been submitted. I anticipated that, by the time we finished this unit, all of the research teams would be approved to begin fieldwork. For the first three weeks of the final third of the semester, I had scheduled one class period for ongoing, collaborative data collection and the other for coding and analytical memoing. The last two weeks of the semester were reserved for the students to finish writing up their findings and to prepare their final presentations to share their work with the class (see appendix E).

Across both cohorts, the student researchers designed a total of thirteen collaborative studies on topics of their own choosing. I encouraged the research teams to select a campus-based research question to facilitate collaborative fieldwork and to align their research with the EUI models, course readings, and learning activities. For example, the first paper for the ethnography course, an autoethnographic analysis of how the students' own subcultural affiliations affected teaching and learning practices, was designed to scaffold campus-based microethnographies. Consequently, several research teams focused on subcultures within the student population (e.g., commuters, resident students, working students, sorority members, veterans, student-athletes) or specific field sites on campus (e.g., the student center, recreation center, classroom buildings). As students brainstormed research questions, I steered them away from the kinds of projects they had done in high school or first-year classes, such as job shadowing, and cautioned them about the ethical complexities of researching vulnerable populations. Institutional policies specifically prohibited the education majors from doing research related to their practicum experiences. This restriction was frustrating for many of the preservice teachers. However, it is not atypical since "it is not yet standard practice for all students to participate in what is considered undergraduate research during their teacher-education programs" (Manak and Young 2014: 35). Nevertheless, four of the fourteen participating education majors (Lisa, Hannah, Danielle, and Theo) made explicit connections between what they had learned through their microethnographies and how they would use teacher research in their careers to, as Theo put it, "consider the needs of all their students."

The students tended to form research teams based on their personal relationships rather than on shared research interests, which caused some difficulties with group dynamics as the projects unfolded. Some of the groups took longer than I anticipated to complete their proposals. Every study was exempted or approved within the IRB's stated window of two to four weeks, which had guided my original plan for the schedule, but the IRB review process was fraught with difficulties ranging from technical issues with the online application system to seemingly endless revision to find just the right language for the IRB audience. The time from initial submission to final approval varied from fourteen days with one resubmission to twenty-nine days with five resubmissions; the average was twenty-one days with two resubmissions. The first resubmission was typically required due to a simple omission or a technical glitch.

As the window for conducting fieldwork grew narrower, some student researchers changed their methods in response to the IRB's feedback. For example, they opted to forego audio recording or to substitute written questionnaires for face-to-face interviews. Although I was concerned that the IRB's recommendations were propelling some of the projects away from ethnography, the IRB's intention was to help the student researchers succeed within the time constraints of the course. Mary Brydon-Miller and Davydd Greenwood (2006: 122) observe that even experienced researchers sometimes "' play it safe' as a strategy for streamlining the approval process and completing their research in a timely manner." Nicole reflected that her research team "didn't want to push [their] luck" by audio recording interviews with campus police officers because they knew the risks for those participants were already relatively high. Nicole thought that decision "hurt the project in the end," but she articulated exactly how she would design a larger follow-up study if she could.

Despite my own previous successes with IRB applications (the one for this study was approved within a week, without a hitch), I learned valuable lessons about research ethics and research design alongside the student researchers. The IRB personnel we consulted were unfailingly supportive and patient. Especially in cohort A, the students had difficulty following the directions for required modifications, which led to what felt like "relentless rejection" of their well-intentioned but naive efforts to comply with the IRB's specific instructions. Some of the reasons for applications being returned stemmed from a lack of attention to detail: missing a checkbox, using the wrong file format. The more substantive issues typically involved students' incomplete understanding of IRB discourse and the genre of the IRB application—even though we had worked collaboratively on the proposals in class, as Brydon-Miller and Greenwood (2006) recommend. Through the trials and errors of cohort A's review process, I realized that my inclination as a writing instructor to read drafts for the students' intended meaning and to take a nondirective approach to revision was incompatible with the IRB reviewers' expectations of precise terminology. For example, when the students used phrases like "select people *randomly* for *anonymous* interviews," they used the italicized terms generically, whereas the IRB read them as technical terms that evoke specific methodologies and methods.

Students' inexpert attempts to produce language acceptable to the IRB audience resulted in what Ellen Barton (2008: 606) describes in her study of research recruitment practices as "vague reformulations" of the federal regulations. Students tried to paraphrase the language from IRB checklists, perhaps because they thought it was improper to copy and paste. They avoided being "repetitive" by varying their wording, which the IRB viewed as inconsistency. Cory, who had prior experience with IRB-approved research, reflected that writing an IRB application is "really hard the first time and really easy the second time," because the language "doesn't need to be creative or original"; it needs to be "consistent, safe, inescapable language."

The IRB review process produced tensions and resistance in cohort A, similar to Rogers's "frustrated and even resentful" (2010: 81) students. For example, Ned described the IRB process as "somewhat of a nightmare." With each setback, I reassured the students that trial and error—even failure—is part of both the learning process and the research process. Despite their anxiety, the cohort A students also exhibited a "sense of accomplishment" (Rogers 2010: 87), as well as an "unexpectedly strong positive reaction when their research was officially approved by the IRB" (Kallgren and Tauber 1996: 23). Lucy, whose group held the record for the rockiest road to IRB approval, put it best in her reflective essay:

> What I will remember the most from doing this project is the interaction with the IRB. I have never been as frustrated as I was each time we had our application come back as denied I developed a new respect for ethnographers at that point, having to go through such hurdles because you are dealing so intimately with the research of people and their cultures, and their protection is the biggest priority. I have

never before worked on a group project that was this intense. We fully experienced the frustration and elation of the final IRB approval.

Although cohort A had the most problematic IRB reviews, ten of the twelve participating cohort A student researchers viewed the experience as productive. "I wasn't happy about it at the time," Danielle laughed. "It was a learning experience, and I'm glad I went through it. Who knows? I might do a research project again, and I'll actually know how to do it properly and not get myself in trouble." By the second semester, the IRB had a clearer idea of what we were trying to accomplish in our microethnographies. Cohort B also had the advantage of my experiences helping cohort A navigate the IRB, but there were still delays, misfires, and required modifications that I had not anticipated. With cohort A's hard-won successes to guide them, cohort B rose to the challenge with markedly less resistance, and I was delighted when two of cohort B's applications were returned for minor revisions with the comment, "Thank you for submitting a well-written IRB application."

Despite their vivid descriptions of the "tedious," "stressful," and sometimes "overwhelming" review process, in retrospect, seventeen of the twenty-four participating students expressed positive attitudes about the IRB. None of the remaining seven were interviewed, but in their reflections, three did not discuss the IRB at all, and four described the IRB requirements only in negative terms, such as "long" and "restrictions." However, most students credited the IRB review process for raising their awareness of ethical issues in research. In fact, several of them reported that they knew about or had done primary research projects in other courses where things had "gotten out of hand," ethically speaking. Cory observed, "Obviously [they] haven't gone through IRB because no one would approve this." In Carl Kallgren and Robert Tauber's study, "going through the IRB process added to the students' perception that they had conducted real research" (1996: 23). My students all experienced IRB reviews; however, neither that experience nor the students' attitudes about the IRB could account for whether the students viewed their research as "real" or as "just for a grade."

"No Benefits, No Study": Personal Goals versus Contributive Research

Based on observational data and reflections from cohort A participants, I predicted that Mary had engaged with "real research," but Lucy had completed the ethnography project "just for a grade." I was wrong on both counts. Bob Broad (2012: 204) argues that qualitative researchers must "actively seek out interpretations contrary to what they might have hoped or expected to find, and to ensure that interpretations and findings are 'emic,' that is, that they are deeply rooted in the interpretive framework(s) of research participants." By her own admission, Mary dragged her feet until the very end of the semester, when her fieldwork experiences suddenly ignited her interest. In contrast, Lucy was enthusiastic at the beginning, but the tensions within her group and her frustration with the IRB sapped her energy. In her interview, Lucy described her attitude by the end of the semester as "let's just get this over with." Lucy's and Mary's accounts of their research experiences and their ethnographic reports yielded disconfirming data: They "disrupt[ed] neat interpretations" and brought another issue into focus (Smagorinsky 2008: 397–98). Lucy and Mary shared many characteristics, but they differed in one key area: how they perceived the benefits of their research.

Mary and her research partner conducted the only off-campus microethnography, investigating how tattoo artists learn their craft. Mary reflected, "Being able to learn from experience isn't something that I've often done in a college classroom. It was a nice change from reading out of a book all semester and you learn so much more." It is possible that if Mary had participated in an interview, in retrospect, she might have articulated some benefits of her study that extended beyond having a personally rewarding learning experience. The IRB application for her study, of course, claimed such benefits: "This research project will benefit individuals who wish to pursue tattoo artistry by further educating them on various topics regarding [tattoo] culture . . . [and will] provide . . . insight on the necessary skills and dedication that are required." During the IRB presentation for cohort B, the students asked how they should fill out the benefits section of the application if their proposed research would not really benefit anyone. "No benefits, no study," the guest speaker shrugged. The IRB will not approve any proposed study that fails to make a persuasive argument that the research has the potential for direct benefits to the participants or indirect benefits to society. Although the ethical principle of beneficence in human subjects research (National Commission for the Protection of Human Subjects 1979: sec. B) had been discussed in the IRB presentation for cohort A also, it was this memorable exchange in the second semester that illuminated the distinction between Mary's engagement on the level of personal goals and Lucy's engagement with contributive research.

Neither Mary nor her partner was an aspiring tattoo artist, but in her ethnographic report, Mary's purpose statement shifted, making herself and her co-researcher the beneficiaries: "The intended purpose of our study is to learn as much as we can about the culture, such as the types of people who get tattoos, why they get them, and common misconceptions that are often associated with them." Had Mary actually used her data to address "common misconceptions," her research project might have crossed the threshold from personal to contributive. Instead, Mary's report was entirely inward focused. Pedagogical benefits for Mary and her co-researcher (their own learning) would not have been sufficient for the IRB to approve their study, but, in Mary's hands, the study did not live up to its potential to be beneficial to others. Although Mary's coursework demonstrated one of the most dramatic shifts in attitude toward the IRB process—from open resistance to appreciation of the need to protect participants as she "witnessed, firsthand, why the IRB was so important"—there was no evidence whatsoever that Mary viewed her research as "real."

In contrast, Lucy's apparent lack of engagement on a personal level stemmed from the dysfunctional communication within her group in response to the IRB's efforts to streamline their research design. Lucy reflected that her agency as a researcher had been affected: "You come up with all these ideas of what you want to do, but by the time you're done with the IRB, it's their research project because the way they changed it there's none of your own suggestions or personality left in it. So then you feel like you're completing somebody else's research project and you're not as into it anymore." Lucy lost the connection to the problem that she initially wanted to investigate; thus, her study could easily have become an exercise "just for a grade." However, in her report, Lucy stressed that, despite its limitations, her research represented an opportunity for "putting our knowledge into action." More than any other factor, this outward-focused stance marked the difference between students who viewed the project as a classroom activity and those who engaged with it as "real research."

"But This Was Different": Student Engagement with "Real Research"

Sheila Cavanagh argues that students should "do 'real work' in their research. Like faculty, they need to set the parameters of their projects, determine the best way to proceed, and learn how to contend with unexpected or unwanted outcomes" (2010: 139). By engaging in such projects, students "have the experience of creating an academic endeavor they can claim as their own more readily than a typical assignment that is crafted, assigned, and then graded by their professor" (139). Each of the twenty-four participating students in my study indicated that they were engaged in their microethnographies to a greater extent than they usually were in typical group projects or traditional research paper assignments.

In addition to this pedagogical value of increased student engagement, the presence of a wider audience is often cited as the factor that makes students view their research as "real": "As opposed to simply writing a paper and turning it in, the stakes in presenting at [an undergraduate conference] might be higher, and perhaps more worthwhile in the end" (Hersh, Hiro, and Asarnow 2011: 398). Similarly, Hunter (2012: 40) observed that her EUI students "were excited to be conducting 'real' research that an audience outside the course . . . might care about" and that "though their results were preliminary, all students believed they had something valuable to say about and *to* the university." My student researchers' perceptions of what constituted "real research" were not nearly so clear-cut: ten of the twenty-four participating students, including Mary, viewed their research primarily as a learning experience that helped them to achieve personal goals, such as acquiring useful skills, gaining information, or getting good grades. Cindy reflected, "I have gained so much knowledge from this course, not only about ethnography but working in a collaborative research group." Tanya related her research findings only to her own experiences as a working student, and her self-assessment that she had "learned a great deal of new information" was based on procedural knowledge, such as writing in American Psychological Association style, which would help her be successful in future coursework. None of these students described their work in the course as "real research."

In contrast to the students whose engagement with the research hinged on personal goals, the fourteen student researchers who did describe their experiences as "real" research, including Lucy, all focused on how their findings could effect change beyond their own lives. Brian stated that he and Samuel became "a real research team" and that the most important aspect of the course was "our ability to conduct research that yields some real results that may help those that don't understand the 'commuter' [student]." Samuel also commented on his collaboration with Brian: "Usually group work is a pain But this was different. It was always messy, but I think we worked well together." Samuel described the typical research project as a "low stakes" activity that is "not valuable outside of that classroom. It's 'Do this so you can see how to do it' not 'Do this because you can produce something as an undergraduate.'" When he reviewed his first fieldwork activity, Samuel called it "amateurish": "It felt like a practice. It *was*. I would never look for those very superficial things if I was doing something—now, after taking this class—[as] *real* research."

Similarly, Lisa appreciated the opportunity to conduct "substantial research" that produced "authentic information": "We weren't just writing a paper to write a paper and turn it in for a grade We wanted to know how it affected us and how it affected other people This process has made me feel as if I am actually contributing to, or may be able to contribute to, the area that will help others and me grow and become better teachers, and possibly instruct future teachers as well." As a result of her research experiences in the course, Lisa embraced Frank's (1999: 1) argument that "ethnographic eyes" improve both teaching practices and teacher education. In fact, Lisa reported in her interview that she had changed her plans for graduate education so that she could continue to conduct "future teacher research and action research in [her] career [and] contribute to the body of knowledge in the field of education."

Kallgren and Tauber (1996: 20) found that "some undergraduate research escapes IRB scrutiny based on the false premise that, because [it] is primarily educationally motivated, IRB review is not required 'It's just student research' and thus is not thought of as 'real' research." Although not all of the participating student researchers in this study viewed their undergraduate experiences as "real research," those who did recognized both pedagogical and contributive benefits. Even when the student researchers acknowledged that their studies were too limited to be publishable, those who viewed their projects as "real research" articulated the unrealized potential of their studies to benefit others.

Conclusion: Speaking from Experience

Why did some students take up the microethnography as "real research" while others did not? The conditions for creating student engagement at the level of authentic, contributive research are more complex than previous models of undergraduate research have indicated. Indeed, as Dewey emphasized, "Everything depends on the quality of the experience" ([1938] 1997: 27). The one quality that consistently characterized the "real research" learning experience for participants in this study was the outward-focused stance of the student researcher. Without this orientation toward both an audience and a purpose beyond themselves, the student researchers in this study did not engage with the research beyond the level of a learning experience— valuable as that experience may have been for achieving personal or pedagogical goals, such as expanding their definition of research, increasing their awareness of research ethics, and gaining information or procedural knowledge.

Downs and Wardle (2010: 178) argue that students' research "might be viewed as contributions to the immediate class's knowledge rather than to the discipline." This inward-focused stance narrows the scope of the audience that could benefit from the research to the student researchers themselves. Rogers (2010: 90) argues that students "gain a sense of how research matters by the process of disseminating results within the community of those examined." As a result of this teacher research study, I have revised my approach to teaching the course: I now invite community stakeholders to attend the students' final presentations to encourage students to consider how their research can benefit others. Recently, student researchers in my ethnography course have presented their findings to faculty, program directors, support staff, and deans— all of whom have honored the student researchers' work by asking thoughtful questions and engaging them in serious discussion. Yet even the physical presence of a wider audience does not guarantee that students will take up their projects as "real research." Like Hunter's students who "fail[ed] to make the 'university link'" in their EUI projects (2012: 37), the students in my study who viewed their research as projects "just for a grade" missed opportunities to speak from their data. Although they recognized how they had benefited from conducting their studies (e.g., they articulated what they had learned or how their findings might impact them personally), they did not confront the larger community issues that their studies were poised to address.

The results of this teacher research study shift the focus of the argument for ethical review of undergraduate research from potential risks to potential benefits for participants or community stakeholders. Human subjects research attends to the needs and vulnerabilities of the participants and the populations they represent. IRB reviewers must weigh potential risks against potential benefits (National Commission for the Protection of Human Subjects 1979: sec. C.2). Discussions of ethical review for undergraduate research typically focus on the risk side of that ratio (e.g., Kallgren and Tauber 1996; Traywick 2010). Some faculty do not think the level of risk in their students' studies warrants IRB oversight, and they may even "suggest to their students that they are better equipped to protect human subjects than IRBs" (Kramer, Miller, and Commuri 2009: 511).

As long as undergraduate research is defined in terms of risks rather than benefits, it will not be viewed as research from the IRB's perspective: no benefits, no study. Heidi McKee (2003: 491) urged professionally trained writing researchers to "argue for the legitimacy of our research, particularly when confronted with institutional oversight committees that may operate with different research paradigms in mind." I argue that educators also need to advocate for the legitimacy of contributive undergraduate research by subjecting it to outside ethical review via IRBs or locally sanctioned committees—not because it might pose risks, but because those risks, however minimal, must be balanced by benefits to someone other than the researcher.

When we reframe undergraduate research to focus on its potential benefits beyond the pedagogical ones, we refocus our students' attention on the purposes of their research that reach beyond their own learning experiences. The IRB review process creates a rhetorical situation that demands that researchers consider who, besides themselves, could potentially benefit from the study. Yet it is certainly possible for researchers to articulate theoretical benefits for the IRB audience that they never operationalize—as Mary did. As educators, it is our responsibility to help our student researchers to keep those potential benefits in focus: to develop their articulation of their research purposes recursively throughout the entire research process.

In my own teaching, I now scaffold learning activities that prompt student researchers to revisit the potential benefits they identified through the ethical review process as they engage in the recursive data collection and analysis process and as they develop their reports and presentations through drafting and revising. Ethnography is a messy business that does not always turn out as expected, and all researchers face the possibility of a failed study due to insufficient data or other factors. Recognizing that the legitimate potential benefits of one's research have not been realized, as Lucy did, does not negate its status as "real research." Instead, like Dewey's "continuous spiral" ([1938] 1997: 79), it can lead to unanticipated findings, new research questions, and refined methods. As firsthand undergraduate research becomes more prominent in writing studies programs because of its pedagogical benefits for students, the results of this study can help educators guide student researchers through an ethical review process that also obliges them to take seriously the potential impact of their research to benefit others.

Appendix A: Syllabus Excerpts

Catalog Description
Development of analytic and collaborative writing skills in the context of ethnographic study. Emphasis on written analysis in a variety of forms including case study analysis and ethno-methodological investigation. This class satisfies the General Education requirements in the Knowledge Applications, U.S. Diversity, and Writing Intensive areas.

Course Overview
This course focuses on ethnography as a research method in the scholarship of teaching and learning. We will use the local context of our campus and our own classroom as sites for exploring the subcultures of college students, the construction of classroom culture, and the cultures of academic disciplines. We will consider a variety of different approaches to ethnography and examine how ethnographic research

methods that were originally developed in anthropology have been adapted and applied to education, literacy studies, writing studies, and rhetorical studies. We will pay special attention to issues of race, ethnicity, and gender as they relate to ethical guidelines for human subjects research, to ethnographic research practices, and to teaching practices. You will work as part of a collaborative, student-directed research team to design and conduct a microethnography. You will also be invited to participate in a scholarly teacher-research project that explores how undergraduates learn to do qualitative, ethnographic research. Because this is a writing-intensive course, we will pay particular attention to using writing as a way of learning and to the relationship of rhetoric to ethnography. As we read the work of professional ethnographers, we will consider not only the content of the readings but also the writing conventions and rhetorical strategies used for particular audiences and purposes.

Learning Outcomes

- Demonstrate how knowledge in rhetoric and ethnography can be evaluated and applied to solve problems across a range of applications.
- Demonstrate knowledge of the personal, professional, ethical, and societal implications of ethnographic inquiry.
- Demonstrate knowledge of how diverse value systems and societal structures are influenced by at least two of the following: race, gender, ethnicity.
- Identify major challenges and issues these differences raise in society.

Appendix B: Participants

Cohort	Major	Year
Cohort A		
1. Samuel*	Writing and rhetoric	Senior
2. Brian	Writing and rhetoric	Senior
3. Leslie	Writing and rhetoric	Junior
4. Lisa*	Elementary education	Senior
5. Theo*	Elementary education	Junior
6. Lucy*	Elementary education	Junior
7. Danielle*	Elementary education	Junior
8. Sheila	Elementary education	Junior
9. Gwen	Elementary education	Junior
10. Ned	Elementary education	Junior
11. Mary	Elementary education	Junior
12. Tanya	Communication	Junior
Cohort B		
1. Lee	Writing and rhetoric	Senior
2. Cory*	Writing and rhetoric	Junior
3. Kayla	Elementary education	Senior
4. Cindy	Elementary education	Junior
5. Christie	Elementary education	Junior
6. Sabrina	Elementary education	Sophomore
7. Faith	Elementary education	Sophomore
8. Hannah*	Elementary education	Sophomore
9. Richard*	Communication	Junior
10. Rachel	Communication	Sophomore
11. Ken*	Sociology and anthropology	Senior
12. Nicole*	Archeology	Senior

*Phase 2 interview participants

Appendix C: Microethnography Assignment Instructions (Excerpts)

Project Overview

For Project 3, you will work as part of a collaborative research team of 2–4 students to design and conduct a microethnography. During the first half of the course, you will complete the required training for conducting research with human participants, practice ethnographic data collection methods in class assignments, form research teams, design your study, and submit the Institutional Review Board (IRB) application. During the second half of the course, you will conduct fieldwork to gather data using field observation (taking field notes) and at least one other data collection method that we have studied, analyze your data, write up your findings, and prepare a conference-style presentation for the class.

The goal of the project is to contribute to a deeper understanding of the cultural factors that affect teaching and learning within a particular context, such as campus culture, subcultures within the university community, discipline-specific cultures, or classroom cultures. As a result of your study, you may be able to make recommendations for changes that will improve teaching and learning at your field site. I recommend that you choose an on-campus location or group for your study; however, it is possible to do off-campus research that will have relevance to the campus learning community.

IRB Approval

Each research team must submit an application to the IRB and be approved or exempted before fieldwork can begin. In the event that IRB approval is denied or cannot be obtained in time to complete the research, I will assign an alternative project. Research conducted with IRB approval is eligible for possible publication.

Fieldwork

Three regular class meetings have been designated for fieldwork. Research teams should decide how best to use this allotted time depending on individual schedules and field site conditions. Each student will be responsible for maintaining individual records of the research process and contributing to the data collection and analysis process.

Individual Ethnographic Report

Based on the collaboratively collected data, each student will write a 2,000 word ethnographic report in IMRAD report style or in narrative style. Individual members of the same research team may focus on different aspects of the study, construct different arguments, or choose different approaches to ethnographic writing. The report must include at least 1 relevant scholarly source that we did not read in class, as well as 2–3 course texts. The report will be graded holistically based on the following criteria:

- use of secondary sources (background/context, theoretical framework, relationship to previous studies, methodological choices, ethical/diversity issues);
- use of primary data (thick description, excerpts/representations of data);
- researcher's positionality (personal background, theoretical perspective);
- methods (research question and study design, access to the field site, data collection, ethical considerations/IRB, limitations);
- analysis of data (themes/coding, participants' perspectives, social/ cultural/ ethical interpretations, triangulation);
- conclusions (reasonable, data-driven recommendations; new research questions);
- APA manuscript format/citation and editing/proofreading.

APPENDIX D: SHEILA'S CONCEPTUAL DRAWING: "TYPICAL COLLEGE RESEARCH ASSIGNMENT"

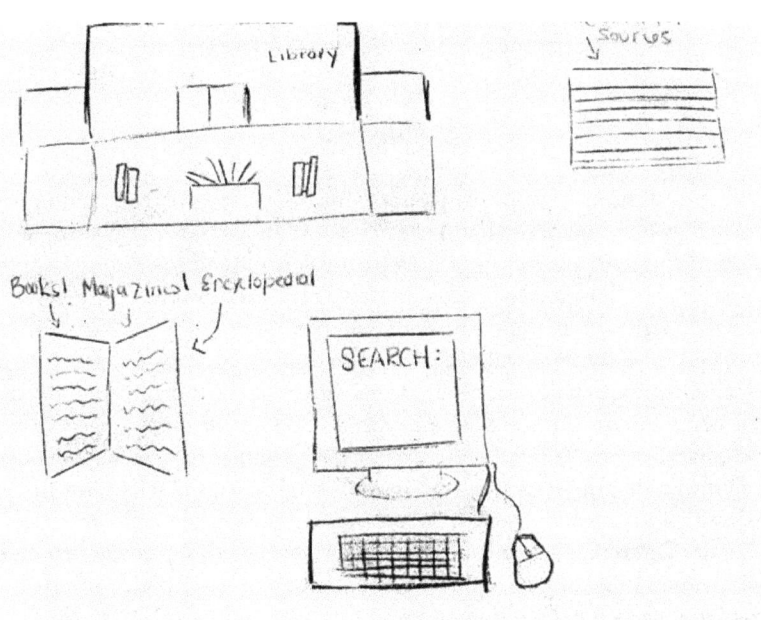

Appendix E: Semester Schedule

Weeks	Learning Activities	Major Assignments
1–5	Introduction to Ethnographic Methods: observational field notes, ethnographic mapping, interviewing, analysis of cultural artifacts Preparation for Collaborative Ethnography: research ethics/CITI; proposal/IRB application	Autoethnography Paper: case study—"thick description" and analysis of campus subculture(s) and teaching/learning issues
6–10	Introduction to Race/Ethnicity in U.S. Culture: analysis of online resources on race/ethnicity; analysis of scholarly ethnographic texts Collaborative Ethnography: IRB application (revisions); begin fieldwork (when approved)	Analytical Paper: examining ethical issues and cultural diversity in published ethnographic research (secondary sources)
11–15	Collaborative Ethnography: fieldwork (cont.); analytical memoing; coding data; drafting research report; preparing collaborative presentation (with visuals); compiling research portfolio (research records, codebook, etc.)	Collaborative Ethnography: individual research report; collaborative presentation; research portfolio; individual reflective essay

Notes

1. All student names are pseudonyms. All excerpts of participating students' work, quotations from interviews, and descriptions of classroom interactions are used with the written permission and informed consent of the participants. This research was approved by the institutional review board at the university where the study was conducted.

2. The common rule defines research as "a systematic investigation, including research development, testing and evaluation, designed to develop or contribute to generalizable knowledge" (US Department of Health and Human Services 2009: 102d). Exempt status under IRB regulations does not mean that the activity is "not research." In fact, an activity must first be classified as "research" and then as "human subjects research" in order to qualify for exempt, expedited, or full board review. Also, "the intent to publish is not, in and of itself, a reliable indicator" for determining whether an activity meets the definition of research (Public Responsibility in Medicine and Research 2013).

3. See DiPardo 1994 and Greene and Higgins 1994 for discussions of stimulated recall and retrospective account research in writing studies.

4. See Broad 2012: 204 for the benefits of grounded theory coding to avoid "'cherry picking' anecdotes to support conclusions arrived at without a clear system of data analysis."

5. Purdy and Walker (2013: 9) define researcher identity as the "confluence of skills, knowledge, attitudes, and practices that combine when an individual engages in research activities." However, in my coding scheme, researcher identity refers to students' perception of themselves as researchers—not just as learners.

6. Only twenty drawings could be identified as belonging to consenting participants.

Works Cited

American Anthropological Association. 2004. "American Anthropological Association Statement on Ethnography and IRBs," 4 June, www.americananthro.org/ParticipateAndAdvocate/Content.aspx?ItemNumber=1652.

Banks, Will, and Michelle Eble. 2007. "Digital Spaces, Online Environments, and Human Participant Research: Interfacing with Institutional Review Boards." In *Digital Writing Research: Technologies, Methodologies, and Ethical Issues*, ed. Heidi A. McKee and Danielle N. DeVoss, 2–47. Creskill, NJ: Hampton.

Barton, Ellen. 2008. "Further Contributions from the Ethical Turn in Composition/ Rhetoric: Analyzing Ethics in Interaction." *College Composition and Communication* 59: 596–632.

Bishop, Wendy. 1999. *Ethnographic Writing Research: Writing It Down, Writing It Up, and Reading It*. Portsmouth, NH: Heinemann.

Broad, Bob. 2012. "Strategies and Passions in Empirical Qualitative Research." In *Writing Studies Research in Practice: Methods and Methodologies*, ed. Lee Nickoson and Mary P. Sheridan, 197–209. Carbondale: Southern Illinois University Press. Brydon-Miller, Mary, and Davydd Greenwood. 2006. "A Re-examination of the Relationship between Action Research and Human Subjects Review Processes." *Action Research* 4: 117–28, DOI: 10.1177/1476750306060582.

Cavanagh, Sheila T. 2010. "Bringing Our Brains to the Humanities: Increasing the Value of Our Classes While Supporting Our Futures." *Pedagogy* 10.1: 131–42.

Collins, Nina, Shirley Hymon-Parker, Dorothy I. Mitstifer, and Briana Nelson Goff. 2010. "Perceptions of the Value of Undergraduate Research: A Pilot Qualitative Study of Human Sciences Graduates." *Family and Consumer Sciences Research Journal* 38: 303–16, DOI: 10.1111/j.1552-3934.2009.00026.x.

Conference on College Composition and Communication. 2003. "Conference on College Composition and Communication Guidelines for the Ethical Conduct of Research in Composition Studies," National Council

of Teachers of English, November, www.ncte.org/cccc/resources/positions/ethicalconduct.
Conliffe, Mark. 2014. "Turning Unexpected Resources into Undergraduate Research in the Humanities." *CUR Quarterly* 35.1: 43–47.
Council on Undergraduate Research. 2011. "About CUR," www.cur.org /about_cur/ (accessed 14 November 2014).
Dewey, John. [1938] 1997. *Experience and Education*. New York: Simon and Schuster. DiPardo, Anne. 1994. "Stimulated Recall in Research on Writing: An Anecdote to 'I Don't Know, It Was Fine.'" In *Speaking about Writing: Reflections on Research Methodology*, ed. Peter Smagorinsky, 163–81. Thousand Oaks, CA: Sage.
Downs, Doug, and Elizabeth Wardle. 2004. "Teaching about Writing, Righting Misconceptions: (Re)Envisioning 'First-Year Composition' as 'Introduction to Writing Studies.'" *College Composition and Communication* 58: 552–84.
———. 2010. "What Can a Novice Contribute? Undergraduate Researchers in First-Year Composition." In *Undergraduate Research in English Studies*, ed. Laurie Grobman and Joyce Kinkead, 173–90. Urbana, IL: National Council of Teachers of English.
Frank, Carolyn. 1999. *Ethnographic Eyes: A Teacher's Guide to Classroom Observation*. Portsmouth, NH: Heinemann.
Greene, Stuart, and Lorraine Higgins. 1994. "'Once upon a Time': The Use of Retrospective Accounts in Building Theory in Composition." In *Speaking about Writing: Reflections on Research Methodology*, ed. Peter Smagorinsky, 115–40. Thousand Oaks, CA: Sage.
Grobman, Laurie, and Joyce Kinkead, eds. 2010. *Undergraduate Research in English Studies*. Urbana, IL: National Council of Teachers of English.
Hersh, Cara, Molly Hiro, and Herman Asarnow. 2011. "The Undergraduate Literature Conference: A Report from the Field." *Pedagogy* 11.2: 395–404, DOI: 10.1215/15314200-1218112.
Howard, Rebecca Moore. 2014. "Why This Humanist Codes." *Research in the Teaching of English* 49: 75–81.
Hunter, Gina. 2012. "Students Study Up the University: Perspectives Gained in Student Research on the University as Institution." *Pedagogy* 12.1: 19–43, DOI: 10.1215/15314200-1302750.
Kallgren, Carl A., and Robert T. Tauber. 1996. "Undergraduate Research and the Institutional Review Board: A Mismatch or Happy Marriage?" *Teaching of Psychology* 23: 20–25, DOI: 10.1207/s15328023top2301_3.
Kramer, Michael W., Vernon D. Miller, and Suraj Commuri. 2009. "Faculty and Institutional Review Board Communication." *Communication Education* 58: 497–515, DOI: 10.1080/03634520903006208.
Lee, Carol D., and Peter Smagorinsky. 2000. *Vygotskian Perspectives on Literacy Research: Constructing Meaning through Collaborative Inquiry*. New York: Cambridge University Press.

Manak, Jennifer A., and Gregory Young. 2014. "Incorporating Undergraduate Research into Teacher Education: Preparing Thoughtful Teachers through Inquiry-Based Learning." *CUR Quarterly* 35.2: 35–38.

Mancha, Ruben, and Carol Y. Yoder. 2014. "Factors Critical to Successful Undergraduate Research." *CUR Quarterly* 34.4: 38–45.

McKee, Heidi. 2003. "Interchanges: Changing the Process of Institutional Review Board Compliance." *College Composition and Communication* 54: 488–93, DOI: 10.2307/3594176.

Murray, Joseph L. 2014. "Course-Based Research on Students' Own Institution Introduces Historical Inquiry." *CUR Quarterly* 34, no. 3: 30–36.

National Commission for the Protection of Human Subjects of Biomedical and Behavioral Research. 1979. *The Belmont Report*, US Department of Health and Human Services, 18 April, www.hhs.gov/ohrp/humansubjects/guidance/belmont.html.

Nickoson, Lee. 2012. "Revisiting Teacher Research." In *Writing Studies Research in Practice: Methods and Methodologies*, ed. Lee Nickoson and Mary P. Sheridan, 101–12. Carbondale: Southern Illinois University Press.

O'Connor, Mary Katherine, F. Ellen Netting, and M. Lori Thomas. 2008. "Grounded Theory: Managing the Challenge for Those Facing Institutional Review Board Oversight." *Qualitative Inquiry* 14: 28–45, DOI: 10.1177/1077800407308907.

Public Responsibility in Medicine and Research. 2013. "Key Decision Points: Is It Research Involving Human Subjects? Is It Exempt? Is IRB Review Required?," webinar, 28 February, www.primr.org/webinars/2013/decisionpoints/.

Purdy, James P., and Joyce R. Walker. 2013. "Liminal Spaces and Research Identity: The Construction of Introductory Composition Students as Researchers." *Pedagogy* 13.1: 9–41, DOI: 10.1215/15314200-1814260.

Rogers, Jacquelyn M. 2010. "An Undergraduate Research Methods Course in Rhetoric and Composition: A Model." In *Undergraduate Research in English Studies*, ed. Laurie Grobman and Joyce Kinkead, 74–92. Urbana, IL: National Council of Teachers of English.

Sheridan, Mary P. 2012. "Making Ethnography Our Own: Why and How Writing Studies Must Redefine Core Research Practices." In *Writing Studies Research in Practice: Methods and Methodologies*, ed. Lee Nickoson and Mary P. Sheridan, 73–85. Carbondale: Southern Illinois University Press.

Slobodzian, Jean T., and Nadya Pancsofar. 2014. "Integrating Undergraduate Research into Teacher Training: Supporting the Transition from Learner to Educator." *CUR Quarterly* 34.3: 43–47.

Smagorinsky, Peter. 2008. "The Method Section as Conceptual Epicenter in Constructing Social Science Research Reports." *Written Communication* 25: 389–411, DOI: 10.1177/0741088308317815.

Szecsi, Tunde. 2015. "Undergraduate Research in Humane Education: Benefits Gained in Action Research." *CUR Quarterly* 35.4: 42–46.

Traywick, Deaver. 2010. "Preaching What We Practice: RCR Instruction for Undergraduate Researchers in Writing Studies." In *Undergraduate Research in English Studies*, ed. Laurie Grobman and Joyce Kinkead, 51–73. Urbana, IL: National Council of Teachers of English.

US Department of Health and Human Services. 2009. Human Subjects Research (45 CFR 46), 15 January, www.hhs.gov/ohrp/regulations-and-policy/regulations/45-cfr-46/.

SUPPLEMENTAL MATERIAL

Part I: Reflection on the Origins of the Article

Behind every ethnographic researcher's published work is the researcher's own story. Mine begins with a frustrating experience as a graduate student in a qualitative research course in Education. At the beginning of the semester, we were told that our major projects would be reviewed by the IRB. They weren't. I don't know if the professor had a change of heart, or we didn't have enough time, or someone in authority claimed it wasn't necessary. For whatever reason, I was left with a pile of amazing data for a study that I could not publish without the sponsorship of an IRB. I also watched in dismay as some of my classmates collected data in ethically problematic ways that the professor never questioned (at least, not openly).

This was not an isolated incident. While attending professional conferences, I became acutely aware of presenters' approaches to teaching and conducting human subjects research. (Like many in our field, I prefer the term *participants*; however, this is the language of the federal regulations.) In too many dissertations, graduate research projects, undergraduate presentations, and first-year writing assignments incorporating primary research, vulnerable student-researchers and their participants were being put into ethically questionable positions. It came as no surprise, then, when participants in my study "reported that they knew about or had done projects in other courses where things had 'gotten out of hand,' ethically speaking" (p. 264). These researchers and their instructors meant no harm, but what they were doing was, in fact, potentially harmful.

As I prepared to teach qualitative research methods myself in the ethnography course that became my fieldsite, I wrestled with how to design authentic research-based assignments. For me, authenticity meant creating a learning environment that would allow students to design and complete their own small-scale ethnographic research studies that could yield meaningful data and that would safely expose them to the ethical complexities of participant-based research. Researchers—and the instructors and advisors of student-researchers, at any level—have an inherent conflict of interest when it comes to ethical review of their own (or their students') research studies. That's why IRBs exist in the first place. There is no such thing as a "no risk" study.

I began this project thinking about risks. It was, in many ways, a risky business. But the researcher in me could not pass up this opportunity to turn a pedagogical experiment into an ethnographic teacher research study. I did not want to deny myself the opportunity to publish my findings. It was equally important to seek out and foreground student-researchers' emic perspectives. I open the article holding my breath at the beginning of the semester when my initially resistant student Mary asked if IRB review was really necessary. Honestly, I didn't exhale until I opened the sealed envelope containing twelve signed informed consent forms when the semester was over. As it turns out, this study was about benefits. It reframes the risk/benefit ratio in ethical review. It changed my perspective—which is what ethnography should do.

Part II: Description of Research Methods, Findings, and/or Pedagogical Impact

Qualitative researchers often talk about climbing Mount Data. For me, the coding process is more like slogging through wetlands saturated by data. I get bogged down, lost in a dismal swamp. I wade through muddy marshes, picking my way from one solid-looking interpretation to the next. The only way out is through. The "messy, recursive process" feels more like being in the weeds than blazing "a path through the data that led to an unanticipated finding" (p. 250). It's only looking back that reveals the path. The meandering loops that eventually lead back to the original point of departure, the blind alleys, and the sinkholes that require a ladder of re-coding to escape are seldom shared in print.

I began most coding sessions by writing analytical memos in Word documents with colorful backgrounds and funky fonts. I needed the mental break from the landscape of the Atlas.ti coding software. Early on, I chided myself for worrying about getting an article published: "My gut tells me that I just need to table argument and target journal audience decisions for now and let the data speak for itself. It's such a huge undertaking, though." I gave myself permission to whine and vent before "diving back into the data." I second-guessed myself. I asked myself questions. I resisted oversimplification. I trusted the process.

At the half-way point of coding interviews, I knew that I had to refine my initial codes: "As usual, I'm starting to feel like the codes aren't differentiating concepts enough, even though I began with several different aspects of 'research'—attitude, definition, ethics, identity. If everything gets multiple codes and they're all the same, what have I accomplished, really?" After my initial pass of coding interviews, I identified 10 questions that I was tracking, based on "my impressions so far." At the time, I wrote: "There are more, but I'm losing focus. I will need to choose a narrower focus when I try to write this stuff up." Looking back at that early memo, I was surprised to find that the central argument of the article and its key supporting points are all present in that randomly ordered bullet list. Those memos laid down a rough boardwalk that enabled me to retrace my steps, solidifying the path each time.

I am a rhetorician, as well as an ethnographer. Analyzing the IRB review process rhetorically revealed how the students, the IRB reviewers, and I (as their instructor) all contributed to the failed attempts to articulate "a well-supported argument . . . that study conforms to the commonly held values of the academic community" (p. 250). The breakthrough moment came when I rediscovered the phrase "'No benefits, no study'" in my fieldnotes, well into the coding process. I began "poking around in the data looking for evidence" that the student-researcher's focus on *benefits for others* might be the key that explained why some students crossed the threshold from research "just for a grade" that met pedagogical and personal goals to "real research."

Part III: Discussion Questions

1. Imagine that you are conducting an autoethnographic study of your own experiences with research. What data would you include to create what ethnographers call a *thick description* of yourself as a researcher? How many different types of research have you done, and under what conditions? How would you characterize the "'quality of the experience'" (p. 268) that you had as a learner in each case? Based on the argument this article makes, would you classify your research experiences as

"just for a grade" or as "real research"? What evidence would support these interpretations? How would you represent your definition of "real research" visually (see pp. 257-260)? To what extent have you had research experiences that changed your own perceptions of what you were investigating, or of research itself as a knowledge-making process?

2. The ethnographic research assignment discussed in this article required students to work in small groups (see Appendix C). What were the pedagogical reasons for this requirement? Discuss specific examples of the advantages and disadvantages of allowing students to form their own groups for this assignment. (Consider both the students' and the instructor's perspectives.) How else might the research activities have been organized? How might a different approach to designing and conducting a research study affect students' level of engagement? What impact, if any, might these pedagogical decisions have on the IRB review process? If you were implementing this assignment, how would you revise it to adapt it to your own institutional context and teaching philosophy and/or learning style? What opportunities and limitations would result from your decisions about submitting students' research studies to an ethical review committee or IRB?

3. In January 2019, significant changes to the federal regulations governing human subjects research went into effect. Today, the student-researchers' expedited research studies that are described in this article could be exempted or receive limited IRB review for privacy and confidentiality issues only (a new category of review introduced in the 2018 Requirements—Final Rule/Revised Common Rule). While these regulatory changes may streamline the ethical review process, student-researchers (and experienced researchers) still struggle with "incomplete understanding of IRB discourse and the genre of the IRB application" (p. 262). What do the examples included in this article of students-researchers' difficulties with the IRB applications reveal about their writing processes or their assumptions about writing? How can instructors or advisors prepare student-researchers to meet the rhetorical challenges of communicating effectively with the people responsible for ethical review of research at your institution?

WPA: WRITING PROGRAM ADMINISTRATION

WPA is on the web at http://wpacouncil.org/journalarchives

For forty years, *WPA: Writing Program Administration* has published practical, empirical, and theoretical research on issues in writing program administration. As the flagship journal of the Council of Writing Program Administrators, WPA publishes a wide range of research that not only serves administrators of writing programs in a variety of institutional contexts, but also serves as an advocate for the broader discipline of rhetoric and composition.

Inez in Transition: Using Case Study to Explore the Experiences of Underrepresented Students in First-Year Composition[1]

"Inez in Transition" is a case study of a Chicana student's experiences in first-year writing at a Southwestern university. The article addresses the nature of our work as writing program administrators and demonstrates the range of research methods available to scholars in the field. Our editorial board appreciated the blending of the analytical and personal styles exemplified in Saidy's work. Board members felt that the case study methods described in this article can offer WPAs particularly valuable data about students' learning and felt that the article stands as a powerful critique of large-scale assessment modes that sustain inequality. Saidy's article investigates a transitional moment for Inez, a first-generation Chicana student, as she adapts from high school to first-year college writing. Saidy offers her case study method as an opportunity to "understand the experiences and writing development of students who are often misunderstood by other measures" (32).

---

1. *WPA: Writing Program Administration*, vol. 41, no. 2 © 2018 by the Council of Writing Program Administrators.

Inez in Transition: Using Case Study to Explore the Experiences of Underrepresented Students in First-Year Composition

Christina Saidy

This case study reports on the transition from high school to college writing undertaken by Inez, a first-generation Chicana undergraduate student. Through use of interviews, student writing samples, and research memos, the author illustrates how a seemingly smooth transition to college writing is actually complex and raises questions for WPAs about the ways students—especially underrepresented students—experience the transition to college writing. The author suggests that case studies, like this one, may benefit writing programs, via programmatic assessment and pedagogical modeling.

I feel like I'm doing good. I've done so much better. I am happy . . . Because you know at first I felt really, really bad about school in general. It was just like, "No, I don't belong here." But not until the semester has finished I feel so confident about it. I can take on more.

—"Inez"

Above are the words of Inez,[1] a first-generation Chicana[2] undergraduate student I interviewed for a case study of students in the transition between high school and college writing. Inez made this statement in December of her first semester of college. She had finished her first semester, completed her final exams, and was preparing to head home to spend the winter break with her family. Inez ended the semester on this positive note, confident in her academic performance from the first semester. Inez felt like she'd made it as a writer and as a student. She had learned to negotiate the institution and its expectations. She started to feel like she belonged.

In this article, I share the case study of Inez's transition from high school to college writer. This study examines Inez's perceptions and descriptions of her high school writing experiences, shares how she navigated and transitioned to college writing expectations, and describes her experiences in a first-semester composition course. On the surface, Inez's transition appeared smooth with few hiccups along the way. However, as this case study reveals, writing transitions, especially for students from underrepresented groups, are often complex and political events requiring the writer to successfully navigate institutional policies and barriers, sometimes with support and other times without. For writing program administrators, the close examination of one student's writing transition opens opportunities to consider the role of writing programs and first-year composition (FYC) classes in supporting students, especially first-generation and underrepresented students, in their transitions to college writing.

(Writing) Transitions—Institutional and Programmatic

Broadly, much research has examined the transition to college for Latinx students in the United States. This work has found that Latinx students' success in the transition to college is aided by parental support; personal drive and desire to overcome poverty; college preparatory class work despite initial placement in basic or vocational tracks; and specially designed minority retention and recruitment programs (Falbo, Contreras, and Avalos; Gándara, *Over*). While studies have shown that Latinas, as opposed to their Latino counterparts, are more academically successful in high school and college and graduate at higher rates, gender roles and expectations have the potential to significantly impact these success rates (Gándara, *Making*). Furthermore, students from low socioeconomic or ethnically underrepresented groups who do enroll in college are often less likely to have had access to a college-focused high school curriculum and are often placed in remedial college classes. These factors often lead to less confidence in students' beliefs about their abilities to succeed in college-level work and a feeling that they do not fit, which thus contributes to lower retention rates for Latinx students (Engle and Tinto). In writing programs, the first interaction with students often happens at the moment of placement, long before an incoming student steps on campus. Yet, for students like Inez, this moment can be critical to developing a sense of belonging in both college and the writing class.

Placement is the first interaction between the student and the writing program. Holly Hassel and Joanne Baird Giordano note that placement "is a critical moment of contact—when students are being evaluated for the match between their prior educational experiences and their learning needs as first-semester students" ("Blurry Borders," 60). Furthermore, in writing programs, placement is often shaped by institutional and financial constraints. Hassel and Giordano go on to point out "At many campuses, students are placed into first-year writing courses by standardized placement tests (for example, ACT, SAT, Compass, and Accuplacer) that assess students in limited areas such as usage, grammar, and reading comprehension" (60). In addition to the limited scope of measured skills and abilities for placement in FYC, most standardized tests, such as the SAT and ACT, which was used for Inez's placement, tend to privilege white students from middle and upper-middle-class backgrounds. New research on the SAT in the University of California system found that in a 17-year timespan, race and ethnicity were the largest predictors of standardized test scores with white students scoring significantly higher than black and Latinx students on the SAT (Geiser). This research confirms what composition scholars working in developmental writing and academic retention programs have known for years—standardized tests for placement in writing classes lead to less diverse and often segregated classes. In his *Antiracist Writing Assessment Ecologies*, Asao B. Inoue discusses the remedial early start or bridge courses for students with low scores on California State University's English Placement Test (EPT). Inoue states, "Even a casual look into the classrooms and over the roster of all students in these programs shows a stunning racial picture . . . The classes are filled with almost exclusively students of color" (34–35).

WPAs have long understood the impreciseness of standardized tests as placement mechanisms. In their "Toward Writing as Social Justice," Mya Poe and Asao B. Inoue note, "So much of the writing assessment work we do seems complicit in sustaining inequality. No wonder we are drawn to seemingly more democratic assessment methods" (119–20). Among these seemingly more democratic methods, WPAs report exploring placement test replacements such as directed self placement (Royer and Gilles, "Attitude"; Royer and Gilles, *Principles*; Blakesley, Harvey, and Reynolds) and modifications to testing placement (Isaacs and Keohane; Peckham). While these alternate placement methods are often considered more predictive, useful, and just, Hassel and Giordano, citing a report by Fain, note that standardized tests are solely used for placement in 80% of cases ("Blurry Borders," 60). Standardized tests are employed primarily because of budgetary and personnel constraints. However, it is widely accepted that when these tests are used for placement they cannot, or do not, provide the necessary level of sensitivity, especially for students whom standardized testing is known to exclude.

The moment of placement is often a critically important one from a programmatic perspective, since it dictates course numbers, instructional needs, etc. However, this moment is also critically important for students transitioning from high school to college writing because it is the moment in which they are institutionally labeled as prepared or underprepared. A student's writing placement can impact the way the student perceives their abilities, fit in college, and even self-worth. Moreover, Siskanna Naynaha also notes that for traditionally underrepresented students, especially multilingual students, placement or competency exams may "mean they are consigned to a kind of institutional purgatory. They are neither in nor out; they gain access to college but remain blocked from advancement by required courses or chosen programs of study" (197). For students from traditionally underrepresented backgrounds, the moment of placement is often the first time, but certainly not the last time, they experience the gatekeeping aspect of college writing. In her 2004 keynote, "Made Not Only in Words: Composition in a New Key," Kathleen Blake Yancey urged, "Suppose that if instead of focusing on the gatekeeping year, we saw composition education as a *gateway?* Suppose that we enlarged our focus to include *both* moments, gatekeeping and gateway" (306). If we are to heed Yancey's call, to make the first year more than a gatekeeping year, Naynaha argues "unjust placement and curricular models must become the focus of critical inquiry into our institutional practices and especially the ways those practices impact particular student populations" (200). One starting point for this critical inquiry is investigating students' experiences of transition, which includes students' writing backgrounds and experiences and their experiences in our programs. This is information that traditional data sources—test scores, grades, demographic information, and even portfolios of student work—do not provide.

Case Study and the Transitioning Writer

Using case studies for critical inquiry and programmatic fact-finding, research, and assessment offers the opportunity to understand writing transitions, especially for students who are typically underrepresented in our institutions. Case studies are in-depth studies of individual representatives of a group, organizations, or phenomena in the natural context (Hancock and Algozzine). Case studies do not typically provide generalizable findings. Rather, they provide stories and real examples that raise additional questions about decision-making and practice (Dyson and Genishi; Yin). For WPAs, case studies offer an additional layer of information to consider in institutional and programmatic assessment. Although case studies may only reflect the experiences of one person at a time, they offer us glimpses into the student's experience of our programs that we typically cannot obtain from other types of data available to us such as grades, retention rates, student academic indicators, course evaluations, or even student portfolios.

Case studies ranging from anecdotal stories to more formal uses of the methodology have a history in FYC for offering a picture of what writing classrooms look like. For example, in his 1989 book *Lives on the Boundary*, Mike Rose uses anecdotes to represent students who, "By the various criteria the institutions use . . . deserve admission—but they are considered marginal, 'high risk' or 'at risk' in current administrative parlance. 'The truly illiterate among us,' was how one dean described them" (2). Rose goes on to show that the specific students he describes, those placed into the university's lowest level writing course, are as one might assume of students accepted into a competitive university, highly intellectual and critical thinkers who are both aware of their placement and struggle with feelings of inadequacy because of it.

In recent years, these anecdotal accounts have been enhanced by research that focuses on using case study methodologies to further provide insight into the academic and cultural experiences of students in writing transitions. For example, in his book *Transiciones*, Todd Ruecker follows language minority students from high school into college and offers suggestions for ways that writing programs and institutions can better serve underrepresented and language minority students. In his article "From Journals to Journalism," Kevin Roozen tracked a writer from a college bridge program, through college writing and college, and into a career in journalism. Roozen explored ways that the student's personal journals were significant in her writing transitions. The work of Ruecker and Roozen have begun to illustrate the role of case study in exploring writing transitions, especially for students who are traditionally considered underrepresented in university settings. My case study of Inez adds further complexity to discussions of writing transitions, writing placement, and the institutional and political considerations WPAs face as they address these transitions.

As a case study researcher, it is important to disclose my own subjectivity. My interest in Inez and in her transformation as a writer is rooted in my experience as a former secondary English language arts teacher and FYC instructor, and now as an assistant professor of English teaching writing methods courses for secondary teachers and as a writing researcher examining writing transitions from secondary school to college. My research focuses on complex stories of writing transitions as a way to influence the field's thinking about institutional policies and practice. However, this interest is also informed by my personal transition into college and college writing. Like Inez, I was a first-generation college student. My father, an immigrant from Brazil, had a high school education, and my mother, a white woman born and raised in the United States, graduated high school and then attended technical school when I was a child. After technical school, she had a successful career in healthcare, but she had no formal college education. My parents very much wanted me to attend college, and I did. Like Inez, I remember throughout college feeling on and off like I did not belong. Fortunately, I participated in a college bridge and retention program for students like me at UCLA: first-generation college students, underrepresented students, and students from low-income families. I often credit that program and its academic and community support system for keeping me in college.

As a researcher, I am aware that stories like mine and Inez's are often told in aggregate form. Our experiences of education are typically reduced to statistics about postsecondary success and retention or, on the flip side, postsecondary attrition and dropout rates. Therefore, as a university researcher and teacher committed to understanding writing transitions, I believe it is important to contribute work that is reflective of the nuance, complexity, and detail of writers' experiences as they transition from high school to college and that accurately reflect people, experiences, and institutional policies/practices that help or hinder students. In addition to understanding the statistical norms and outliers that constitute data about writing programs, it is important to continue adding real examples and stories that impact programmatic and institutional decision-making and change.

In the following pages, I will share Inez's story. At the most basic level, her story represents the experience of one Chicana student and her writing transition as she enters a large public university. I will use Inez's story to raise questions and make observations about her experience. Furthermore, I will argue that Inez's case, while only one student's experience, invites us to consider case studies as a form of programmatic fact-finding and assessment. This form of assessment encourages us to engage in critical inquiry that serves students, strengthens teaching, and provides information about who and how programs serve or fail to serve their students, especially traditionally underrepresented students.

Learning about Inez

To learn about Inez's transition to college writing, I met with her monthly from August to December of her first year of college. I collected a pre-survey in August and post-survey in December. At each monthly meeting, I interviewed Inez. These interviews were voice recorded. They lasted anywhere from 20–45 minutes. Inez was an engaging interviewee, and she shared very openly with me. She told me on more than one occasion that she liked being involved in "the research" and asked questions about my research methods, practices, and areas. I collected copies of all Inez's writing assignments from her first semester writing course. I invited Inez to bring her writing from her composition class to our interviews and each time she would read a passage to me. This would give us the opportunity to talk about her writing choices and progress, and it would help me to understand the elements of her writing that were most important or interesting to her. Finally, at the end of each interview session, I wrote research memos. The purpose of the research memos was twofold: (1) they were a reflective practice for me, and (2) Inez would often continue talking as we walked to the copy machine to copy her assignments or prior to leaving my office. Often, I learned much about Inez, her family, and her experiences from these side conversations that were not voice recorded, and I used my memos to keep track of these added details. At the end of our meetings, I kept in touch with Inez via email.

I recruited Inez for participation in my study from her high school. Inez attended an urban high school in the Southwest that I call Community High School. Prior to meeting Inez, I had conducted research and provided professional development to teachers at Community High School. The school currently enrolls 1,800–2,000 students yearly. The school population is comprised of 94% Latinx/Chicanx students, 2% Anglo, 2.5% African American, and 0.8% Native American students. Some 89% to 94% of students receive free and reduced lunch. The school reports a four-year graduation rate of 66.2% percent. Out of Community High's graduating class, 11% plan to obtain a postsecondary education. The majority of these students attend local community colleges. In the year I recruited Inez into the study, approximately 15 students planned to attend the nearest state university. Through my work at Community High School, it became evident that even the school's highest achievers were often labeled at-risk or underprepared when they entered college, and I wanted to understand why.

Inez is a first-generation college student, but not the first in her family to enroll in postsecondary education. Inez's older sister attended a local community college until she became pregnant and needed to work longer hours to support her son. Inez's parents are both immigrants from Mexico. Her father immigrated to California as a teenager and attended high school in California for a short time where he learned English. Inez's mother graduated from high school in Mexico before immigrating to Arizona. Inez's parents met and married in the United States and Inez, her older sister, and her younger brother were all born in Arizona. The family primarily speaks Spanish at home. However, all Inez's education has been in English. She was never classified as an English-language learner in school and all schooled reading and writing has been in English since kindergarten. Inez's father works as custodial staff at a local college, and her mother works as housekeeping staff at a large hotel. Inez's mother is a union activist, and her sister has become an activist as well. Inez told me a number of stories of working on activist campaigns alongside her mother and sister. Her mother, who is not a citizen, is very active in registering community members to vote.

Inez chose to attend the in-state, local university, Southwest State University, primarily for financial reasons. She qualified for financial aid, and her parents were able to help her pay for the costs of schooling and housing not covered in her aid package. Southwest State is the state's largest public university. As part of its mission, Southwest State seeks to increase access to postsecondary education for traditionally underrepresented students, including Latinx students. In the semester Inez entered Southwest State, approximately 18.5% of the student population identified at Chicanx/Latinx, while the state Chicanx/Latinx population in the same year was 31% (*Demographic*).

Upon admission to Southwest State, Inez declared a criminal justice major since she planned to go to law school. Her parents were excited that Inez wanted to be a lawyer. However, before even beginning her freshman year of college, Inez changed her major to psychology when realized she did not want to be a lawyer. At the midpoint of the first semester, Inez once again changed her major, this time to elementary education. On her "About Me" page of her online writing portfolio, Inez states: "My passion is children. I want to pursue a career as a teacher. I want to teach 3rd graders. After I have had the experience, I eventually want to work my way up into becoming a principal." Inez told me that another motivating factor for becoming a teacher is that her younger brother, who is in elementary school, has had trouble in school and she is interested in helping students in the way she wants her brother to be helped.

WRITING IN HIGH SCHOOL—SUCCESS AND SUPPORT

Inez started her high school career in what she called "normal" English. At Inez's school, normal or regular English was the class for students who were not tracked into honors. However, early on, Inez was moved to the honors class. She said, "I started in normal English, but then the teacher thought that I would be good in honors." Although Inez's teacher perceived her writing and reading abilities to be above average performance, Inez was at first insecure in the honors track. She told me, "When I took that leap into honors I felt really discouraged by everybody just because they wrote wonderful papers. I really had something simple. That was the awkwardness about being in honors. Either you were too smart to be normal, or I felt too dumb to be in honors." Despite Inez's insecurities about her writing and fit in the honors track, she reports excelling in her high school classes, especially English language arts. On more than one occasion Inez said that high school was easy or that she didn't have to work very hard. Inez's hard work on writing in school was rewarded with good grades.

She received A's in language arts every semester. Inez's early experience as a writer in high school was shaped by her teacher's perception of her writing as honors-level material. This teacher's act of moving Inez to honors greatly shaped her experience of learning to write in high school because she remained tracked in more challenging writing courses throughout her high school experience.

To be successful in high school, Inez regularly completed "A lot of independent writing where it was just like, write about this and that. We had to write five pages every time." She noted that most of the writing topics were things she did not care about, or topics she did not choose, and that often papers would be returned with just a grade and no comments. Inez told me that she completed the five-page writing assignments easily and regularly. Although Inez wrote regularly and at length in her English language arts honors classes, writing was minimal in classes outside of English. Inez reports doing PowerPoints in biology but no sustained writing in classes other than English. This supports Applebee and Langer's findings that writing in high school classes is minimal and that, on average, students write 2.1 pages per week of writing combined in social studies, math, and science. The majority of this writing is fill-in-the-blanks (15).

When asked what mattered most in her high school writing, Inez noted, "That we didn't plagiarize . . . Just that it [the writing] was ours. That it was our opinion. That's what was valued the most." Inez told me that writing original work in high school was easy, which is part of the overall picture of her high school writing experience. In high school, Inez wrote regularly, by senior year five pages at a time, and was rewarded with high marks on her assignments. Although she did not necessarily receive detailed feedback on her writing, she met the ethical expectations for writing in high school and grew beyond her ninth-grade lack of confidence to feel like a fairly successful writer.

During her high school years, Inez also developed into a successful writer outside of school. She told the story:

> There was this one time in my junior year. I volunteered for political campaigning. I wrote an essay just on what I thought about it. The person that I worked for in the campaign, she loved it so much that she cancelled somebody else's speech and she put me in there.

Writing in this particular context brought together the family commitment to politics and campaigning and Inez's schooled strengths. Furthermore, this experience of being publically selected to share writing solidified Inez's confidence in her writing abilities. Although Inez started high school feeling apprehensive about being on the honors track, she developed into a successful and confident writer both inside and outside of school.

Placement and the Institution

When Inez entered college, her confidence in her writing quickly faded. Because of her ACT score, Inez was placed into Stretch writing, a course that stretches the first composition course (English 101) over two semesters. The first-semester course is counted as an elective course and students take English 101 in the spring semester of their first year and English 102 in the fall of their second year. The Stretch course is intended to give struggling writers more writing practice and to increase retention rates.

Inez saw her placement in Stretch as a misunderstanding of institutional structures. For example, she told me, "My ACT score was 17. I was put in [Stretch English]." When she talked about the ACT, she said, "We thought it was a required test. We didn't know it would affect us in college, so we didn't really try, or I didn't. If I could go back I'd probably try." Inez's comments point out some of the challenges of using standardized tests for placement. In our standardized testing culture, students learn not to take tests all that seriously since they are regularly evaluated formally. Furthermore, as Hassel and Giordano point out, using standardized tests for placement often leads to incorrect placement of students who do not test well ("Blurry Borders"; "Transfer Institutions"). Research shows that SAT and ACT tests privileges white, affluent males and that women, black and Latinx students, and students from lower socioeconomic backgrounds regularly test lower (Geiser and Studley). There is no way to know whether Inez could have tried harder and done better, but this particular placement mechanism made her feel, in her words "lower about my writing." She goes on to say, "I think the idea of being in that class discouraged all of us because we felt like, I guess dumb in a way." While the Stretch course was designed to increase retention and give Inez extra practice, she saw it as remedial and an indicator that she was not good enough for the institution.

Although Inez saw her placement as a mark of her deficits as a test taker and writer, she was also aware of the political implications of placement. In talking about her Stretch course she told me, "When I go in there, basically all you see is nothing but minorities. We're all either Hispanic and one African American girl. It makes me feel like we're all . . . Here's all the Hispanic people for [State University]." I was not able to confirm the ethnic makeup of Inez's class, but I was impacted by Inez's perception of her experience and clear articulation of the students who made up her class.

Becoming a College Writer

As a writer, Inez excelled in her Stretch writing class. She maintained an A grade the entire semester, and her final grade in the course was a 96%. Inez's writing was well received by the instructor and by fellow students in her writing class. In a sense, the Stretch class was the first time that Inez's schooled writing became public in a number of ways. Inez told me that in high school she never received feedback on her writing. She suspected her writing teachers did not really read her writing, and she never read other students writing via peer review. This contrasted dramatically with Inez's experience in college in which it was clear that her teacher read her writing and she often shared writing with her classmates as part of the composition process. What impacted Inez most was her teacher often asking if she could share aloud Inez's writing with the rest of the class. In this writing, Inez was invited to write about her experiences and things she cared about deeply. In one of these examples, Inez wrote:

> I grew up in the Hispanic community. I only spoke English in class. I used to get grounded for speaking English at home. Going to Mexico is really funny because here I am such a Mexican. I eat Mexican food, I have dark skin, my height is 4' 11", and I have trouble pronouncing certain words. I've been yelled at to get out of this country. How can I leave my own country? I was born here. Just because Mexican blood runs through my veins, I am not American enough? When I go to Mexico I am considered a Gringa. Why? Because I love country music, I don't really eat real Mexican food, and I'm

rich over here. It's really hard finding who you really are in a world where society characterizes you based on appearance."

After the teacher read this aloud, Inez reports a classmate turned to her and said, "Whoa. That was deep. You wrote that?" In the passage, Inez interrogated what it means to belong, which is something she struggled with in her personal life, transition to college writing, and transition to the university more broadly. Furthermore, Inez appreciated the attention that came from being recognized for her writing, and this helped her to see that writing for an audience gave her writing a sense of purpose.

Deficits and Belonging

Throughout the semester, Inez was successful in her writing class, and toward the end of the semester, Inez was able to express a sense of accomplishment and feeling that she had made it by learning how to negotiate her writing transition and, more broadly, her university transition. Furthermore, as the semester progressed, the topic of Inez's placement in Stretch came up, in some way, every time we met. However, the discussion of Inez's placement changed dramatically. Inez's early description of the students in her writing class showed a critical awareness of the racial politics of tracking and sorting and a sense of anger and injustice about institutional policies and practices to which she did not have access. However, beginning in the middle of the semester, her anger was quickly replaced with shrinking confidence in her abilities as a writer. She told me that placement in the Stretch course made her feel "lower about [her] writing" and went on to say, "I think the idea of being in that class discouraged all of us because we felt like, I guess, dumb in a way." Inez left high school a successful writer who regularly wrote on demand up to five pages at a time. Yet, as a result of her placement, a placement she did not completely understand, she began to feel dumb and lower.

As the semester went on, Inez's feelings of inadequacy transformed. She enjoyed her writing class, and she felt successful since she shared her writing with other students via peer review, was invited to write about things that *mattered* to her, and had her writing read aloud to the class by her instructor. However, as Inez's personal feelings about the class became more positive, the way she represented her work became more problematic. Inez began to internalize the deficit that she resisted at her initial placement. For example, in our November interview, Inez justified her placement saying, "They told me I had to take the class for a reason, you know?" Later that day, as we walked to the copy machine, Inez told me that her instructor told the students how important the Stretch class was and that students who took that class often passed English 102 at higher rates than students who did not take the class. Inez had come to trust her instructor and how the instructor valued her writing, so too Inez came to trust the instructor's defense of the course as supportive of Inez's future writing success.

Furthermore, Inez often talked about how students from her community were slower or behind. She told me academic reading and writing

> takes me longer, I think, because I'm exposed to new vocabulary that I wasn't used to back in my community. It's a lot of new vocabulary that I know I'm expected to know by my age but since I haven't had practice in it, I am a little slower at it. I'm getting there. I'm trying.

Inez focused on a perceived cultural deficit and assumption that she is missing knowledge because of her experience with language and her cultural background. Inez's experience of internalizing her deficits operates separate from her success in her writing class and separate from the fact that introductory college-level reading and writing is challenging for many students. Inez stopped seeing her placement as a function of her missing institutional knowledge and began seeing it as a function of her deficient writing skills and abilities.

Asking Questions, Seeing Gaps

On the surface, Inez made a successful transition to college writing. She came to college as an accomplished and successful high school writer and continued that success in her FYC class by finishing the class with a high grade and feeling accomplished as a writer. If I had only looked at Inez's test scores, demographics, grades, and a portfolio of her work, I would assume that Inez's transition was smooth and uncomplicated. Yet, through my case study, I came to see Inez's story as a more complex and nuanced story about the politics and experiences of placement and the transition to college writing for a student who was traditionally underrepresented at my university. Case studies, such as my study of Inez, offer an additional layer of information about students that complements existing teaching and programmatic assessment materials such as test scores, grades, course evaluations, and student portfolios.

Inez had been tracked and sorted throughout her academic career. In high school, she was tracked into honors based on abilities perceived by her teachers. Inez's comments about honors and normal English language arts show a sophisticated understanding of the ways tracking and sorting work. Furthermore, Inez seemed aware that what constituted honors at her urban high school may have been different than honors in other schools where students had socioeconomic privilege. Inez's experience of tracking and sorting changed dramatically when she was placed, via test scores, into the Stretch course. Inez believed that her placement, which she perceived as a remedial, was the function of missing institutional knowledge and a lack of understanding regarding the role of standardized testing in college placement processes. While Inez did not link this missing institutional knowledge to standardized test biases, she did clearly note that her Stretch course was primarily comprised of students with similar ethnic backgrounds as hers, and she expressed great disappointment that "all of the brown kids" would be in a class she considered remedial.

As in many writing programs, the large program at Southwest State University relies solely on test scores for placement. Funds are not provided for other placement measures, and the writing program's courses are typically filled to capacity at the beginning of the semester, which limits the mobility of students who may have been misplaced. These institutional constraints, paired with the political implication of using standardized testing for placement seem to be the perfect recipe for the type of segregation Inez described.

Case studies have the potential to raise questions and provide rich description to evaluate student experience and learning in situations where institutional constraints impact programmatic practice and decision-making. For example, the early data from the initial implementation of the Stretch program showed that the demographics of the classes matched the university's demographics. However, Inez's comments about all the brown kids in the room counters this early data and suggests that a closer examination of the segregation in these classes may be warranted. A 2008 Pell report by Jennifer Engle and Vincent Tinto finds that first-year college students from underrepresented groups who are placed in remedial classes are more likely to drop out of school because they feel they do not belong. Rather than dropping out, Inez attempted to understand her placement and the necessity of the Stretch course. In doing so, Inez internalized deficits related to writing ability, which she did not actually seem to have. If the Stretch courses are disproportionately comprised of "the brown kids" as Inez perceived, are they actually increasing retention? If so, at what cost? Using case studies for programmatic assessment has the potential to make questions and programmatic concerns visible in ways that retention data, such as grades and percentages, cannot.

Case Study as Instructional Complement

While case studies certainly have the potential to raise programmatic questions, an added benefit of the case study approach was Inez's informal learning about university research, writing, and even publishing. Inez regularly asked me about my research and writing. She wanted to understand how it worked and why it worked that way. She saw connections between the interviews she conducted for the research for her writing class and the case study research I was doing. While I was not Inez's instructor, it was empowering for her to think that her experience could impact the way instructors, WPAs, and university-level administrators think about a writing program. Through the case study, I came to see that Inez saw me as a form of literacy sponsor (Brandt). Via this case study methodology, Inez, a student who was struggling to navigate the university and its practices, felt integrated into the research that is integral to the way her university works.

In her "Definitive Article on Class Size," Alice Horning notes that the small size of composition courses adds to student engagement and learning, offers space for in-depth writing process activities since teachers have time to respond to many drafts of writing, and contributes to higher retention rates for incoming students. Because of the familiarity between instructors and students in the FYC course, students have the opportunity to see their instructors not only as subject matter experts in composition but also as researchers and learners who are continually developing. Integrating case studies into individual practice is one way for FYC instructors to model research for their developing writers who are also conducting research and to develop a deep understanding of their students in the transition to college writing.

In programs where a large number of graduate teaching assistants take responsibility for teaching FYC courses, a case study model could both benefit the program, the graduate students' research, and the FYC students who are case study subjects. For example, case studies could be assigned in the writing practicum to help developing TAs to learn about their students in order to directly impact curriculum and retention. For programs with graduate-level, WPA-focused seminars, this methodology can be used in a semester-long programmatic assessment. This helps future WPAs learn a specific method for qualitative research while also learning how to regularly conduct in-depth programmatic assessments on a continuing basis. Finally, in programs that use portfolio assessment for direct assessment of student writing, case studies may offer a way to complement, or even replace, student portfolios. For example, throughout the semester, Inez's portfolio showed that she was an accomplished writer. However, the additional information I gathered about her gave context to her placement, class work, and the overall experience of writing in FYC that I could not have gleaned from her work alone.

The integration of case studies into the work of writing program instructors and graduate students also invite instructors to see ways that assessment, as Staci M. Perryman-Clark notes, "creates or denies opportunity structures" (206). At Southwest State, as in many programs across the country, faculty in writing programs are often far less diverse than students taking their classes. Perryman-Clark argues that to support students of color and linguistically diverse students,

> white, monolingual instructors and graduate students are challenged to work differently from the practices to which they have been accustomed, and by working differently, white, monolingual instructors and graduate students often see themselves as unsure of what exactly they should do. (210)

Integrating case studies into the work of writing instructors and graduate students opens up the opportunity to more clearly see and address the institutional and pedagogical elements that deny opportunity structures in order to consider ways to better support traditionally underrepresented students and create opportunity structures.

Conclusion

Case studies open up opportunities to understand the experiences and writing development of students who are often misunderstood by other measures. As Mya Poe and Asao B. Inoue remind us, "So much of the writing assessment work we do seems complicit in sustaining inequality" (119) and Inez's story confirms this. Inez was highly ranked out of high school but, according to her test scores, at risk in FYC. Via this case study, I want to suggest that transitioning writers like Inez have much to teach us about programmatic policies, practices, and assessment in our programs. The integration of case study methodology offers an opportunity for instructors to conduct research alongside their students, get to know these students and their stories of transition more deeply, and alter instruction to meet the needs of transitioning writers. Case studies offer programs a way to develop a deep understanding of their students, especially their traditionally underrepresented students, via data that can be used to complement, or even challenge, traditional and more quantitative data sources that are typically used in writing programs or by upper level university administrators.

Notes

1. The names of all people and institutions appearing in this article are pseudonyms. This research was institutional review board (IRB) approved.

2. I am using the term Chicana specifically to describe Inez's ethnicity and the gender-neutral Chicanx or Latinx in situations where I am speaking generally. At the beginning of the case study, Inez used Chicana, Hispanic, and Mexican interchangeably to describe herself, as evidenced by her writing samples. However, as the semester moved on, and she continued in a Chicanx studies class, Inez began using Chicana when talking about her ethnicity. Therefore, to honor Inez's own choice of language, I use Chicana when I am specifically writing about her.

Works Cited

Applebee, Arthur N., and Judith A. Langer. "A Snapshot of Writing Instruction in Middle Schools and High Schools." *English Journal*, vol. 100, no. 6, 2011, pp. 14–27.

Blakesley, David, Erin J. Harvey, and Erica J. Reynolds. "Southern Illinois University Carbondale as an Institutional Model: The English 100/101

Stretch and Directed Self-placement Program." Royer and Gilles, *Directed*, pp. 207–41.

Brandt, Deborah. "Sponsors of Literacy." *College Composition and Communication*, vol. 49, no. 2, 1998, pp. 165–85.

Demographic and Economic Profiles of Hispanics by State and County, 2014. Pew Research Center, www.pewhispanic.org/states.

Dyson, Anne Haas, and Celia Genishi. *On the Case: Approaches to Language and Literacy Research*. Teachers College P, 2005.

Engle, Jennifer, and Vincent Tinto. "Moving Beyond Access: College Success for Low-Income, First-Generation Students." Pell Institute for the Study of Opportunity in Higher Education, 2008, pellinstitute.org/downloads/publications-Moving_Beyond_Access_2008.pdf.

Falbo, Toni, Helen Contreras, and Maria D. Avalos. "Transition Points from High School to College." *Latinos in Higher Education*, edited by David J. León, Emerald Group Publishing, 2003, pp. 59–72. Diversity in Higher Education 3.

Gándara, Patricia C. *Over the Ivy Walls: The Educational Mobility of Low-Income Chicanos*. State U of New York P, 1995.

—. *Making Education Work for Latinas in the US*. UCLA: The Civil Rights Project / Proyecto Derechos Civiles, 2013, civilrightsproject.ucla.edu/research/college-access/underrepresented-students/making-education-work-for-latinas-in-the-u.s/gandara-longoria-report-2014.pdf.

Geiser, Saul. "The Growing Correlation Between Race and SAT Scores: New Findings from California." *Center for Studies in Higher Education Research and Occasional Paper Series*, vol. 10, no.15, 2015, pp. 1–43.

Geiser, Saul, and Roger Studley. "UC and the SAT: Predictive Validity and Differential Impact of the SAT I and SAT II at the University of California." *Educational Assessment*, vol. 8, no. 1, 2002, pp. 1–26.

Hancock, Dawson R., and Bob Algozzine. *Doing Case Study Research: A Practical Guide for Beginning Researchers*. Teachers College P, 2011.

Hassel, Holly, and Joanne Baird Giordano. "The Blurry Borders of College Writing: Remediation and the Assessment of Student Readiness." *College English,* vol. 78 no. 1, 2015, pp. 56–80.

—. "Transfer Institutions, Transfer of Knowledge: The Development of Rhetorical Adaptability and Underprepared Writers." *Teaching English in the Two-Year College*, vol. 37, no. 1, 2009, pp. 24–40.

Horning, Alice. "The Definitive Article on Class Size." *WPA: Writing Program Administration*, vol. 31, nos. 1–2, 2007, pp. 11–34.

Inoue, Asao B. *Antiracist Writing Assessment Ecologies: Teaching and Assessing Writing for a Socially Just Future*. WAC Clearinghouse / Parlor P, 2015, wac.colostate.edu/books/inoue/ecologies.pdf

Isaacs, Emily, and Catherine Keohane. "Writing Placement That Supports Teaching and Learning." *WPA: Writing Program Administration*, vol. 35, no. 2, 2012, pp. 55–84.
Naynaha, Siskanna. "Assessment, Social Justice, and Latinxs in the US Community College." *College English*, vol. 79, no. 2, 2016, pp. 196–201.
Peckham, Irvin. "Online Placement in First-Year Writing." *College Composition and Communication*, vol. 60, no. 3, 2009, pp. 517–40.
Perryman-Clark, Staci M. "Who We Are(n't) Assessing: Racializing Language and Writing Assessment in Writing Program Administration." *College English*, vol. 79, no. 2, 2016, pp. 206–11.
Poe, Mya, and Asao B. Inoue. "Toward Writing as Social Justice: An Idea Whose Time Has Come." *College English*, vol. 79, no. 2, 2016, pp. 119–26.
Rose, Mike. *Lives on the Boundary: The Struggles and Achievements of America's Underprepared*, The Free P, 1989.
Roozen, Kevin. "From Journals to Journalism: Tracing Trajectories of Literate Development." *College Composition and Communication*, vol. 60, no. 3, 2009, pp. 541–72.
Royer, Daniel J., and Roger Gilles. "Directed Self-Placement: An Attitude of Orientation." *College Composition and Communication*, vol. 50, no. 1, 1998, pp. 54–70.
—. *Directed Self-Placement: Principles and Practices*. Hampton P, 2003.
Ruecker, Todd. "Transiciones: Pathways of Latinas and Latinos Writing in High School and College." Utah State UP, 2015.
Yancey, Kathleen Blake. "Made Not Only in Words: Composition in a New Key." *College Composition and Communication*, no. 56, vol. 2, 2004, pp. 297–328.
Yin, Robert K. *Case Study Research: Design And Methods*. Sage Publications, 2013.

Supplemental Material

Part I: Reflection on the Origins of the Article

"Inez in Transition" developed out of questions I had been asking for years about the ways that students experience transitions in writing. These questions began to develop out of my own experiences as a first-generation college student and really took shape as I moved through my career teaching writing in middle school, high school, and college. In each of these teaching contexts, I would listen to colleagues discuss students' lack of preparedness for writing. Over time, I came to see writing transitions as complex events that students often bear the brunt of negotiating on their own.

When I moved to the Arizona in 2011, I was determined to tackle my questions about writing transitions in a multi-pronged approach. The state regularly scored low in performance measures of public schools, schools were severely underfunded, and SB 1070, the racist and restrictive anti-immigration law, was deeply and negatively felt in Arizona's schools and communities. In response, I committed myself to working in settings where my research and teaching could increase access to college for students who are traditionally underrepresented and underserved. In my research and teaching, I worked with secondary-school students, high school teachers in professional development and coursework, and in our university writing program and retention program. My work on "Inez in Transition" was sparked by a teacher inquiry group I led in a local high school. As I worked with the teachers, I realized that the teachers, too, were working to identify and overcome deficit views of their students as writers and learners. This high school, like many urban high schools in our large metro area, has a very low 4-year college graduation rate, which reflects our statewide low 4-year college graduation rate. With all of these factors in mind, I wanted to understand the complex writing transitions of students from this high school as they entered our university. With help from the school's instructional coach, I recruited a handful of students for a study in the fall semester of their first-year of college. Inez (a pseudonym) was one of these students.

When I met Inez, I was interested, but not surprised, in how much experience she had as a writer in her personal life and the ways that writing had and had not been cultivated in school. Inez had also placed into our stretch writing course, and she provided much insight into what that meant for her as a writer and as a student. Through my interviews and informal discussions with Inez and through the writing she shared, I saw how Inez's placement in the Stretch writing course made her doubt her abilities as a writer and a learner. This case study highlighted the ways that current methods of placement and assessment can potentially sustain inequality. I learned much from Inez, and I thought the field could learn from her too.

Part II: Description of Research Methods, Findings, and/or Pedagogical Impact

I am both a researcher and a teacher of writing. My researcher side wants to ask questions that generate data and findings that can be replicated. As the field moves more toward 'big data' informed decisions about teaching and learning, my teacher side sometimes feels like something is lost in this process. Teachers have a deep way of knowing that is not always captured in aggregate data. In deciding on a research methodology for this research project, I took a methodological approach that best brings together the writing researcher and the teacher.

In "Inez in Transition," I employed a case study approach to study Inez's transition into college writing. As I note in the article, case studies are in-depth studies of individuals in their natural context. While case studies do not provide generalizable findings, they do offer us a deep way of knowing that can help us ask questions about decision-making and practice. This methodology seemed most fitting for my study of Inez. I wanted to deeply understand her experience and her writing in a way that would help the field to understand the complexity of a first-generation and traditionally underrepresented writer's transition into college writing.

In my case study, I collected pre and post surveys from Inez and samples of her writing from her first-semester course. I conducted semi-structured interviews and wrote research memos after each of our meetings that contained my reflections on the interviews and on our small talk when the recorder was turned off. I listened and learned from Inez as a writing researcher and teacher. As I analyzed the data, I saw that Inez had much to teach writing program administrators (WPAs), researchers, writing teachers, and even university administrators tasked with recruiting and retaining first-generation and traditionally underrepresented and underserved students.

In writing this piece, I position the methodology centrally. I encourage WPAs to use big data but also complementary methods, such as case studies, to complement what we learn from big data. I suggest that case studies give us a way of deeply knowing the students our program serves – not just in aggregate form. Since writing this article, I am planning on incorporating case studies into the teaching of my practicum course for incoming teaching assistants. This offers new teaching assistants a way to see their classrooms as a site of research and provides programs with descriptive data that helps us to deeply understand who the program serves and how those students are served.

Part III: Discussion Questions

1. What are the conditions that impact students' transitions to college writing at your institution?

2. Inez was frustrated by her placement in the stretch writing course because she felt that it did not accurately represent her ability as a writer. What does it mean for a writer to be "prepared" for college writing? How is this shaped by your local context? By other factors?

3. This article positions case studies as a way to deeply understand students and their experiences in our writing classes. How might you implement a case study methodology to answer a question about teaching and learning in your course?

TEACHING ENGLISH IN THE TWO-YEAR COLLEGE

TETYC is one the web at http://www2.ncte.org/resources/journals/teaching-english-in-the-two-year-college/

Teaching English in the Two-Year College (TETYC) publishes articles for two-year college English teachers and those teaching the first two years of English in four-year institutions. We seek articles in all areas of composition (basic, first-year, and advanced); business, technical, and creative writing; and the teaching of literature in the first two college years. We also publish articles on topics such as program and curriculum development, assessment, technology and online learning, writing program administration, developmental education in writing and reading, speech, writing centers in two-year colleges, journalism, reading, ESL, and other areas of professional concern.

A Critical Time for Reform: Empowering Interventions in a Precarious Landscape

Warnke and Higgins's article stands out for several reasons. Two-year colleges and two-year college writing programs in particular are often testing ground for national initiatives intended to intervene in and improve the educational attainment rate in the US. This is likely because of the large proportion of college students who attend two-year colleges, their relatively low status among institutions of higher education—thus possessing less cultural capital and prestige than four year and research campuses, and the often administratively topic heavy hierarchy that relies less on faculty governance than residential four year campuses, As a result, the literacy programs and writing courses at two-year colleges are often subject to well-funded initiatives such as Achieving the Dream, Guided Pathways, and other philanthropic organizations' agendas for their work. Situated within this context, Warnke and Higgins offer strategies for navigating and engaging external change initiators and internal stakeholders around issues like placement methods, learning support curricular, developmental writing and reading, accelerated learning programs, curriculum and learning support for multilingual students, writing studio, and other components of writing programs at open-access institutions that are particularly susceptible to external change mandates. Their piece offers strategies for critically engaging with such mandates.

A Critical Time for Reform: Empowering Interventions in a Precarious Landscape

Anthony Warnke and Kirsten Higgins

This article defines a principled, critical orientation towards reform initiatives based on two instructors' experiences as well as interviews with two-year college instructors across the country.[1]

Larger discussions about persistence and retention from groups like CCRC, Lumina Foundation, the Bill and Melinda Gates Foundation, and AtD have really put the pressure on developmental ed. There have been some scathing critiques of dev. ed. I disagree with much of that, but some criticism was warranted. Best practices and what works based on solid research for developmental education has been around for 20 years. We know what works, but we do not always embrace these practices. Criticism of the field has helped us examine what we're doing and why we're doing it, and this has moved us toward making changes. I'm not against critique and criticism, and if we can't answer criticisms then maybe we're in the wrong business.

—Jane Denison-Furness, developmental literacy coordinator and assistant professor of English, Central Oregon Community College

I don't think people pushing those kinds of reforms necessarily have the best needs of students in mind. "That is not on the schedule for you. Yeah, diversity classes are interesting, but you're going into physics. You just keep on this path. You don't need that." It demeans people. It lessens them.

—Carol Perdue, retired fulltime reading instructor, Green River College

---

1. *Teaching English in the Two-Year College*, vol. 45, no. 4 © 2018 by the National Council of Teachers of English. All rights reserved.

I always try to imagine what my heroes Mina Shaughnessy, Adrienne Rich, Audre Lorde, and June Jordan (all of whom taught in the early years of Basic Writing/open admissions at City College of NY) would have done in the current climate in our field. Their ethos as BW teacher/scholars/innovators leads me to believe that they would have resisted efforts at austerity and precarity, and resisted quite strongly. In fact, as financial conditions for public colleges worsened in New York City, Rich, Lorde, and Jordan did stop teaching in Mina Shaughnessy's program (Maher). However, none of these teacher/scholars ever stopped writing and teaching about the imperative of equitable education for poor and working class people. For these three feminist activist poets, BW was always already connected to education as liberation, and linked to the Kairos of the freedom struggles of the late 1960s and early 1970s. As we know from the dilemmas that we currently face, those struggles never really ended.

—Susan Naomi Bernstein, co-coordinator, Stretch Writing Program lecturer in English, Arizona State University, Tempe

It's a familiar scene of enthusiasm and anxiety—the first all-campus instructional meeting of the school year. Longstanding tensions between instruction and administration simmer below the cordial surface. After an ostensibly humorous video that features a high-ranking administrator "cloning" himself, the same administrator informs faculty that the principles for achieving institutional goals this year are called "WIGs." WIGs, he explains amid somewhat stifled laughs, stand for "Wildly Important Goals." Taken from *4 Disciplines of Execution: Achieving Your Wildly Important Goals* by Stephen Covey (an innovator of the managerial self-help genre),WIGs, this administrator argues, provide a top-down framework for making a concerted effort across campus toward achieving our objectives. His WIGs for us concern retention and completion. Although his remarks are couched in condescension toward faculty, this administrator laudably advocates for a student-focused approach for improving the institution and encouraging structural reforms that will increase student success. Following the orientation, this same administrator leads a breakout session designed to scrutinize retention and persistence data, particularly data that track the completion of students of color. The administrator asks us to consider strategies for closing the achievement gaps for our students of color, thus building on his sustained commitment to serving a diverse student population. The session, however, is soon sidetracked when faculty members stress the importance of a new—and fair—faculty contract. Faculty argue that doing meaningful work, such as attending to the success of students of color, requires a commitment to the worth of instructors. Although framing his presentation on the achievement-gap data within social justice rhetoric, the administrator refuses to even acknowledge faculty concerns.

As we sat in the breakout session on the achievement gap—with data from our own developmental English sequence clearly demonstrating disparate results for various at-risk groups—we couldn't help but agree to the importance of closing the gap. This work required critically examining English's lengthy developmental pipeline and its complicity as a barrier to students of color. Although we felt solidarity with the faculty labor struggle and perception of administrative hypocrisy, we also saw the shift in focus to the contractual dispute as obfuscating the story the data told—students' race correlated with their chances of success at our college. Rather than understanding the labor dispute and the racial achievement gap as separate conversations, we viewed them as two issues related to the overall ethic of just practices for all stakeholders at the college. We felt stuck between those faculty resisting reforms that might better serve students and those in power advocating for them. If we joined in the critique of the administration's labor practices, we risked turning a blind eye to our program's structural impact on some of the most marginalized students on campus. If we voiced commitment to program redesign in light of this data and joined forces with administration to address these disparities, we risked alienating ourselves from our colleagues and their legitimate concerns. Luckily, as tenure-track faculty, our silence in the debate was tolerated. But beneath that silence, we felt ambivalence and unease.

This story dramatizes a perhaps familiar clash—corporate-minded forces seeking to address demonstrable gaps in equitable student success against instructional solidarity that, in its righteousness, obscures a more nuanced connection between labor and student equity. A bind results from the conflict—us versus them—that leaves some instructors feeling unmoored and conflicted. As newer English faculty, we longed for a "third space" of resistance to both corporatization *and* the instructional status quo. We longed for a position of critical engagement with issues of reform. Our conversations with fellow two-year college faculty across the country tell us that our position is not uncommon.

Positions toward Reform

Community colleges across the country have been facing increased scrutiny and calls for reform. Frequently framed in terms of neoliberal efficiency, these calls for reform have had far-reaching impact on many aspects of the two-year college (TYC) ecology, from funding models to placement. As Patrick Sullivan points out in his recent book *Economic Inequality, Neoliberalism, and the American Community College*, the "neoliberal business model has . . . led to an extraordinary diminishment of the public and civic functions of higher education" (193). In this article, we survey the landscape of writing program reform, especially involving developmental English, through examining the postures available to faculty in two-year college writing programs. As it stands now, two primary postures seem available to faculty: reform resister and enthusiastic reformer.

We argue for the value of staking out a "critical reform" position, in hopes of allowing faculty to move from an ad hoc, defensive posture to a consistent, offensive position with a reliable framework and value system. Albeit simplistic, the framing of three positions helps to clarify the fraught terrain and create opportunities for greater understanding and effective engagement. *Critical reformer* provides an identity position around which faculty can coalesce and equip themselves with tools to fight for principled reform. First, there are a large number of faculty, particularly longtime, tenured faculty, who operate primarily from a reform-resistant stance. Reform resisters' loyalties lie with faculty autonomy and a "good intentions" model of literacy. They adopt a posture of totalized resistance to protect a legacy of faculty autonomy, academic rigor, institutional knowledge, and humanist endeavor.

A second, growing, group of institutional actors, including faculty and administrators, might be called *enthusiastic reformers*. Enthusiastic reformers see moving the needle on student success as the primary impetus for engaging in reform work. They work to design, implement, and scale reform models within the local context, often with little more than cursory knowledge of national trends or disciplinary grounding. At their worst, these reformers are driven by questions of economic solvency, career advancement, and national recognition by the Gates Foundation and others.

The third position, one of critical reform, is one that we see already existing in many English departments and within the scholarship of basic writing and two-year colleges. However, we think it is most in need of energetic people to flesh it out, draw its boundaries, and create an interinstitutional community. On the one hand, we are not committed enough to instructional autonomy and solidarity that we neglect our own complicity in constructing barriers to student success. On the other hand, we are not unaware of the risks of allowing administrative and legislative mandates to dictate programmatic reform.

This third position requires reassessing basic writingTYC scholarship in light of the proliferation of research from the Community College Research Council (CCRC) and others on the need for reform. For us, *critical reform* synthesizes and applies a variety of aspirational and inspirational critical dispositions. These include foundational and radical critiques of higher education and access—from Burton Clark's "'Cooling-Out' Function in Higher Education," which questions how community colleges compel some students to internalize failure, to the history of students of color in 1968 storming the gates of City University of New York and demanding access. We draw on the basic writing scholarship that critically examines the structures of basic writing courses, the curriculum we use to teach "basic writers," and the tenuous construction of *basic writer* as a category itself (Shor; Shaughnessy; Bartholomae; Horner and Lu). Critical reform picks up on the productive debate over "mainstreaming" basic writers into first-year composition, in which Peter Adams, the innovator of the Accelerated Learning Program (ALP), figured prominently.The critical reform positions draw from the progressive scholarship in this journal, such as Patrick Sullivan's call to consider ourselves as teacher-scholar-*activists* and the harrowing account of realizing change in "The Risky Business of Writing Reform" (Coleman et al.).

As importantly, we draw on the on-the-ground, and often undersung, work of our fellow two-year college faculty. The critical reform position attempts to live out the disciplinary values and underappreciated instructor values that have underpinned the most progressive work with regard to basic writers, two-year college students, and underserved populations in higher education. This position, we argue, involves taking up the teacher-scholar-activist mantle to its fullest extent to act both within and beyond the classroom. Critical reformers, we suggest, make it their business to engage with the structural consequences of reform. We see this work as akin to Christie Toth's metaphor of "hacking" nascent reforms. This article outlines four components of a critical framework so that faculty can equip themselves for principled work in their local institutions.

Sometimes, in our own individual contexts, faculty like us feel relegated to the triangulated margins. We believe that we are a part of a growing subset of faculty who we are calling *critical reformers*. We position critical reformers between forces for reform—often administrators and corporate-funded nonprofits such as the Gates Foundation—and reform resisters—often faculty who see themselves as doing inherently good work beyond reproach, the "good intentions" model. We explicitly outline this position as one that is not merely a compromise between reform-resistant faculty and enthusiastic reformers.

As part of our inquiry, we reached out to TYC faculty to hear their insights about engaging in community college reform. For this article, we used criterion-based sampling to select interview participants; our interviewees are community college developmental writing and reading faculty interested in developmental reading and writing reform. By sending a query out on the TYCA Listserv as well as contacting people in our professional networks, we strove to include colleagues from several states and college systems as well as with different disciplinary affiliations and institutional statuses (i.e., adjunct, tenured, English, writing, reading.) We utilized a general interview guide approach that allowed us some flexibility in terms of question order, word choice, and follow-up, and we believe these methods are in keeping with a grounded theory approach. One of our interviews was conducted via email, while all others were conducted via phone or Skype. All in all, we interviewed nine TYC faculty from eight different colleges in seven states (Arizona, California, Connecticut, NewYork, Montana, Oregon, and Washington).

In our interactions with interviewees as well as conversations with faculty on our own campus, we've heard many describe their work in quasi-sacred terms, using words like *calling* or *devotion*; most refer to an ethos of public service, a deep commitment to equity and a view of their role as instrumental to democracy; some referred explicitly to notions of class- and race-based inequities; a few drew parallels between their own experiences as outsiders in various contexts and their students' experiences. Carol Perdue, retired tenured reading instructor at

Green River College, notes that her father could barely read. She said, "Teaching at the community college has always been sort of a mission. Literacy is a human right. I always thought there were people who didn't want others to be literate" (Perdue, interview).

Furthermore, their views clearly inform not just their decision to teach at the two-year college but how they position themselves as teachers, scholars, and activists. Karen Henderson of Helena College notes: "The big picture is, if students come to us, we're an open-access institution. We have to meet them where they are" (Henderson, interview). Stephanie Hunter, an adjunct at Skagit Valley College in Washington, emphasized that empathy for students is paramount to this work. She frames her work in terms of student-centered values: "A community college is supposed to be for everyone. We're here for the community. I don't see myself as a gatekeeper. I'm a facilitator" (Hunter, interview). Such comments demonstrate instructors' student-centered motivations—and help enrich our understanding of how they engage with reform.

The Reform Landscape

We use the term *reform* to neatly refer to a variety of recent initiatives. We come to critical reform as English instructors, with English being a particularly important vector in the landscape of reform initiatives. In terms of course placement, for example, critiques of the validity of standardized placement tests have led many colleges to turn to placement mechanisms such as multiple measures, GPA placement, and directed self-placement in order to, at the least, more accurately place students and sometimes, more aspirationally, help students gain more agency in the placement process (see Klausman et al.).

Beyond placement, colleges are asking: Into what kinds of course sequences are we placing students? And how do these sequences promote or hinder student progress? Again, recent empirical research has questioned the efficacy of lengthy developmental English sequences. These sequences sometimes consist of multiple courses and, in our program's case, unintegrated reading and writing tracks. This research suggests that many students are underplaced into English courses—they could have been successful with fewer "remedial" courses or, perhaps, none at all (Scott-Clayton). Some reformers have developed various models for rethinking developmental English, such as ALP, with this data in mind. Beyond English-specific reforms, reform projects such as Guided Pathways ask colleges to more holistically address the impediments that students face across their experience in open-access institutions (see Bailey et al.).

Nonprofit organizations such as the CCRC, MDRC, and Complete College America (CCA) often produce the research that empirically demonstrates what follows from much basic writing theory: developmental English can actually act as a barrier to students, many of whom are already marginalized within institutions of higher education. However, these nonprofits regularly receive funding from corporately underwritten sources, including the Gates Foundation and the Lumina Foundation. By "throwing open the gates" of access, as Peter Adams encourages us, some worry that we are conceding higher education to the "Gates" of private industry and the unfettered free market (Adams et al.).

Karen Henderson at Helena College notes that representatives of organizations like CCA often utilize neoliberal rhetorical positioning in conversations with faculty, potentially raising the hackles of educators committed to the student-centered ethos of community colleges. Henderson describes her experience on a Montana higher education task force:

> All I ever heard from the CCA guy was numbers. I never heard him talk about a human. I work with humans every day. It's about the humans. . . . While I still believe that they are only looking at the numbers, I can also say that the co-req class was a positive thing. I'm humble enough to say I didn't see the whole picture.

In her interview, Henderson described how the big picture view revealed that the traditional developmental pipeline was inflicting unintended harm on some students—and engaging in reform work opened her eyes to that bigger picture. Why was it hard for the "CCA guy," with his immersion in the research, to convince a passionate, open-minded educator like Karen Henderson that he was coming from a principled position that had the best interests of her community college students at heart?

It's not just the foundation philanthropists' rhetorical trappings that may alienate community college faculty. Carol Perdue described her discomfort with the material excess she encountered at an Achieving the Dream conference in Anaheim:

> After years of going to NADE and CRLA, I was like, holy cow. This is how the other half lives. I've never had food at a conference like that.They had sponsorship that . . .That bothered me. The fact that there's a lot of money being spent here. Chocolate covered strawberries and petit fours. What bothered me was the religious fervor. It was like going to a rah-rah. There was a lot of software being sold there ATD and Disney, how appropriate, right?

Achieving the Dream and Disney, indeed. Given that talk of acceleration is consistently coupled with "austerity" framing, it's little wonder faculty are suspicious. These nonprofits rarely—if ever—articulate their values in terms of a radical commitment to social justice. In fact, their critiques often come with a neoliberal understanding of the value of education that, ideologically, clashes with the Marxism of Ira Shor or the liberal humanism of Mike Rose. Neoliberalism describes the current, hegemonic iteration of capitalism that puts the free market at the heart of all aspects of social life (Brown). A neoliberal orientation asks of higher education:

What is the return on investment for college students—not only their personal return, but society's return? This return on investment is quite literal; it's about career prospects, earnings potential, and contributions to the economic health of the nation. We argue that nonprofit interests uncritically adopt the neoliberal paradigm. Admirably, they value students and place their needs front and center. However, students are often entirely understood within a market logic.T hey are future workers, and their education is a commodity that they can trade in for a more valuable market position. Within this market logic, reforming developmental education becomes an efficiency move for the institution—fewer courses, fewer instructors, fewer resources used on languishing students. Reforms such as acceleration also privilege market-framed efficiency. As Susan Naomi Bernstein, a pioneer in basic writing scholarship, told us, "The kairos of ALP hinges on the word 'accelerated.' Speed and efficiency remain at the heart of conditions of austerity and precarity and add an additional burden for writers who, for any number of reasons, need more time to learn and grow into maturity as writers" (Bernstein, personal interview). CCRC and MDRC do not, to be clear, seem to construct their work with an eye toward this kairos, and their arguments draw mostly on data and big-picture efficiency modeling. We believe noncritical reformers' neoliberal tendencies are pervasive and, if not placed within critical frameworks that privilege robust, nuanced constructs of student success, can damage the institutions they purport to help. Christie Toth, Patrick Sullivan, and Carolyn Calhoon-Dillahunt note in their article "A Dubious Method of Improving Educational Outcomes: Accountability and the Two-Year College":

> neoliberal ideologies are contributing to structural inequities in higher education, not ameliorating them, and this makes us skeptical of discourses of educational accountability rooted in the language of consumerism. Issues of class, social standing, and family resources should be a crucial variable in discussions of public policy, particularly those policies affecting two-year colleges because of these institutions' open admissions policies and their historic mandate to help democratize the U.S. higher education system. (396)

As critical reformers, we are tasked with linking what we know empirically with our values and vision for the community college. When interests converge, we are responsible for reframing and reimagining ostensibly apolitical reform research. Extending critical race theorist and legal scholar Derrick A. Bell Jr.'s concept of "interest convergence" to basic writing, Steve Lamos argues that systemic, racialized structuring out of basic writing students has historically only changed when intersecting with the interests of power. He argues, "During periods of convergence, a certain amount of racially egalitarian change within disciplinary and institutional discussions did occur, albeit change that was bounded in important ways by mainstream concerns regarding the need to preserve racialized standards, including Standard English" (8). This concept of interest convergence places critical reform within the historical trajectory on issues of civil rights and equity. When our interests overlap partially with those in power, we may stand a chance of achieving progress through careful, structurally aware engagement.

These complexities and competing values, however, might leave some faculty feeling alienated, discouraged, as though they are in the Labyrinth, possibly facing the minotaur, with no path forward. With cleareyed recognition of these dangers and complexities in the reform landscape, we offer a set of critical frames and questions that highlight opportunities that the obvious dangers so often obfuscate. In each section, we offer critical reformers suggestions as to how to approach reform-resistant colleagues and reform-minded administrators and colleagues through questions and opportunities for collaborative work. These suggestions support critical reformers so that they may engage with reform efforts in the teacher-activist-scholar tradition. These suggestions, therefore, aim to support critical reformers in reasserting the values of the open-access college sometimes structured out of efficiency-minded reforms.

Dialoguing between the National and the Local

Sometimes, in the spirit of protecting their college's mission, faculty position the uniqueness of their local contexts against national trends. In the context of current reform conversations, this is not a productive defensive strategy. With one eye on the ground and the other on the national terrain, critical reformers navigate the intersection of the national and the local as a productive tension that rewards an orientation toward scholarship and expertise. Yet community college cultures are often suspicious of outside entanglements. As Toth and Patrick Sullivan explain, "[Faculty] sometimes operate within institutional or departmental cultures that neither expect nor appreciate their efforts to engage with scholarship" (251). In the highly contentious atmosphere at our own college, administration referred to "community college curmudgeons" to explain why faculty would not join their initiatives for reform (O'Banion), and longtime faculty tended to denigrate the scholarly interests of newer faculty. In their article "Distinct and Significant: Professional Identities of Two-Year College Faculty," Christina M. Toth, Brett M. Griffiths, and Kathryn Thirolf contend that two-year college faculty often conflate national conversations about developmental education policy with administration-driven reform agendas, and they recoil (12). Symbolically but importantly, the trend of removing "community" from two-year college names—implemented in the push to expand four-year degrees at community colleges—speaks to the devaluing of local knowledge and a lack of commitment to the unique and heterogeneous service areas, the actual communities, that these colleges serve. We understand that disciplinary scholarship and administratively palatable data often do not acknowledge locally generated knowledge. The anecdotes, experiences, and intuitions of instructors provide a kind of data that do not always speak to the neoliberal orientation toward the quantitative, the generalizable, and the economically meaningful. These experiences provide the necessary understanding of the complexities of every college, their cultures and students, on which the success of any reform relies.

On the other hand, two-year colleges undoubtedly share traits, orientations, and challenges despite their local particularities. With a lack of professional engagement outside of individuals' institutions, faculty sometimes position their local contexts as institutions sui generis. While this move intends to hold onto the complex experiences, histories, and needs of every college, it also threatens to cut off two-year colleges from understanding larger systemic issues as well as cutting off faculty from shared communities and interests, which could result in more powerful collective actions.

These tensions do not need to be resolved, with either the local trumping the national or the national eliding the nuances of the local. In fact, we suggest that the local contexts—and those who have labored within them—must be the starting point for implementing any reform. Holly Hassel and Joanne Baird Giordano argue that "the intersections between research and teaching can translate a problem or professional frustration into an engaging line of scholarly inquiry" (133). Critical reformers' most powerful move is to not only recontextualize their situations within national conversations, but also to recontextualize the way these conversations reflect historical/disciplinary knowledge and histories. For example, we were motivated to revise and remodel ALP for our local context because we had some concerns about the general lack of attention to its replication of the racial and socioeconomic equity gap. While studies have repeatedly demonstrated that ALP increases completion rates across demographic categories, we also know that the racial and socioeconomic equity gaps are still replicated in this increase—in other words, nonwhite students might do better because of ALP, but they still lag behind white students, and low-income students in ALP do better than they do without it but still lag behind middleclass students (Cho). For us, in-depth knowledge of the scholarship on ALP as well as recognizing our local context's rapidly diversifying student demographics empowered us to create a model whose validity was grounded in its service to diverse students. While we based the acceleration model on what had been developed nationally, we tied its success to the way it responded to the needs of our most marginalized students. We wedded our iteration of ALP to the mission of promoting access and success for our service area's population.

Scenario

Administration claims they want to reform developmental education by offering a corequisite structure—perhaps ALP, the Accelerated Learning Program. They claim, "Look at how well ALP is working at college X!" And they offer one short PowerPoint presentation that includes snippets of research and data that support their claims.

Lines of Inquiry for Critical Engagement

In order to engage in the above scenario, the critical reformer must have a larger understanding of the national conversations and data regarding ALP while also having a complex understanding of their local context.

Engaging Enthusiastic Reformers

The presentation above implies a direct correspondence between the national data and reforms and the specific needs and structures of the local context. To ascertain the relationship between the national and local contexts, a critical reformer might ask questions along the following lines:

- What were the demographics of the two-year colleges represented in the data? How do these student populations compare to the student populations of our college?
- What did the developmental sequences look like before the proposed reforms? And how do those sequences compare to our college's?
- What resources were given to college faculty to implement the changes, or were faculty given agency at all within the reforms? What impact on adjunct faculty, in particular, did these changes have?
- How old is the data? Where does the data come from? What understandings of student success might not be represented by the data?

Engaging Reform Resisters

In light of these proposed changes, reform resisters might argue that this reform further threatens to introduce an already underprepared student body into higher-level courses and lessen the rigor of the first-year composition class. In light of this resistance, questions a critical reformer might ask include the following:

- To what extent is the local context different from other contexts that have successfully implemented these reforms?
- What are the current placement mechanisms into the college composition courses? In light of scholarship on placement, to what extent do they produce valid student placements into composition courses?
- Beyond the anecdotal, what evidence of underpreparedness are faculty offering?

SEPARATING AGENCY FROM AUTONOMY

Longtime faculty so often present the greatest resistance to even well-crafted, student-centered reforms, but their resistance tactics rarely amount to more than a protracted period of institutional critique. In "What Happens When Ideological Narratives Lose Their Force?," Jeanne Gunner concedes that "[w]e manage and are managed according to institutional values increasingly difficult to distinguish from corporate values." However, she questions the efficacy of ideological critique in response. Gunner argues that to move beyond mere symbolic victories, we must lessen the grip of pure, ideological critique, thereby "lessening the risk of inducing a kind of closed and unresolvable mirror stage, in which the oppressor we encounter leads us to construct ourselves as a totalized body of resistance" (159). In many institutions, longtime faculty are, by default, reform resisters who dismiss and oppose administratively driven changes and cite preserving faculty autonomy as the rallying cry against reform.

The reflexive recourse to autonomy is, at best, shortsighted, especially as it often in practice equates to lack of engagement as the structural bells ring for us all. As Brett Griffiths notes, "When instructors constrain their definitions of teaching to the activities of classroom instruction and grading, they constrain their own autonomy and limit their impact on departmental and institutional change" (62). Uncritical autonomy is increasingly untenable, undesirable, and unethical in the face of reform initiatives that impact institutions across the country. Fulltime faculty who wash their hands of reforms by affording themselves of arguments for absolute autonomy sidestep an opportunity to bring rich local knowledge and equity framing to the negotiation table on behalf of their students (and also in alliance with their hardworking and undervalued adjunct colleagues).

Under the pressures of reform and the anti-faculty sentiments embedded in accountability narratives, many faculty understandably retreat to the domains where they still feel empowered—the classroom. In one interview, an anonymous fulltime instructor at a Connecticut community college described self-serving, shortsighted faculty orientations toward reform that had a negative effect on her college's writing sequence. Faculty leaders at this institution, according to our interviewee, sometimes joked that faculty "are gods in the classroom"—and implied that they would do everything in their power to preserve the status quo in the face of pressure to reform. Thus, at first fulltime faculty "dragged their feet" on creating an acceleration model. Eventually, they bowed to administrative pressure and implemented a hastily constructed, untested model that exacerbated labor inequities, undermined academic standards, and, in the words of our interviewee, placed some students into a less-rigorous, "segregated" corequisite course (interview, 12 Sept. 2017). When reform is performed with facile autonomy as a central value, *austerity* as administration's watchword, and a partial understanding of the impetus for developmental reform, it is a recipe for incoherent changes that do not follow a consistent, principled ethic.

What if we faculty who teach basic writing and college composition had as much exposure to the research on persistence and retention rates and national models of reform as administrators? What if we were able to sit at the table in a powerful stance of negotiation, able to elaborate on the local implications of findings from articles written by Shanna Jaggars Smith, Sung Woo Cho, or Judith Scott-Clayton? What if, in addition to our knowledge of the history of the community college, basic writing scholarship, and our own students and their needs, we could fully articulate how various reforms square with a deep commitment to social justice and a theoretically robust equity construct? What if we knew the literature of CCRC better than our institutional researchers and administrators did, and we could construct arguments and build or reenvision models based on that knowledge? What if, instead of adopting a posture of subversion and absolute resistance as our reflexive move, we adopted a reflective, strategic, flexible position that allowed us to critique without losing our place at the table? What if we became key agents of reform so that, in collaboration with constituents and colleagues, every model we built could be informed by our robust equity framework? Perhaps this vision, this "agency" we call for—which we think is a flexible, endlessly curious orientation to a teacher-scholar-activist in this particular context—seems utopian. When we interviewed Wendy Smith, she noted that Junot Díaz has suggested we should be envisioning utopias in dystopian times (Smith, interview). As Keith Kroll's 2012 article predicting the decimation of the two-year college composition professoriate suggests, we are certainly approaching dystopian times.

Scenario

Administration intends to implement a pathways reform, including potentially significant cuts to the arts, humanities, social sciences, and some sciences.Though they say their reforms are based on "the pathways book" (*Redesigning America's Community Colleges*), most of them only seem to have cursory knowledge of the structural and pedagogical implications of the reforms. Some of your colleagues, most of them deeply dedicated to the community college as a place of opportunity, advocate for a wholesale rejection of creating clearer pathways for students' programs of study, despite evidence that overwhelming and confusing options – what Bailey, Jaggars, and Jenkins call the "cafeteria model" of community colleges – do, in fact, impede some students' likelihood of success.

Lines of Inquiry for Critical Engagement

In order to engage in the above scenario, critical reformers must develop an historical awareness of the promise of access that two-year colleges offer and extrapolate from that a values-driven framework that lead to the following questions:

Engaging Enthusiastic Reformers

Know "the numbers" and engage them, but ask reformers to engage at the level of values as well. Scrutinize the efficiency and accountability narratives, and keep the community college's values at the center of every conversation without assuming that those values are inherently opposed to efficiency or accountability.

- How does the implementation support opening access to all, not foreclosing possibilities to make the college's completion rates or graduation rates more impressive?
- Have other colleges studied the unintended consequences of reforms, especially in terms of avoiding "tracking" of historically marginalized students?
- How do the conditions on the ground, including local context, culture, funding models, and so on, resemble or differ from those at other campuses that have adopted the model? How can we work together to ensure that those factors are well accounted for in our model?

Engaging Reform Resisters

Gently call attention to the dangers of "closing the classroom door" or attempting monolithic resistance. A faculty united in open, respectful negotiations can powerfully influence reforms.

- What are they losing when they "close the classroom door"—and in what ways are they symbolically and actually refusing to be a voice at the table on behalf of marginalized students?
- In what ways does a reflexive posture of resistance reinforce the worst narratives in reform, that of out-of-touch faculty who refuse to respond to reasoned argument?
- How can faculty engage in restructuring programs for student success without undermining their own positions and beliefs—and, in fact, how can they reenergize both through reform?

RETHINKING A "DEFICIT MINDSET"

Recently, faculty on our campus risked their livelihoods in a three-day strike that concerned issues of social justice. As administration closed down vocational programs and threatened academic ones, faculty storytelling in conversations with the public emphasized the open-access, community-serving mission of two-year colleges. Throughout the labor dispute, faculty rhetoric highlighted the institution's commitment to serving immigrants, refugees, first-generation students, students of color, and working-class students. On the picket lines with student activists and community members, faculty asked the community to reclaim with us the narrative of the two-year college as a place for increased access and economic justice for traditionally underserved communities.

However, our college's legacy of curricular practices engaged a strikingly different narrative. A very few years ago, our English Division had a course placement protocol that explicitly privileged mythical and incoherent standards over access, a protocol that unfairly penalized multilingual students and students of color. Furthermore, our developmental course sequence compelled many students to take twenty-five credits of unintegrated, developmental writing and reading courses before stepping foot into a transfer-level English course. In other words, our curricular walk didn't match our ideological talk.

In the face of widespread resistance across campus, we convened a place ment study committee in 2013 with two other colleagues and began a process of placement and developmental education reform that emphasized mitigating equity gaps that disadvantaged marginalized students. Some faculty perceived our efforts as an attack on standards, instructional autonomy, and local institutional history. Framing their resistance as a standards-preserving response to a new breed of telescopic philanthropists and penny-pinching administrators, these faculty firmly braced themselves to resist change. Invoking a totalizing "deficit" framework for our students, faculty across campus engaged in heated discussions about why "students can't write" and why "international students shouldn't be allowed to take classes if they can't understand what we're saying." Many faculty suggested that, in fact, a *more* rigorous placement process, perhaps one including a test of speaking and listening skills, was needed. As far as most faculty were concerned, the problem was readily apparent: too many underprepared students, especially students who "just couldn't understand English," were getting into their classes.

Despite faculty's larger progressive ideological commitments, it is difficult to reframe deficit in the context of the two-year college. As

Stephanie Hunter, a faculty member at Skagit Valley College, pointed out:

> The problem with CCs is that they are staffed by people who loved school and do not always understand that the students who come to community colleges aren't [typically] like that. They've got substantial barriers, and when we throw up more of them, often unintentionally, we're keeping them from achieving whatever goal they might have I believe the mentality in the past was everyone has the right to fail, and we're trying to shift that to everyone has the right to succeed. And I believe that. Everyone does have the right to succeed.

In order to shift away from the "right to fail" mindset, critical reformers must lead the way in interrogating deficit framing. We believe narrative making around access, on the one hand, and recourse to student deficits as reasons not to reform, on the other hand, are incompatible. A deep, lived commitment to the social justice, open-access mission of the community college collides with universal and colorblind notions of "standards," which position students as having to constantly prove their worth. Critical reformers can aspire to the institutional activism and value-driven resistance that we witnessed during our labor struggle, yet also challenge a two-year college professoriate that is progressively oriented but reliant on reductive frames about "community college students." Much of the "good intentions" rhetoric positions faculty and students in an unnecessarily adversarial relationship. Such antagonism undermines the potential faculty and students have to coalesce around a shared vision of access that the larger mission of the two-year college represents. We argue that to reform critically, and successfully, we must uncover the standards-preserving discourses' reliance on what Ruth Frankenberg has termed "color- and power-evasive paradigms" (qtd. in Prendergast 37)—paradigms so naturalized in our thinking about students that we may forget the ways in which they create and obfuscate barriers to access.

We do not intend to dismiss conceptions of rigor and challenge; in fact, we fully subscribe to Rebecca D. Cox's call for high challenge and high support. However, we turn to the *strengths-* or *asset*-based language of recent higher education research and the rich work in basic writing that treats students as capable, diverse intellectuals. As Louise Hull argues, "For almost two centuries the dominant way to think about underachieving students has been to focus on defects in intellect or character or differences in culture or situation that lead to failure, and to locate the causes within the mind and language of the individual" (qtd. in Ostman 51). The diverse language practices of multilingual students, in particular, inform some of the current iterations of "deficit" narratives being circulated at many community colleges.

The recent language turn in writing studies, informed by the work of translingual scholars such as Trimbur, Horner, Lu, Canagarajah, and others, offers a productive rethinking and reframing of deficit, particularly as it concerns the diversity of language use in the two-year college. Jonathan Hall, in "Multilinguality Is the Mainstream," argues that we must reframe our institutional and classroom practices around the notion that most students are multilingual or plurilingual. Hall asks how we can rethink our constrictive Standard English framework as we redesign our courses:

> Up until now, we have created our courses on the supposition, conscious or unconscious, that our mainstream student is monolingual—and then, as we have become more aware of the existence of multilingual students among us, we have attempted to adapt or accommodate for them. What would happen if we reversed that process—if we start with the conscious assumption that multilinguality is the mainstream? (40)

Explicitly valuing multilingual students speaks to a larger repositioning of difference as worthwhile and productive rather than as something to be policed or dismissed as not meeting monolithic standards.

Although we believe that clear, transparent standards coupled with rigorous teaching can improve students' reading, writing, and critical thinking abilities, how do we come to terms with the empirically disparate impacts of our practices? It is here, in fact, that we find the key to the question of deficit modeling: Assessment scholars have demonstrated that student groups must not be forced to bear the burden of assessment for which they have not been provided a robust, multidimensional opportunity structure. Scholars of assessment, in fact, argue that adherence to vague, immutable standards without recognition of the undue burden placed on students, particularly students of color, puts access in peril. Fairness to students is not about helping them meet abstract standards, but a cleareyed recognition that enforcement of standards sometimes structures in disparate impacts on particularly vulnerable students. Scholars on assessment see a perpetual devaluing of marginalized students that consistently results in the privileging of white, middle-class, Standard English norms. Of course, we cannot guarantee success; we can only offer the "opportunity to learn," but we can remake the OTL in the most robust, multidimensional manner possible.

In "Occupy Writing Studies: Rethinking College Composition for the Needs of the Teaching Majority," Holly Hassel and Joanne Baird Giordano highlight the disjuncture between how writing studies privileges composition at the four-year college with the reality that two-year colleges offer the majority of composition courses in American colleges. They propose "[A] scholarly reimagination that repositions two-year college teaching at the center of our disciplinary discourse about college composition" (118).We extend this same reimagination to the differences that constitute our student populations at two-year colleges. Rather than seeking to elide or remediate differences in pursuit of a "mythical norm" (Tatum), we ask: How can we affirm and harness the heterogeneity of our student populations—whether in terms of how they use language, how they learn, their life experiences, and other identity characteristics? While not turning a blind eye to the real struggles that students face or the real needs that we must meet, we suggest that we hold back the work of critical reform, and ultimately undermine the place of two-year college composition in our disciplinary discourse, when we position our students as perpetually failing to live up to abstracted, and politically problematic, ideals. If we assert that two-year college students perpetually miss the marks they need to meet, what does that say about the efficacy of our two-year colleges and the efficacy our own positions?

Scenario

On your campus, the reform resisters consistently lament the state of their underprepared student population. Common complaints include suggestions that "some students can't learn" and "I wasn't trained to teach ESL." Some faculty want to propose a lengthier developmental sequence with direct grammar instruction or to segregate "ESL" students from monolingual English speakers. Finding opportunity in these faculty complaints about student preparedness, administration argues for decreasing access for certain students. Citing data that demonstrates that very few students make it through precollege sequences, administration argues that students can either start in a corequisite structure or, if their placement test scores are too low, access adult education and ESOL services available at local high schools and community centers. Perhaps for different reasons, reform resisters and enthusiastic reformers share a conception of two-year college students as "deficient" and unable to progress if they cannot start at college-level composition with support.

Lines of Inquiry for Critical Engagement

Based on the above scenario, the following lines for engagement ask faculty to reframe student abilities in a way that is both realistic about their diverse needs but does not ignore their strengths and assets.

Engaging Reform Resisters

Challenging commonplace understandings of students' capabilities requires bringing to light assumptions and distinctions that often go unexamined and unchallenged.

- When students are cast as deficient, ask for finer distinctions among the students to whom they're referring: For example, who do we mean by "ESL" students? International students? Students for whom English is a second or third language? Students who are bilingual or multilingual? Students who have English preparation from a young age and come from a country that teaches English in primary education or where English is a widely spoken language? Students who have recently begun to learn English?
- In what, exactly, are students "deficient," and to what extent do those deficiencies map onto the skillsets, aptitudes, and "habits of mind" that professional documents, such as the WPA Outcomes Statement and the Framework for Success in Postsecondary Writing, outline? How well are our classes and program utilizing communicative skillsets that students already bring into the classroom, such as communicating across language difference and utilizing multimodal composition—skillsets that perhaps flip the script, requiring professional development on the part of composition instructors?

Engaging Enthusiastic Reformers

Advocate for seeing student access as part of a larger "ecosystem" that must be supported writ large.

- To what extent are enthusiastic reformers selectively invoking the rhetoric of access and student success while advocating for changes that, in effect, limit access?
- What lessons have enthusiastic reformers learned from states, like Florida, where access has been reduced? To what extent do they even care?
- The call for access seems to be opposed to the austerity framework. How are reformers accounting for students' needs—and how is access to education also framed in terms of equitable access to resources? To what extent are enthusiastic reformers willing to "put their money where their mouth is"— especially when evaluating money spent on other priorities, such as adding administrative positions?

IV: MAINTAINING VALUES, EMBRACING FLEXIBILITY

In order to speak to multiple stakeholders and engage with their myriad agendas, critical reformers must remain committed to their values despite sometimes competing contexts and pressures. However, just as we teach student writers to do, we must work to transfer our critical frameworks to many conversations and audiences. For example, while more explicit discussion of social justice might win over some progressive faculty, appropriation of neoliberal discourse—speaking in terms of quantitative data and dollars and cents—might work better in front of certain administrators. Furthermore, in our scholarly communities, we might value more complex, data-driven epistemologies that serve our goals. This rhetorical balancing act can be precarious, if not disconcerting. While we are not advocating for duplicity, we also do not think that an "authentic" identity position really exists in such a complicated landscape. We argue for strategic rhetorical approaches that remain true to our values. The diverse ideologies and evidence bases within reform conversations require nimble navigation and adaptability.

Here, Richard Earl Miller's work on effecting institutional change in *As If Learning Mattered: Reforming Higher Education* can help us consider how to develop pragmatic but also idealistic dispositions. He encourages faculty members and administrators to consider themselves within the "hybrid persona of the intellectual-bureaucrat" (41). Miller argues that "bureaucracies are certainly good at generating data, producing information about the social world" (41). However, he warns that "there is little evidence to support the idea that bureaucracies are driven by some internal compulsion to interpret the collected data in ways that *effectively* result in a more egalitarian distribution of educational and employment possibilities" (41). While critiquing the utopian impulses of some who seek to remake institutional structures, Miller suggests that engaging with bureaucracies with a critical orientation results in actual change (25). We take up this critical realism in advocating for adaptable and flexible rhetoric and dispositions. Sometimes, it might work to our advantage to smile and enjoy the strawberries—without forgetting where they came from.

While this article attempts to flesh out *critical reform* as a framework for approaching changes and initiatives in today's community colleges, we hope to offer *critical reformer* as an identity position that teacher-scholar-activists can embrace even when, within their institutions, they feel caught between loyalties and value systems. Embracing flexibility as a necessary strategy for making change is a hallmark of this identity position, as Miller explicates above. Our hybridity is a source of power for navigating complicated conversations and initiatives. Karen Henderson of Helena College exemplifies the role that a robust, equity-framed communication and assertive negotiation grounded in local knowledge can play. She explains her work on a statewide legislative task force:

> Right away, I was advocating for students. My students include veterans, people with criminal records, first-generation college students, parents, etc. They won't be successful at college writing if we just put them in there. My voice was important at that time. No one else had experience with those students coupled with the lack of wisdom to speak out. I was able to collaborate with those on the committee who had more cultural capital—and we came up with a statement encouraging MT to utilize the ALP. We got some of the things we wanted. Don't throw out the baby with the bathwater.

Though she knew that her state would probably commit to a model of acceleration at some point, she saw the value in bringing her perspective and skills to the table. If she hadn't been there, if her voice hadn't been there, what babies would've been thrown out with the bathwater? Henderson's willingness to adapt to the needs of the situation kept her at the table in the negotiation process, yet her voice was consistently raised to humanize and make present the students for whose futures the negotiations were ultimately being held. By continually reframing the work they were doing in terms of real students of whom she had extensive knowledge, she infused a nonnegotiable, robust commitment to students who have been traditionally underserved or even marginalized in institutions of higher education.

Scenario

A tense faculty meeting centered on proposed reforms engages in worst-case scenario thinking. It is followed by an administrative conversation on retention with a regional conference over the weekend. Some faculty complain that administrators have been "bludgeoning" them with data about poor completion rates and using coercive tactics to force them to adopt reforms. Morale is low, and the general feeling on campus is moroseness spiked with resentment; however, the critical developmental reform work on your campus has had modest successes that you're presenting at the regional conference.

Lines of Inquiry for Critical Engagement

In this section, our interviewees help to frame the lines of inquiry: Use rhetorical flexibility and adaptable, nimble inquiry while clearly articulating the values that drive you as an educator. While not accepting an uncritical role as peacemaker, you do hope to bring to bear the progressive values of your colleagues and the potential of the reforms.

Scrutinizing Enthusiastic Reformers

Synthesize and embrace a mixture of methodologies and values when examining the seemingly apolitical knowledge that enthusiastic reformers might use and produce.

- How can the data be used to learn about the way that current structures have placed an undue burden on students, especially students of color?

- What elements of a robust construct of student success cannot be addressed by the available data, and how can faculty expertise and local knowledge make a fuller picture of the obstacles students face?
- How can the data be understood when framed in terms of key concerns articulated in basic writing scholarship, particularly in terms of equitable access for students and the civic and humanist framing of the value of education?

Engaging Reform Resisters

Reform resisters might be tempted to adopt postures of absolute, monolithic resistance, questioning everything from the financial interests of the foundation philanthropists who promote the reform models to the college administrators' own desire for career advancement. While it is true that engaging in critical reform involves careful scrutiny of neoliberal narratives of the community college and accountability, we might position our rhetoric more in terms of the "mutual responsibility" framing offered by Toth, Sullivan, and Calhoon-Dillahunt than the outright rejection of any accountability. Getting longtime faculty involved in the conversation requires the ability to be rhetorically flexible but centered on values and vision.

Adaptability and translation are important when speaking to other instructors across the curriculum. As Marc Pietrzykowski explains, "Developmental education affects the whole school, so it's important to get the whole campus involved to understand its importance. I did work on informing [the] whole campus on what those faculty doing developmental education want versus what administrators want. It was the strategy of the former president to keep people from talking to each other, so we went about intentionally connecting with other faculty" (Pietrzykowski, interview).

Wendy Smith, basic skills coordinator at San Diego Mesa College, describes how she and others have successfully undertaken equity-centered reforms by not only explaining reforms but also listening to various stakeholders. An ultimate belief in their colleagues' commitment to the community college mission paid off when they approached colleagues with humility and openness. Smith urges:

> Talk to people individually. Hear them out when they're not defensive at a meeting. Convene panels of students to describe

how they came to college, what it was like to take a placement exam, how it felt to be placed into developmental education classes. Use data and professional development. Talk to people at other colleges. Talk to people in curriculum.

The words from our colleagues in the trenches do not boil down to just "words, words, words" but emphasize the ways in which community college faculty are already attempting to engage in critical reform.

Conclusion

These principles, we admit, are incomplete and aspirational. We do not necessarily know the unintended consequences of engagement with reform, no matter how strategic and cleareyed we think we are. We also recognize that *critical reform* itself sounds as though we are laying claim to a brand that we control when, in actuality, critical reform has been happening across institutions for many years. We would also be remiss if we did not recognize that *critical reform* often implies a certain level of institutional authority, and that reform conversations may not fully welcome and support contingent faculty members. A consistent ethic of equity cannot elide power differences within our institutions. Although largely unexplored here, we see addressing equity for adjunct faculty as key for developing a social justice framework.

Despite these caveats, we outline our engagement with reform in order to more clearly define a critical community to take on this work as powerfully as possible. We suggest that effective, progressive faculty members will need all of our available postures, from resistance to embrasure, to thoughtfully undertake this work in the service of advancing the communal values of the community college. Humbly, we face the fact that our programs, with their foundations in good intentions, have been enmeshed in the crafting of structural inequity. We suggest that many have often adopted the least helpful posture, the posture of absolute resistance, in the context of reforms. And we acknowledge that we and our colleagues have sometimes jumped to conclusions and short-circuited student-centered reforms.

In this work, we will need our openness and nimbleness. We will need our unwavering belief in equity and social justice, our commitment to the mission of the two-year college. And, most of all, we will need the collaboration and creative thinking of colleagues near and far. With the resurgent fashionability of hate and discrimination and in the age of privatized public resources, we hold out hope that two-year college instructors will continue to commit to their passion for justice. As Susan Naomi Bernstein reminds us:

> Education is a human right, and given current conditions, we cannot dismiss hope as an idealistic construct. Hope is one of the most important prerequisites for teaching and learning in Basic Writing. The systems that are imposed upon us, or that we have inherited, replaced other systems that were very far from perfect. These earlier systems were dismantled with little regard for the students who stood to lose the most, and for many people the current systems also have proven to be unsatisfactory because of their inattentiveness to the intersectionality of students' lives. In order to create a more sustainable future, we need to intervene and interrogate these systems, and we need to imagine and enact equitable visions of education for Basic Writing. Our students' and all of our lives depend on it.

Works Cited

Adams, Peter, et al. "The Accelerated Learning Program: Throwing Open the Gates." *Journal of Basic Writing* vol. 28, no. 2, 2009, 50–69. Accessed 21 Sept. 2017.

Anonymous instructor. Personal interview. 12 Sept. 2017.

Bailey, Thomas R., et al. *Redesigning America's Community Colleges*. Harvard University Press, 2015.

Bartholomae, David. "The Tidy House: Basic Writing in the American Curriculum." *Writing on the Margins: Essays on Composition and Teaching*, edited by David Bartholomae, Macmillan, 2005, pp. 312–26.

Bell, Derrick A., Jr. "Brown v. Board of Education and the Interest-Convergence Dilemma." *Harvard Law Review*, vol. 93, no. 3, 1980, pp. 518–33.

Bernstein, Susan Naomi. "Re:TETYC Article Quote Check." Received by Anthony Warnke and Kirsten Higgins, 11 Nov. 2017.

Brown, Wendy. *Undoing the Demos*. MIT Press, 2015.

Cho, Sung-Woo, et al. "New Evidence of Success for Community College Remedial English Students: Tracking the Outcomes of Students in the Accelerated Learning Program (ALP)." CCRC Working Paper No. 53, 2012. *Community College Research Center, Columbia University*.

Clark, Burton R. "The 'Cooling-Out' Function in Higher Education." *American Journal of Sociology,* vol. 65, no. 6, 1960, pp. 569–76. Accessed 21 Sept. 2017.

Coleman, Taiyon J., et al. "The Risky Business of Engaging Racial Equity in Writing Instruction: A Tragedy in Five Acts." *Teaching English in the Two-Year College,* vol. 43, no. 4, 2016, pp. 347–70. Accessed 21 Sept. 2017.

Cox, Rebecca D. *The College Fear Factor.* Harvard University Press, 2010. Griffiths, Brett. "Professional Autonomy and Teacher-Scholar-Activists in Two-Year Colleges: Preparing New Faculty to Think Institutionally." *Teaching English in the Two-Year College,* vol. 45, no. 1, 2017, p. 47.

Gunner, Jeanne. "What Happens When Ideological Narratives Lose Their Force?" *Composition in the Age of Austerity,* edited by Tony Scott and Nancy Welch, Utah State UP, 2016, pp. 149–61.

Hall, Jonathan."Multilinguality Is the Mainstream." *Reworking English in Rhetoric and Composition: Global Interrogations, Local Interventions,* edited by Bruce Horner and Karen Kopelson, Southern Illinois UP, 2014, pp. 31–48.

Hassel, Holly, and Joanne Baird Giordano. "Occupy Writing Studies: Rethinking College Composition for the Needs of the Teaching Majority." *College Composition and Communication,* vol. 65, no. 1, 2013, pp. 117–39.

Henderson, Karen. Personal interview. 14 Sept. 2017.

Horner, Bruce, and Min-Zhan Lu. *Representing the Other: Basic Writers and the Teaching of Basic Writing.* National Council of Teachers of English, 1999.

Hunter, Stephanie. Personal interview. 31 Aug. 2017.

Klausman, Jeffrey, et al. "TYCA White Paper on Placement Reform." *Teaching English in the Two-Year College,* vol. 44, no. 2, 2016, pp. 135–57.

Kroll, Keith. "The End of the Community College English Profession." *Teaching English in the Two-Year College,* vol. 40, no. 2, 2012, p. 118. Accessed 21 Sept. 2017.

Lamos, Steve. *Interests and Opportunities: Race, Racism, and University Writing Instruction in the Post-Civil Rights Era.* U of Pittsburgh P, 2011.

Latham, Eleanor, and Jane Denison-Furness. Personal interview. 12 Sept. 2017. Miller, Richard Earl. *As If Learning Mattered: Reforming Higher Education.* Cornell UP, 1998.

O'Banion,Terry. "Who Are the Curmudgeons?" *Community College Week,* 16 Feb. 2015. Accessed 21 Sept. 2017.

Ostman, Heather. *Writing Program Administration and the Community College.* Parlor P, 2013.

Pietrzykowski, Marc. Personal interview. 14 Sept. 2017. Perdue, Carol. Personal interview. 14 Sept. 2017.

Prendergast, Catherine. "Race: The Absent Presence in Composition Studies." *College Composition and Communication,* vol. 50, no. 1, 1998, pp. 36–53. Accessed 21 Sept. 2017.

Scott-Clayton, Judith. "Do High-Stakes Placement Exams Predict College Success?" CCRC Working Paper No. 41, 2012. *Community College Research Center, Columbia University.*

Shaughnessy, Mina P. *Errors and Expectations: A Guide for the Teacher of Basic Writing.* Oxford UP, 1977.

Shor, Ira. "Our Apartheid: Writing Instruction & Inequality." *Journal of Basic Writing,* vol. 16, no. 1, 1997, pp. 91–104. Accessed 21 Sept. 2017.

Smith, Wendy. Personal interview. 12 Sept. 2017.

Sullivan, Patrick. *Economic Inequality, Neoliberalism, and the American Community College.* Springer, 2017.

—. "The Two-Year College Teacher-Scholar-Activist." *Teaching English in the Two-Year College,* vol. 42, no. 4, 2015, p. 327. Accessed 21 Sept. 2017.

Tatum, Beverly Daniel. "The Complexity of Identity: Who Am I?" *Readings for Diversity and Social Justice,* vol. 2, 2000, pp. 5–8.

Toth, Christie. Personal conversation. With Anthony Warnke and Kirsten Higgins. 14 Oct. 2017.

Toth, Christina M., et al. "'Distinct and Significant': Professional Identities of Two-Year College English Faculty." *College Composition and Communication,* vol. 65, no. 1, 2013, pp. 90–116.

Toth, Christie, et al. "A Dubious Method of Improving Educational Outcomes: Accountability and the Two-Year College." *Teaching English in the Two-Year College,* vol. 43, no. 4, 2016, pp. 391–410.

Toth, Christie, and Patrick Sullivan. "Toward Local Teacher-Scholar Communities of Practice: Findings from a National TYCA Survey." *Teaching English in the Two-Year College,* vol. 43, no. 3, 2016, p. 247.

Supplemental Material

Part I: Reflection on the Origins of the Article

We initially conceived of this piece on a drive from Seattle to Corvallis, Oregon, for the Two-Year College Association Pacific Northwest conference in the fall of 2015. Hydroplaning down I-5 through a rainstorm, we used the convivial space of the car to interrogate our approach to community college reform initiatives while one of us drove and the other one typed. Two-year college faculty are accustomed to maximizing temporal and spatial resources, no matter how constrained, to the hilt.

Moving from the context of our college to the context of a scholarly conference triggered a familiar identity shift and inspired the conversation that created this piece. Our college and department cultures often marginalize scholarly identities and downplay our engagement with writing studies scholarship or at least subordinate that engagement to entrenched power structures; however, presenting at conferences regularly invigorates our attachments to our scholarly networks and academic values. In spaces like these conferences, we are not outsiders weirdly obsessed with scholarship. Rather, we are part of a network whose collective knowledge and stories help us to navigate dilemmas while centering progressive values. This shared scholarly disposition facilitates breaking the double-bind that too often holds us in hierarchical, familial bonds at our home institutions, which sometimes resist responding and changing according to student needs. Spaces and networks like those at TYCA-PNW offer a counterbalance to the social pressures of campus politics and provide necessary perspective on the struggles within our department (struggles that center around questions like integrating reading and writing, accelerated writing courses, and breaking out of racialized, monolingual norms).

Moving in the car from one context to the other symbolized the "in-betweenness" we inhabited as instructors at our institution. Perhaps it is no coincidence, then, that the idea of "critical reform" that we offer in our piece arose literally in transit. Critical reform attempts to broker competing pressures that, through our conversations with colleagues at peer institutions, we knew others also felt indebted to, constricted by, galvanized by, and wary of. We wanted to explicate that ambivalence and create language for what could feel like an unmoored, unrecognized position that we attempted to stabilize by naming "critical reform." The term "critical" attempts to broker the powerful, corporately underwritten influences on "reform" movements—namely those that emphasize improving retention and completion by rethinking deeply embedded structures like developmental reading and writing sequences in community colleges. In the car, we began staking out the positions that we felt we were perpetually negotiating. The desire for a taxonomy that would support discussion without creating a hierarchy of wokeness led us to create the heuristic for understanding "Enthusiastic Reformers," "Reform Resistors," and "Critical Reformers." If generating the language to describe the categories is one step in improving understanding and broker the complexities of our roles as teacher-scholar-activists, we feel that this taxonomy, while potentially reductive, offers a framework for opening space for conversation.

Part II: Description of Research Methods, Findings, and/or Pedagogical Impacts

As we sought to corroborate and enrich our perspectives, we wanted to more deeply explore, as well as codify, what we heard during informal conversations with like-minded colleagues. Although our personal experiences have a significant role in the article, we wanted to highlight other voices that intersected with our experiences, concerns, and dispositions. To find these compelling external voices, we solicited interviews from the TYCA national listserv. Those who responded agreed to go on the record about their experiences balancing institutional cultures with the desire to create change. Our methods were inspired by scholars who attempted to capture the often silenced voices of two-year college professors who engage in curricular and program change initiatives. We had previously read work like Caroline Calhoon-Dillahunt's "Writing Programs without Administrators: Frameworks for Successful Writing Programs in the Two-Year College," and Jeffrey Klausman's "Mapping the Terrain: The Two-Year College Writing Program Administrator," and we appreciated the depth of their qualitative representations that we know they had produced within seriously constrained resource contexts. Furthermore, while the research from the Community College Research Center and other large bodies uses quantitative and qualitative methods to study results of reforms, such research rarely asks the practitioners how they do their work or how they construct their agency and position themselves within entrenched power structures and social structures on their campuses.

The positive responses of the interviewees when we explained the parameters of our project buoyed us as we worked. They were interested in the sort of fish-bird creature of critical reform as they, too, had found that being pro-reform yet critical of processes and top-down models left them without a camp from which to seek support. We acquired a wealth of information from what our interviewees shared with us and felt privileged by the opportunity to represent and synthesize their voices. We, unfortunately, could only publish a fraction of the insights that they offered us.

On the pedagogical level, "critical reform" as a concept has led us to revamp our curricula and rework our pedagogies by, in part, making us critically adopt potentially overdetermined concepts and frames that frequently circulate in higher education. These include concepts such as grit, growth mindset, and asset-based orientations, among others. These pervasive terms have remarkable potential for improving the lives of underserved students as well as the hollow ring of trendy buzzwords. Adopting a critical reform stance has allowed us to feel comfortable with incorporating popular concepts and terminology while asking ourselves hard questions about how they individualize success and rely on "bootstraps" ideologies that ignore pernicious systemic inequities. Naming an orientation "critical reform" has compelled us to center equity frames in our pedagogies, emphasizing affective, rather than cognitive, approaches and centering students' identities. Scholars such as Steve Lamos and Dawn Coleman have helped us put equity and social justice at the heart of any reform conversation. We also continue to think through how equity-minded reform should account for the inequities of an exploitative instructional labor system.

Part III: Discussion Questions

1. How can someone seeking to do critical reform work acknowledge and value local knowledge and experience while still pushing beyond local resistance?

2. To what extent are these categories of "reform resistors," "enthusiastic reformers," and "critical reformers" reductive? What are the limits of this heuristic? What nuances might be lost?

3. What kind of curriculum/pedagogy follows from a "critical reform" stance? How is a critical reform stance similar to and distinct from critical pedagogy?

4. While reform is often centered on course structures and placement mechanisms, how can questions of undercompensated and undervalued labor become integral to the reform conversation? To what extent does the adjunct labor system belie the ethos of critical reform if left unchanged?

5. How can we make progressive traditions in writing studies referenced in this article—such as translingualism—more readily available to and clearly practical for the two-year college professoriate? What responsibility does writing studies have for making the voices and work of two-year college instructors a larger part of the knowledge-making in and about composition?

RESEARCH IN THE TEACHING OF ENGLISH

RTE is one the web at http://www2.ncte.org/resources/journals/research-in-the-teaching-of-english/

Research in the Teaching of English (RTE) is a broad-based, multidisciplinary journal composed of original research articles and short scholarly essays on a wide range of topics significant to those concerned with the teaching and learning of languages and literacies around the world, both in and beyond schools and universities.

Translanguaging, Coloniality, and English Classrooms: An Exploration of Two Bicoastal Urban Classrooms[1]

This article represents cutting edge research in writing studies, supplying new insights in the field's scholarship on translanguaging practices as they emerge in the discipline of rhetoric and writing and come to be deployed in K-12 settings.

---

1. *Research in the Teaching of English*, vol. 52, no. 1 © 2017 by the National Council of Teachers of English. All rights reserved.

Translanguaging, Coloniality, and English Classrooms: An Exploration of Two Bicoastal Urban Classrooms

Cati V. de los Ríos and Kate Seltzer

While current research focuses on the marginalization and educational crises of students classified as English language learners—whom we identify as emergent bilinguals (García & Kleifgen, 2010)—this article highlights some of the contexts for learning that help these students thrive academically, culturally, and socially in two urban English classrooms. We explore the concept of translanguaging (García, 2009a; García & Li Wei, 2014) through the writing of two students who took up this practice as a challenge to coloniality in English classrooms. We also outline how two secondary teachers in New York City and Los Angeles adopted a translanguaging pedagogy (García, Johnson, & Seltzer, 2017). Through our analysis of two focal emergent bilingual students, we demonstrate how a translanguaging pedagogy—one that puts students' language practices at the center and makes space for students to draw on their fluid linguistic and cultural resources at all times—is a necessary step forward in twenty-first-century English instruction. Our findings illustrate that the teachers' translanguaging pedagogies disrupted the inherently monolingual and colonial tendencies of English classrooms through curricula that promoted metalinguistic awareness and reflection about their own linguistic and cultural identities, and integrated students' diverse language practices to push back against colonialist ideologies. Our study adds to the nascent body of literature that translates theories of translanguaging into practical pedagogical approaches in secondary English classrooms.

As one of the largest school-aged populations, Latinxs[1]—with their concomitant diverse demographic profile—are far from a monolithic entity. However, despite their diversity and unlike most immigrant groups, Latinxs share a history of US domination, intervention, and occupation that spans centuries in Latin America and in the United States itself (González, 2000). Within the United States, García (2009b) notes that the linguistic colonization of Latinxs unfolded through"a policy of eradicating Spanish by encouraging a shift to English"(p. 111). She explains that the United States has done this "by adopting a policy of debasing and racializing Spanish, linking it to subjugated populations, immigration, poverty, and a lack of education" (García, 2009b, p. 111).

Power-laden social, linguistic, and racial hierarchies saturate the lives of Latinxs in myriad ways, primarily through the "coloniality of being" (Mignolo, 2000), where Latinx children's lived experiences, schooling, and languages are surveilled through restrictive policies. While studying the translingual practices of Latinx youth is not a new phenomenon, few empirical studies examine how secondary English classrooms use translanguaging pedagogies. In addition, the colonial roots intertwined with English education, especially for Latinx youth, make these classrooms fertile ground for decolonial and translingual approaches.

This article focuses on releasing Latinx youth's translingual voices as they write against colonial language ideologies in two bicoastal cities. As Latinx youth constitute the largest student population in both California and New York, we examine Latinx students from two urban English classrooms taught by two teachers (one monolingual and the other bilingual) to understand how translanguaging pedagogies transpired across contexts. Rather than separate students' language practices, the teachers adopted "discursive and pedagogical practices that break the hegemony of the dominant language in monolingual classrooms" (García, Flores, & Woodley, 2012, p. 45). Our collaboration between a Chicana researcher and a White researcher lent insight into one another's examination of curricula that encouraged "border thinking" (Mignolo, 2000), or the knowledge generated from the exterior borders of the modern/colonial world. For the mostly Mexican and Dominican youth in our studies, their existence in and ties to the United States are laced with tumultuous colonial pasts and unique but similar histories of immigration (González, 2000). These histories became the subject of inquiry and resistance through a translingual approach to English instruction.

Morrell's (2015) call to action for more "courageous leadership" (p. 317) in dismantling the linguistic racism in our nation's English classrooms inspired our research collaboration. Our data, which include participant observation, field notes, and analysis of student writings, illustrate how the teachers' implementation of a translanguaging pedagogy—particularly their *stance*, or their set of beliefs about students and their language practices, and their *design*, their organization of classroom life that brought to the surface the diversity of students' language practices (García et al., 2017)—benefited Latinx bilingual students. Thus, our collaboration inspired two interrelated questions: (1) *How do two teachers in English classrooms implement translanguaging pedagogies?* and (2) *When such pedagogies are implemented, what language and literacy practices emerge from Latinx bilingual students?* Through our analysis, we illustrate that the two teachers' reimagining of the English classroom through a translanguaging lens made space for students to reflect on their linguistic and cultural identities and use their rich language practices to resist colonial ideologies.

The term *translanguaging* describes the language practices of our participants. Rather than start with socially constructed "languages" (and thus discuss how students "switch" between such "languages"), we start with the *speakers*, whose creative and critical enactment of their holistic repertoire (Makoni & Pennycook, 2007; Li Wei, 2011) cannot be separated into such dualities as "first/second" or "standard/nonstandard" language. We believe that translanguaging transcends these false dichotomies that reproduce monoglossic language ideologies and continue to shape the discourse about language in our society (García, 2009a).

SUBVERTING THE ENGLISH-MEDIUM CLASSROOM

We connect the theoretical contributions of Mignolo's (2000) "border thinking" with sociolinguistic conceptions of bi/multilingualism as dynamic (García, 2009a). Both Mignolo's work and the concept of translanguaging are integral to the cultural, epistemic, and discursive borderlands (Anzaldúa, 1987) that US Latinx immigrant youth often navigate in "English-medium" classrooms. We draw from these theories to examine the educational discourses and practices that value the depth of knowledge production of Latinx youth.

Coloniality and Border Thinking

According to Quijano (2001), *coloniality* refers to long-established systems of power that surfaced as a result of colonialism and continue to control labor, social relationships, and the sanctioning of knowledge. Coloniality manifests in various domains in society: (1) the coloniality of *power* references the relationship between modern forms of exploitation and power (Quijano, 2000); (2) the coloniality of *knowledge* represents the impact of colonization and racism in the construction of knowledge (Mignolo, 2000; Quijano, 2000); and (3) the coloniality of *being* primarily affects everyday lived experiences and language, with language being the primary place where knowledge is inscribed (Mignolo, 2000, as cited in Maldonado-Torres, 2007). Throughout the Americas, and in the United States specifically, the coloniality of being persists through the monolingual and monocultural schooling of Indigenous and Latinx youth.

As equity-minded scholars dedicated to the "epistemic democratization" (Mignolo, 2011, p. 169) of our nation's classrooms, we draw on Mignolo's (2000) notion of "border thinking" to explore how colonial histories continue to inform restrictive educational contexts, especially as they pertain to the languaging2 (Makoni & Pennycook, 2007) of emergent bilinguals. Mignolo (2000) conceptualizes border thinking as "an other thinking" (p. 66), which includes thinking "between two languages and their historical relations in the modern world system" (p. 74). According to Mignolo, the current world system lies at the nexus of modernity and coloniality and cannot be explained or analyzed without foregrounding colonialism. Current ethnic, racial and social hierarchies are the product of European colonialism in the Americas that dates back to 1492. These legacies of colonialism grant power to certain people while dehumanizing others through what Mignolo identifies as the *colonial difference*. In turn, border thinking emerges within the interstitial spaces of the colonial difference and emanates from the very epistemic borderlands where the colonial/modern global design intersects with local histories. As a theoretical framework, border thinking is primarily concerned with recognizing the subaltern knowledge production of people living in ongoing colonial or formerly colonized nations, and is also concerned with the subjectivities of those who did not physically cross borders, but rather had borders cross them.

Coloniality and English-Medium Spaces

English-medium spaces are particularly mired in coloniality. Part of the poststructuralist process to "disinvent" English is the recognition that "languages were, in the most literal sense, invented, particularly as part of the Christian/colonial and nationalistic projects in different parts of the globe" (Makoni & Pennycook, 2007, p. 1). Elements of this coloniality are still at work in US schools, namely in restrictive language policies that police those students whose language practices do not align with "Standard English" (Silverstein, 1996). Because students in English classrooms are tasked with learning "English"—treated as a bounded and teachable subject—their language practices are especially scrutinized (Martínez, 2016). To disinvent the "subject" of English in schools is, in effect, an effort to redefine English-medium spaces that leave little room for alternative ways of languaging. By jettisoning the idea that the inclusion of other languages "interferes" with English, our studies embrace the reality of linguistic contact and highlight the fluid ways that bilingual Latinxs language in urban contexts. We take up Pennycook's (1995) argument for a new understanding of the role of English in the classroom, one "in favour of a critical paradigm that acknowledges human agency and looks not only at how people's lives are regulated by language, culture, and discourse but also at how people both resist those forms and produce their own forms" (p. 48). In other words, though English most certainly shapes Latinx students' education, Latinx students also *shape English* in ways consistent with their location on the borderlands. Taking this stance, English classrooms can invite "the process of using language against the grain, of the empire writing back to the centre . . . of using English to express the lived experiences of the colonized and to oppose the central meanings of the colonizers" (Pennycook, 1995, pp. 51–52). To use English in this way defies its standardized uses in the classroom. For the Latinx youth in our two classrooms, the use of English was always intertwined with Spanish. Students' ways of languaging were aligned with García's (2009a) conceptualization of dynamic bilingualism, which views bilingual speakers' languages not as static or balanced, but flexible and responsive to the communicative context.

According to García et al. (2017), *translanguaging* refers to "both the complex language practices of multilingual individuals and communities, as well as the pedagogical approaches that draw on those complex practices to build those desired in formal school settings" (p. 2). Thus, to adopt translanguaging means taking linguistic fluidity as the norm and building pedagogy from students' language practices. Translanguaging holds "the potential to release ways of speaking of subaltern groups that have been previously fixed within static language identities and hierarchical language arrangements and that are constrained by the modern/ colonial world system" (García, Flores, & Woodley, 2012, p. 48).

With this in mind, we follow Young's (2009) argument for a shift away from teaching students of color to "code-switch" because of the term's implicit separation of their language practices, which he relates to the Jim Crow construct of "separate but equal." Teaching students to code-switch reifies language ideologies that designate one language (i.e., "Standard English") as powerful and simultaneously relegate others to the margins. Instead, students of color should be taught to "become more effective communicators by doing what we all do best, what comes naturally: blending, merging, meshing dialects" (Young, 2009, p. 72). We use *translanguaging*, moreover, to describe both the pedagogical approaches our teachers took in their classrooms and Latinx students' language practices because of the term's inherently transgressive nature. Teaching students to engage in translanguaging, rather than code-switching, supports the border thinking necessary to challenge coloniality through borderlands language and literacy practices (Cervantes-Soon & Carrillo, 2016).

Latinxs, Colonization, and Resistance

Despite xenophobic ideologies that continue to propagate English Only policies, Latinx communities in the United States continue to be highly bilingual (Krogstad & González-Barrera, 2015). Schools, as institutions of assimilation, operate under the ideology of the coloniality of being, where the colonizer's qualities are deemed superior to those of subjugated populations (Mignolo, 2000). Thus, this review of literature: (1) provides a brief examination of the ways in which Latinxs have been colonized, (2) points to literature that demonstrates the ways in which K–12 Latinx emergent bilinguals resist colonialist classroom ideologies, and (3) explains our choice of *translanguaging* over terms of "appropriateness" (Flores & Rosa, 2015) such as *code-switching*.

The Colonization of Latinxs

Mignolo (2005) notes that Latin America is a constructed idea that emerged from Christian expansionism and the modern/colonial roots of racism. Colonialist wars waged against the Indigenous Americas beginning in the sixteenth century continue to bear heavy and oppressive legacies five centuries later, spanning the racial violence, religious persecution, linguistic colonization, slavery, and genocide (Mignolo, 2005) that comprise Western civilization's foundational logic. These legacies have been inscribed in contemporary racial, political, and social hierarchies throughout Latin America (Mignolo, 2000).

Coloniality is not solely covert subjugation, but also the West's enduring economic, political, and epistemological presence and force throughout Latin America (Mignolo, 2005). The surge of immigration from Latin America to the United States and the accompanying demographic shift, which González (2000) calls the "Latinization of the United States," are the product of the United States' expansionist economic and territorial history. González distinguishes Latinx immigration and presence in the United States as different from European immigration to this country in at least three ways: (1) Latinx immigration is closely tied to the needs and growth of the US empire; (2) racial and language ideologies in this country have had the effect of moving Latinxs not from immigrant to mainstream status, but from an immigrant to a linguistic/racial caste status; and (3) the greatest number of Latin Americans have arrived since the United States became the dominant world power. In direct relation to these increasing Latinx immigration trends, the economic circumstances that allowed European immigrants to assimilate and rise socioeconomically are no longer present (González, 2000).

The disjuncture between histories of immigration, language policies, and the realities of the lives of immigrants coalesce into a tempest that shapes the K–12 experiences of the majority of Latinxs in our nation's schools (Gándara & Hopkins, 2010). The education of Latinx children in the United States continues to be shaped by legacies of imperialism, where colonial schooling buttresses "a single system of thought" (Willinsky, 1998, p. 10) and an internalized oppression by the colonizer (Urrieta, 2009). Furthermore, Latinx youth have been subjected to both de jure and de facto schooling segregation (González, 1990; Laosa, 2001; Orfield, 2004), where colonialist curricula continue to strip Latinx youth of their cultural, racial,

and linguistic identities. Forms of "subtractive schooling" (Valenzuela, 1999) persist and often portray Latinx children as "missing" so-called dominant forms of language (Rosa, 2016) and cultural capital (Yosso, 2005), and locate educational inequalities in "deficiencies" in students' communities rather than in structural systems of power (Gutiérrez, 2006). Lastly, the 2010 legislative attacks on Mexican American studies in Tucson Unified School District best represent state-sponsored assaults on Latinx histories, literacies, and ways of knowing (Cammarota & Romero, 2014). Border thinking as a critical response to coloniality helps us honor the knowledge production that is often silenced within Whitestream curricula (Urrieta, 2009) that center the histories and contributions of Euro-Americans (Sleeter, 2005). In addition, as we outline below, by releasing students' voices from monolingual ideologies that separate their languages into the "two solitudes" (Cummins, 2008), translanguaging becomes a method of theorizing and enacting pedagogies for Latinx bilinguals that enables them to speak and write from the margins and
against empire.

Translanguaging as Resistance

Restrictive language policies have been implemented all over the United States, but especially in California, Arizona, and Massachusetts, which have banned bilingual education despite large numbers of Latinx students. Many scholars (Crawford, 2000; Gándara, 2000; Uriarte, Tung, Lavan, & Diez, 2010) have taken a critical view of these policies, citing the negative effects of a linguistically subtractive education. By limiting and devaluing students' language practices, they argue, we also limit and devalue who they are and what they can do. Despite this hostile climate, teachers and students have subverted such restrictive policies by translanguaging, drawing on their diverse language practices for both academic and socioemotional well-being. The term *translanguaging* has mainly been used to describe pedagogies in classrooms geared toward teaching emergent bilinguals English, such as English as a second/new language (ESL/ENL) and TESOL, as well as bilingual settings. Growing numbers of empirical studies on the use of translanguaging have been conducted in PreK–8 dual-language settings (Durán & Palmer, 2014; Gort & Sembiante, 2015; Martinez, Hikida, & Durán, 2015), afterschool contexts with bilingual/multilingual K–8 learners (Daniel & Pacheco, 2016; Martínez-Roldán, 2015), the college composition classroom (Canagarajah, 2013), and community or heritage-language classrooms outside the United States (Creese & Blackledge, 2010). Fewer studies have examined the use of translanguaging in secondary English classrooms in the United States.

Efforts to translate theoretical work in translanguaging into pragmatic approaches in secondary classrooms are emerging. For example, promising translanguaging pedagogies in English classes include García and Leiva's (2014) examination of a teacher who leveraged students' proficiency in bilingual hip-hop to mobilize their biliteracy and to challenge the cultural and linguistic privileging of monolingualism in English classrooms. Due to the intense focus on text analysis in secondary English classrooms, some studies have explored the use of genres such as poetry (Seltzer & Collins, 2016) and monologue (de los Ríos, 2016) to understand how translanguaging relates both to literacy development and socioemotional well-being. Additionally, Stewart and Hansen-Thomas's (2016) case study of one bilingual youth underscores the need for sanctioning translanguaging spaces in secondary classrooms through the leveraging of students' transnational worlds and literacies.

Translanguaging against "Appropriateness"

Our study extends this body of translanguaging scholarship by focusing specifically on the transgressive nature of translanguaging. We argue against what Flores and Rosa (2015) call *appropriateness-based approaches* to language education. As in Young's (2009) argument against code-switching, Flores and Rosa assert that these approaches do little to challenge the underlying racism that designates certain language practices as "standard" or "academic"; instead, these terms must be understood as "language ideologies rather than discrete linguistic practices" (p. 152). This means that teaching students that an ability to "switch" between their "home languages" and "academic language" leads to success ignores the reality of White supremacy and coloniality by which the White listening subject others the non-White speaking subject in racialized ways.

By taking up the theoretical perspectives and pedagogies associated with translanguaging—as opposed to appropriateness-based approaches steeped in what Flores and Rosa call raciolinguistic ideologies—the teachers in our studies invited students' fluid bilingual language practices that voiced border thinking and challenged coloniality and related ideologies. Our studies illustrate that translanguaging does far more than simply "scaffold" instruction for emergent bilinguals; it functions as a "border tongue"(Mignolo, 2000) that enables students to critique the coloniality still present in their lives and schooling.

Two Cities, Two Classrooms, Two Students

This article draws from two yearlong ethnographic studies that explored the literate and linguistic practices of Latinx youth enrolled in English classrooms that employed translanguaging pedagogies. Specifically, we looked for instances of students using translanguaging in both their writing and classroom conversations to push back against the kinds of language ideologies that go hand-in-hand with coloniality. By training our eyes and tuning our ears to students' translanguaging, we became aware of how this languaging went hand-in-hand with border thinking and saw how students drew on their multiple language practices and cultural positionings to write back to empire (Ashcroft, Griffiths, & Tiffin, 2003). In the following sections, we briefly describe our individual research settings and participants. We then discuss our individual processes of data collection and analysis while also explaining our positionalities as racially diverse researchers. Last, we explain how we moved from the analysis of our individual studies toward the collaborative process of analysis across both studies.

Settings and Participants

De los Ríos's 10-month study took place in an 11th- and 12th-grade English elective Chicanx/Latinx studies course offered at an urban public high school in the greater Los Angeles area. According to California Department of Education data, the school demographics at the time were 85% Latinx, 12% African American, and 3% undisclosed; 81% of the student body received free or reduced lunch. About 42% of the student body was classified as English language learners, with the primary language being Spanish. The Chicanx/Latinx studies course was composed of first- and second-generation Chicanx students (of Mexican descent) at various points on the bilingual continuum (Hornberger, 2003). The teacher, Arturo Molina,3 was a first-generation bilingual Chicano male who was born and raised in the working-class immigrant community where the school was located. Prior to this research in his classroom, Mr. Molina was not aware of the term or theory of translanguaging, yet he had already developed curricular and pedagogical approaches that reflected translanguaging. Mr. Molina, then in his seventh year of teaching, shared that "it only makes sense" to use a pedagogy that values both Spanish and English when working with bilingual youth (Field note, November 13, 2014). His existing engagement with translanguaging was one of the primary reasons his classroom was selected for inquiry.

Seltzer's study took place in an English classroom at a small public high school in a borough of New York City. Of the approximately 460 students at the school, 70% were Latinx and 28% were African American, nearly 90% qualified for free or reduced lunch, and 23% were labeled as English language learners. Though the large majority of these students spoke Spanish, there were also Fulani speakers from West Africa and small numbers of Arabic, Urdu, and Albanian speakers. Lauren Ardizzone, a White, English-speaking woman who had taught at the school for nearly 10 years, taught the English class. Because of the school's emphasis on inclusion, students classified as ELLs were programmed into Ms. Ardizzone's "mainstream" English classroom and received push-in services from an ESL teacher. This meant that Ms. Ardizzone's English classroom contained Latinx students from across the bilingual continuum, as well as non-Latinx students traditionally viewed as monolingual. The two focal student participants from our classroom studies were chosen through criterion-based purposive sampling (Corbin & Strauss, 2008). Though border thinking and translanguaging were pervasive in both Mr. Molina and Ms. Ardizzone's classrooms, we include Lourdes's[4] and Anna's writing because these students were particularly representative of these language and literacy practices. Lourdes, a student in Mr. Molina's classroom, was a first-generation Chicana student who grew up in a bilingual and bicultural immigrant household in a working-class neighborhood east of Los Angeles. As a self-identified "brown-skinned woman," she embraced both her Mexican and American identities. In Ms. Ardizzone's classroom, Anna was a vocal participant and sophisticated thinker. A self-described "dark-skinned Latina" of Dominican descent, Anna often used both English and Spanish to respond to texts and participate in classroom discussions, though she reported more comfort with English than Spanish.

A Word about Our Participants

We use the term *emergent bilinguals* to refer to the population the federal government has called *LEP* (*limited English proficient*) and many call *ELLs* (*English language learners*). Some scholars attempt to break down these categories further, using terms like *SIFE* (*student with interrupted/incomplete formal education*), *newcomer*, *LTELL* (*long-term English language learner*), or *RFEP* (*redesignated fluent English proficient*) to describe participants. Though we agree that terms like *ELL* or *LEP* are far too simplistic and reductive to describe these young people, we are also wary of the myriad labels placed upon bilingual students in school (Gutiérrez & Orellana, 2006). Though the two young women in our studies were at different points on the bilingual continuum and were classified by different terms in the eyes of the state, we refer to them as *emergent bilinguals* to emphasize their linguistic strengths and the fluid, shifting nature of their practices as they "do" being bilingual (Auer, 1984).

Data Collection and Analysis

Data were collected from two ethnographic classroom studies with bilingual/ multilingual learners in secondary schools in Los Angeles and New York City. For de los Ríos's study, data collection consisted of participant observation with field notes and analytic memos, semistructured interviews with students, and the analysis of students' literacy artifacts. For Seltzer's study, data collection consisted of participant observation with field notes and analytic memos, analysis of artifacts from students' classroom work, and audio recordings and transcriptions of classroom talk.

Our Positionality

Who we are has influenced both our individual studies and our scholarly partnership. Like Ms. Ardizzone, Seltzer is a White woman who taught English in New York City for six years to students with whom she did not share an ethnic, racial, linguistic, or socioeconomic background. De los Ríos, more like Mr. Molina, is a bilingual Chicana who was raised in an immigrant household. During her six years as a secondary literacy and ethnic studies teacher, she shared an ethnic, racial, and linguistic background with her students in California. Rather than distancing us, these differences have enabled us to "read" one another's data through different lenses, highlighting our inherent assumptions and biases. We believe that active and critical reflection on our own positionality has enabled us to uncover deeper understandings of our participants' words, which not only makes for more compelling scholarship, but respects and honors the young people who have lent us their voices. In addition, as we discuss in the Implications section, we believe that our scholarly partnership has important implications for future research in linguistically diverse English classrooms.

From Individual Studies toward Collaborative Analysis

To begin our collaborative data analysis, we first took an iterative approach to our own data that combined both inductive and deductive approaches (Maxwell, 2013). Deductive codes were used from existing literature and our own pilot studies and included translanguaging, language ideologies, and linguistic creativity. Inductive codes were derived from data analysis. For this, we adapted Luttrell's (2010) three-step analytical process, in which data were sorted, indexed, and read through a total of three times: the first reading consisted of looking for "recurring images, words, phrases and metaphors"(p. 262); a second reading consisted of looking for "a coherence among the string of stories" (p. 262); and a third reading consisted of a coding that used concepts from our theoretical framework. During the third reading, we looked for examples of border thinking in students' conversations and writing, translanguaging as a mechanism for students speaking back to coloniality, and the parts of Mr. Molina's and Ms. Ardizzone's classroom designs that created space for students to voice their border thinking through translanguaging. When comparing our data, we found strong overlap and connection with the codes *metalinguistic awareness, translanguaging,* and *reading their social/linguistic/cultural worlds*. With this in mind, we revisited our data to recode and pull relevant instances of these codes from students' writing.

To enhance the validity of our qualitative research, we served as peer debriefers (Lincoln & Guba, 1985) for each other's data analysis—we considered one another's methodological activities and provided feedback regarding the accuracy and completeness of our data collection and data analysis procedures. We engaged in cross-case analysis to mobilize our knowledge beyond our individual studies, to compare and contrast cases, and ultimately to produce new knowledge (Khan & VanWynsberghe, 2008). Additionally, we triangulated data from student journal writing, essays, and poems with classroom observations and field notes, and corroborated findings with one another.

Mr. Molina's Classroom

Through historical and literary texts and multimodal popular media, the yearlong Chicanx/Latinx studies class examined notions of colonialism, hegemony, and racism in the United States and how they affect communities of color, particularly Chicanxs and Latinxs. A veteran ethnic studies teacher, Mr. Molina taught the elective course, which met daily for 55 minutes. A hallmark of ethnic studies and Chicanx/Latinx studies literacy curricula is the aim of encouraging students to explore themselves as racial formations (Omi & Winant, 1994) and to effect social change (de los Ríos, López, & Morrell, 2015). This was done through engaging multiple writing genres, one of which was autoethnography. Within oppressed communities of color, autoethnographic writing has been a tool for decolonial thought and praxis (Aldama & Quiñonez, 2002) and a powerful mechanism for youth of color to write against the forms of coloniality that manifest in their everyday lives (Camangian, 2010). Pratt (1992) defines autoethnography as "instances in which colonized subjects undertake to represent themselves in ways which engage with the colonizer's own terms"(p. 6). If ethnographic texts have been historically used by the West to study the "Other," then Pratt argues that autoethnographic texts are a means for subjugated populations to respond to and dialogue with such colonial representations. As in the compelling work of Camangian (2010), Mr. Molina used autoethnography as an anticolonial pedagogical tool for students to examine the ways their identities were deeply entangled with colonial legacies.

In one lesson, Mr. Molina incorporated students' interest in the Mexican literary genre *corridos*. Corridos—historically written in Spanish—have long been central to the self-determination and literary landscape of Mexican people (Paredes, 1958). As a "border rhetoric" (Noe, 2009), corridos have origins in the nineteenth century and are short ballads that often narrativize heroes, border-conflicts, and struggles for justice (Simonette, 2001). Students listened to a border corrido in Spanish, "La Jaula de Oro," written by Norteño ensemble band Los Tigres del Norte, because it personifies "the spirit of border strife" (Paredes, 1958, p. 205) and explores the multiple identities that immigrants experience in the United States. The title, "La Jaula de Oro" or "The Golden Cage," serves as a poignant metaphor for the "American Dream," which often forces immigrants to assimilate in exchange for social and political acceptance. Students listened to the corrido in Spanish, annotating alongside the lyrics the words and themes that resonated with them. Students were then asked to write autoethnographic essays that explored the racial, cultural, and linguistic identities they had developed while navigating physical and metaphorical borders that are not always accepting of bi-/multilingual and transnational Latinx youth identities.

Upon listening to the corrido as a class, students were encouraged to think about the intergenerational relationships that exist within Latinx immigrant families and how Latinx children in the United States are often pushed to strip away their cultural and linguistic markers (Bejarano, 2005), which in turn can cause cultural tensions and a disconnect with their elders. The father figure in this corrido's lyrics states, *"Mis hijos no hablan conmigo, otro idioma han aprendido y olvidado el español. Piensan como americanos, niegan que son mexicanos, aunque tengan mi color."* (My children don't speak with me, they've learned a new language and have forgotten Spanish. They think they are Americans, and deny they are Mexican, even though they have my color.) One student, Lourdes, explored in her essay how, as a child, she would regularly answer her Spanish-speaking loved ones in English: I began to identify as Mexican when I was young. That's because when I was little I would often talk English in front of my abuelita [grandmother]. I will always remember how she would yell at us saying "Cuando yo estoy aquí, se habla español," and in English that means "when I am here, you only speak Spanish" but I specifically remember that because one of my cousins then said, "Abuelita, this is America, We can speak English." She then said "ustedes son mexicanos, no son gringos!" We all knew we were Mexican but didn't understand why she would make such a big deal, until later we realized that my abuelita could've let us speak English if she wanted because she understood a little bit, but she didn't want us to forget Spanish or where we came from. After that I was proud to identify as Mexican, because I was able to speak two languages and have two cultures.

As we see in Lourdes's writing, her abuelita reminds Lourdes that she is *Mexican,* and that in her abuelita's presence, she and her cousins need to speak in Spanish. Lourdes's use of both Spanish and English to recount this pivotal childhood experience exemplifies her use of her fluid linguistic repertoire to describe how language ideologies have affected her life, as well as the ways in which her abuelita has helped her resist colonialist practices.

In Lourdes's essay, she continues to highlight the tensions encountered in colonial liminal spaces. Akin to the father's description of his children in the corrido, Lourdes highlights the ways that she has been perceived and treated because of her cultural and linguistic markers:

> My other Latina friends who don't speak Spanish would think that it's weird for me to speak it or others who spoke a different kind of Spanish, como el español formal [like a formal Spanish], would also say the way that I spoke it was weird, like un español quebrado [like a broken Spanish]. As time went on I stopped caring how I was seen for being Mexican and I got past how I was treated for it, because it was them who had the problem, not me.

Lourdes's lived experiences were marked by coloniality through her peers' stigmatization. She was either an English-speaking Mexican who dared to speak Spanish or an English-speaking Mexican who spoke "broken" Spanish, both perspectives that reflect colonial gazes and function to police and shame young people like Lourdes. In this context, Lourdes was not *allowed* to be a Spanish speaker of any kind, which highlights the racialized language ideologies through which Flores and Rosa (2015) argue that Spanish speakers are held to colonial standards of correctness and linguistic purity governed by privileged White listening subjects. Translanguaging, however, moves discourses away from deficit notions of "brokenness" and offers the alternative of performing a dynamic bilingualism that releases speakers from the constraints of an "Anglophone" and "Hispanophone" ideological binary (García & Leiva, 2014) which has historically rendered US Latinx immigrant youth "languageless" (Rosa, 2016).

Moreover, Lourdes's writing is a type of "syncretic text" (Cruz, as cited in Gutiérrez, 2008), or a testimony that is "situated in subjective particularity" (p. 149) and contests dominant discourses about Latinxs. Lourdes's syncretic text—one which cultivated critical consciousness, linguistic and cultural pride, and historical memory—might not have occurred had Mr. Molina not intentionally created a translanguaging classroom design for this type of border thinking and writing. The combination of autoethnography and the teacher's classroom design enabled Lourdes to question and critique the stigmatization that bilingual people like her receive, even from Latinx peers.

Ms. Ardizzone's Classroom

Ms. Ardizzone took a metalinguistic approach to her curricular design and introduced students to the idea that instead of speaking one "language" (English, Spanish, etc.), we employ any number of *language practices* with different people, in different contexts, and for different reasons. Students investigated their own language practices as well as the connections between language and identity and language and power. Through various multimodal texts, students encountered writers and other artists who engaged in metalinguistic exploration of their own language practices. Because Ms. Ardizzone wanted to bring students' language practices to the surface, she designed lessons around texts that provided students with representations of the kinds of metalinguistic awareness and exploration she wanted them to take up themselves.

The two examples discussed here employ spoken-word poetry. Like autoethnography, spoken-word poetry is deeply rooted in critical reflection and transgression. Many literacy scholars have pointed to the power of poetry to engage students of color in discourses that denounce colonial and narrow representations of their rich literate practices (Camangian, 2008; Fisher, 2005). Here, Ms. Ardizzone purposefully chose spoken-word poetry that was metalinguistic in nature, modeling the kind of thinking she wanted students to engage in as well as the use of a translingual border tongue.

During a unit that unpacked the links between language and identity, students watched a spoken-word performance by Melissa Lozada-Oliva entitled "My Spanish." Lozada-Oliva's poem explores her own language practices and attempts to make sense of how those practices connect to her evolving identity. After watching a recording of the performance and doing a close reading of the poem, Ms. Ardizzone invited students to write their own poems that explored their relationships to their language practices.

As students wrote their poems, many took the opportunity to translanguage using English and Spanish practices to engage in border thinking about monoglossic norms imposed upon their identities. For example, Anna reflected on her fluid, changing language practices, acknowledging that her audience might or might not understand her:

> My English is good enough, yet . . .
> Mi ingles a veces se cambia,
> it's okay, you'll get the idea, no es
> muy complicado. Understand? No . . . OK.
> Doesn't matter!

When Anna writes that her English is "good enough" but still sometimes changes, she communicates to her audience that this contradiction "no es muy complicado" (is not very complicated). For Anna and other urban bilinguals like her, this understanding and awareness of her own fluid, dynamic bilingualism is uncomplicated. However, in the line that follows, she anticipates her audience's lack of understanding of this basic bilingual truth. Anna acknowledges this inevitable misunderstanding *and* pushes back against the need for her audience to understand her. The last line, "Doesn't matter!" speaks to her confidence as a bilingual and her refusal to change her language practices to conform and make herself comprehensible to a monolingual audience.

In a subsequent unit, Anna engaged in translanguaging to interrogate language ideologies that question bi-/multilingual speakers' competence. The idea that a language other than English might mix with and thus "contaminate" English erases the reality of linguistic contact and, in turn, silences those speakers whose ways of languaging do not align with an ideology of separateness and purity. Interestingly, the other text that Ms. Ardizzone chose, a spoken-word poem by Jamila Lysicott entitled "3 Ways to Speak English," does not discuss bilingualism in the traditional sense. In her brilliant performance, Lysicott explores her different *English* practices: one associated with her academic life, another with her Caribbean family, and another with her friends and community in urban Brooklyn, New York. Rather than view these practices as distinct, Lysicott characterizes them as interconnected and integral to her identity as a "tri-lingual orator." The poem celebrates her linguistic complexity and indicts language ideologies rooted in coloniality. For example, she writes of her own English, "But you can't expect me to speak your history wholly while mine is broken / These words are spoken / By someone who is simply fed up with the Eurocentric ideals of this season."

Lysicott's characterization of her English as "broken" is one that students in the class investigated at length. Though some took issue with the phrase, others understood Lysicott's wording to mean that if her language was "broken," it was only because it had been "stolen" and "raped" away throughout history. This text, like Lozada-Oliva's poem, is metalinguistic in nature, engaged in writing from the borders back to empire, and served as a mentor text for students' own border thinking. In a journal entry, Anna responded using her own interrelated language practices to the following lines of Lysicott's poem:

> But do not judge me by my language and assume
> That I'm too ignorant to teach

In response, Anna wrote:

> This was powerful for me. To me, a person that could speak more than one language is the best person to teach due to the fact that students won't be learning things in just one simple language but in multiple ones. When people tell her she can't teach it's like saying, "Oh yo no se why you so ignorant, para que you want to teach." What I liked about this was that people that know many languages are not ignorant, they are really living their lives in different languages at the same time. To me, being able to mix languages is something everyone should be proud of and should share with the rest of the world.

Anna's reflection on the poem reveals both her grappling with the ideas put forth in the poem and her pride in her own "mix" of language practices. She begins by aligning herself with Lysicott and talking back to the same people Lysicott did. To do so, Anna engages in translanguaging and takes down those who judge Lysicott as ignorant. Anna uses English and Spanish fluidly in her rebuke, which can be read in two ways. In one way, it is an authentic representation of how she uses both languages together to go after someone she sees as ignorant. Over the course of the year, translanguaging was often used in this way, both when students joked around and when they expressed real anger or frustration.

In another way, the translanguaged castigation could be read as a pointed critique of this line of thinking. By using two of her language practices so fluidly in this line of her journal, she challenges the idea that Lysicott—and she herself, as a bilingual speaker—would be judged too ignorant to teach. Instead, Anna turns the tables and calls this imagined group of people ignorant themselves, all while using language practices that only she and other bilinguals would understand. In her journal, Anna grapples with and talks back to the kind of linguistic discrimination that Lysicott (and, perhaps, she) encounters through a transgressive "other tongue" (Mignolo, 2000, p. 249). Anna's translanguaging here adds power and nuance to her rebuke, emphasizing that this monolingual, colonial ideology—not Lysicott or urban bilinguals like her—is indeed ignorant.

Making Space for Translanguaging

In putting our data side by side, we wondered how the two different classrooms and students' writings interacted with one another. Though the studies differed in focus, our shared interest in one another's work enabled us to see important connections, noteworthy differences, and implications in and across our data. First, we saw that an educator's commitment to enacting a translanguaging stance through a transgressive curricular and instructional design could result in border thinking and border writing, no matter the context. Given the malleable nature of a translanguaging approach in English education, racially, linguistically, and culturally diverse teachers can implement translanguaging pedagogies. Although Mr. Molina shared much with his students by way of ethnicity, class, and language background and Ms. Ardizzone did not, they both were able to leverage their students' bilingualism through student-centered, culturally sustaining (Paris, 2012) curricula. Both teachers created literacy units that paired translingual texts with critiques of linguistic colonization to mobilize students' racial, ethnic, and linguistic social worlds towards the center of their writing.

Second, Lourdes's and Anna's writing explores the possibility of evading the colonial expectation that their language practices (and they themselves) be "legible." In their writing, Lourdes and Anna normalize and make sense of their own language practices and engage in a discourse of resistance to coloniality in a translanguaged "other tongue." This opens up space for an alternative, proudly bilingual enunciation of themselves. The kinds of classroom activities we saw in Mr. Molina's and Ms. Ardizzone's classes—including the use of metalinguistic mentor texts that encouraged border thinking and translanguaging—highlight what Mignolo (2000) calls "cracks" in the "modern world system" (p. 23). Both teachers' translanguaging designs were integral to creating an environment where students began to take risks and break out of the monoglossic mold of school writing. By providing students with models of translanguaged writing, Mr. Molina and Ms. Ardizzone set the stage for the student writing that occurred in the classroom.

Last, the distinct geographical contexts of our two studies are important to consider. Los Angeles and New York City have had divergent immigration patterns, and thus students in the two classrooms had unique sociopolitical histories and experiences. The differences we saw in the two focal students' classroom writing indicate that the sociohistorical context of translanguaging matters. Though both pedagogical contexts built off students' locally situated histories, knowledges, and experiences and made space for the emergence of language and literacy practices we had not seen in other more "traditional" English classrooms, we nevertheless noted distinctions between Anna's and Lourdes's writing. In Los Angeles, Lourdes more explicitly identified herself culturally and linguistically throughout her writing than Anna. This could be because Lourdes was participating in an English class with an ethnic studies focus while Anna was in a "mainstream" English course. The actively antiracist and decolonial thinking evident in Lourdes's writing requires us as researchers and practitioners to reorient the English classroom to what Emma Perez (1999) identifies as a "decolonial imaginary," a place where people can imagine themselves as decolonial subjects whose futures will be on their own terms. A decolonial imaginary means moving past simply "allowing" students to draw on their everyday language practices and instead centers instruction and curricula around who and where students are as historically colonized and racialized subjects.

Reimagining the English Classroom

Restrictive language policies in US schools continue to work against students' translanguaging. Even in"bilingual"programs—and particularly in the burgeoning "dual language" programs across the country—students are held to monoglossic standards that separate their languages into bounded categories. As a result, students like Anna and Lourdes have not been exposed to pedagogy that emphasizes the interconnectedness of their language practices and the possibilities inherent in their translanguaging. Bilingual/multilingual students must be made aware that their ability to translanguage is integral both to their academic success and to their positioning as border thinkers who have the power to critique their English-medium learning spaces. The Every Student Succeeds Act includes what the Obama administration called "Investing in Innovation," which provides grants to schools and other educational organizations that wish to "expand the implementation of, and investment in, innovative practices that are demonstrated to have an impact on improving student achievement" (U.S. Department of Education, 2016). We believe that as one such innovation, translanguaging could be part of a larger reimagining of the education of emergent bilingual students across the country. Perhaps due to the lack of practice and explicit teaching, it is important to note that students' translanguaging did not appear in abundance in either classroom. While Anna and Lourdes were emergent bilinguals, and their teachers encouraged them to draw from their fluid linguistic repertoires, they still wrote primarily in English. This fact reminds us that Anna and Lourdes are products of years of monolingual, subtractive, and highly audited forms of schooling. Emergent bilinguals like Anna and Lourdes are constantly required to "perform linguistically in the dominant language according to a standardized variety imposed by the majority language community" (García, 2015, p. 131). The coloniality of these students' ways of languaging and being is always at work, even when teachers invite them to critique the very notion of linguistic colonization in their lives.

Early in our analysis, we found ourselves anticipating the question from scholars and educators, "How much translanguaging must there be in order to call it *translanguaging*?" Upon further reflection and discussion, we have come to see that our work invites a critique of this very line of questioning. Though students in both studies drew mostly on English in their classroom work, we do not believe this points to a deficit in students' bilingualism or indicates that the use of language practices other than English are unnecessary, two common arguments against translanguaging in the English classroom.

We will never know the extent to which bilingual students engage in translanguaging. As educators, we are only privy to the external manifestations of students' voices—the words they speak aloud and the words they write on the page. We do not know the sound of students' intrapersonal voices (García et al., 2017), those they hear as they alone make sense of their lived experiences in and out of school. To try to define translanguaging as a countable phenomenon, to track and organize students' fluid language practices in order to make them legible, is itself a colonialist process. Instead of attempting to control and "count" translanguaging, then, we urge educators to adopt a translanguaging stance that cedes some of that control and allows students' voices—however they emerge—to take center stage. It is our belief that taking up a translanguaging lens can allow room for more insurgent knowledges to destabilize and subvert the colonialities of power, knowledge, and being inscribed in dominant literacy and language classrooms.

Acknowledgments

We are deeply appreciative of Ofelia García and Danny C. Martínez for their instrumental feedback on earlier versions of this manuscript. We are also very thankful to *RTE* editors Ellen Cushman and Mary Juzwik, the anonymous reviewers, and Carolina Valdéz, who strengthened this article as well. Above all, we are indebted to the teachers and students highlighted in this article for trusting us with their brilliance. The Ford Foundation and NCTE's Cultivating New Voices among Scholars of Color program supported part of this research.

Notes

1. We recognize the contradictions embedded in the colonial label *Latino*. As researchers studying Mexican and Dominican youth, we use *Latino* to describe geographically derived national origin groups that compose a larger US racialized language community from Latin America. Additionally, we use *x* in *Latinx* as a gender-inclusive alternative to the masculinist *Latino* and the gender binary in *Latina/o*.

2. *Languaging*, according to Makoni and Pennycook (2007), refers to the selection and utilization of social features by speakers "in a seamless and complex network of multiple semiotic signs" (García, 2011, p. 7).

3. With the permission of the teachers, we use their actual names to highlight real teachers enacting the courage and pedagogical innovations that Morrell (2015) calls for in twenty-first-century literacy classrooms.

4. Students' names are pseudonyms.

References

Aldama, A. J., & Quiñonez, N. (2002). *Decolonial voices: Chicana and Chicano cultural studies in the 21st century.* Bloomington: Indiana University Press.

Anzaldúa, G. (1987). *Borderlands/La frontera: The new mestiza.* San Francisco: Jossey-Bass.

Ashcroft, B., Griffiths, G., & Tiffin, H. (2003). *The empire writes back: Theory and practice in post-colonial literatures.* New York: Routledge.

Auer, P. (1984). *Bilingual conversation.* Amsterdam: Benjamins.

Bejarano, C. L. (2005). *¿Que onda? Urban youth culture and border identity.* Tucson: University of Arizona Press.

Camangian, P. (2008). Untempered tongues: Teaching performance poetry for social justice. *English Teaching: Practice and Critique, 7*(2), 35–55.

Camangian, P. (2010). Starting with self: Teaching autoethnography to foster critically caring literacies. *Research in the Teaching of English, 45,* 179–204.

Cammarota, J., & Romero, A. (eds.). (2014). *Raza studies: The public option for education revolution.* Tucson: University of Arizona Press.

Canagarajah, A. S. (2013). Negotiating a translingual literacy: An enactment. *Research in the Teaching of English, 48,* 40–67.

Cervantes-Soon, C., & Carrillo, J. F. (2016). Toward a pedagogy of border thinking: Building on Latin@ students' subaltern knowledge. *High School Journal, 99,* 282–301.

Corbin, J., & Strauss, A. (2008). *Basics of qualitative research* (3rd ed.). Los Angeles: SAGE.

Crawford, J. (2000). *At war with diversity: U.S. language policy in an age of anxiety.* Tonawanda, NY: Multilingual Matters.

Creese, A., & Blackledge, A. (2010). Translanguaging in the bilingual classroom: A pedagogy for learning and teaching? *The Modern Language Journal, 94*(1), 103–115.

Cummins, J. (2008). Teaching for transfer: Challenging the two solitudes assumption in bilingual education. In J. Cummins & N. H. Hornberger (Eds.), *Encyclopedia of language and education* (2nd ed., Vol. 5, pp. 65–75). New York: Springer.

Daniel, s., & Pacheco, M. B. (2016). Translanguaging practices and perspectives of four multilingual teens. *Journal of Adolescent & Adult Literacy, 59,* 653–663.

de los Ríos, c. v. (2016). Writing from *La Panza!*: Exploring monologue literacies with emergent bilinguals. *English Journal, 105*(5), 75–80.

de los Ríos, C. V., López, J., & morrell, e.(2015). Toward a critical pedagogy of race: Ethnic studies and literacies of power in high school classrooms. *Race and Social Problems, 7,* 84–96.

Durán, L., & Palmer, D. (2014). Pluralist discourses of bilingualism and translanguaging talk in classrooms. *Journal of Early Childhood Literacy, 14,* 367–388.

Fisher, M. (2005). From the coffee house to the school house: The promise and potential of spoken word poetry in school contexts. *English Education, 37,* 115–131.

Flores, N., & Rosa, J. (2015). Undoing appropriateness: Raciolinguistic ideologies and language diversity in education. *Harvard Educational Review, 85,* 149–171.

Gándara, P. (2000). In the aftermath of the storm: English learners in the post-227 era. *Bilingual Research Journal, 24,* 1–13.

Gándara, P., & Hopkins, m. (eds.). (2010). *Forbidden language: English learners and r strictive language policies.* New York: Teachers College Press.

García, O. (2009a). *Bilingual education in the 21st century: A global perspective.* Malden, MA: Wiley-Blackwell.

García, O. (2009b). Racializing the language practices of US Latinos: Impact on their education. In J. A. Cobas, J. Duany, & J. R. Feagin (Eds.), *How the United States racializes Latinos: White hegemony and its consequences* (pp. 101–115). New York: Routledge.

García, O. (2011, November–December). From language garden to sustainable languaging: Bilingual education in a global world. *Perspective: A Publication of the National Association for Bilingual Education,* pp. 5–10.

García, O. (2015). Translanguaging and *abecedarios ilegales*. In T. M. Kalmar (Ed.), *Illegal alphabets and adult biliteracy: Latino migrants crossing the linguistic border* (pp. 131–136). New York: Routledge.

García, O., Flores, N., & woodley, h. (2012). Transgressing monolingualism and bilingual dualities: Translanguaging pedagogies. In A. Yiakoumetti (Ed.), *Harnessing linguistic variation to improve education* (pp. 45–75). Oxford, United Kingdom: Lang.

García, O., Johnson, S., & Seltzer, K. (2017). *The translanguaging classroom: Leveraging student bilingualism for learning.* Philadelphia: Caslon.

García, O., & Kleifgen, J. (2010). *Educating emergent bilinguals: Policies, programs, and practices for English language learners.* New York: Teachers College Press.

García, O., & Leiva, C. (2014). Theorizing and enacting translanguaging for social justice. In A. Blackledge & A. Creese (Eds.), *Heteroglossia as practice and pedagogy,* New York: Springer.

García, O., & Wei, L. (2014). *Translanguaging: Language, bilingualism and education.* Basingstoke, United Kingdom: Palgrave Macmillan.

González, G. G. (1990). *Chicano education in the era of segregation.* Denton: University of North Texas.

González, J. (2000). *Harvest of empire: A history of Latinos in America.* New York: Penguin Books.

Gort, m., & Sembiante, S. F. (2015). Navigating hybridized language learning spaces through translanguaging pedagogy: Dual language preschool teachers' languaging practices in support of emergent bilingual children's performance of academic discourse. *International Multilingual Research Journal, 9,* 7–25.

Gutiérrez, K. D. (2006). *Culture matters: Rethinking educational equity.* New York: Carnegie Foundation.

Gutiérrez, K. D. (2008). Developing a sociocritical literacy in the third space. *Reading Research Quarterly, 43,* 148–164.

Gutiérrez, k. d., & orellAnA, m. (2006). The "problem" of English learners: Constructing genres of difference. *Research in the Teaching of English, 40,* 502–507.

Hornberger, N. (ed.). (2003). *Continua of biliteracy: An ecological framework for educational policy, research and practice in multilingual settings.* Clevedon, United Kingdom: Multilingual Matters.

Khan, S., & Vanwynsberghe, R. (2008). Cultivating the under-mined: Cross-case analysis as knowledge mobilization. *Forum: Qualitative Social Research, 9*(1).

Krogstad, J. M., & González-Barrera, A. (2015, March 24). *A majority of English-speaking Hispanics in the U.S. are bilingual.* Retrieved from Pew Research Center website: http://www.pewresearch.org/fact-tank/2015/03/24/a-majority-of-english-speaking-hispanics-in-the-u-s-are-bilingual/

Laosa, L. M. (2001). Segregation of children who migrate to the US from Puerto Rico. *Education Policy Analysis Archives, 9*(1), 1–49.

Lincoln, Y. S., & Guba, E. G. (1985). *Naturalistic inquiry.* Beverly Hills, CA: SAGE.

Los Tigres Del Norte (2006). La jaula de oro. Retrieved from http://lostigresdelnorte.com/ main/music/view/7/Banda-Del-Carro-Rojo

Lozado-Oliva, M. (2015). My Spanish. Retrieved from https://www.youtube.com/ watch?v=fE-c4Bj_RT0.

Luttrell, W. (2010). *Qualitative educational research: Readings in reflexive methodology and transformative practice.* New York: Routledge.

Lysicott, J. (2015). Three ways to speak English. Retrieved from https://www. ted.com/ talks/jamila_lyiscott_3_ways_to_speak_ english?language=en.

Makoni, S., & Pennycook, A. (2007). *Disinventing and reconstituting languages.* Clevedon, United Kingdom: Multilingual Matters.

Maldonado-Torres, N. (2007). On the coloniality of being: Contributions to the development of a concept. *Cultural Studies, 21,* 240–270.

Martínez, D. C. (2016). Emerging critical meta-awareness among Black and Latina/o youth during corrective feedback practices in urban English language arts classrooms. *Urban Education.* Advance online publication. Retrieved from http://journals.sage pub.com/home/uex

Martínez, R. A., Hikida, M., & Durán, L. (2015). Unpacking ideologies of linguistic purism: How dual language teachers make sense of everyday translanguaging. *International Multilingual Research Journal, 9,* 26–42.

Martínez-Roldán, C. M. (2015). Translanguaging practices as mobilization of linguistic resources in a Spanish/English bilingual after-school program: An analysis of contradictions. *International Multilingual Research Journal, 9,* 43–58.

Maxwell, J. (2013). *Qualitative research design: An interactive approach* (3rd ed.). Thousand Oaks, CA: SAGE.

Menken, K. (2008). *English learners left behind.* London: Multilingual Matters.

Mignolo, W. D. (2000). *Local histories/global designs: Coloniality, subaltern knowledges, and border thinking.* Princeton, NJ: Princeton University Press.

Mignolo, W. D. (2005). *The idea of Latin America.* Malden, MA: Blackwell.

Mignolo, W. D. (2011). *The darker side of western modernity. Global futures, decolonial options.* Durham and London: Duke University Press.

Morrell, E. (2015). The 2014 NCTE Presidential Address: Powerful English at NCTE yesterday, today, and tomorrow: Toward the next movement. *Research in the Teaching of English, 49,* 307–327.

Noe, M. (2009). The *corrido*: A border rhetoric. *College English, 71,* 596–605.

Omi, M., & Winant, H. (1994). *Racial formation in the United States: From the 1960s to the 1990s.* New York: Routledge.

Orfield, G. (2004). *Dropouts in America: Confronting the graduation rates crisis.* Cambridge, MA: Harvard Education Press.

Paredes, A. (1958). *"With his pistol in his hand": A border ballad and its hero.* Austin: University of Texas Press.

Paris, D. (2012). Culturally sustaining pedagogy: A needed change in stance, terminology, and practice. *Educational Researcher, 41,* 93–97.

Pennycook, A. (1995). English in the world/ The world in English. In J. Tollefson (Ed.), *Power and inequality in language education,* Cambridge: Cambridge University Press, pp. 34–58.

Perez, E. (1999). *The decolonial imaginary: Writing Chicanas into history.* Bloomington: Indiana University Press.

Pratt, M. L. (1987). Linguistic utopias. In N. Fabb, D. Attridge, A. Durant, & C. MacCabe (Eds.), *The linguistics of writing: Arguments between language and literature* (pp. 48–66). Manchester, England: Manchester University Press.

Pratt, M. L. (1992). *Imperial eyes: Travel writing and transculturation.* New York: Routledge.

Quijano, A. (2000). Coloniality of power, Eurocentrism, and Latin America. *Nepantla: Views from South, 1*(3), 533–580.

Quijano, A. (2001). Globalización, colonialidad y democracia [Globalization, coloniality and democracy]. In *Tendencias básicas de nuestra* época*: Globalización y democracia* (pp. 25–61). Caracas, Venezuela: Instituto de Altos Estudios Diplomaticos Pedro Gual.

Rosa, J. D. (2016). Standardization, racialization, languagelessness: Raciolinguistic ideologies across communicative contexts. *Journal of Linguistic Anthropology, 26,* 162–183.

Seltzer, K., & Collins, B. (with Angeles, K. M.). (2016). Navigating turbulent waters: Translanguaging to support academic and socioemotional well-being. In O. García & T. Kleyn (Eds.), *Translanguaging with multilingual students: Learning from classroom moments* (pp. 140–159). New York: Routledge.

Silverstein, M. (1996). Monoglot "standard" in America: Standardization and metaphors of linguistic hegemony. In D. Brenneis & R. H. S. Macaulay (Eds.), *The matrix of language: Contemporary linguistic anthropology* (pp. 284–306). Boulder, CO: Westview Press.

Simonette, H. (2001). Banda*: Mexican musical life across borders.* Middletown, CT: Wesleyan University Press.

Sleeter, C. E. (2005). *Un-standardizing curriculum: Multicultural teaching in the standards-based classroom.* New York: Teachers College Press.

Stewart, M. A., & Hansen-Thomas, H. (2016). Sanctioning a space for translanguaging in the secondary English classroom: A case of a transnational youth. *Research in the Teaching of English, 50,* 450–472.

Uriarte, M., Tung, R., Lavan, N., & Diez, V. (2010). Impact of restrictive language policies on engagement and academic achievement of English learners in Boston public schools. In P. Gándara & M. Hopkins (Eds.), *Forbidden language: English learners and restrictive language policies* (pp. 65–85). New York: Teachers College Press.

Urrieta, L. (2009). *Working from within: Chicana and Chicano activist teachers working in whitestream schools.* Tucson: University of Arizona Press.

U.S. Department of Education. (2016). Programs: Investing in Innovation Fund. Retrieved from http://www2.ed.gov/programs/ innovation/index.html

Valenzuela, A. (1999). *Subtractive schooling: U.S.-Mexican youth and the politics of caring.* Albany: State University of New York Press.

Wei, L. (2011). Moment analysis and translanguaging space: Discursive construction of identities by multilingual Chinese youth in Britain. *Journal of Pragmatics, 43,* 1222–1235.

Willinsky, J. (1998). *Learning to divide the world: Education at empire's end.* Minneapolis: University of Minnesota Press.

Yosso, T. J. (2005). Whose culture has capital? A critical race theory discussion of community cultural wealth. *Race Ethnicity and Education, 8,* 69–91.

Young, V. A. (2009). "Nah, we straight": An argument against code switching. *JAC, 29,* 49–76.

Supplemental Material

Part I: Reflection on the Origins of the Article

Cati and Kate met as graduate students. They were both studying language and literacy and had enrolled in one of Dr. Ofelia Garcia's classes at The Graduate Center, City University of New York. The course explored "Critical Urban Literacies" and as students were invited to connect the course readings to their individual research studies, Cati and Kate soon saw important similarities across their yearlong case studies of English Language Arts classrooms. For their dissertation research, Cati and Kate were each working side-by-side with a teacher and documented how those teachers sought to reorient their classrooms into "translanguaging spaces" (Li Wei, 2012), by creating a classroom ecology and literacy curriculum that placed students' fluid language practices and creative and critical literacies at center of the classroom for learning. While the two teachers had different racial, ethnic, socioeconomic backgrounds, and teaching trajectories, Cati and Kate wondered what they would learn by placing their studies of these individual teachers alongside one another. Our many discussions about and across our work culminated into a transformative collaboration and a series of co-authored papers illuminating the possibilities of translanguaging for both teachers and students.

Part II: Description of Research Methods, Findings, and/or Pedagogical Impact

This article draws from two yearlong ethnographic studies – one in Los Angeles and one in New York City – that explored the literate and linguistic practices of Latinx youth enrolled in English classrooms that employed translanguaging pedagogies. Specifically, we looked for instances of students using translanguaging in both their writing and classroom conversations to push back against the kinds of language ideologies that go hand-in-hand with coloniality. Both researchers utilized ethnographic methods to gather a variety of data including field notes and analytic memos, semi-structured interviews with students, students' literacy artifacts and classroom work, and audio recordings and transcriptions of classroom talk.

To begin our collaborative data analysis, we first took an iterative approach to our own data that combined both inductive and deductive approaches (Maxwell, 2013). Deductive codes were used from existing literature and our own pilot studies and included *translanguaging, language ideologies, and linguistic creativity*. Inductive codes were derived from data analysis. For this, we adapted Luttrell's (2010) three step analytical process, in which data were sorted, indexed, and read through three distinct lenses. Through this collaborative coding process, we found strong overlap and connection with the codes *metalinguistic awareness, translanguaging, and reading their social/linguistic/cultural worlds*. With this in mind, we revisited our data to recode and pull relevant instances of these codes from students' writing. We served as peer debriefers (Lincoln & Guba, 1985) and mobilized our knowledge beyond our individual studies, to compare and contrast cases, and ultimately to produce new knowledge (Khan & VanWynsberghe, 2008). Additionally, we triangulated data from student journal writing, essays, and poems with classroom observations and field notes, and corroborated findings with one another.

Our two studies yielded a number of important findings. First, we saw that given the malleable nature of a translanguaging approach in English education, racially, linguistically, and culturally diverse teachers can implement translanguaging pedagogies. Although Mr. Molina, the teacher in de los Ríos's study, shared much with his students by way of ethnicity, class, and language background and Ms. Ardizzone, the teacher in Seltzer's study, did not, they both were able to leverage their students' bilingualism through student-centered, culturally sustaining (Paris, 2012) curricula. Second, we saw the writing of our two focal students, Lourdes and Anna, as engaged in an exploration of the possibility of evading the colonial expectation that their language practices (and they themselves) be "legible." In their writing, Lourdes and Anna normalized and made sense of their own language practices and engaged in a discourse of resistance to coloniality in a translanguaged "other tongue." This opened up space for an alternative, proudly bilingual enunciation of themselves. Lastly, we found that the two distinct geographical settings of our two projects lent insight into the differences we saw in students' writing. Los Angeles and New York City have had different immigration histories and patterns, and thus students in the two classrooms had unique sociopolitical histories and experiences. The differences we saw in the two focal students' classroom writing indicate that the socio-historical context of translanguaging matters.

Part III: Discussion Questions

1. What could a translanguaging pedagogy look like within different disciplines?

2. Where do you see evidence of coloniality in the ways that writing is traditionally taught? How, if at all, have you grappled with this evidence in your own pedagogy?

3. In what ways could traditional writing pedagogy be reimagined through a translanguaging lens for bi-/multilingual students?

WRITING CENTER JOURNAL

Writing Center Journal is one the web at http://www.writingcenterjournal.org/

The *Writing Center Journal* is the primary research journal in the field of writing centers and is an official journal of the International Writing Centers Association, an Assembly of the National Council of Teachers of English. The journal is committed to publishing strong empirical research and theoretical scholarship relevant to writing centers. In addition, we seek to build a stronger research community for writing centers. The *Writing Center Journal* aims to reflect the diversity of writing center contexts and other environments.

Unmaking Gringo-Centers[1]

Romeo Garcia's article, "Unmaking Gringo-Centers," extends the anti-racist work and agendas of writing centers by pointing to a problematic white-black paradigm that has emerged in the field's discussion and interrogation of race. This article asks us to listen deeply to the needs and attentions of all bodies who enter our writing spaces, substantiating an argument that progressive politics in writing center work have excluded other racial/ethnic groups such as Mexican American writers in their conversations on race and identity. This article is especially timely as it brings attention to the plight of Mexican Americans and the need for writing centers to include their voices and lived experiences as the field continues to research on power and race and advocate for social justice work. This article provides a thorough landscape of the field's work on race and a strong theoretical framework on listening and power to advocate for a need to deepen our conversations on power dynamics and race. We believe this work is especially important to nominate given the current political climate and rhetoric.

---

1. *Writing Center Journal*, vol. 36, no. 1 © 2017 by the International Writing Centers Association.

Unmaking Gringo-Centers

Romeo García

The article focuses on the topics of race and power and how they have been addressed in writing center scholarship. It asks the writing center community to listen, well and deeply, to how members have discussed and pursued anti-racist agendas. The article points to the emergence and presence of a white/black race paradigm. It is argued that this paradigm both limits what a writing center might do and undercuts the efficacy of anti-racist agendas. A method of listening is deployed in multiple ways to substantiate an argument that while pockets of progressive politics have taken place in writing center scholarship, the failure to attend to the conditions experienced by and the needs and interests of other racial/ ethnic groups such as Mexican American student writers is a limitation to writing centers' democratic desires. The article brings attention to the plight of Mexican Americans, both local and global, and moves to discuss what might be afforded in accounting for Mexican American students within writing center conversations on race and power.

Recuerdos[1]

Tengo un recuerdo. Over the weekend, I'd observe my tío work on cars. He'd pop the hood, turn the vehicle on, and listen. He'd step back and look at me and say, "Listen mi'jo to the car." He'd lean back in and work to locate the problem. My tío taught me about the capacious work involved in listening, the type of listening that centers the corporeal body as sensuous within and between the physical, temporal, and symbolic. Learning to listen as such situated me in space, place, and time. My ethos and politics of being, seeing, and doing emerged from these points of references.

---

1. This section pays homage to the importance of memory, which as Víctor Villanueva (2004) discusses, is central to understanding how the body is a corporeal vehicle of past and present.

I was born in the U.S., raised along the frontera of the Lower Rio Grande Valley (LRGV). Situated in-between the geopolitical border that separates two nations and the internal checkpoints that run parallel, I came to embody and experience the legacies behind the phrase *The Mexican*. It is a palimpsest of identity that is resounded in the mythology of normalcy and deviancy. The border/internal checkpoints and the archetypical inscription of *The Mexican*, together, function to accentuate who and what is "in place" and "out of place." From early on, I understood what it meant to carry the burden of meaning associated with this region's histories. You see, sin padre, raised by a single mother who was a high school dropout, I was just another statistic experiencing what it meant to be poor with limited access to resources and opportunities. But, I also learned how to practice survivance, resiliency, and agency through listening. Listening emerged in the crux of incoherencies and disjunctions. It became a form of expression that I found to be transformed and transformative. From listening, I understood that I was situated within a historical space and connected to historical bodies. In the liminal spaces created from my physical and metaphorical crossings and my awareness of how borders and internal checkpoints function and operate in my everyday, my body was thrusting the spaces between societal limitations and new self-definitions.

Tengo otro recuerdo. At grandma's kitchen table I'd sit after school every weekday. "¿Como te fue en la escuela?" she'd ask as soon as I walked in. I believe she'd ask both out of concern and a longing for the educational experience denied to her once she crossed la frontera. "Siéntate," she'd say to me. On the table would be her worksheets where she'd write in English and Spanish and a recorder where she'd practice translating Spanish to English (and vice-versa). She was told she could not go to school, but she eventually learned how to read and write in Spanish and English for herself. In our exchanges, at the table and on our daily walks, by means of cuentos and testimonios, she'd look at me and ask if I was listening and if I understood what she was saying. She'd say two things, "te digo esto para que sepas y aprendes" and "no te dejes mi'jo." Grandma was always teaching me. She was not content with the saying, "Así son las cosas," despite her tribulations. She expected no less from me. "Te digo esto para que sepas y aprendes" underscored "no te dejes," both educating me on what it meant to put in the work involved in listening to my surroundings, to know and learn, and what it meant to cultivate listening as a form of resolve in being heard and seen. Today, I continue to listen in these ways for the Mexican American of the LRGV continues to struggle with being heard and seen.

Último recuerdo. I am on my way to the university on a bus. I wait at the Sarita, Texas checkpoint. I've been here before, but this time it was different: I was entering gringoland on my way to gringodemia. "¿Tu papeles y a dónde vas?" the agent asked. The questions were part of his strategy of "checking" me, reminding me that the interpellation of my traceable history and palimpsest of identity (*The Mexican*) made permissible the "checking" of who I was and where I was going. I handed him my Texas identification card and stated I was going to college. This "checking" typifies my experiences beyond the LRGV. My grandma believed in higher education, and I did too. But, as a first-generation college student, accepted conditionally at a conservative and predominately white institution, what was at stake, among other things, was being an accomplice to my own degradation. The accumulation of white student protest against diversity (and students' treatment of people of color) and feedback from my professors had me thinking that maybe higher education was not meant for me. I could not change my accent, mi color, or the fact that I was not as academically prepared as others. I could not write, communicate, or be white. I shouldn't have had to. My tío once told me, "Tienes que enseñarles que puedes abrí un libro y leerlo también." I had to prove myself daily for I was always being "checked." I could not change who I was, but I listened as to know and learn and as to negotiate ways to be heard and seen. Then and now, I have learned that to engage in social action, I must listen in ways that centers my body as sensuous within and between the physical, temporal, and symbolic.

I have turned to listening to speak and research back to an academic community that knows little about students like me. Gringoland and gringodemia are functional and operational terms for me, because they reflect the circulation of rhetorics of assemblage, the surveillance and monitoring done on behalf of the hegemonic family, and the branding of "other" upon the body, all of which are meant to heighten the internalization of otherness for people of color. In my experiences, writing centers are not absolved from such cultural violence. The idea behind "un-making gringo-centers" implicates the writing center in such violence, but also calls attention to the opportunity for a community of scholars to make and re-make writing centers in productive and meaningful ways.

A Call to Action

Writing centers function within a tapestry of social structures, reproducing and generating systems of privilege. Even writing center mottos that are constructed with the best intentions disguise privilege, falling short of "challenging the links between ideologies of individualism and racism" (Grimm, 2011, p. 76). The power of whiteness continues to shape contemporary forms of management and control of practices and writing center scholarship, in particular the imperative to retrofit Mexican Americans into a white/black race paradigm.

The writing center community has witnessed the benefits o f cultural and/or critical-race approaches. For example, Anis Bawarshi & Stephanie Pelkowski (1999) illuminate the interplay between colonial power and writing centers. At the same time, however, the reductive racial frames—black struggles and white concessions—constitute a limit to what a writing center might do and reduces the efficacy of the postcolonial turn. The failure to name students of color who are not black, to address their conditions and experiences, and to discuss their needs as an essential aspect in writing center practices and theories illustrates a type of colorblindness at work.

To this day, I know of only one writing center article that responds to the needs of Mexican American students, more specifically Mexican American students at writing centers in borderlands institutions. I want to reiterate, then, Beatrice Mendez Newman's (2003) arguments briefly. By and large, border students are not ESL writers or speakers, they do not fit the non-traditional student definition, and they have specific needs and expectations that quite frankly cannot be approached by "traditional" instructional training. I am a border student. I am concerned—we should all be concerned—about how access and success can be hindered by the tendency to reduce or retrofit students of color. This concern requires an appropriate response, one that builds on the work of advocating for student voices and the work of providing pathways so that students can negotiate the academy successfully. This begins with listening, both in the sense that Krista Ratcliffe (2005) discusses it—as a code for cross-cultural communication—and as I conceive of listening—as a form of actional and decolonial work.

I am interested in applying the kind of listening—*para que sepas y aprendes*—discussed in the previous section as a form of intervention to writing center work on race, racism, and power. Writing centers, as previous scholarship has reminded us, are not free from power relations (see Geller, Eodice, Condon, Carroll, & Boquet, 2007; Greenfield & Rowan, 2011a; Grimm, 1996a, 1999, 2011; Villanueva, 2006). So, I call upon the members of the writing center community to engage in transformative listening. I do my part, first, by tracing the writing center's racial economy, quantitatively and qualitatively. Then, in resisting the retrofitting and/or reductionism of students of color, I focus on cultivating a *mindfulness of difference* by describing the geo, body, and mobile politics of knowledge that student's from the LRGV carry with them. In these ways, listening is functional and operational towards actional and decolonial work that can expand the role and work of writing centers.

We have been shown and, perhaps, share a vision of progressive politics in the writing center. Unfortunately, no matter how well intentioned and progressive a writing center has been, the "center" cannot hold without accounting for Mexican Americans (and other students of color) in the heterogeneous sense. I believe we can be engineers of theory and praxis, but committing to ethical and epistemically geared projects of social justice requires the undertaking of both transformative listening and "work." What that work entails is up to the writing center community; as for me, it involves unmaking gringo-centers and bringing into focus students from a community on the cusp of invisibility.

Experimenting with a Macro(Analytic) Approach

Imagine a disciplinary community of writing centers where a politics of knowledge is linked through networks and nodes. Instead of thinking of such politics as constantly being reproduced, consider how information is networked across space and time by language and ideology. Consider how writing center scholars and tutors have performed a "closed" close reading of Mexican American students and their writing. Absent some intervention into those "closed" reading approaches, they, too, function as checkpoints.

The idea of experimenting with a macro(analytic) approach emerged out of a concern for how my arguments in this article would be taken up. My intentions were to conduct a close-reading approach, but this method can be linear and, at times, limiting. As a novice to digital humanities, I undertook a macro(analytic) approach to visualize relevant topics inside and across texts, as nodes, as nodes in relationship with one another, and as nodes across a range of time(s) and space(s). I complemented my close-reading approach with computational tools that would allow me to contextualize my close-readings in new and meaningful ways.

For this essay, I collected over 30 years of writing center articles, many from The Writing Centers Research Project database and some from outside collections. I used two computational online text-mining tools: *Voyant Tools* for the purposes of revealing "frequency" and "distribution" of data across this 30-plus-year span and *Textexture* for the purposes of revealing the most influential keywords and most influential contexts of such data. The following are the results:

- 1980s: No-to-Low frequencies for identity terms "Black," "African," "African American," "Mexican," "Mexican American," "Chicano," "Latino," and "Hispanic."
- 1980s: No-to-Low frequencies for keywords "race" and "diversity."
- 1980s: High frequency for keyword "collaboration."
- 1990s: Mid-to-High frequencies for identity terms "Black," "African," and "African American."
- 1990s: No-to-Low frequencies for "Mexican," "Mexican American," "Chicano," "Latino," and "Hispanic."
- 1990s: No-to-Low frequencies for keywords "race" and "diversity."
- 2000s: High frequencies for "Black," "African," and "African American."
- 2000s: No-to-Low frequencies for "Mexican," "Mexican American," "Chicano," "Latino," and "Hispanic."
- 1980s–2000s: Most influential keywords and most influential contexts in the corpus: "writer," "tutor," "student," "experience," and "identity."

Although not conclusive, this data is significant for multiple reasons. First, there is the incorporation of "diversity" or "collaboration" without any clear understanding or articulation of how diversity might inform the practice of collaboration or how power dynamics materialize both within centers and their practices. This is indicated, for instance, with the High frequency for the term "collaboration," but Low frequency in regards to racial identities. This incoherent narrative of "diversity" and "collaboration" is evidence of the degrees in which whiteness shapes the imagining of both centers and practices as "safe" and "inviting." That is, although the interplay of buzzwords such as "writer," "student," and "identity" are in play, the centering of one (white/black) and the occlusion of all others erases difference with a white/black paradigm.

A Close-Reading Approach

In this section, I look at six texts chronologically, texts that have been recognized as participating in conversations pertaining to race and take up cultural and/or critical-race approaches. This approach is not meant to minimize the contributions of other writing scholars (see Bennet, 2008; Davila, 2006; DeCiccio, 2012; Dees, Godbee, & Ozias, 2007; Denny, 2010; Diab, Godbee, Ferrel, & Simpkins, 2012; Zhang, Amand, Quaynor, Haltiwanger, Chambers, Canino, & Ozias, 2013). I use these six texts, however, to substantiate an argument that while there are pockets of progressive politics reflected in writing center scholarship,[2] such scholarship is limited by a white/black race paradigm. While productive, theoretically and practically, current scholarship fails to attend to the conditions experienced by and the needs and interests of other minoritized and racialized groups other than African Americans, such as Mexican American student writers.

Nancy Grimm, a prominent writing center figure, in her multiplicity of works, continuously demonstrates an understanding of both the complicity of writing centers in institutional racism and the need for sustainable dialogue based on race for writing centers. In "The Regulatory Role of the Writing Center," Grimm (1996a) implicates the disciplinary community of writing centers:

---

2. See also Kail & Trimbur (1987), Lunsford (1991), DiPardo (1992), Grimm (1996a, 1996b, 1999, 2011), Bawarshi & Pelkowski (1999), Pemberton & Kinkead (2003), Murphy & Stay (2006), Geller, Eodice, Condon, Carroll, & Boquet (2007), and Greenfield & Rowan (2011a).

> I am going to take an unhappy approach to writing center work and suggest that we don't always accomplish as much as we think we do and that in the long run we sometimes do more harm than good. (p. 5)

Grimm's (1996a) work brings awareness of how the writing center's politics of knowledge creates social order and acts in service of maintaining the status quo of academic literacy. In explaining how important it is to think beyond the "local" and move towards reflecting on the politics and issues that underlie a "global" structural system, Grimm's (1996a) goal of developing an ideological model of literacy and an articulatory model of social change reveals how narratives of modernity as "progress" hide racist and classist agendas. In asserting the importance of confronting normalizing cultural beliefs as they bleed into a range of social spaces, Grimm (1996a) insists we must view literacy as multifarious and as possessing political and ideological significances. While not the first to establish the relationship between writing centers, social structures, and ideological processes (see Ede, 1989; Lunsford, 1991), Grimm's (1996a) article does stand as one of the few significant writing center publications of the time to recognize that theories of knowledge are unfolding during tutoring moments and are always contextually bound to race.

Bawarshi & Pelkowski (1999) problematize the relationship between race, language, and the idea of a writing center from a postcolonial stance. In "Postcolonialism and the Idea of a Writing Center," they expand upon the cultural theorist approach by Grimm (1996a) by articulating a relationship between colonialist agendas and the work of writing centers. As they discuss the consequences of subordinating marginalized discourses, they hold responsible institutions and institutional spaces that force upon student writers (e.g., basic and marginalized writers) a subjectivity of "other" all the while inculcating a rhetoric of modernity as emancipation. Coded within this rhetoric is the inscription of a colonial subjectivity onto exchanges between tutors and student writers, which are always already shaped by hegemony. In proposing a postcolonial writing center, Bawarshi & Pelkowski (1999) open space in the scholarship for a more efficacious account of race and racism by emphasizing that centers should take an active role in "postmodern" positioning—guiding and translating—and in engaging critically with students to "examine the axioms upon which academic structures are formed" (p. 54). This article demonstrates a critical turn in writing center scholarship that mirrors other larger critical conversations on critical literacy, culture, and postcolonial discourse.

The vein of progressive politics continues with Nancy Barron & Nancy Grimm (2002) whose resistance to colorblindness and racism shares a commitment to racial, generational, and cultural perspectives. "Addressing Racial Diversity in a Writing Center" centers the relationship between race, tutoring moments, and writing centers. Barron & Grimm (2002) write:

> Colorblindness is a way of avoiding the mess of racial history by pretending that racial differences don't exist. Students of color are supposed to write as their color didn't matter We suspect that many writing center workers have encountered students from diverse cultures who have implicitly been expected to engage in literacy in ways that deny their difference. (p. 59)

In moving from theorizing "productive diversity" to materializing "social change" in practical ways, Barron & Grimm (2002) discuss critically what it means to raise questions about race in tutoring moments and within writing centers. Thinking about racial difference, Barron & Grimm (2002) reflect on narratives of modernity as salvation (e.g., education as the road to equity) and progress (e.g., liberal ideology) and begin to consider how race affects almost every aspect of what we do in writing centers. They conclude that because racial encounters occur in unproductive ways every day in the writing center, the way to make transformative change is to make actionable peer tutor commitments to social responsibility within writing centers, particularly with regard to anti-racism.

In "A Call for Racial Diversity in the Writing Center," Margaret Weaver (2006) explores the philosophical and pedagogical contours of whiteness as it manifests within writing centers. Weaver (2006) holds culpable writing center scholars for their complacency with whiteness by analyzing and applying interventionist models that illuminate the gaps and limits of writing center discourse as it pertains to race. Weaver (2006) writes:

> Whether or not we like it and whether or not we acknowledge it, White writing center administrators are enmeshed in the maintenance of a racial educational system. We must begin to interrogate what is at stake in managing racial diversity. (p. 88)

Weaver (2006) concludes by asserting directors and tutors need to avoid being the "White Center" and learn how to be the "Write Center" (p. 89). She concludes with the conviction that writing centers will continue to face ethical and complex issues surrounding race and power. In *The Everyday Writing Center: A Community of Practice*, Anne Ellen Geller, Michele Eodice, Frankie Condon, Meg Carroll, & Elizabeth Boquet (2007) explore the degree to which, on one hand, the writing center has championed itself as a site of diversity and collaboration, while on the other, has been complicit by championing practices that reproduce dominant hegemony. Geller, Eodice, Condon, Carroll, & Boquet (2007) mount an argument for "dwelling" in uncomfortable places, and in the process they implicate the writing center community of practice in focusing too intently on safety and comfort. In combining theoretical and practical explorations, the "betwixt-and-between state" of writing centers and the everydayness of writing center work, Geller, Eodice, Condon, Carroll, & Boquet (2007) argue writing centers possess the structural authority to contribute to institutional change. Further, they call upon members of the writing center community of practice to recognize and resist the temptation to posit writing centers as politically neutral spaces. In their chapter on identity and racism, they relate racism within and across writing centers as social spaces to everyday manifestations of racism embedded within cultural logics and patterns. In discussing the deployment of racist rhetoric, aimed at an African American tutor, for example, they shed light on effects a nd affects o f r acism. U ltimately, t hey c all f or t utors a nd w riting c enter scholars to become "change-agents" who actively engage in anti-racism work.

Writing Centers and the New Racism, edited by Laura Greenfield & Karen Rowan (2011a), builds on existing frameworks established by prior scholars and attempts to respond to Harry C. Denny's (2010) questions about the importance of identity politics, social and cultural forces, and writing centers. The authors in this collection explore how writing centers are already raced (see Greenfield & Rowan, 2 011b), how they are not immune to racism (see Esters, 2011), and how centers contribute to the reproduction of white privilege with center "mottos" that disguise systems of privilege (see Grimm, 2011). Learning how whiteness works requires that tutors become theorists of race and racism (see Geller, Condon, & Carroll, 2011). In this process, there must be recognition of the absence of racial harmony in tutoring moments (see Valentine & Torres, 2011) and careful attention must be paid both to the type of anti-racist agendas implemented and the local and institutional culture in which such agendas are conceived and enacted (see Ozias & Godbee, 2011). Like the previous examples, this edited collection attempts to sustain conversations on race and racism and offers support for interventionist work in writing centers.

THE INSUFFICIENCY OF A WHITE/BLACK RACE PARADIGM

As well intentioned and progressive as the writing center community has been in taking up race and racism, the insufficiency of a white/black race paradigm—the black subject as the default "colonial" subject and the white tutor as a functional colonizer—poses a limitation. Remember, this paradigm does not need to be reproduced overtly, because it is sustained through its affective value. Consider Ratcliffe's (2005) description of how whiteness functions "overtly as a racial category that is privileged even if all white people do not share identical and economic privileges" (p. 12). A similar cultural logic works within a white/black race paradigm. My point is that because this paradigm is a consubstantial part of a dominant presentation and representation of race, writing centers may not be as equipped to account for how race operates and manifests. To move beyond the limits of a white/black race paradigm, and into a pluriversality of anti-racist agendas, a cultural dialogue of recognition, critique, accountability, and responsibility is needed.

Grimm's (1996a) argument to shift from the local to the global to understand colorblindness and racial injustice is constructive. But, before we can make this shift, we have to recognize how a white/ black race paradigm functions as a scalar logic that minimizes the plight of Mexican American history (see Carrigan & Webb, 2003; Delgado, 2009; Kaplowitz, 2005; Perea, 1997). Members of the writing center community should be aware and critical of the ways in which blackness in this paradigm is meant to stand for all struggles, as well as of the failure of this paradigm to account for the particularities of the experience of people of color who are not black. Grimm (1996b) writes, "Writing centers are supposed to deal with heterogeneity…and writing centers are expected to master and control this heterogeneity rather than interpret it" (p. 524). There is now a dialogue on race, power, and the status quo, but still, there remains a gap "between theorizing about difference in higher education and working with differences in the writing center" (p. 524). To see into fruition our democratic desires we must "work" to make that of which has remained absent present—other students of color. This means acknowledging difference and recognizing the differences within difference that play out in the particularities of the local and global.

Barron & Grimm (2002) do argue that race is much more complex than the historical binary construction of white and black. And, yet, there is still this false impression that Mexican Americans were not targets of white consolidation or participants in the struggle and discourse of civil rights. Members of the writing center community should be aware of the particular histories they privilege and those they simultaneously deny. Some scholars have taken up this argument, but inadequately—as if to apologize for not accounting for race beyond a white/black paradigm would be sufficient. There are alternatives to the apology. As a starting point, it is our responsibility as members of writing center communities to listen, well and deeply, in space and time, to material social conditions and social relations. This would counteract the reductionism and retrofitting of students. It is also our responsibility to acknowledge how writing centers are sites of space and place, memory, meaning, and knowledge making. The opportunity is there for cultivating relationships of difference and for strategically circulating how those relationships inform our pedagogies and contribute to the (re)-making of our centers. This involves so much more than theory, because what is at stake is the exclusion of others. What is further at stake is the opportunity to learn from the encounters and interactions that take place in our writing centers.

Anne Ellen Geller, Michele Eodice, Frankie Condon, Meg Carroll, & Elizabeth Boquet (2007) and Weaver (2006) argue race and racist legacies inform writing centers and practices and call for a writing-centered anti-racist approach. But again the writing center community lacks critical awareness of how much or the degree to which a white/black paradigm limits this call. So when Anne Ellen Geller, Michele Eodice, Frankie Condon, Meg Carroll, & Elizabeth Boquet (2007) focus on the example of discrimination against a black tutor without identifying and theorizing the experiences of other students or tutors of color, or when Weaver (2006) situates her critiques of whiteness within the frameworks of other scholarship that focuses on black subjectivity, they participate in this limiting. This occlusion, regardless of intention, continues to deny the lived experiences of racism that condition the writing lives of other students, such as Mexican Americans, as well as our membership and agency within writing center communities. What is needed is a transdisciplinary approach to the topics of race and power. This will help develop a different type of analysis, one that reevaluates the exigencies within which students are actually situated. To change the terms and content of writing center work on race and power, listening (para que sepas y aprendes) is needed in order to work beyond the limitation of a white/black paradigm. A transdisciplinary approach calls attention to space, place, and time.

Bawarshi & Pelkowski (1999) situate writing centers within a postcolonial context to attend to race, academic structures, and power. However, we must acknowledge that there are colonized subjects across the U.S. and around the globe still not living in a postcolonial world. The writing center community must be conscious of how histories of racial violence continue to be ignored and suppressed in the present. We must also be conscious of the extent to which students of color who are not black continue to suffer from this suppression. Some incorporate the concept of contact zones to describe students of color interactions. I am hesitant towards the use of contact zones. Yes, contact zones are about space, social relations, and negotiations. Problematic, however, are the fixity of space and the absence of time. Local contexts and circumstances require a more nuanced application of listening. Students carry with them the burden of their histories and geographies, they are marked with difference, and this is a truth for which we must account. It is our responsibility then to recognize the degrees to which historical and material conditions generate and reproduce everyday practices, as well as to acknowledge how the performativity of those practices are in the production of space and time. If we listen, well and deeply, writing centers are not stable or fixed, but the degree to which we offer up this space to be changed and transformed by student writers has yet to be observed. Writing centers have spatial and temporal attributes, and because of this, they are always becoming in the sense that centers are made through the particularities of bodily movements and actions. The degrees to which these actions are attributed to student writers, as makers of space and negotiators of macro and micro contexts, have remained to be discussed.

The idea of tutors as theorists of race and racism is bold (see Geller, Condon, & Carroll, 2011). As Ozias & Godbee (2011) illustrate in their conversation on grounding discussions of racism, there are substantive frameworks for envisioning and engaging in anti-racism. But, even the most well conceived political agendas continue to be permeated by Western thought. In this global current, difference seems to matter less and less, and with the erosion of local culture due to the production of homogenized global spaces (see Cresswell, 2004), it seems commonplace to flatten and/or erase the coexistence of other histories. But, difference matters. It is not possible to enact and engage in anti-racism agendas without a more robust analysis of race and power. The writing center community is in a unique position to research capaciously and position itself as a leader of critical discourse on race and power. But, in this struggle for changing the terms of conversations—to tutors as theorists of race and racism—the content and structure of the conversation must be revealed and altered. To attend to ideological apparatuses and structural oppressions (see Davila, 2006; Grimm, 1999), to "re-make our consciousness" (Condon, 2007, p. 30) and be "designers of a new world" (Barron & Grimm, 2002, p. 72), and to undertake a project of identity politics (see Denny, 2010) is messy work. While this work is taxing, we should rest assured that when we situate the locality of our centers and practices within sociohistorical and political contexts, we are improving the ways we listen and work with student writers.

I am invested in the anti-racism movement because I believe tutors can become engineers of critical praxis and theory. The question we must answer as a community is what is our rhetorical imperative? If our rhetorical imperative is anti-racism, then our transformative task must go beyond the white/black race paradigm. I mentioned earlier that we must reevaluate the exigencies within which students are actually situated and do so through a transdisciplinary approach. In the next section I apply listening, as passed down to me and cultivated through experiences, to the historical and material conditions of the LRGV. I incorporate space-time and materialist analysis, focusing on spatio and temporal difference and local/regional expressions of action and agency. I do so to bring attention to the exigencies in which these students are situated. Such analysis is required to move anti-racism agendas in the direction of pluriversality, to re-orient the writing center to the dynamics of space and time, and through this re-orientation, begin to see tutors not only as theorists of race and racism, but also as decolonial agents.

Towards a Mindfulness of Difference and a Mobile-Decolonial Framework

In listening to the historical sense of place (e.g., the LRGV) and bodies (e.g., Texas Mexican Americans), a simple analysis of colonialism from a postcolonial lens cannot suffice. I draw upon decolonial scholars to understand the intricate entanglements of a colonial matrix of power, spatio and temporal colonial difference, and a modern/colonial world. I do so, because even though colonialism as a political order has been destroyed in the U.S., there exists very effective means of management and control in the LRGV. I am interested in how the successive mapping of people and territories as "in place" and "out of place," "of time" and "stuck in space and time," applies to the Texas Mexican American in the LRGV. How, specifically, that is, does the colonial traffic in the present. I am also interested in the cultural displays of expression that adapt, reject, and/or transform global meaning. The following is not meant to be capacious in review; rather, it is meant to open up a space for a more nuanced type of analysis. I do, though, offer a list of references, parenthetically.

Race and ethnicity played an important role in the aftermath of the "discovery" and "conquest" of the Americas. Aníbal Quijano & Immanuel Wallerstein (1992) connect the discovery and conquest of the Americas with the construction of a "new" modern/colonial world system. Capitalism, according to Quijano (2000), produced a new mental category to codify the relations between inferior and superior. This new mental category would center on the idea of race—biologically and structurally—and racial classifications, creating an "interstate system" of hierarchal layers for control and rank order. The role of modernity (salvation, emancipation, and progress), uniquely, would be to conceal, and yet reproduce, imperial epistemologies and homogenous totality. Imperial epistemologies denied the dominated people their geographical locations and body-graphical politics of knowledge, while the imperial concept of totality, under the names of modernity and rationality, led to theoretical reductionism and the metaphysics of a macro-historical subject (see Mignolo, 2007; Quijano, 2007). For the Americas, race and the logic of coloniality, cloaked in the rhetoric of modernity, became the locus and testing ground for management and control over domains of power, knowledge, and subjectivity.

Decolonial scholars argue the modern/colonial world and its power differentials are unavoidable.[3] I find this to be true in listening to the local and regional histories of the LRGV and the effects of spatio and temporal colonial difference. The LRGV was the space where the barbarians lived (see De León, 1983). The "other" needed to be saved and civilized, or so goes the rhetoric of colonization. Yet, what ensued was the ideological strategy of delineating space for the "other" and the ideological belief that the "other" should be taken out of cultural and social life (see Pratt, 1992). To ensure inferiority, a subject/object paradigm of rational knowledge would emerge, wherein the "rational" subject would characterize the "other" either as absent or present in objectivized ways (see Quijano, 2007).[4] We see this today both in the lack of acknowledgment of Mexican Americans in history books and the legacy of *The Mexican*. As noted, *The Mexican* is a palimpsest of identity, a racialized imaginary that functions as an archetypical inscription of racial symbols and myths. The ability of this marker of difference to transcend space and time says something about how the colonial continues to traffic in the present. Nonetheless, spatial colonial difference created a social structure wherein *The Mexican* would remain "out of place."

In addition to the colonization of space and construction of spatio colonial difference, the colonization of time and construction of temporal colonial difference reflect yet another ideological strategy and belief. Arnoldo De León (1983), in his study of Texas Mexicans, writes, "What whites found in Texas…was that Mexicans were primitive beings who during a century of residence in Texas had failed to improve their status and environment" (p. 12). The shift from barbarism to primitive reflects an ideological strategy of temporalization. Johannes Fabian's (1983) notion of *denial of coevalness* and Walter D. Mignolo's (2007) *modern-time consciousness* are valuable here in that they offer insight into how temporalization meant the "other's" time was not the time of civilized history. Fabian writes, "temporalization is not an incidental property of historical discourse," it is an intentional

---

3. Mignolo (2000) writes that the "imaginary of the modern/colonial world system is not only what is visible and in the ground but what has been hidden from view in the underground by successive layers of mapping people and territories" (p. 24).

4. Quijano (2000) writes, "The inferior races are inferior because they are objects of study or of domination/exploitation/discrimination, they are not subjects, and most of all, they are not rational subjects" (p. 221).

practice of distance that requires "time to accommodate...one-way history: progress, development, modernity" (p. 78; 141). Stuck in space and apart from evolution, *The Mexican* would become and remain the "essential alterity of modernity" (see Dussel, 1993, p. 74).

The logic of coloniality would lead to historical and structural transformations that continue the oppression of the Texas Mexican American in the present. "The Mexican" problem took center stage on a local (and national) level. Texas Mexicans were displaced from their lands (see Carrigan & Webb, 2003; De León, 2009), politically and socially disenfranchised (see Bedolla, 2009; Rodriguez, 2007), taught inferiority both in the context of inferior schooling equipment and facilities (see Castellanos & Jones, 2003; Guajardo & Guajardo, 2004; San Miguel, 1998; Spring, 2005; Valencia 2000) and the undertaking of a pedagogical approach (see Blanton, 2007), and exploited for labor (see Gutiérrez, 1995). Because of a white/black race paradigm, this history is ignored or forgotten. Yet, I carry the weight of civilizing *The Mexican* people and saving "it" from itself, while struggling for political, social, and educational rights. Henry Giroux writes, "Colonizing of differences by dominant groups is expressed and sustained through representations in which the Other is seen as a deficit, in which the humanity of the Other is posited either as cynically problematic or ruthlessly denied" (p. 130). The colonial wounds remain fresh, because we are still seen as the "other" in society and approached as deficient in the academy. We continue to occupy a space in the American imagination, which my experiences can attest to, as "wetbacks" and "aliens." I carry the weight not only of the effects of colonization of space a nd t ime, but also that of the mind and body. The inequity gap in higher education between whites and Mexican Americans is just one example of this history trafficking in the present.

What the colonizing campaign found was that in this *Tejano cultural zone*, a people refused to reject their languages, traditions, and cultural identity and that this region was a distinctive subcultural area that reinforced cultural identity to place (see Arreola, 2002; De León 1982). Now consider this. Take U.S. 77 South towards the LRGV. No passport is needed. Yet, the almost 100-mile border that edges this region to the south, and the internal checkpoints that run parallel 70 miles north of it, are features that suggest a design meant to limit mobility. A border(ed) land is created, signaling the perception that "we"—my people in the LRGV—are stuck in space and outside of time. Literally, these features create a geography of exclusion (see Peters, 1998). We are interpreted as an othered space, monitored, and deprived of resources. There is no coincidence that this region has one of the highest concentrations of Mexican Americans, with some of the highest statistics for people living in poverty and some of the lowest statistics for high school completion and literacy acquisition. We do not live in postcolonial conditions. Yet, we do not remain in our past nor are we contained by the colonial legacies behind *The Mexican*. The rhetoric and culture of the LRGV is our identity and helps form our expression of representation. We adapt, reject, and transform global flows through our geo-graphical, body-graphical, and mobile-graphical displays of expression that continues to make and re-make place and geography. What is needed in rhetoric and composition and within the writing center community is a *mindfulness of difference*, a framework that re-imagines the common local and global distinction as a dialectical relationship and that begins at the scale of human practice and a community's political economy (see Pred, 1995; Tsing, 2000).

The LRGV has its own language, memory, and meaning making practices, as well as its own historical and collective memories and political economy, which may or may not connect with other Mexican American community's. It should go without saying that Mexican Americans have evolved in disparate ways. Yet, because of this global current of interconnections and universal cultural logics, Mexican Americans from the LRGV remain on the cusp of invisibility. I propose a mobile-decolonial interpretive framework to counteract this global effect of no units or scales counting except for that of the global (see Tsing, 2000). In this modern/colonial world, it is imperative for me to briefly account for how we, in the LRGV, respond to the rhetoric of stillness and fixity through place, knowledge, and meaning-making practices. This involves accounting for geo-body-and-mobile-graphical displays of expression (human practice) and how these cultural displays of expression say something about locality, regionality, and globality.

The idea of historical spaces and bodies suggests social and cultural practices and actions that are constellative (see Scollon & Scollon, 2004). This is partly central to the significance of the *Tejano cultural zone* and the meaning and knowledge-making practices that make it possible. In the LRGV, our integration of Spanish and English in the everyday occurs both in the physical (public and home) and material forms (billboards, documents, etc.).[5] This is a bilingual and binational area. Our ethnolinguistic and ethnocracial identities stem from historical discourse, but also from our experiences with macro and micro forces. They are reflective of our meso-political negotiations that are created and performed in the locality of language practices (see Pennycook, 2010). The type of language practice that occurs in the LRGV undercuts English as the lingua franca and deserves to be studied in-depth for its structural and linguistic features. It deserves such study, because it is the circulation and flow of bilingualism that makes the LRGV a unique subcultural area.

It can be a challenge to evidence a local and regional identity, especially because I am aware and critical of the romantic essentialism that takes place in the academy. In this context, I find myself thinking about the importance of communicating and circulating stories. Judy Rohrer (2016) writes,

> We are the set of stories we tell ourselves, the stories that tell us, the stories others tell about us, and the possibilities of new stories. I am these stories. I lived them or I inherited them, and they live vibrantly and turbulently in and around me. All stories are political; they involve power that has structural underpinnings and material consequences. (p. 189)

Stories, as Malea Powell discussed in her 2012 CCCC Chair's address, "take place" and "practice place into space" (p. 391). The essence of storytelling is discourse and rhetoric in action. I believe it is possible for both to delineate a collective ethos and regional identity. If places are about relationships and the "place of peoples, materials, images, and the systems of difference that they perform" (Sheller & Urry, 2006, p. 214) and if place is a "meaningful component in human life" (Cresswell, 1996, p. 51) "produced through action" (Cresswell, 2004, p. 7), what is the import of a regional identity and what does it say about locality and globality? There is a phrase from a billboard that can be seen and read in and across the LRGV. It reads "Pa' Los Que Saben," which translates into "For those who know." Pa' los que saben, we say, "soy del Valle y somos Valle." This form of self-representations

---

5. Michelle Hall Kells (2002, 2004), in her longitudinal studies of language practices in South Texas, argues Tex Mex functions as a code, which promotes social cohesion and solidarity against the homogeneity of the English language.

undercuts the totality of national identity and is a statement of how Western values and systems breakdown. Our bodies are constellative, evidenced in the stories we tell, but we are the possibilities of new stories too as we have and continue to make and re-make place and geography in ways that illuminate our decolonial imperative—to be seen and heard. "Valley/ Valle" is a regional form of representation.

The import of "soy del Valle y somos Valle" is made possible through the flow and circulation of *politics of mobility* in place (see Cresswell, 2010). Micro-bodily movements have traceable histories and geographies. The rhetoric and culture of the LRGV does not exist on its own. Movement, Tim Cresswell (2006) argues, is "rarely just movement" because it "carries with it the burden of meaning" (p. 4). The gente of the LRGV, with their historical and definitional struggles over creating meaning, have made and continue to re-shape a political economy by which dissent is possible. Attentiveness to the entanglements of meaning, representation, and praxis involved in mobility illuminates, according to Cresswell (2006), how people are agents in the production of space and time. The people of the LRGV are not stuck in space or behind in time, quite the contrary. Being literate in "contexts for movement" and "product of movement," I see the LRGV as constantly being made in ways that allow the people to be heard and seen in and on their own terms. Yes, micro and macro structural properties generate and reproduce time-space specific social systems and social/ cultural practices. But, our meso-political negotiations offers insight into our residual cultural displays of human agency and practice, as well as the emergent features of our politics of being, seeing, and doing. This is where the possibility of new stories exists and where bodies thrust the spaces between societal limitations and new self-definitions to be heard and seen. This is where contested modernities meet alternative modernities.

Pa' los que saben, the LRGV has and continues to be a stronghold for Mexican values and traditions. Despite the legacies of colonization and the manifestations of coloniality, our movement, representation, and praxis have created a kind of slippage that results in a "sad oppressor complex." The people of the LRGV have, to some degree, flipped relations with whites who live and move through that region. The "oppressor" becomes "sad" as the "other" has understood and overcome, at least partially, their racist and material conditions.[6] Whites continue

---

6. The idea of a "sad oppressor" emerged out of conversations with colleagues at the 2016 Conference on College Composition and Communication.

to exert domination in this region, but their practices of domination have to be adaptive. While full decolonization has not been achieved, social relations have been changed and transformed.

Look, my point is this: the flattening of difference, the representation of sameness within difference that so saturates writing center talk about race, is untenable and damaging to people like me who come from the LRGV or from other Mexican American communities. If we are going to talk about and attend to race in writing centers, either in the historical or contemporary sense, Mexican Americans cannot be absent. Civil rights' is so often regarded as a predominantly black effort. Pa' los que saben, there are court cases that preceded and created legal precedent for *Brown v. Board of Education* (1954): *Del Rio ISD v. Salvatierra* (1930s), *Alvarez v. Lemon Grove School District* (1931), *Mendez v. Westminster* (1947), and *Delgado v. Bastrop ISD* (1948). We have and continue to struggle with being heard and seen. As a site of place, meaning, and knowledge-making, the writing center is about interactions and encounters, co-existing histories and trajectories, and is always in the process of being made. Imagine, then, if we included other groups into conversations on race and power and engage in micro-scales of observation. We'd not only be able to see all students as shaped by meaning, but also obverse them in production of space-time. Our writing centers would be forever transformed for the better. Mexican Americans like me, are knocking on the door, will we acknowledge them?

Decolonial Initiatives and Agents

There is impact, regardless of intention, when anti-racist writing center scholars make a call for action for members to be agents of change, and yet, in the historicizing and premising of this change, occlude the lived experiences of racialized others. Members of the writing center community need to continue to make an explicit commitment to addressing race and power. This much, prior scholars in our field have gotten right. But, any acknowledgment that does not account for differences will be insufficient. We need to change the terms and content of writing center work. For instance, there is a contradiction when the objective is to create a "safe space" and articulate an ethical appeal of anti-racism. The terms have changed, but the cultural logic surrounding the notion of "safe space" is still steeped in the dialectic of management and control. To redefine and re-orient our work, I offer the following suggestions.

Tutors need to cultivate a mindfulness of difference and be mindful of spatio and temporal attributes. The writing center was once promoted as a "safe space" or "home." Let me remind you, this space has been historically, culturally, and rhetorically marked by whiteness and white culture (see Grutsch McKinney, 2005; Zhang, Amand, Quaynor, Haltiwanger, Chambers, Canino, & Ozias, 2013). For me, the writing center is neither my safe space nor my home. To be mindful of difference is to: call attention to the structural practices in which re-create realities of dwelling; engage in social justice goals by a retraining of the mind that works to understand capaciously how race and power influences all; and participate in a different logic that invests in a pluriversal understanding of differences. A mindfulness of spatio and temporal attributes approach-es students as makers of place, shapers of subjectivities, and engineers of negotiated linguistic and literate practices. Alastair Pennycook (2010) argues that a "focus on movement takes us away from space being only about location, and instead draws attention to a relationship between time and space, to emergence, to a subject in process—performed rather preformed—to becoming" (p. 140). I suggest that we imagine student writers as having the capacity to change and/or transform face-to-face consultations, and, having the capacity to change and/or transform the writing center as a whole. We must remember that space and place is the product of interrelations and social and cultural actions that is always in the process of being made (see Massey, 2005). I believe the writing center can be re-made from being a "white center" to being a center in the process of becoming.

Tutors need to become decolonial agents. This "work" will look and be different from tutor to tutor. Laura Greenfield (2011) in, "The Standard English' Fairy Tale" writes,

> If most educators allow their unchecked racism to guide their beliefs about language, it stands to reason that the teaching and tutoring practices long advocated in the fields of composition and rhetoric and writing center studies that are premised on these attitudes are necessarily racist, too. Included in this indictment are those contemporary pedagogies—especially those contemporary pedagogies—celebrated by those of

> who fancy ourselves 'progressive' in the world of teaching and tutoring writing. (p. 35)

Progressives continuously return to the idea of contact zones. Mary Louise Pratt (1992) defines the contact zone as a site "where disparate cultures meet, clash, and grapple with each other, often in highly asymmetrical relations of domination and subordination" (p. 7). Consider Greenfield's (2011) argument that tutoring practices and contemporary pedagogies cannot go unchecked. It stands too, then, that in approaching consultation sessions from the approach of "contact zones," the projection of fixed finite sets of rules and features in space and time too needs to be checked. We cannot just accommodate differences nor should we approach differences as that to be solved. I suggest that we consider and "check" tutoring practices and contemporary pedagogies for how they maintain center/periphery binaries and uphold other forms of management and control. To be a decolonial agent is to be ethically and socially committed to social justice for all. It is having those critical conversations that question even the well-intended progressive and leftist practices.

Tutors need to become theorists of race and racism. Cecilia Shelton and Emily Howson (2014) pose the question, "How, then, do writing centers 'escape'—even if imperfectly or incompletely—from cooperation in racially-biased academic practices on an institutional level" (n.p.). It begins, I argue, in conversations on race and racism (blatant and micro-aggression), no matter how uncomfortable it makes us, especially in this age of celebration of diversity in writing centers. In, "Blind," Victor Villanueva (2006) suggests, "Those of us dedicated to anti-racist pedagogy, to addressing the current state of racism find ourselves everyday trying to convince folks that there really still is racism, and it's denied" (p. 11). He argues that "We can't buy into the silencing of what we know is still racism" (18). I agree. Consultants must acknowledge the material reality of race and the reality of racism. But, this is not enough. I suggest that consultants add a rhetorical feature to their pursuance in becoming theorists of race and racism. So while we may be told not to worry about race and racism, with an education in rhetorical discourse, we know this to be a matter of articulation from the centers of power, rather than truth. To become theorists of race and racism, we must have a greater understanding, then, of how rhetoric works.

Tutors need to engage in reflection and reflexivity. I suggest tutors become researchers of their everyday experiences and researchers of the everyday of writing centers. The idea of rhetorical listening and thick description complement each other, and so, I propose the use of portfolios as a meditational and reflexive activity of decolonial action. Portfolio writing should start at the beginning of the academic year, with the tutor initially responding to what it means to engage in anti-racist work. With weekly or monthly reflections, it would be in the best interest of the tutor to begin describing the everyday thickly, accounting for the ways in which power, issues of race, and social relations play out. In the process, the tutor should be working towards a transdisicplinary approach in putting race and power into dialogue. This way, race and power go beyond the content and scope of writing center work and into the global issue of race and power. This way, the tutor does not only work to reveal and alter the structures that limit social justice agendas and goals in the writing center, but takes on this ethical and epistemically geared project beyond the writing center space. I see the directors playing a critical role in this type of transformative learning and praxis. The director should be the one to initiate these conversations on race and power, holding professional development sessions and monthly meetings dedicated to such topics. On the individual level, the director should hold accountable the tutor and their contributions to a portfolio. That being said, the director should open up space for the tutor to present and discuss what has been learned and practiced and what remains to be learned.

On a final note, tutors as decolonial agents should not make assumptions about students, no matter how well intended those assumptions are. Part of engaging in decolonial initiatives and action is to change the content and terms of conversations. So, in preparation for working with the Mexican American population, for example, you might read a text such as Gloria Anzaldúa's *Borderlands/La Frontera*. But, tutors might also find books like Américo Paredes's *George Washington Gomez* or José Limón's *Dancing with the Devil* useful. This will provide a greater perspective on the dynamic and complex community of Mexican Americans. To universalize Mexican Americans in the experience of Gloria Anzaldúa, as is the case with academics, is to perpetuate the same logic of sameness of difference, which fails to see differences within difference.

The history for professionalization by the writing center community of practice and its efforts towards sustaining a vital positionality in the academy are well documented (see Barnett, 1997; Carino, 1995, 1996; Harris, 1982; Kail, 2000; Riley, 1994; Simpson, 1985; Summerfield, 1988; Yahner & Murdick, 1991). We are now in a position to create new knowledges and practices and to create meaningful coalitions that can work together for sustainable change. To be pedagogical and epistemic engineers, new perspectival horizons must be explored, and in charting those horizons, new tools must be used. In this process, a new design must be engineered for attending to race in the writing center. At the center of this design should be a new, not merely renewed, practice of listening: listening as a form of understanding and action.

Conclusion

Some might say: "my writing center does not have students from the Valley." You will. Remember, not accounting for the Mexican American community in conversations of race and power is to be complicit in a white/black race paradigm. My own academic viaje has taken me from the LRGV to Upstate New York. While my circumstances have changed as a writer, my experience of being in "white" centers with all their many manifestations of "whiteness" continues to make me conscious of being a writer and now a tutor of color. But, like my grandma used to say to me, "no te dejes." So, when I hear some argue that race or racism does not exist in their writing center, I challenge this assertion. I've seen white students switching their appointment in order to work with a white tutor. I've heard white tutors apologize for other students' discrimination. In those moments, I am reminded of how important it is to continue to listen. My grandma was a great mentor in this way. I carry with me those memories of sitting in the kitchen, learning from her how to listen to the world. Listening to the world, well and deeply, is a lesson that all of us should learn, whoever and wherever we are. Like my grandma would say, para que sepas y aprendes. This type of listening will help nuance what it means to talk about race and difference(s).

Acknowledgments

Thanks needs to be given to Frankie Condon whose constant support and investment in this project has re-assured me of the importance of my work. To the editors of WCJ, thank you for first seeing my vision, working through it with me to ensure it comes into fruition, and for believing in the importance of my work for the writing center community.

References

Arreola, D.D. (2002). *Tejano South Texas: A Mexican American cultural province*. Austin: University of Texas Press.

Barnett, R. W. (1997). Redefining our existence: An argument for short and long-term goals and objectives. *Writing Center Journal, 17*(2), 123–133.

Barron, N., & Grimm, N. (2002). Addressing racial diversity in a writing center: Stories and lessons from two beginners. *Writing Center Journal, 22*(2), 55–83.

Bawarshi, A., & Pelkowski, S. (1999). Postcolonialism and the idea of a writing center. *Writing Center Journal, 19*(2), 41–58.

Bedolla, L. G. (2009). *Introduction to Latino politics in the U.S.* Cambridge: Polity Press.

Bennet, B. C. (2008). Student rights, home languages, and political wisdom in the writing center. *Writing Lab Newsletter, 32*(5), 7–10.

Blanton, C. K. (2007). *The strange career of bilingual education in Texas, 1836-1981*. College Station: Texas A&M University Press.

Carino, P. (1995). Early writing centers: Toward a history. *Writing Center Journal, 15*(2), 103–115.

Carino, P. (1996). Open admissions and the construction of writing center history: A tale of three models. *Writing Center Journal, 17*(1), 30–48.

Carrigan, W. D., & Webb, C. (2003). The lynching of persons of Mexican origin or descent in the United States, 1848 to 1928. *Journal of Social History, 37*(2), 411–438.

Castellanos, J., & Jones, L. (Eds.). (2003). *The majority in the minority: Expanding the representation of Latina/o faculty, administrators and students in higher education*. Sterling: Stylus.

Condon, F. (2007). Beyond the known: Writing centers and the work of anti-racism. *Writing Center Journal, 27*(2), 19–38.

Cresswell, T. (1996). *In place/out of place: Geography, ideology, and transgression*. Minneapolis: University of Minnesota Press.

Cresswell, T. (2004). *Place: A short introduction*. Malden: Blackwell Publishing.

Cresswell, T. (2006). *On the move: Mobility in the modern western world*. New York: Routledge.
Cresswell, T. (2010). Toward a politics of mobility. *Environment and Planning D: Society and Space, 28*, 17-31.
Davila, B. (2006). Rewriting race in the writing center. *Writing Lab Newsletter, 31*(1), 1–5.
DeCiccio, A. (2012). Can the writing center reverse the new racism? *New England Journal of Higher Education*. Retrieved from http:// www.nebhe.org/thejournal/can-the-writing-center-reverse-the-new-racism/
Dees, S., Godbee, B., & Ozias, M. (2007). Navigating conversational turns: Grounding difficult discussions on racism. *Praxis: A Writing Center Journal, 5*(1).
De León, A. (1982). *The Tejano community, 1836-1900*. Albuquerque: University of New Mexico Press.
De León, A. (1983). *They called them greasers: Anglo attitudes toward Mexicans in Texas, 1821-1900*. Austin: University of Texas Press.
De León, A. (2009). *Mexican Americans in Texas: A brief history* (3rd ed.). Malden: Wiley-Blackwell.
Delgado, R. (2009). The law of the noose: A history of Latino lynching. *Harvard Civil Rights-Civil Liberties Law Review, 44*, 297–312.
Denny, H. C. (2010). *Facing the center: Toward an identity politics of one-to-one mentoring*. Logan: Utah State University Press.
Diab, R., Godbee, B., Ferrel, T., & Simpkins, N. (2012). A multi-dimensional pedagogy for racial justice in writing center. *Praxis: A Writing Center Journal, 10*(1), 1-8.
DiPardo, A. (1992). "Whispers of coming and going": Lessons from Fannie. *Writing Center Journal, 12*(2), 125–144.
Dussel, E. (1993). Eurocentrism and modernity (introduction to the Frankfurt lectures). *Boundary, 20*(3), 65–76.
Ede, L. (1989). Writing as a social process: A theoretical foundation for writing centers. *Writing Center Journal, 9*(2), 3–13.
Esters, J. B. (2011). On the edges: Black maleness, degrees of racism, and community on the boundaries of the writing center. In L. Greenfield & K. Rowan (Eds.), *Writing centers and the new racism: A call for sustainable dialogue and change* (pp. 290–299). Logan: Utah State University Press.
Fabian, J. (1983). *Time and the other. How anthropology makes its object*. New York: Columbia University Press.
Geller, A. E., Condon, F., & Carroll, M. (2011). Bold: The everyday writing center and the production of new knowledge in antiracist theory and practice. In L. Greenfield & K. Rowan (Eds.), *Writing centers and the new racism: A call for sustainable dialogue and change* (pp. 101–123). Logan: Utah State University Press.

Geller, A. E., Eodice, M., Condon, F., Carroll, M., & Boquet, E. H. (2007). *The everyday writing center: A community of practice*. Logan: Utah State University Press.

Giroux, H. (1992). *Border crossings: Cultural workers and the politics of education*. New York: Routledge.

Greenfield, L. (2011). The 'standard English' fairy tale: A rhetorical analysis of racist pedagogies and commonplace assumptions about language diversity. In L. Greenfield & K. Rowan (Eds.), *Writing centers and the new racism: A call for sustainable dialogue and change* (pp. 33-60). Logan: Utah State University Press.

Greenfield, L., & Rowan, K. (Eds.). (2011a). *Writing centers and the new racism: A call for sustainable dialogue and change*. Logan: Utah State University Press.

Greenfield, L., & Rowan, K. (2011b). Beyond the 'week twelve approach': Toward a critical pedagogy for antiracist tutor education. In L. Greenfield & K. Rowan (Eds.), *Writing centers and the new racism: A call for sustainable dialogue and change* (pp. 124-149). Logan: Utah State University Press.

Grimm, N. (1996a). The regulatory role of the writing center: Coming to terms with a loss of innocence. *Writing Center Journal, 17*(1), 5–29.

Grimm, N. M. (1996b). Rearticulating the work of the writing center. *College Composition and Communication, 47*(4), 523–548.

Grimm, N. M. (1999). *Good intentions: Writing center work for postmodern times*. Portsmouth: Heinemann.

Grimm, N. (2011). Retheorizing writing center work to transform a system of advantage based on race. In L. Greenfield & K. Rowan (Eds.), *Writing centers and the new racism: A call for sustainable dialogue and change* (pp. 75–100). Logan: Utah State University Press.

Grutsch McKinney, J. (2005). Leaving home sweet home: Towards critical readings of writing center spaces. *Writing Center Journal, 25*(2), 6–20.

Guajardo, M., & Guajardo, F. (2004). The impact of Brown on the brown of South Texas: A micropolitical perspective on the education of Mexican Americans in a South Texas community. *American Educational Research, 41*(3), 501-526.

Gutiérrez, D.G. (1995). *Walls and mirrors: Mexican Americans, Mexican immigrants, and the politics of ethnicity*. Berkeley: University of California Press.

Hall Kells, M. (2002). Linguistic contact zones in the college writing classroom: An examination of ethnolinguistic identity and language attitudes. *Written Communication, 19*(1), 5–43.

Hall Kells, M. (2004). Understanding the rhetorical value of Tejano codeswitching. In M. Hall Kells, V. M. Balester, & V. Villanueva (Eds.),

Latino/a discourses: On language, identity, and literacy education (pp. 24-39). Portsmouth: Boynton/Cook.

Harris, M. (1982). Growing pains: The coming of age of writing centers. *Writing Center Journal, 2*(1), 1–8.

Kail, H. (2000). Writing center work: An ongoing challenge. *Writing Center Journal, 20*(2), 25–28.

Kail, H., & Trimbur, J. (1987). The politics of peer tutoring. *Writing Program Administration, 11*(1/2), 5–12.

Kaplowitz, C. A. (2005). *LULAC: Mexican Americans and national policy.* College Station: Texas A&M University Press.

Lunsford, A. (1991). Collaboration, control, and the idea of a writing center. *Writing Center Journal, 12*(1), 3–10.

Massey, D. (2005). *For space.* London: SAGE Publications.

Mendez Newman, B. (2003). Centering in the borderlands: Lessons from Hispanic student writers. *Writing Center Journal, 23*(2), 43–62.

Mignolo, W. D. (2000). *Local histories/global designs: Coloniality, subaltern knowledges, and border thinking.* Princeton: Princeton University Press.

Mignolo, W. D. (2007). Delinking: The rhetoric of modernity, the logic of coloniality and the grammar of de-coloniality. *Cultural Studies, 21*(2), 449–514.

Murphy, C., & Stay, B. L. (Eds.). (2006). *The writing center director's resource book.* Mahwah: Lawrence Erlbaum Associates.

Ozias, M., & Godbee, B. (2011). Organizing for antiracism in writing centers: Principles for enacting social change. In L. Greenfield & K. Rowan (Eds.), *Writing centers and the new racism: A call for sustainable dialogue and change* (pp. 150–176). Logan: Utah State University Press.

Pemberton, M. A., & Kinkead, J. (Eds.). (2003). *The center will hold: Critical perspectives on writing center scholarship.* Logan: Utah State University Press.

Pennycook, A. (2010). *Language as a local practice.* New York: Routledge.

Perea, J. F. (1997). The Black/White binary paradigm of race: The normal science of American racial thought. *California Law Review, 85*(5), 127–172.

Peters, E. J. (1998). Subversive spaces: First nations women and the city. *Environment and Planning D: Society and Space, 16*(6), 665–685.

Powell, Malea. (2012). Stories take place: A performance in one act. 2012 CCCC Chair's Address. *College Composition and Communication, 64*(2), 383-406.

Pratt, M. L. (1992). *Imperial eyes: Travel writing and transculturation.* New York: Routledge.

Pred, A. (1995). Out of bounds and undisciplined: Social inquiry and the current moment of danger. *Social Research, 62*(4), 1065-1091.

Quijano, A. (2000). Coloniality of power and Eurocentrism in Latin America. *International Sociology, 15*(2), 215–232.

Quijano, A. (2007). Coloniality and modernity/rationality. *Cultural Studies, 21*(2-3), 168-178.

Quijano, A., & Wallerstein, I. (1992). Americanity as a concept, or the Americas in the modern world-system. *International Social Science Journal, 134*, 549–557.

Ratcliffe, K. (2005). *Rhetorical listening: Identification, gender, whiteness.* Carbondale: Southern Illinois University Press.

Riley, T. (1994). The unpromising future of writing centers. *Writing Center Journal, 15*(1), 20–34.

Rodriguez, G. (2007). *Mongrels, bastards, orphans, and vagabonds: Mexican immigration and the future of race in America.* New York: First Vintage Books.

Rohrer, J. (2016). *Staking claims: Settler colonialism and racialization in Hawai'i.* Tucson: The University of Arizona Press.

San Miguel, G. (1997). Roused from our slumbers. In A. Darder, R.D. Torres, & H. Gutierrez (Eds.), *Latinos and education: A critical reader* (pp. 135-157). New York: Routledge.

Scollon, R., & Scollon, S. W. (2004). *Nexus analysis: Discourse and the emerging Internet.* New York: Routledge.

Sheller, M, & Urry, J. (2006). The new mobilities paradigm. *Environment and Planning A, 38*(2), 207-226.

Shelton, C.D., & Howson, E.E. (2014). Disrupting authority: Writing mentors and code-meshing pedagogy. *Praxis: A Writing Center Journal, 12*(1). Retrieved from http://www.praxisuwc.com/ shelton-howson-121/

Simpson, J. H. (1985). What lies ahead for writing centers: Position statement on professional concerns. *Writing Center Journal, 5/6*(2/1), 35–39.

Spring, J. (2005). *The American school 1642-2004* (6th ed.). Boston: McGaw Hill.

Summerfield, J. (1988). Writing centers: A long view. *Writing Center Journal, 8*(2), 3–9.

Tsing, A. (2000). The global situation. *Cultural Anthropology, 15*(3), 327–360.

Valentine, K., & Torres, M. F. (2011). Diversity as topography: The benefits and challenges of cross racial interaction in the writing center. In L. Greenfield & K. Rowan (Eds.), *Writing centers and the new racism: A call for sustainable dialogue and change* (pp. 192–210). Utah State University Press.

Valencia, R.R. (2000). Inequalities and the schooling of minority students in Texas: Historical and contemporary conditions. *Hispanic Journal of Behavioral Sciences, 22*, 445 – 459.

Villanueva, V. (2004). Memoria is a friend of ours: On the discourse of color. *College English, 67*(1), 9–19.

Villanueva, V. (2006). Blind: Talking about the new racism. *Writing Center Journal, 26*(1), 3–19.

Weaver, M. (2006). A call for racial diversity in the writing center. In C. Murphy & B. Stay (Eds.), *The writing center director's resource book* (pp. 79–92). Mahwah: Lawrence Erlbaum Associates.

Yahner, W., & Murdick, W. (1991). The evolution of a writing center: 1972-1990. *Writing Center Journal, 11*(2), 13–28.

Zhang, P., St. Amand, J., Quaynor, J., Haltiwanger, T., Chambers, E., Canino, G., & Ozias, M. (2013). "Going there": Peer writing consultants' perspectives on the new racism and peer writing pedagogies. *Across the Disciplines: A Journal of Language, Learning, and Academic Writing, 10*(3). Retrieved from http://wac.colostate. edu/atd/race/oziasetal/family.cfm

SUPPLEMENTAL MATERIAL

Part I: Reflection on the Origins of the Article

I wrote "Unmaking Gringo-Centers" on sheets of paper one day while working at the Writing Center at Syracuse University. The day I started brainstorming and sketching the outline for the essay, I was fresh out of a postcolonial course taught by Chandra Mohanty. That day, I presented on the work of Anibal Quijano, and his criticism on the coloniality of power, knowledge. His work, both exhibited in coloniality as an analytic and de-linking as a prospective vision, was inspirational to me. It gave me language to discuss my experiences in the Lower Rio Grande Valley of Texas, a border(ed)land or a geography of exclusion. (To the south, there is the geopolitical border and to the north internal checkpoints that span approximately 100 miles east and west). This region is a quintessential example both of historical colonial management and control of land, resources, and people, as well as how a rhetoric of modernity is deployed to cloak this violence in the name of a modern nation-state. The modern/(de)colonial project presented an option, a de-colonial option, one that denounces and fractures hegemonic structures of thought and feeling and works towards changing the terms (concepts) and contents (histories) of conversations. Optimistically, I began to think that day that I was brainstorming and drafting whether the academy and the writing center could be a site for such work. Because coloniality and modernity gain much of its currency at the epistemic level, I wondered both about the possibilities and impossibilities. If, as I argued in "Unmaking Gringo-Centers," history and memories stand at the nexus of collective identity and consciousness, how might this same statement resound within the WC? Writing center work has and continues to not sit well with me. All this talk about being progressive and yet the WC community reduces and retrofits students of color (García, 33). My position of critique, at least it was my hope, would scaffold how to be de-colonial engineers and agents. That is, how to not purchase into the rhetoric of modernity while at the same time working to de-colonize spaces/ places and knowledge productions. A de-colonial option instilled in me a renewed sense of hope. Without hope, what is there?

Part II: Description of Research Methods, Findings, and/or Pedagogical Impact

So often, institutional spaces like the Writing Center like to prematurely celebrate "diversity." The sophistication of Gringoland and Gringodemia are its capacities to absorb and then tokenize resistance. A close-reading approach, such as the one I deployed, focused on seminal pieces of WC scholarship that have allowed the WC community to tout narratives of salvation, progress, and development. Albeit the WC community knows the WC is an institutional structure, the postulation of needing to "save" it (and "save" thy selves) inculcates this idea that it can be anything but colonial all the while recycling and reproducing power cloaked by ideas of progress. The close-reading approach I engaged in says, wait and hold up. As I read various pieces of scholarship, I kept arriving at a similar thought, the "reductive racial frames—black struggles and white concessions—constitute a limit to what a writing center might do" (32). My intention by no means was to take away from the critical turns these seminal texts took the WC in. Rather, as I note, "As well intentioned and progressive as the writing center community has been in taking up race and racism, the insufficiency of a white/black race paradigm—the black subject as the default 'colonial' subject and the white tutor as a functional colonizer—poses a limitation" (38). Anti-racism and social-justice work fail by design with the occlusion of other experiences and reveals rudimentary levels of hegemonic ideologies in play.

I also experimented a little by deploying a macro-analytic approach alongside a close-reading approach. I took over 30 years of writing center work and through computational methods I focused on how themes emerged across time. Although no conclusive conclusions could be made, I deployed this method to illuminate how, over 30 years, the WC has been invoking terms such as "diversity" and "collaboration" within black and white contexts.

Central to the essay are community concepts such as community listening (para que sepas y aprendes), collective memory, and recollection. "Unmaking Gringo-Centers" is where I began to explore my understanding of community listening through recuerdos. A central question for me continues to be, ¿dónde comenzamos? Where do I begin, with regard to my politics of memory and my understanding of responsibility and justice? What happens, however, when all we have are scattered memories, loose-leaf papers, and photographs? For me, the very question of "where to begin" is already an expression of responsibility that necessitates a re-learning process. How might we begin to listen (rather than hear) for sound and see (rather than look) presence from absence? Inevitably, I am transported back "home," to my family and friends, and to my community. By no means is this an expression of nostalgia. "Home," for me, has always been a contentious notion. Rather, "home" is where I learned about historical places such as the Lower Rio Grande Valley and historical bodies such as the Mexican American body. "Home" is where I learned firsthand about the "plight" of the Mexican American that is so often captured by tropes of tragedy and hope. As I argued in "Unmaking Gringo-Centers," these are people on the cusp of invisibility, a people who continue to struggle to be "heard" and "seen." From the Sarita, Texas checkpoint to the writing center, all these were sites that interpellated my body and constantly pursued to "check" me for "mis papeles." These are sites where the "other" can never truly be "heard" and "seen." The writing center will always re-write itself as colonial.

Part III: Discussion Questions

1. What are the possibilities and impossibilities of deploying a decolonial option within the WC?

2. How do every day practices ensure the "re-making" of Gringo-Centers?

3. How might we begin to "take on ourselves" rather than simply deploy the language of politics?

JOURNAL OF BASIC WRITING

The Journal of Basic Writing is on the Web at http://wac.colostate.edu/jbw/index.cfm

The Journal of Basic Writing is a refereed print journal founded in 1975 by Mina Shaughnessy, who served as the journal's first editor. *JBW* is published twice a year with support from the Office of Academic Affairs of the City University of New York. Its editors are full-time CUNY faculty. Basic writing, a contested term since its initial use by Shaughnessy in the 1970s, refers to the field concerned with teaching writing to students not yet deemed ready for first-year composition. Originally, these students were part of the wave of open admissions students who poured into universities as a result of the social unrest of the 1960s and the resulting reforms. Though social and political realities have changed dramatically since then, the presence of "basic writers" in colleges and universities—and the debates over how best to serve them—persist. *JBW* publishes articles related to basic and second-language writing using a variety of approaches: speculative discussions that venture fresh interpretations; essays that draw heavily on student writing as supportive evidence for new observations; research reports written in non-technical language that offer observations previously unknown or unsubstantiated; and collaborative writings that provocatively debate more than one side of a critical controversy.

Cultivating Places and People at the Center: Cross-Pollinating Literacies on a Rural Campus[1]

Wendy Pfrenger's "Cultivating Places and People at the Center: Cross-Pollinating Literacies on a Rural Campus," expands notions of "who is the basic writer" by emphasizing the overlaps of identity among writing consultants and their students on a rural, regional campus. As Pfrenger shows, writing consultants who grew up and still participate in the community lives of their students are able to translate literacy tasks by setting them in a place-based literacy context. Such interactions sustain both writing consultant and student in their academic aspirations across divides of deepening poverty and widening opportunity gaps in this rural setting. Pfrenger shows the rural-cultural leverage of place that a writing center can potentialize, with positive identity impacts for writing consultants and basic writers alike.

---

1. *The Journal of Basic Writing*, vol. 36, no. 1 © 2017 by City University of New York

Cultivating Places and People at the Center: Cross-Pollinating Literacies on a Rural Campus

Wendy Pfrenger

Students in rural communities often describe themselves as unsuccessful readers and writers in a university context, yet off-campus their literacy lives may be avidly experienced and richly valued. This article investigates the layered literacies of student clients and writ-ing center consultants on a rural, regional campus in an Appalachian county of Ohio with particular attention to the dissonance between students' success in extracurricular contexts and their perceived inadequacies in academic contexts. The theoretical frame for this inves-tigation draws upon place-based pedagogies, extending notions of literacy sponsorship and multiple literacy strands to a strongly place-identified, age-diverse student body negotiating college composition courses on an open enrollment regional campus. The author describes the varied means by which peer writing consultants and students may work together to construct hybrid academic literacies, highlighting an appreciation for the value of their community-based literacy practices.

I am observing a writing session in which a consultant and a client, both young men, are struggling to make progress. The client, pleasant but uncommunicative, gives brief replies to the consultant's questions. The consultant, attempting to draw attention to the immediacy of the assignment's central question, asks the writer to talk about how a relationship to audience impacts his choices as a writer. The writer shrugs and grins apologetically, expressing the opinion that he is not, in fact, much of a writer. The consultant, in desperation, grins back and takes an unexpected tack.

Consultant: "Are you a grade A or a grade C sexter?"

Client: "What?"

After a quick flush of initial embarrassment, the writer warms to the task of describing the rhetorical moves involved in texting romantic partners and comparing those moves (somewhat more hesitantly) to those used in intellectual writing.

Out of many visits throughout the semester, this was one of the few moments we had with this client in which he was able to take a more active role in constructing a metadiscourse about his own literacy practices, and he did it through applying knowledge of his everyday practices to what he supposed was expected in his basic writing course. The writing consultant, in maneuvering the client outside of the role he had chosen (passive, empty of relevant knowledge), and into a more humorous, self-critical perspective, made it possible for the client to stand with feet planted in a new, third space. After this session, I began paying closer attention to the role that extracurricular literacies were playing in the Learning Center on the regional, rural Kent State campus where I have worked as Learning Center Coordinator for the past five years. When were they explicitly explored in a session and who brought them up? To what use were they put? When did they have a more subtle, but still apparent, influence? And what webs of connection (or disconnection) gave shape to the hybridization of literacies in these sessions? The consultant's dual role as a literacy sponsor and a member of the client's home community clearly seemed to have a significant impact on the shape of a writing session. In order to understand what was happening, it seemed necessary to consider more fully the ways that writing centers, particularly in small campuses like ours, can become places where community-based literacies and academic literacy practices come together in a confluence of diverse expectations, practices, knowledge systems, and cultural associations. In our community, everyday literacy practices look like this: Melanie journals for her counseling sessions. Mark watches historical documentaries and discusses them with his father. Nick argues politics in the apartment complex courtyard with his elderly neighbors, while Sarah uses her Facebook posts to share her poetry and songs. Brittany, a mechanic's wife, assists friends with advice grounded in a combination of experience and research on car purchases and repair. Justin analyzes draft picks and interprets ambiguous girlfriend-texts with his brother, and Erin produces textual commentary regularly for her Bible study group.

The dissatisfaction both students and professors express with the writing produced in entry-level college composition courses seems oddly dissonant when contrasted with the students' own avid and personally valued literacy lives.

The literacy practices students bring to academia are resources too often left largely untapped; at best, they are acknowledged only so they may be consciously set aside in the composition course to be replaced by the communicative norms of the university: literacy code-switching. The profoundly personal enthusiasms and deeply felt, shared experiences captured through these literacy practices do not often enough receive our respectful, sustained attention as we assist students in their efforts to develop academic literacy practices.

Some college writing instructors may invite elements of those extracurricular literacies and communicative norms into student writing for portions of the semester in the form of literacy narratives, but the understanding is that, for the most part, the stylistic aesthetics, cultural orientations, and habits of mind characteristic of these literacies will not be incorporated into the students' more "developed" academic work if they are to succeed in later courses. Anne-Marie Hall and Christopher Minnix argue that, contrary to what they refer to as "the bridge metaphor" of the literacy narrative, in which the narrative serves as a "bridge" for "easing students into" more conventionally valued forms of academic writing, we might instead enhance transference by exposing for students the ways that "the literacy narrative [like other genres] gains its power and meaning from its relationship to other genres and the hierarchies of value that shape particular contexts of writing," explicitly demonstrating for students the ways that "Writing a text about oneself (the familiar part) and turning it into a sophisticated critical analysis is a problem-solving skill that transports to other areas of learning" (78). What Hall and Minnix are advocating with their emphasis on the social construction of textual value in the university is a shift in how we encourage students to imagine their literacy purposes in various contexts and transposed to multiple settings.

Regional campuses occupy an advantageous position with regard to the question of contexts for understanding literacy, because the mission of a regional campus is specifically to serve place-bound students in a geographically defined area. This affords professors and students alike opportunities for deeper, more sustained engagement with literacy contexts because so much of the body of knowledge, practices, and values around literacy are shared in common. As part of a discussion of the physical spaces of composition learning and instruction, Nedra Reynolds has pointed out that the "actual locations for the work of writing and writing instruction coexist with several metaphorical or imaginary places where we write" (13). Rather than accepting as "transparent" the spaces and settings of higher education, she argues that we must work to recognize these places and their features, interpreting the layerings of space and place in ways that inform and enrich a critically reflective approach to writing and writing instruction in the university. For Reynolds, composition classrooms and writing centers are given form by their physical spaces, by the place-based metaphors that shape our thinking about writing, and by the geographies within which our campuses are situated. She, like Hall and Minnix, advocates for a shift in emphasis toward a more intentional examination and use of the contexts of reading and writing as they are learned, taught, and tutored on university campuses which are in turn, as physical buildings and as ideas, situated within layered histories, geographies, and spaces.

I would suggest that when we consciously make similar shifts in our writing center practice, pointing explicitly and regularly to ways that students' literacy lives outside the university give meaning and shape to their emergent academic literacy lives, we are making a subtle but important change. By doing so, we encourage the purposeful valuation and cultivation of extra-curricular literacy practices in the hope that they might thrive alongside and even cross-pollinate with the intellectual work students perform throughout their time in the university. If writing centers are to successfully address themselves to strongly place-identified clients, they must recognize and make use of the unique resources possessed by peer writing consultants who are similarly place-identified. Peer consultants fluent in translating the literacies they have learned *outside* the university into practices useful *within* the academy may prove effective in assisting other students as they attempt to do the same. In identifying approaches to a client's agenda that include a sustained engagement with personal and place-based literacies, writing consultants may then be prepared to "follow more deliberately those 'detours' taken by the writer that challenge our habitual way of viewing the self in relation to the world" as Min-Zhan Lu has suggested (Brandt et al. 54). As both consultants and clients come to view such detours less as evidence of academic illiteracy than as evidence of other literacies with potential utility for academic projects, they open the way to a more personally meaningful, place-based experience of higher education.

This article takes as its starting place a concern with the gap between students' often successful and personally valued community-based literacy experiences and their perceived inadequacy as they struggle to acquire the literacy practices required by their coursework. We have taken an ethnographic approach to the study of these processes in our own writing center, focusing primarily on the work of systematic observation and interpretation. Over the course of two semesters, peer writing consultants were asked to reflect in brief, informal writings about the relationship of their "outside" literacy practices and experiences to the literacy practices they were engaged in developing as university students. I also participated as a writing consultant, both observing and participating in sessions described here. The ways in which we have shifted our writing center practice to include routine consideration of non-academic literacies are documented in these session reports, reflections, and audio recordings, providing an ethnographic portrait of consultants and students on a rural campus engaged in a project of self-study. The resulting vignettes of consultants' and students' work illustrate the fruitful potential of directing our writing center practice toward the cultivation of what Deborah Brandt terms "hybrid" (182) or "re-appropriated literacies" (179).

The theoretical frame for this investigation draws upon place-based pedagogies, extending notions of literacy sponsorship and multiple literacy strands to a strongly place-identified, age-diverse student body negotiating college composition courses on an open enrollment campus in a rural corner of Appalachian Ohio. I examine the means by which peer writing consultants and student writers may work together to construct hybrid academic literacies, combining an appreciation for the value of their community-based literacy practices with an awareness of academic literacy practices; such an account, I hope, may provide a compelling case for the role writing centers may play in recasting the enculturation of first generation and nontraditional rural college students.

Placing the Rural Writing Center

In Columbiana County, where our Kent State University regional campus is located, there are many kinds of divides and many kinds of conversations that result because of them. There are divides between incorporated townships and villages; between farmers and small manufacturers; between the broad, rolling corn/soy fields and Quaker-born towns *north* of the Lincoln highway and the forested hills and hollows, the Copperhead heritage *south* of the Lincoln highway.

The portrait presented by socioeconomic data shows a county divided within by barriers of opportunity and divided from the surrounding region by deepening poverty and economic isolation. 3.3% of the population of Columbiana County earns a household income of $150,000 or more annually, while 45.7% of the population report earnings below the county's median wage of $43,700 (Ohio Development Services Agency). Our county earned mention in *The Upshot*'s 2014 analysis of U.S. Census data, ranking it in the top third of most difficult counties for American families to live in, based on a variety of measures including unemployment, disability, poverty rates, health, and affordable housing (Flippen). Educational barriers present obstacles to available jobs, frustrating area employers as well as aspiring workers. Just 22.4% of Columbiana County residents over 25 reported attaining an associate's degree or higher compared to 34.3% of the broader Ohio population of residents over 25 (U.S. Census Bureau). These numbers are especially daunting given that Georgetown's Center on Education and the Workforce projects that 64% of jobs available in Ohio in 2020 will require at least some post-secondary credential or degree (3). In part, this is because academic preparation has lagged in Ohio. Though progress has been made in recent years due to implementation of new standards, just 18.7% of the high school classes of 2014 and 2015 in our county graduated with remediation-free ACT scores (Ohio Department of Education), and 81% of students enrolling at our local Kent State campuses in the last year placed into at least one remedial course (Kent State University IR, *Remediation Rates*). These statistics have prompted dialogue throughout our university system and our region, but conversations around retention and improving student preparation are sometimes inhibited by the same barriers they are meant to address.

The writing center is one place where students themselves—peer writing consultants and student writers—may step into the space between these divisions, a third space in which no one is quite on one side or another—and sometimes find ways to do something better than merely cross the divide. The writing center on the Kent State University Salem campus serves approximately 14% of the overall campus population every year, affording us many opportunities for the kind of close engagement between consultants, student clients, and professors that may offer alternatives to failure or, alternatively, transformation and outmigration. Attempting to pause in that alternative, third space as we have done in the process of this study may allow us to take stock of our students' literacy resources, measuring the potential to grow a hardier, more resilient and adaptive academic literacy than the more limited literacies we usually aspire to cultivate for students emerging from college composition courses. If we assume that college student writers like the ones described above possess in some measure "rural literacies . . . the kinds of literate skills necessary for sustaining life in rural area" (Donehower et al. 4) or, in the case of younger students, may be in the process of acquiring them, cultivating both academic and rural literacy may strengthen both for our writing clients and for our writing centers more broadly. In her seminal study of literacy sponsorship, Deborah Brandt remarked the multiple domains and points of contact that shape literacy in communities—in faith communities, the workplace, and the justice system, for example—pointing to the "deep hybridity" inherent in such overlapping. Brandt suggests that we, as educators in the university, should respond to this awareness by creating literacy models that "more astutely account for these kinds of multiple contacts, both in and out of school and across a lifetime" (179). I would argue that writing centers can and should help students foster a richness of meaning through the cultivation of hybrid literacies, and that we are best prepared to do this work by immersing ourselves as writing consultants in hybridity, in reflection on the layered literacies that we and our clients bring into the university. Such an approach requires an explicit embrace of the moves readers and writers make, and of the relationships and social contexts that lend meaning to lives led on our campuses and in our rural communities.

Rural education researcher Michael Corbett has written extensively about the need to differentiate between the challenges rural students face on college campuses and the challenges faced by other student populations. In reflecting on the contrast between his own educational journey, rooted in an appreciation for mobility and the abstract, thanks to his proximity to the railroad life, and the place-based educations of his students in a rural, coastal community, Corbett suggests that although the "place-specific identity constructions" of rural college students "represent a complex set of resistances and accommodations" (1) to the educational setting of the university, their ability to successfully navigate this territory is uneven and fraught with obstacles. The obstacles posed by the university setting may not significantly impact students fluent in the decontextualized, comparatively rootless identity constructions of the contemporary suburban middle class in the same way that they impact rural students. For this reason, these obstacles—of uncommunicated assumptions about authority, the purpose of education, how to read and study, how to generate ideas and write—may go unaddressed by the university even as they impact metrics for persistence, achievement, and post-graduation outcomes.

The presence of these obstacles at Kent State's Salem campus is evident in the number of students placing into developmental composition courses and then failing to complete these courses successfully. During the period from fall 2013 through spring 2016, 27% of the students enrolled in composition courses on our regional campus were enrolled in developmental courses. D-F-withdrawal rates during the same period for those developmental courses averaged 32.7 percent (Kent State University IR, *Grade Distribution Reports*). 34.6% of the students enrolled in the first of the developmental courses never appear in the record of composition courses a second time, suggesting that they dropped out of the university altogether. Why they vanish and where they go, we don't know, because our university, as is the case with many, has no formal method of systematically tracking students like these who fail to persist or graduate. We suspect that they disappear for the reasons they gave us when they missed classes and assignments before leaving: they didn't feel like they were "college material"; they didn't understand "what the professors were asking for" because they weren't like the high school teachers; or that caring for the farm and an ailing father while going to college got to be too much and the family told them that family should always come first. We are sure that the students are still nearby, just down Route 45, but place has played a role in ending their educations just as surely as it played a role in getting them started at our campus originally.

Institutions of higher education in rural areas are often the inadvertent purveyors of two kinds of loss. Lamenting "the routinization of failure, its virtual acceptance amongst typical educators, and the all too common acquiescence in the process on the part of most failing students themselves," Corbett calls for greater attention to the problem of the links between education, rural outmigration, and access to resources. When rural students succeed in higher education, on the one hand, their success may contribute to the problem of outmigration. A recent United States Department of Agriculture report notes that "Rural outmigration is highly concentrated among young adults, especially those possessing or acquiring education and skills" (2). The second kind of loss, failure in the realm of higher education, contributes to a larger narrative of systematic loss and decreased quality of life in areas where access to economic resources has eroded over time.

Identifying Corbett's account as one which delineates "the educational discourse of loss and place," (1) Ursula Kelly emphasizes not only the consequences Corbett has identified but also the ways we interpret those consequences and the inevitability of loss as a result of rural education. For Kelly, loss has transformative potential—but only if it is intentionally addressed within the educational framework. More routinely, we accept loss and failure as inevitable outcomes of the clash between institutional uniformity and the heterogeneity of the students who pass through our doors. If we assume that failure is simply a function of the system as it sorts those that belong from those that do not, there is no mechanism for considering possible paths leading to hybridity, transmutation, or other collaborative imaginings of literacies that might bridge the everyday and the academic. Alternatively, Kelly argues for an "acceptance of loss . . . [that] would create a space in which one might plan and preserve, turning love of place into an ethic of responsibility and sustainability" (3), viewing loss as an opportunity to create new knowledge.

For an adult entering the university and undertaking the educational project of acquiring a new literacy, some loss may be an inevitable part of succeeding, but complete loss, total change should not be treated as a desirable or unavoidable side effect of assimilation. Collaboration between the student and the university in generating a new, hybrid literacy grounded in both the local and the global may prove a stronger, more resilient foundation than displacement can provide. Because writing centers employ peer consultants who, in the case of commuter campuses especially, are likely to come from the same communities as their clients, writing centers can offer a uniquely place-based form of literacy sponsorship for students.

Writing center pedagogy has long privileged the agenda and agency of the client in a way that would suggest an asset-based approach to each session. Yet we may not always do enough in the writing center to consider the social and practical context of literacy itself. For a symposium published in *College English,* Richard E. Miller suggested that it is important to be "as interested in the expectations that we bring to the activity of writing as . . . in the writing we produce to meet those expectations" (Brandt et al. 50). If we consider the foundation of literacy to be "the culturally appropriate way of thinking" for a given society (Langer 13) and the expectations generated by these cultural paradigms, then we must move beyond discussing skills and strategies, even beyond demystifying one specific cultural context (the academy), and instead invite examination of the multiplicity of cultural contexts layered within the campus setting. In a case study of an off-campus writing center, a space described as "both curricular and extracurricular" (678) Deborah Minter, Anne Gere, and Deborah Keller-Cohen noted that peer tutors often "initially [take] literacy to be a context-independent bank of knowledge of a set of skills" (678) leading them to focus on guiding a writer in developing those skills rather than developing an examination of the *context(s)* of those skills. However, the longer the peer tutors in the study worked in the writing center, housed in an urban community center and serving local elementary-aged students, the more they were challenged to "respond to or manage the surplus of meaning" (678) resulting from the overlap in space usage, the juxtaposition of work and community roles, and the layering of various kinds of literacy practices and values held by both adults and children involved with the center. As the peer tutors gained their own cultural competency in the extracurricular space of a community-based writing center, they came to see the features of their clients' texts as more than mere deviations from (or models of) academic literacy; rather, they were able to see them as literacy products constructed at the intersection of the cultural contexts of school and home, of decontextualized, national standards-based instruction and their familiar, urban neighborhood.

Writing centers, then, can become a critical intervention for students struggling to participate in the literacy culture of the university at the same time that they strive to find their place in the global economy. By offering a space where students may sort through the layered literacies of their extracurricular experiences, they assist students in finding ways to make use of these literacies for academic purposes, though perhaps in an altered form, and open new ways of considering narratives of mainstream cultural supremacy. A "surplus of meaning" may manifest in student texts in ways often regarded by professors or skilled peers as evidence of disadvantageous differences. In response to this negatively tinged lens, we may very well need "conceptual frameworks that *simultaneously* assert shared cognitive and linguistic competence while celebrating in a non-hierarchical way the play of human difference" (Hull et al. 326); such frameworks could instead shift the focus of a writing session from excising all evidence of difference from a text and toward leveraging that difference productively, converting a surplus of meaning into a richness of meaning.

In the first chapter of *Rural Literacies*, Kim Donehower, Charlotte Hogg, and Eileen Schell make the case that in higher ed "we need to work with students to help them see the economic, social, and political issues encountered in rural areas as interconnected with the larger social and political patterns present in urban and suburban contexts and vice versa" (30). They advocate such work as the basis of a critical public literacy of greater utility to all students, no matter where they are from or where they choose to locate themselves. Donehower recommends that "By acknowledging how loaded the topic of literacy may be for [rural] students, by exploring ways to validate students' existing knowledge and literate practices, and by encouraging appropriative relationships with the types of literacy we offer," (76) we may be more effective as literacy sponsors serving place-bound students and even, I would suggest, problematize our institutional models of success and failure in significant ways.

Offering Literacy Sponsorship

Many studies have noted the critical role that literacy sponsors may play in the success of traditionally underrepresented students (Brandt; Carrick; Heath; Shepley; Webb-Sunderhaus), and both new literacy and social constructivist learning theories suggest that the educational impact of sponsors is amplified when they share with learners a common set of communicative norms and cultural contexts. For these reasons, writing consultants on local, non-residential campuses may offer their clients a unique form of literacy sponsorship, unique because, though located within the university as successful students, the consultants nonetheless share in common with writers a location within the community.

Deborah Brandt, introducing the notion of literacy sponsorship suggested the tension of power inherent in the role of a sponsor, defining sponsors as "any agents, local or distant, concrete or abstract, who enable, support, teach, model, as well as recruit, regulate, suppress, or withhold literacy-and gain advantage by it in some way" (166). Noting that sponsors unavoidably wield disproportionate power in the relationship and "represent the causes into which people's literacy usually gets recruited" (167) Brandt expressed a sense of unease as a self-declared "conflicted broker" (183) of literacy in the classroom. In the nearly two decades that have passed since Brandt's initial research, we have sought to make peace with this power dynamic through various reformulations of the literacy transaction, through altering its terms and players. In the writing center, sponsors proficient in navigating what geographer Doreen Massey terms "the simultaneous multiplicity of spaces" available to the specific locale of their campus may be particularly effective in constructing together with their clients a meta-discourse about the choices they can make as readers and writers, selecting moves from their literacy repertoire outside the university for adaptation to the expectations of academe and perhaps simultaneously modifying the terrain of academe through manipulation of their local rhetorical space. The discursive nature of these analyses of writing "moves," informed by the "simultaneous multiplicity of spaces" shared by writing consultants and clients alike, may diminish, to an extent, the conflicted nature of literacy sponsorship in the rural writing center.

Writing consultants in our center, for example, often find writers favoring "short and to the point" as a writing aesthetic that causes problems when they are expected to sustain complex reasoning in essays. Rather than simply explain academic aesthetics and begin the process of re-writing, however, our consultants inquire into what "short and to the point" means to a writer and why it seems desirable. Many of our clients tell us they learned this style in the military, or as prison guards, or as they completed government documents for various purposes. As a consultant learns more about why and how a writer favors a set of choices, she can help a writer recognize 1) that these are indeed choices; 2) that they can be savvy ones, not "wrong" choices demonstrating their lack of writing ability; 3) that the reasoning behind those choices might have utility in an academic context, even if stylistic adaptation may be needed.

For our purposes here in considering students' lived experiences of literacy, its mutability and adaptation, the notion that literacy is fundamentally a social practice is key. Understood in this way, the literacy required to assess, for example, the information gleaned in Columbiana County's most widely circulated newspaper, *Farm and Dairy*, is given form and meaning by social context. An article about valuing antiques (written by one of my student's mothers) draws upon locally lived experience of history, the rapid passage of generations, and the disruption/repetition of cultural trends as experienced by Columbiana County residents. The writer's purpose is shaped by her knowledge of a local audience of contemporaries, nostalgic for a past their children may never wish to celebrate and enriched by a material culture which she understands to be changing, though not perhaps in the sense of diminishing which we often associate with change. She advocates for celebration and use of treasured family items, remarking that, "The memories will keep moving forward as we fold these items into our lives," (Seabolt). For Kym Seabolt and her readers, locally sourced literacy is clearly not simply an all-purpose tool, but one embedded in a social context that includes articles about turkey-hunting and grain storage alongside antique valuation.

Extending our interest in literacy promotion to include development and hybridization of extracurricular literacies shifts our practice toward an appreciation for our students' potential as adults knowledgeable in their communities who may themselves "fold" literacies, as they may do memories, into their layered lives. Noting the damaging ethnocentrism of skills-based notions of literacy, Francis Kazemek has called instead for an acknowledgement "that literacy is constrained by social and cultural practices and is not merely a private accomplishment" (473), thus liberating literacy education from reductive approaches that emphasize individual effort and "acquisition" of modular, decontextualized literacy practices. Adults in the literacy programs that Kazemek studied were spending time performing reading tasks often identical to those used with primary school children despite the inappropriateness of such tasks and topics for the literacy contexts of adult life. The alternative, shifting from skills-based instruction to creating socioculturally-motivated, context-based literacy instruction grounded in the adult needs and applications of the students, encouraged students to adaptandrevise their existing literacy strategies, has become a model for contemporary adult literacy programs (Hull; Muth; Weiner) though not, typically, in basic or first-year university courses. If we are to create in university spaces the opportunity for students, whether traditional or nontraditional, to make use of their primary literacies, we need forms of academic literacy sponsorship that draw upon extracurricular literacies and social contexts, and we need ways to talk about the academic setting itself as a particular site for literacy within a larger community of spaces where literacy is constituted. Space must be made for conversations about discontinuity and disruption at the same time that we foster an appreciative recognition of the literacies students bring with them into the university.

Cultivating Hybrid Literacies: Three Writing Consultants in Context

As we have observed, university students acquiring academic literacy practices are engaged in a social transaction composed of literacy histories specific to them personally, to the practices and traits of the individual teacher and class, and tothe place and time in which they are being educated. Assisting adult students as they adapttheir literacy toacademic requirements must make *social* sense, not only academic sense, perhaps particularly in communities and on campuses where students aspire not to use education to leave, but to return equipped to succeed there, as many of our students do. The old adage of writing centers, that we make "better writers, not better writing" (North 68) might as well be adapted to include "better connections, not better grades." In the working class southern towns where she did her ethnographic work, Shirley Brice Heath suggested that both teachers and learners could better "learn to articulate relations between cultural patterns of talking and knowing, and, understanding such relations [could] make choices" (13) when they shared cultural context. The construction of literacy through shared inquiry and relationship makes sense in an education inclusive of situated learning, with writing consultants or tutors assisting their peers in becoming part of the university's community of practice.

My own investigation of this process has formed itself around the encounters of individual students interacting in our campus spaces, giving particular attention to the value of multiplex relationships in promoting the formation of hybrid literacies. What Beth Daniell terms "The little narratives of literacy [that] connect composition to culture" (405) can illuminate the dark corners of our classrooms and writing centers. To collect these little narratives, I worked with undergraduate writing consultants employed in our regional campus Learning Center to gather and interpret reflective accounts of writing sessions. I also requested that the peer writing consultants create literacy reflections detailing their own adaptation and use of extracurricular literacies within the university. Most of the material described in this article derives from the consultants' experiences as developing academic writers and as literacy sponsors working with their clients. The consultants' reflection papers described the evolution of their tutoring pedagogies and, in the process, remarked the ways that their own literacy lives had influenced their growth as academic writers. I had also instructed the writing consultants in periodic staff meetings to look for opportunities to learn about students' extracurricular literacies and, where appropriate, make use of those practices in the course of ordinary writing sessions. They were given a specific set of questions addressing conversations about extracurricular literacy to answer in their session reports.

Ultimately, the accounts chosen for inclusion here were selected because the consultants and clients involved were typical of our student population—most of them non-traditional students, none of them having graduated high school with an intention to enroll in college, all of them born and raised in the county where our campus is located. The consultants had each distinguished themselves as being particularly invested in their personal literacy lives, though only one was a self-identified aspiring professional writer. In addition, their ability torepresent in their reflections specific aspects of the ways extracurricular literacies had influenced the formation of their academic literacy practices made rendering their experiences for research purposes a more equitable and accurate process, as they provided ongoing clarification and feedback for this article. I have chosen to emphasize the accounts of the consultants rather than those of the clients in large part because I feel they tell in their own words (better than I could and in a way the client writers were not asked to) the story of how the extracurricular literacies they practice off campus influence the academic literacy they have acquired as college students. Three out of the five consultants who were active that year have accounts represented here.

It is worth noting that the remaining two consultants (both traditional-aged students) perceived themselves to be less located in place due to family background and socioeconomic class, so their accounts of their literacies were strikingly place-less by contrast with the three accounts of the writing consultants represented here. The focus in their accounts is on learning the superficial conventions of academic work (e.g. accuracy in citation style, avoiding the "five paragraph essay") and acquiring habits of mind characteristic of the disciplines in which they were learning to write.

The accounts of writing sessions in the subsequent section offer, by contrast, a suggestion of how consultants fluent in both place-based and academic literacy practices may help writers explore their extracurricular literacies and make use of them in cultivating academic literacy. These were selected on the basis of a greater availability of descriptive information (some writing consultants wrote fuller session reports than others, and in some cases I myself was the consultant and had available recordings). I only used information from clients whom I'd had the opportunity to observe in session at least once or with whom I had worked myself.

Stacie Crawford—A Literacy with Many Roots, Many Purposes

Stacie Crawford, in her time as a Human Development and Family Studies major on our campus, was one of our most sought-after consultants. Her story suggests a complex of economic and personal motives, the richness of her experiences prior to college, and the value of stitching a college education into the larger patterns of her life. In her reflection, she writes, "I certainly am not an early achiever (way passed [sic] the 20 something mark) . . . I am a mother whose husband is on disability and just want to have some security in a society where the financial climate has gone haywire . . . I certainly have been known to say 'Algebra 3? . . . Why do I need so much math for Human Services?'"

At the time when she was employed in the Learning Center, Stacie had a college-aged son enrolled at the campus, and he was the one who had encouraged her to return to school and get a degree. Stacie entered the university motivated by economic need and was, at first, puzzled by requirements she saw as unrelated to her purpose in seeking a higher-paying job. She seems more willing, however, to mark the value of a broader, less instrumentally driven education when she describes in her account the indirect routes by which she had pursued education in her youth. In relating her "vagabond years" after high school graduation, she refers to her experiences as "an education of a different kind that is irreplaceable." This contrast between an impulse to education as economic necessity and one driven by curiosity and a taste for novelty is striking, suggesting as it does one more tension inherent in the acquisition of new literacies. Higher education with its general education requirements and graduation formulas does not always seem to students particularly conducive to either of these more personal educational aims. Even Stacie's emphasis on her age as a returning student points to an assumption she shares with many others—that book-based education is for younger, inexperienced people and may prove inaccessible or even redundant for those schooled in the book of life. For Stacie, travel provided a way to gain knowledge about the world that she could bring back and use in her home community. Her educational experience in the university, though motivated by pragmatic purposes, only became more satisfying as it took on other, more personal, dimensions.

As an adult student, Stacie was initially uncertain whether her ways of thinking and learning would work within the university, an uncertainty refracted into a different shape by friends who worried that rather than struggling to adapt to the university, she would adapt too successfully and so be changed. Prior to entering the university, she was known for her skill at facilitating a Bible study group that met at her house, and she was also an avid reader and poet. As her first writing instructor on the campus, I watched her initial hesitation and nervousness turn to confidence and even joy as she found through her academic writing a new form of exploration not unlike the types of writing she already valued: her inspirational Facebook postings or the contemporary spiritual music she composed. In the composition classroom, Stacie's writing—initially rich with ideas, but fragmented in structure—reflected a mind conversant with textual analysis and a writing life that placed value on the connotative potential of word choice. These characteristics, derived from her experiences as a poet and student of the Bible, became valuable in the service of composing essays, and they were ones that I, as her instructor, emphasized as strengths to be cultivated even as she tried out new skills and approaches needed for academic essay writing. This sense that her skills prior to entering the university were valuable ones helped Stacie relax into her role as a university student, since it did not necessarily require a rejection, as her friends had feared, of her preferred forms of expression, her personal convictions and beliefs. In fact, Stacie describes in her reflection "realizing that there is so much more to know" and that "by knowing something more . . . I become more. Well at least I open the door to the possibilities of more."

Stacie did indeed find much success. Although she became a high-achieving student in many courses and in her major, a highly-sought-after consultant in the writing center, she remained a member of her close-knit community as a leader of her Bible study group, a musician performing at local churches, and a good friend to her high school classmates. When she graduated with her associate's degree in Human Services, she celebrated with a bonfire in her backyard attended by friends, family, and professors alike.

Joseph Pritchard—Relational Literacy

Another writing consultant on our campus, Joseph Pritchard, has found his place as an English major and is currently working to complete his honors thesis while his wife pursues a nursing degree. Joe is known in the Learning Center for his patient silences and thoughtful, open questions, his willingness to sit with uncertainty and vulnerability. On Fridays, his sessions often run long as students sit beside him, writing independently while he does his own work, untroubled by the hectic pace characteristic of the rest of the writing center weekly schedule. In his approach to his writing sessions, Joe is thoughtful about how the pressures of "real life" schedules and health problems and family commitments make investing in time-intensive homework assignments (like essays) particularly challenging for students on our campus. His pacing and relational style encourage student clients to treat writing sessions as a social space separate from their college lives (less scheduled, less instrumental) and perhaps resembling more the kinds of personally meaningful forms of literacy he (and they) practice in their everyday lives in the community.

In his second year of college and his first year as a writing consultant, the reflection Joe composed relates the overlap between his on- and off-campus literacy lives and comments on how his own experiences compared to those of his peers. As a self-described "recluse" Joe writes: "I get my sports news from my wife's dad who's an encyclopedia on the matter; and I just shoot the shit with my crazy, old neighbors if I desire human interaction." He compares this to the literacy practices he associates with university work, noting that in his community, "People don't read, it certainly wasn't emphasized at . . . [my high school]." Joe does not see his home community as a community of readers, and yet he describes in a brief, vivid burst the literacies prized by his family and neighbors, literacies which he, too, values: sports, politics, history, and outdoorsmanship. In conversation, Joe often refers to the pleasure he takes in online interactions and friendly argumentation with his neighbors.

Before the motorcycle accident that placed him in a wheelchair, Joe lived a physically active life, hunting and fishing and generally (by his own account) not taking school too seriously. But once his mobility became limited, Joe turned to reading as an alternative to the activities he could no longer manage. Reading and writing have since re-formed themselves in his life as social activities connecting him to others in ways that his previous hobbies once did.

The social role of reading and writing practices derives its meaning and shape in Joe's life from the relationship contexts within which those literacy acts take place, and in turn these relationships take their form from the rural town where he grew up and the online spaces which, for many in rural areas (particularly those with limited mobility), provide a valuable alternative place for dwelling and for exchanging information. Continuing with a discussion of what he believes to be his peers' difficulties in acquiring academic ways of reading and writing, Joe describes "main campuses" as "full of scholarship chasers [and] early achievers," noting that regional campus students are more likely to be "rusty on time management (hell, I still am), basic writing skills (still sharpening that sword myself), and trying new things (luckily, I kind of enjoy this)." Joe also writes about the social interchange of his off-campus life with the arbitrariness and performative pressure of on-campus literacies, conditions which favor, perhaps "the scholarship chasers." In Joe's first semester as a student, his ability to see diverse points of view and craft nuanced positions on topics new to him were a strength, even as he struggled with issues of syntax and paragraphing. By the time he became a writing consultant, Joe had forged strong mentoring relationships with several professors in the English Department, having met frequently with them to request assistance in improving as a writer. As a writing consultant, his embrace of a style of interaction more consistent with the laidback, unfocused exchanges of off-campus life simultaneously replicates for many students the more socially-motivated dynamic of interpersonal relationships in the community while still accomplishing the intellectual objectives of the academic writers he is assisting.

Heather Haueter—Reading with and against Place

I will offer one further story of a student writing consultant whose account contributes another facet to the diversity of literacy as it is experienced in our local community and the uses to which place-based literacies may be put when combined successfully with academic literacy. Heather Haueter entered the university as a developmental writing student and, after a year or so, was recommended by her instructors to be a writing consultant in our writing center. She was known for her blunt but empathetic approach to peer review, her skill at making explicit the conventions of intellectual writing for the university in a way her fellow students found easy to apply. Her experiences as a student in developmental courses may have provided a helpful grounding for her unique skill in demystifying academic conventions, but her experiences as the daughter and confidante of an alcoholic taught her at an early age that *everything* could be a text, subject to interpretation and re-interpretation. In her reflection, which ultimately became a paper she delivered in a joint presentation with me at the Eastern Central Writing Center Association Conference in 2014, Heather writes, "My literacy does not come from books and what I've learned to write came from passion to leave a world I didn't want to be a part of but had no control over" (Haueter). In Heather's account, acts of reading and writing become critical for survival, tools for pulling the tangled web of her life apart and reassembling it in ways that made sense.

She describes how her father used to wake her up after returning home drunk because he was looking for someone to talk to. Heather acknowledges that "as bad as that sounds, because we're raised in world that teaches us that's bad parenting, it really wasn't horrible" (Haueter). She portrays her father as "a logical man with a sarcastic attitude [who] knew he wasn't prepared for the world" (Haueter) and who wished to provide her with a critical perspective on how to read people and their actions. When other children were learning the authority of received knowledge as it was taught by parents, grandparents, and schools, Heather was learning that truth and knowledge were social constructs, dependent on one's position in an eroding rural, rust-belt economy in which family and future and jobs were ever-changing, and that acts of reading, of interpretation, of that world were essential to survival.

Heather spoke with her dad about this section of her paper before presenting it, perhaps as a way, after years of sorting through her complicated feelings, to acknowledge both the pain and the value of this part of her childhood. She says that gaining access to the messiness of the adult world through the critical eyes of her father as he told his stories late at night played a key role in forming her skeptical, analytical approach to intellectual work, an approach that later was valued and further developed by her university education. Heather writes, "When I was young, I would write poetry to handle the pain and smile through the storm" (Haueter). Her response to the strong emotions of her childhood—writing poetry—planted the seeds of a fundamental confidence in writing as a meaningful form of expression and communication.

A Meta-Review of Cross-Pollinating Literacies in Practice

Students from rural or Appalachian backgrounds may experience the process of "inventing the university" in the college classroom very differently from suburban and middle class students for whom there may be more overlap in the literacies of home and university, and in many ways this difference may prove an advantage. Discourse in writing sessions about the assumptions and uses of literacy in its various contexts can prevent writers from experiencing erosion and loss, particularly when the conversation is led by peer writing consultants who practice literacy with skill both in the community and in the university. Placing a value on the knowledge that peer writing consultants and their clients already bring to the questions and challenges presented in the classroom represents an inversion of conventional models of literacy sponsorship in which, as Deborah Brandt has described, "although the interests of the sponsor and sponsored do not have to converge (and, in fact, may conflict) sponsors nevertheless set the terms for access to literacy and wield powerful incentives for compliance and loyalty," (166-7). Campuses that enroll significant percentages of their students from their home communities should make use of the full range of their writing consultants' literacy knowledge, not merely that which they use in classroom contexts. In their study of a rural community college campus, Howley et al. problematize what they term "the deficit views of rural life" (10), suggesting that on rural campuses students find the overlapping system of relationships and connections familiar to them from the home community. The complex web of interconnected relationships and roles evident on such a campus may make it easier for rural students, particularly non-traditional students who may be displaced workers or otherwise economically disadvantaged, to more effectively navigate the challenges of college because they can leverage relationships and operational modes from the community. Howley et al. contend that, as a result of this embeddedness, students under pressure from family, work, and economic distress may be more likely to persist and transplant to the college environment successfully because "rural community members are more likely to respond to each other in ways that do not threaten their multiple commitments but rather support and maintain them" (8). The stories of the three writing consultants described above point to the rich promise that an embrace of multiplicity in the writing center may offer university students as they construct their academic literacies.

Stacie's story remains, in some ways, something of an exception on our campus. Whatever losses she sustained as her relationships were strained by the changes she experienced were incorporated into the unbroken fabric of her life narrative because of the way education, for her, came to represent continuity with her past literacy life and practices. Stacie, with her bonfire and friendships maintained after graduation, succeeded in integrating her campus and community lives more fully than most. For students motivated primarily or solely by economic need, cultivating academic literacy on a rural, commuter campus may ultimately prove to be unnecessarily difficult if the process can be completed only at the cost of displacement or a devaluation of one's prior experiences. Cultivating a garden of sweet corn, tomatoes, and greens, the familiar things, in one's backyard is a long way from cultivating a soyfield in the monoculture of contemporary agriculture. As Stacie's story demonstrates, when we encourage students to locate and employ their personally and community-valued literacies in the service of their academic growth, rather than displacing those literacies with some imagined, homogenized academic literacy, there is greater potential for productivity and sustained growth both for students and the university community itself.

For Joe, the integration of campus and community literacy has become far more than a success strategy or an area of personally satisfying growth (though it is, of course, those things). Since writing his reflection piece, Joe has published several poems in literary journals and contributed to the growth of an active literary community on our campus and in our county. He speaks often of what it has meant to connect to others on our campus with whom he found common experience and could cultivate shared aspiration grounded in both the local community and a college education. His insight into the range of students' primary identities underlying their "student-at-university" identities and his perception that "people don't read" illustrates the gap between students' perceptions of their community context and university context, but in writing sessions his stylistic embrace of an appreciation for the texture of social exchange and the ambiguous feelings students have for acquiring academic literacy position him as a highly effective tutor. As the experiences and practices of Stacie and Joe suggest, such sponsorship may be most effective when such validation takes social forms recognizable to students and explicitly acknowledges the moves required by these shifting literacy contexts.

Heather's adult experiences of literacy in the community as a single mother offer insight into the ways that critical literacies may be cultivated through oppositional encounters with authority and through storytelling imbued with relationally-constructed meaning. Her literacy practices in the community—producing statements for court and completing paperwork for the county bureaucracy, helping her children with their own educations— became to an extent acts of resistance to what she perceived as the prevailing narrative about who she was and what her potential might be. Just as Heather sought to take control of the narrative of a childhood that included late-night chats with an alcoholic father (parenting which "wasn't all that horrible"), she formed her aspirations around a life of writing in resistance on behalf of others. That very positioning as an outsider became an asset once she decided to apply to her local Kent State campus and pursue a degree in Human Services. As Heather saw it, she was bringing to the university valuable insights and literacy experiences that would enrich her value as a student and professional. Heather continues her account by observing the ways that her integrated, hybridized literacy practices in college enabled her transition to full adulthood as a parent and professional in the community:

> Everything in my life has been [a search] for meaning and the exchange of information, but I had never realized it. . . . It all

was starting to form a web and connecting in the middle to this one goal: to make a difference. College is my way of trying to make a positive change in such a negative world. (Haueter)

Heather's observations about her application of previous literacy practices and experiences in the development of academic literacy illustrate not only the practical benefits of gaining fluency in academic writing (making progress toward a degree and career goals) but also the healing power of living a life undivided by uneasy barriers between the worlds of on and off-campus. Her ability to read texts critically, taking them apart and then rebuilding meaning, offers another example of the means by which place and community may prepare a student for college in a fashion that the university does not typically anticipate or access.

For Stacie and Joe, continued engagement with their own non-academic literacies and those of their clients offers them what they perceive to be accelerated and personally meaningful progress toward becoming more proficient academic writers. As Heather puts into practice some of her community-based notions about literacy, critical thinking, and identity in her role as a writing consultant, she advances her own skill and confidence at the same time that she assists other students in doing so. Heather concludes her reflection by noting that "the most compelling literacy . . . [she has] been involved with in the Learning Center is the writing for [developmental writing courses]" (Haueter) because of the value she sees in helping other students gain a more nuanced and compassionate view of others and of themselves. These students' stories of reading and writing began with literacies they had practiced alone and with others in Columbiana County long before they entered college, and their extracurricular literacy experiences continue to contribute in powerful, positive ways to their formation as academic writers.

TUTORS CO-SPONSORING LITERACY/ HYBRIDITY

Given their tremendous resource base and their rootedness in place, consultants can promote hybridization by encouraging students to explore the literacy knowledge and practice they employ outside the university in a variety of other settings. Doing this requires a willingness to follow conversational tangents and personal stories, indeed to build them into a session's agenda. In one case, Joe related to me a difficult session in which a student trying to analyze the movie *Freaks* was able to made progress after Joe discovered the student had been avidly following news of an NFL scandal; Joe used the student's knowledgeable analysis of the news reporting to encourage him to make similar reading moves as a viewer of *Freaks*. As Joe has suggested above, many students also perceive themselves a non-readers and non-writers, so recasting this perception through curiosity about personal and place-based literacy practices valued by the student may help clear the ground of counterproductive notions about the difference between academic life and "real" life. Here follow a few similar cases of consultants assisting students to see the academic moves in light of their extra-curricular literacies.

Adam[1]—An Aesthetic Move

A student, "Adam," who is himself an avid reader and non-traditional student working in manufacturing, brought a nearly-complete draft into the Learning Center, hoping to work on what he felt were problems with how he was making use of his lens text, Friedrich Nietzche's *Thus Spake Zarathustra*. In working with him, I could see his enthusiasm for the material and that he clearly had synthesized the material in order to investigate U2's *Zooropa* album as required by the assignment, yet he was not doing so in a way a reader fresh to the material would be able to interpret. As the writing consultant, I began the session by responding to his stated goal for the session by describing a section in his work where the problem seemed apparent. He responded by suggesting that he was "trying to be vague" in order to produce "better writing" that would not be "glaring" in making the point he wished to make.

At that point in the session, rather than "correcting" his perception of academic style, I asked why he had made the aesthetic choice he was making, where he had developed his mental model of "good" writing. At this point Adam, warming visibly to his subject, briefly described the ending of *The Life of Pi*, its ambiguity and appeal, explaining that the novel was typical of the reading he preferred to do. He explained, "I really like metaphors is what I'm saying as opposed to like a simile . . . Simile dumbs it down." He went on to explain that he found similes predictable and they don't "challenge the reader to use his own mind." He added that he felt it was beneficial to allow a metaphor to play out in his essay because it "leaves a reader time to try and figure it out."

The emphasis on extending time in his essay is also significant, reflecting as it does the different rhythm of Adam's reading life off-campus, in which ideas and literature are consumed for pleasure, as opposed to the more instrumentally-driven consumption of academic work in university life. Once I understood that Adam wanted to engage his reader as an active partner in interpretation, I could help him identify the moves he needed to make in order to support his reader.

Melody—Why We Write

Stacie was partnered on aweekly basis with "Melody," a non-traditional student who expressed at first a great deal of self-doubt and concern about writing. She was direct in relaying to us that much of the trouble she was experiencing related to trauma and ongoing medical issues, and that as a high school student she had been "a really good writer" according to her teachers. Stacie, responding to Melody's visible agitation, reassured her that they would take the reading and writing tasks piece by piece so she could stop at any point if she began to feel overwhelmed. My account here covers multiple sessions over the course of a semester which are summarized for the purpose of offering a longer view of the process of cultivating hybrid literacies.

Stacie began most sessions by asking Melody to read the assigned text aloud and discuss as she went so they could identify any problems with comprehension as they occurred. This had the effect of focusing Melody's attention on the act of simply reading aloud rather than worrying about how she was measuring up. Very early on it became clear that she did have some difficulty comprehending, but once she did, she readily connected the texts to her own life experiences and feelings. Because Melody was generating so many thoughts that seemed only loosely associated with one another, Stacie encouraged her to note them down as she was reading. Melody immediately recognized in this common reading strategy a connection to advice her counselor had given her, suggesting that she journal in order to process her feelings. This insight led toa conversation about why both student client and student consultant write, what role the act of writing plays in their lives. Stacie shared that she also keeps a journal of her thoughts, though for her they represent a more spiritual investigation. Both women talked about identity, how it changes in response to experience, and how writing can be a way to track those changes, making sense of them through re-reading and revision.

In their sessions together, Stacie was able to re-direct conversation from the purposes of their extracurricular literacy practices to the question of why we write intellectually, pointing out to Melody that her professor was asking her to use writing to think through the problems of the text, just as she used it in her journaling to process her emotions and make sense of her experiences. Melody noted that her professor did not want her to use lots of "I think" or "I feel" language, and she expressed frustration with the problem of how to represent her own ideas about the text without marking the origin of her thoughts in this way. This led to a brief discussion about the conventions of intellectual writing—why they are different from those of journaling—and how Melody might draw on her journaling practices to develop her reading of texts before using her ideas for more formal papers.

Meta-Review of Tutors Co-Sponsoring Literacy/ Hybridity

What makes these session worth remarking is that, once again, the barrier between these two students was at least partially dismantled by the consultant's decision to work with, rather than work against, the student's extracurricular literacy experiences. By encouraging Melody to see connections between a literacy practice she already valued and the new one which she viewed with such trepidation, Stacie helped restore to her a sense of place. Melody had been under the impression that nothing she thought or could write would be appropriate for the assignment, and though she felt it was expected she should transform herself into a college student, she also seemed determined to assert her sense of herself as a survivor. This latter identity and her healing process were of greater interest and importance to her than her identity as a student. Stacie, in acknowledging the connection between her college literacy experiences and her own non-academic, more spiritual journey, was attempting to demonstrate for the student the possibility of multiplicity, of layered literacies and selves that complement rather than conflict with one another.

Throughout the semester Melody continued to write her way across a spectrum that often resembled journaling more closely than the personal intellectual essay assigned by the professor teaching her basic writing course. Around mid-semester Stacie noted with chagrin that although she had tried her best to show Melody how to make use of her journaling style for pre-writing and then adapt it for her essays, Melody still often chose to turn inward, taking assignments in directions she preferred for their therapeutic value rather than addressing the professor's intent. "But," Stacie said to me, "I think maybe that's just what she needs to do right now, you know? If college is a part of her therapy, that's just how it is. Hopefully when she gets to College Writing I, she'll be ready to change it up a little more."

This consultant's realistic acknowledgement of the gap between the student's purposes and the university's purposes, and her willingness to truly collaborate with the student—which meant, at times, simply offering her choices and then accepting them, whatever they were, without further comment—are exemplary, I think, of many similar stories. Although in other stories it might not be therapy journaling we're working with as a literacy practice—perhaps instead it's politics or religion or story-telling or crime dramas—we need models of literacy sponsorship that include an appreciation for the value of layered literacies in the writing center. In practice, this means that consultants like this one should actively invite those literacies into the discussion so that they can be examined and used rather than resisted. Stacie, while frustrated that she could not assist the student in more rapidly making progress toward success in the class, was only able to make progress with this particularly challenging student because, as the student client acknowledged to me, Stacie had established trust with her by respecting her choices and constructing with her a way for talking about those choices. This trust kept her engaged in her class and engaged with the writing center despite her ongoing extracurricular struggles. In this case, Stacie, by accepting the dissonance between the student's intentions and the university's requirements, was able to continue engaging the student in a conversation about the dissonance itself. This remained productive for the student, helping her continue with her university education.

Differences in purpose may be one challenge that writing consultants sensitive to the idiosyncratic contexts of place and personal history may effectively address; differences in aesthetic and intellectual style may similarly benefit from an approach to literacy sponsorship informedb y curiosity and a receptivity to context. Early in the session with Adam, I had clearly expected to assist him in understanding typical academic essay moves like transitions and claims sentences, moves that would help him bridge between the two texts and give the essay a recognizably academic cast. Instead, the session shifted focus to acknowledging and making use of his interest in offering less explicit guidance for his reader, a guidance more similar to the spiritual adventure novels he favors, works whose meanings "you're kind of left trying to decide" and which, perhaps for thematic reasons, offered an appropriate aesthetic for an essay in which he clearly had engaged in his own spiritual adventure of sorts.

If instead I had viewed his moves as mistakes to be corrected, we might have missed developing a deeper understanding of his intellectual project in the essay, a project mirroring the spiritual quest of both works and adopting something of the Socratic flavor of his preferred recreational reading material. Not only did we gain some needed perspective on the project he was pursuing in his writing, but through metadiscourse about the writing process, Adam also became more aware of himself as a purposeful decision-maker balancing the challenge of satisfying his own aesthetic preferences against the needs of his academic audience.

In each of the above sessions, writing consultants and clients perceive a lack of continuity between their familiar literacy practices and those they must adopt within the university. In the case of Adam, he retains an aesthetic from his recreational reading that influences his academic writing. Making him aware of the moves he's making as a writer, their source and their use, assists him in adapting his aesthetic more intentionally to academic requirements. In this way, he is able to develop rather than erase his distinctive writing style. For the sexter mentioned much earlier in the article and for Melody, active investigations into their non-academic literacy practices evolve into conversations about their identities as academic writers and introduce modes of critical thinking that can be adapted for use in academic contexts.

Toward a Pragmatics of Place

A recent article by Marc Scott written in collaboration with peer writing consultants at Shawnee State University in another corner of Appalachian Ohio suggests that building rapport with first generation college students is fundamental to success and may look different with Appalachian students than building rapport with students of other backgrounds. In particular, Scott and his consultants recommend altering the politeness norms of the middle class university writing center to more regionally appropriate norms, for example, offering a more direct explanation of *why* a particular feature in a paper is successful, then making a clear and direct transition to what is *not* working in a paper and why (58). They also describe writing consultants speaking in regional dialect themselves as they tutor ("this part needs revised") (55) and the value for writers in seeing their own linguistic and literacy journeys reflected in that of the consultants whom they trust to assist them along the way. Extending this discussion of language and social behaviors to embrace the entire complex of literacy practice, we might strive for what Kurt Spellmeyer calls a "way of reading that restores a sense of connection to things, and with it, a greater confidence in our ability to act" (168). Spellmeyer contends that such a "pragmatics of reading" accomplishes the "most essential work of the arts" (168), thus affording students access to their cultural inheritance as a tool for making sense of their contemporary context. Likewise, pragmatics of writing on a rural campus requires an attention to the relationships and social contexts that shape literacy practices on the campus and in the community and a critical examination of loss when—and if—it occurs. Such an awareness supports students' ability to act and make decisions with an authority derived from knowledge grounded in place, relationship, and the academic literacy they are in the act of acquiring.

In his handbook for students, *ReWriting: How To Do Things with Texts,* Joseph Harris unpacks for his audience the "moves" of intellectual writing and reading, emphasizing the need for them to work with the understanding that "Our creativity . . . has its roots in the work of others—in response, reuse, and rewriting"(2). For students learning to identify and make moves between and within multiplex literacies, there is much to be gained from Harris' approach of explicitly commenting to students upon the pragmatic workings of intellectual reading and writing; by sifting the pragmatic from the conceptual, he makes possible the comparability of these moves to the more familiar moves of students' community-based literacies. A student who composes music for her faith community may readily recognize in Harris' descriptions of forwarding or "taking an approach" the moves she makes in referencing a line from a well-known hymn or riffing off a favorite inspirational writer's work in order to bring those insights to a religious context. Harris calls upon students to make conceptually sophisticated choices about their writing moves as readers and writers informed by their own evaluation of the rhetorical spaces they occupy. For the student steeped in making these same moves for other purposes outside the university, the act of naming the moves and demonstrating their utility for intellectual work may be gamechanging. Writing consultants fluent in the use of these moves both on and off campus are more likely to see the potential for making these connections.

In our writing center practice, then, cultivating literacy hybridity requires an intentional pursuit of several aims that may inflect our sessions with a slightly different feel.

- *Establishing community-based identities as writers and readers:* As the experiences of Joe and others described above suggest, when students arrive at rural and regional campuses, they often do not identify as successful readers and writers simply because they do not recognize their non-academic reading and writing practices as having value in an academic context. Many student writers expect, early in their academic careers, to write only "what the teacher wants." Others, like Heather or Adam, may see themselves as successful readers and writers but lack an awareness of the utility of their community-based literacy practices. Writing centers serving strongly place-identified clients may benefit from inquiring into the literacy identities of their clients in order to help them tap into their competence as literate adults, in this way establishing a fertile ground for the cultivation of academic literacies. A writing center that asks not only, "what do you know about this?" but also "*how* do you know it?" may offer students new ways to ground their authority in the classroom.
- *Leveraging our multiple relationships:* Similarly, part of training writing consultants on rural campuses should include drawing their attention to the complex of relationships and knowledge they bring with them into the university, helping them appreciate the ways that their community-based social contexts may animate and enrich their roles as writing consultants and literacy sponsors on the campus. Successful peer tutors like Stacie, Joe, and Heather ground much of their literate practice in community-based social relationships and histories. Their awareness of the contrast between their forms of social, literate exchange and the social literacy exchanges of the academy give them an edge as they seek to make sense of why they think as they do about the questions posed by their professors. The

result may be a generative disruption, both of their position in the academy and their position in the community.

- *Making use of dissonance and a surplus of meaning:* Writing sessions should routinely include questions not only about what a writer hopes to accomplish, but about the choices and histories leading up to what a writer has already done. In this way, dissonance between a writer's accustomed literacy practices and the practices favored in academic settings may lead not to displacement of known practices but instead adaptation and hybridity. A writer might choose to be restrained and direct in language in one portion of an essay while elaborating and taking calculated risks in another. Complementary plantings and hybrid cultivars may, in the end, result in more lively and productive academic work.

Writing centers on rural campuses must cultivate connections between consultants and student clients with particular attention to creating space for the inclusion of the multi-layered literacies of community belonging that, if consciously propagated and combined with academic literacies, have potential to transform both the lives of students and of their university communities. The key here is that notion of cultivation: without planning and intention, the literacies that grow will be wild and variable in their use or else monocultural and lacking in resilience. Because of their position within the academy, writing consultants are uniquely positioned to do this work of cultivating places—and people—at the center.

Note

1. All students were invited to remain anonymous or be named in the article. Consultants chose to be named individually, while clients either had no preference or indicated they would prefer anonymity. The names here given for consultants, then, are their real names while clients' names are pseudonyms. Consultants reviewed the article and, without exception, gave feedback approving the accuracy of the representation of themselves contained here, at times even offering additional insight.

Works Cited

Brandt, Deborah, et al. "The Politics of the Personal: Storying Our Lives against the Grain." *College English*, vol. 64, no. 1, 2001, pp. 41-62.

Brandt, Deborah. "Sponsors of Literacy." *College Composition and Communication*, vol. 49, no. 2, 1998, pp. 165-185.

Carnevale, Anthony P. et al. "Recovery: Job Growth and Education Requirements through 2020." *Georgetown Center on Education and the Workforce*. 2013. https://cew.georgetown.edu/wp-content/uploads/2014/11/Recovery2020.SR_.Web_.pdf

Carrick, Tracy Hamler. "Bootlegging Literacy Sponsorship, Brewing Up Institutional Change." *Community Literacy Journal*, vol. 2, no. 1, 2007, pp. 25-39.

Corbett, Michael. "Rural Schooling in Mobile Modernity: Returning to the Places I've Been." *Journal of Research in Rural Education*, vol. 24, no. 9, 2009, pp. 1-13.

Daniell, Beth. "Narratives of Literacy: Connecting Composition to Culture." *College Composition and Communication*, vol. 50, no. 3, 1999, pp. 393-410. Donehower, Kim, et al. *Rural Literacies*. Southern Illinois University Press, 2007.

Flippen, Alan. "The Upshot: Where Are the Hardest Places to Live in the U.S.?" *The New York Times*, 16 Jun. 2014, https://www.nytimes.com/2014/06/26/ upshot/where-are-the-hardest-places-to-live-in-the-us.html.

Hall, Anne-Marie, and Christopher Minnix. "Beyond the Bridge Metaphor: Rethinking the Place of the Literacy Narrative in the Basic Writing Curriculum." *Journal of Basic Writing*, vol. 31, no. 2, 2012, pp. 57-82.

Harris, Joseph. *Rewriting: How To Do Things with Texts*. Utah State University Press, 2006.

Haueter, Heather. "Untitled." *Paper presented at the annual meeting of the Eastern Central Writing Centers Association*. Oxford, OH, 2014. Conference paper.

Heath, Shirley Brice. *Ways with Words: Language, Life, and Work in Communities and Classrooms*. Cambridge University Press, 1983.

Howley, Caitlin, et al. "'Like Human Beings': Responsive Relationships and Institutional Flexibility at a Rural Community College." *Journal of Research in Rural Education*, vol. 28, no. 8, 2013, pp. 1-14.

Hull, Glynda, and Katherine Schultz. "Literacy and Learning Out of School: A Review of Theory and Research." *Review of Educational Research*, vol. 71, no. 4, 2001, pp. 575-611.

Hull, Glynda, et al. "Remediation as Social Construct: Perspectives from an Analysis of Classroom Discourse." *College Composition and Communication*, vol. 42, no. 3, 1991, pp. 299-329.

Kazemek, Francis. "Necessary Changes: Professional Involvement in Adult Literacy Programs." *Harvard Educational Review*, vol. 58, no. 4, 1988, pp. 464-487.

Kelly, Ursula. "Learning to Lose: Rurality, Transience, and Belonging (A Companion to Michael Corbett)." *Journal of Research in Rural Education*, vol. 24, no. 11, 2009, pp. 1-4.

Kent State University Institutional Research [IR]. *Grade Distribution Reports Fall 2013, Spring 2014, Fall 2014, Spring 2015, Fall 2016 ENG 01001, ENG01002, ENG 11011, Salem Campus* [Data file], 2016.

Kent State University Institutional Research [IR]. *Remediation Rates for East Liverpool and Salem Campuses, Fall 2015* [Data file], 2016.

Langer, Judith A. "Literacy and Schooling: A Sociocognitive Perspective." *Literacy in a Diverse Society: Perspectives, Practices, and Policies*, edited by Elfrieda H. Hiebert, Teachers College, 1991, pp. 9-27.

Massey, Doreen. *Space, Place, and Gender*. University of Minnesota Press, 1994. Minter, Deborah, et al. "Learning Literacies." *College English*, vol. 5, no. 6, 1995, pp. 21-39.

Muth, Bill. "Integrating Social-humanist and Cognitive Approaches to Adult Literacy." *Adult Basic Education and Literacy Journal*, vol. 5, no. 1, 2011, pp. 26-37.

North, Stephen. "The Idea of a Writing Center." *College English*, vol. 46, no. 5, 1984, pp. 433-446.

Ohio Department of Education. *2015-2016 Ohio School Report Cards*, 2017. http://reportcard.education.ohio.gov.

Ohio Development Services Agency. "Columbiana County Profile." 2017, https://development.ohio.gov/files/research/C1016.pdf.

Reynolds, Nedra. "Composition's Imagined Geographies: The Politics of Space in the Frontier, City, and Cyberspace." *College Composition and Communication*, vol. 50, no. 1, 1998, pp. 12-35.

Scott, Marc, et al. "Tutoring 'The Invisible Minority': Appalachian Writers in the Writing Center." *Open Words: Access and English Studies*, vol. 9, no. 1, 2015, pp. 50-61.

Seabolt, Kym. "Use It or Lose It." *Farm and Dairy*, 13 April 2017, farmanddairy. com/columns/use-it-or-lose-it/409854.html.

Shepley, Nathan. "Places of Composition: Writing Contexts in Appalachian Ohio." *Composition Studies*, vol. 37, no. 2, 2009, pp. 75-90.

Spellmeyer, Kurt. *Arts of Living: Reinventing the Humanities for the Twenty-first Century*. State University of New York Press, 2003.

United States Census Bureau. "Columbiana County Educational Attainment." *2011-2015 American Community Survey 5-Year Estimates*. https:// factfinder. census.gov/faces/tableservices/jsf/pages/productview. xhtml?src=CF.

United States Department of Agriculture. "Non-Metropolitan Outmigration Counties: Some are Poor, Some are Prosperous." *Economic Research*

Report Number 107. 2010. https://www.ers.usda.gov/webdocs/publications/44770/8062_err107.pdf?v=41056 .

Webb-Sunderhaus, Sara. "When Access is Not Enough: Retaining Basic Writers at an Open-admission University." *Journal of Basic Writing,* vol. 29, no. 2, 2010, pp. 97-116.

Weiner, Eric J. "Keeping Adults Behind: Adult Literacy Education in the Age of Official Reading Regimes." *Journal of Adolescent and Adult Literacy,* vol. 49, no. 4, 2005, pp. 286-301.

Supplemental Material

Part I: Reflection on the Origins of the Article

As the Learning Center Coordinator at Kent State University's Salem campus, I worked intimately with student writing both in the classroom and in the writing center, often following individual students for years as they progressed toward their degrees. I was fascinated in an anthropological way with the stories students shared about their extracurricular literacy practices and, at the same time, frustrated. I was new to the Midwest and found that I had a lot to learn about how the prevailing cultural narratives around education, success, and the economy shaped students' understanding of their purposes at the university. I saw students who I viewed as successful and interesting writers – effective in the community, making terrific progress in the university – discount the value of their literacy knowledge and fail to adapt to new writing contexts. As they moved from college writing courses into courses in history or psychology or human development, for example, they would re-cast themselves once again as non-writers and express a sense that "every professor" or "every class" had its own, arbitrary writing requirements. Rather than seeing continuity and opportunities for adaptation between their community-based literacies, their literacy practices in college writing, and their literacy practices in other disciplines, they perceived fragmentation, conflicting messages, and failure.

At the same time, I was fortunate to have access to a marvelous and ever-changing staff of talented writers who were also peer writing consultants. Their creativity and relational approach to writing sessions seemed significant to me in its difference from that of other talented peer writing consultants with whom I had worked at my previous institutions. Their novel approaches to writing sessions and their tendency to cultivate mentoring – not just tutoring relationships were reinforced by our campus requirement that writers in developmental courses visit the writing center for a minimum of five to eight visits per semester. Even if consultants didn't know the writers prior to meeting them on campus – though often they did – they had the opportunity to develop rewarding relationships with them over time. These sustained tutoring relationships, repeated throughout their first year of writing instruction, meant that the consultants also had to look for new ways to approach the same writing issues, developing an approach and vocabulary specific to each, unique writer's situation. This familiarity built trust and encouraged more personal sharing in sessions. It also allowed all parties to take risks, because they had the combined benefit of trusting relationships and extended time.

I noticed in particular that when we, as writing consultants, encouraged students to stop worrying about their papers and to instead talk about the writing and reading they enjoyed, we could learn all kinds of things about their strengths and about how they perceived the moves writers and readers make. This article was the result of my curiosity about these observations and my desire to more purposefully embed what appeared to be a promising set of practices into our Learning Center culture.

Part II: Description of Research Methods, Findings, and/or Pedagogical Impact

I took a loosely ethnographic approach to this research, creating a template of questions that structured the routine session reports each consultant produced regularly for all sessions. This created some uniformity in the data I was working with. I also recorded some sessions that occurred when I was present in the Learning Center, afterwards flagging sections of dialogue that demonstrated discourse about extracurricular literacy knowledge and practices. I should note that the act of organizing my curiosity into a research project of this scale has been helpful in a number of ways that extend beyond writing the article itself. In fact, I am about to embark on my PhD, as I've realized that at this point in my career, most of the research questions I have about my work require greater knowledge of qualitative and quantitative methodologies.

All of our peer writing consultants were required to produce pedagogical reflections on their tutoring experiences at the end of each year in the Learning Center. In the year during which this study was conducted, I requested that they comment in their pedagogical essays on the writing and reading practices they bring to the university from the community. The results were far richer in detail and variety than I had expected, which is why they ultimately became a centerpiece for this article. I also preferred to emphasize students' own accounts of their literacy lives rather than my interpretations of their literacy lives, which would have been the case inevitably if I had relied exclusively on accounts of clients' sessions. The writing consultants provided me with their own insights which provided a foundation for my more theoretically grounded analysis of their work. I could also be accountable to the writing consultants in a way that would have been difficult with our writing clients as they lost touch with us or graduated during the process of composing this article. The writing consultants, on the other hand, graduated but were still in touch and eager to read and comment upon my representations of their work in the article.

My own pedagogy, while always student-centered, has undergone a shift as I pursued the work represented in this article and in other spaces. At the same time that I was a composition instructor and writing center coordinator on our campus, I also created and directed a rural college access program. The combination of these experiences has deepened my interest in making use of students' histories, more explicitly creating opportunities for them to strengthen the continuity between past, present, and future. This doesn't mean that we spend all of our time writing literacy narratives in the composition classroom, for example (though we do incorporate those). We spend a lot more time talking about how writing is fundamentally driven by the confluence of the audience's needs, the sociohistorical situatedness of the writing act itself, and the writer's purposes – and how insights related to that confluence can be applied to writing in a variety of contexts. We examine the place and location that inform both the writer's approach and the audience's, and that means talking about the reasons readers and writers make the moves that they make. We share our community-based literacy stories and do scaffolding assignments that cross genres of writing that they have used in the past as well as those, like business proposals, that they may encounter in the future.

In the Learning Center, each writing session is composed of the following rough structure, familiar to most writing center practitioners, with different parts receiving more emphasis depending on the agenda set by consultant and client: 1) introductions made between writer, reader, and text, 2) setting the agenda, 3) getting the story behind the assignment, 4) reacting to the text/making a plan, 5) writing during the session, 6) reviewing progress, and 7) concluding the session with next steps. I think the difference in our Learning Center is the emphasis we place on "getting the story" of a piece of writing and then continuing that discussion throughout the session. We encourage writing consultants to unpack the history of a writer's relationships to a piece of writing or a proposed focus for revision before charging into working with the text. Wherever possible, we work to draw connections between the writer's current academic work and prior reading/writing experiences. As writing consultants, we continue to check in on the whys and hows of a writer's decision-making for the remainder of a session, encouraging the writer to construct a continuous narrative that traces the path from past experience to present choices.

Part III: Discussion Questions

1. In your own experience, which types of community-based or extra-curricular literacy practices might seem to produce the most readily transferable approaches and skills for university work? Which community-based or extra-curricular literacy practices might seem devalued by or in other ways perceived as disruptive to the acquisition of academic literacy? How, why, and by whom are the community-based literacies you have described transmitted?

2. The account in this article focuses in particular on student literacy assets present on a rural, regional campus serving primarily place-bound students. How might its insights translate to a different type of campus environment with different student demographics and campus setting? To a large, R1 campus? A small, liberal arts campus? To an online university environment? How might these different environments challenge or otherwise suggest modification to the ideas presented in this article?

3. This article suggests that we investigate and make use of students' layered literacies in order to promote their holistic development as readers/writers and encourage transference as they encounter new writing contexts in their academic environments. How might you build this embrace of multiplex literacies into your pedagogical practice? What would it look like on the ground? What might be the challenges or consequences of such a practice?

Part IV: Activity Idea

The activity suggested below might be best conducted before students have read this article. The idea is to invite students to inventory their own reading and writing practices, considering the social and personal contexts that shape these acts. Whether or not students complete all of the suggested questions, simply taking a bit of time to reflect on the ways that we categorize acts of reading and writing into "academic" and "non-academic" or enjoyable/boring/nerve-wracking may provide them with a useful starting framework for constructing their own inquiries about the layering and cross-pollination of literacies.

Literacy Practice Inventory

In one minute, list all of the reading and writing acts you have performed in the last 24 hours of your weekday life. Include everything! Even the grocery list and the mom-texts.

Once you've done that, take another minute and list all of the reading and writing acts you typically perform during a weekend.

With a partner, look over the lists you have created and discuss. The following questions may be useful in guiding your discussion.

- Which acts of reading and writing were voluntary? Which were mandatory?
- Which acts of reading and writing gave you energy or pleasure? Why?
- Which acts did not, and why?
- Were any of the acts of reading or writing shared in the company of others? What kinds of exchanges occurred that added meaning to the reading/writing?

- Which acts of reading or writing required you to do interpretive or contextualizing work and which did not? What other moves are required of you on a regular basis as a reader or writer?
- How did your anticipation of audience influence your acts of writing? Did you make different moves for different audiences?
- Do you still practice some of the reading and writing acts that were important to you in your childhood/young adulthood? If you've left some behind, why?
- What can you observe about the patterns of like/dislike, shared experience, and interpretation that characterize your daily literacy habits?
- Which of your literacy practices would you characterize as academic? And which would you characterize as non-academic? How do you construct these categories?

Follow up by attempting to visually map your practices and the "moves" you make as a reader or writer for various purposes in your life onto these categories of "academic" and "non-academic."

Examples of practices and moves might be: re-reading, making notes, using key words, interpreting, crafting headings, drawing connections, introducing another source, alluding to another piece of reading (or information or art or music, etc.), wordplay, use of metaphor, being concise, avoiding personal pronouns, or scanning introductions and conclusions.

Where do you find moves and practices crossing categories? Which are exclusive to one category or another and what do you make of that? Where might there be possibilities for hybridization between your reading/writing practices?

RHETORIC REVIEW

Rhetoric Review is one the web at https://www.tandfonline.com/toc/hrhr20/current

Rhetoric Review (RR), a scholarly interdisciplinary journal of rhetoric, publishes in all areas of rhetoric and writing, and provides a professional forum for its readers to consider and discuss current topics and issues. The journal publishes manuscripts that explore the breadth and depth of the discipline, including history, theory, writing, praxis, philosophy, professional writing, rhetorical criticism, cultural studies, multiple literacies, technology, public address, graduate education, and professional issues.

Integral Captions and Subtitles: Designing a Space for Embodied Rhetorics and Visual Access[1]

Butler's article theorizes the ways in which what she calls "integral captions and subtitles" can be designed to more accurately reflect embodied rhetorics in multimodal literacy practices in ways that benefit both deaf and hearing composers and viewers. The peer reviewers of Butler's article praise the "original and important contribution to our understanding of multimodal accessibility . . . very few people in rhetoric are talking about accessibility in this way and it deserves to be read and considered by rhetoric scholars."

---

1. *Rhetoric Review*, vol. 37, no. 3 © 2018 by Taylor & Francis Group, LLC.

Integral Captions and Subtitles: Designing a Space for Embodied Rhetorics and Visual Access

Janine Butler

Integral captions and subtitles are specific forms of captions and subtitles that are designed to be essential elements of videos in co-ordination with sound, signs, and other modes of communication. Integral captions reflect the importance of embodied rhetorics in Deaf culture, particularly in the kinetic language of ASL and Deaf Space design practices. Designing a (Deaf) space for integral captions that embody multimodal and multilingual communication is an essential multimodal literacy practice that benefits d/Deaf and hearing composers and viewers. Five criteria that characterize integral captions provide instructors and scholars with a tool for captions and embodied rhetorics.

As a Deaf[1] rhetoric and composition scholar who studies accessible multimodal communication, I have been drawn to videos with dynamic captions, such as American Sign Language (ASL) music videos, that enable me to visually access the interplay of multiple modes of communication.[2] In these particular videos, captions are embedded within the space of the video to move with bodies and sound—and to draw the viewer's eye through the meaningful moments of the composition. These videos *integrate* captions in ways that embody, or recreate, the ways that we communicate across multiple modes, languages, and styles at once; thus, I define this form of captions as *integral captions*.

In contrast to standard captioning practices that may place captions at the bottom of the screen, *integral captions* and *integral subtitles* are designed as components of a multimodal message that make sound, meaning, and communication visually accessible. Integral captions and subtitles enhance the *rhetorical* message of a video by: (1) intensifying the interaction of multiple modes in expressing meaning; (2) enriching the *aesthetic* arrangement of a video by purposefully combining visual elements; and making the space of the video visually *accessible* by not forcing viewers' eyes to captions that (3) are added at the bottom of the screen. Multiple modes of communication—visual text, embodied performance on screen, spoken or signed languages, and other elements—coordinate within the space of the screen.

Integral captions are incorporated most vibrantly in ASL music videos—videos that intensely fuse sound, bodies in motion, and kinetic text in movement (Butler). In ASL music videos, captions embody the pulsations of the beat and the vibrations of the music. While captions in ASL music videos may be animated and colored—aesthetic strategies that might not be appropriate in certain contexts, as in professional presentations—videos in other genres can likewise integrate captions into the space of the screen so that captions coordinate with other elements and make holistic meaning accessible for deaf *and* hearing viewers.

A straightforward instance of integrating words on screen in a professional context is evident in Justin Jackerson's signed video presentation on the value of providing deaf infants with access to sign language, which is shown in Figure 1. In his presentation, Jackerson places himself strategically to create space for the subtitles that accompany his signs. The words and phrases in each sentence gradually appear on screen as he signs each element. Because of this placement strategy, viewers can follow his signs, his facial expressions, and his English words in tandem to appreciate his multimodal message. These subtitles recreate his embodied language to make his signed message visually accessible.

While I do not reject standard captions in many contexts, I encourage those in rhetoric and composition and related disciplines to appreciate the design of captions as rhetorical and accessible qualities of multimodal composition practices. Inspired by Jackerson and others who redesign captions and subtitles, I define integral captions and subtitles as embodied and multimodal entities that make possible fluid connections across languages, cultures, and modes. Composers can instill the human quality of rhetoric into captions by considering how we all communicate in interaction with multiple modes of meaning-making so that audiences can make connections between words, signs, speech, and body language in the same space. We can integrate captions into video lectures to reinforce key learning concepts, emphasize our particular messages in conference presentations, and show students the rhetorical connections that can be created between writers and audiences when they infuse captions with character. In order to distinguish integral captions from other forms of captions, I identify essential features of integral captions and I present these features as five criteria near the end of this article. The criteria consider how composers of integral captions design space, visual access, embodied rhetorics, multimodal/multilingual communication, and rhetorical and aesthetic qualities into their videos. These principles serve as an analytical tool through which composers can assess, in tangible terms, how participants design a shared space for communicating in accessible and multiple ways with other bodies. Shared spaces may include video-based interactions, cultural exchanges, sites of translation, or other situations in which individuals consciously construct connections across modes, cultures, and languages through integral captions and accessible practices.

Figure 1: Jackerson stands along the right side of the screen facing the camera. He is wearing a black shirt against a white background and signs the word "Language." The words "American Sign Language" appear in large black font on the left side of the screen. The word "Language" fades into view to show that Jackerson is signing that word (Jackerson 0:27)

To work toward the five criteria for identifying integral captions, this article establishes the embodiment and multimodality of integral captions. I first explain research in the growing field of caption studies, including kinetic captioning, and further develop the distinct definition of integral captions and subtitles. I then merge the study of integral captions with scholarship on embodied rhetorics and multiple and multimodal literacies. My discussion of multimodal composition transitions to the centrality of embodied rhetorics in Deaf culture. I show that the kinetic language and values of Deaf culture inform the design of Deaf Space in *Gallaudet: The Film*, a Deaf-created film in which integral subtitles interweave throughout the frame to embody different speakers and situations. As I discuss, designing a (Deaf) space for integral captions that embody multimodal and multilingual communication is an essential multimodal literacy practice that can benefit d/Deaf and hearing audiences because audiences are able to access the composition's holistic meaning. In the conclusion, my discussion of embodied rhetorics and the five criteria provide scholars with a tool for integrating captions rhetorically.

CAPTION STUDIES AND INTEGRAL CAPTIONS

As a Deaf woman who communicates through body language and eye contact, I acknowledge my own embodied response to words on screen that move in tandem with signs or that draw my eyes to a presenter's face. Integral captions that *show* inflections in meaning are the textual recreations of sign language performances and interpretation. The body of the sign language interpreter and the visual design of the captions embody the rhetorics of the message—which resembles Abby Knoblauch's definition of embodied rhetorics as "productive *rhetorical* uses of the body" (57). I am drawn, then, to the design of integral captions that make a rhetorical and aesthetic message accessible to deaf *and* hearing viewers. Integral captions are distinct from other forms of captions, including traditional closed captions and kinetic captions, as I will discuss in this section.

First, in alignment with generally accepted U.S. definitions for captions and subtitles, I use the term *captions* to refer to same-language text, or contexts in which the caption text is the same language as the language being spoken on screen; in contrast, I use *subtitles* to refer to foreign language subtitles, or contexts in which the spoken or signed language is different from the textual language. For instance, closed captions are created predominantly for deaf and hard-of-hearing audiences and provide textual descriptions of sound, while subtitles are created predominantly for general audiences that may not understand the primary language on screen. So, if ASL is the primary language on screen, then I write that English *subtitles* on screen provide access to ASL.

Now, *closed* captions are different from *open* captions. *Closed* captions, such as those provided on television sets, can be turned on and off—in contrast to *open* captions that are permanently placed on screen so that they are seen by, or open to, viewers of media at any time. For instance, when speakers of a different language speak in a television show or movie, open subtitles appear on screen for viewers to be able to understand what the speakers are saying. Integral captions are open captions because they are designed to be part of the viewing experience, but they go further because they are *integrated* into the space of the video, interact with other elements of multimodal communication, and provide visual access to embodied rhetorics, as I will discuss.

While there is a large number of published studies on captions in various fields (including Deaf studies and usability studies), the rhetorical study of captions can arguably trace itself to Sean Zdenek's extensive research on closed-captioned television shows and films. Noting that rhetorical studies and disability studies have not "paused to pay attention to captioning as rhetoric, even as we've held up captioning as one of the centerpieces of an accessible web," Zdenek argues that the rhetorical nature of captioning is highly relevant to multimodal composition and technical communication since caption studies allow us to consider "how sound and writing interact," "how to transcribe rhetorically," and "how to deepen and complicate our understanding of audience and access" (6; 14–15). Zdenek's research is careful to define closed captioning in terms of accessibility with the following statement: "*[C]losed captioning provides access to audiovisual content for deaf and hard-of-hearing viewers*" (34). His closed captioning research demonstrates how captioners make rhetorical choices in expressing sound textually that shape viewers' experiences and access to media. Closed captions have traditionally been created so that deaf and hard-of-hearing viewers can access televised media and films. Closed captions are an undeniably necessary means of access; however, as Zdenek observes, professional captioners often are not in contact with the producers or directors of popular media and so can be free to make choices in how they caption pre-recorded material. Different captioners could then make different decisions about how to describe sounds in a film or show. In a similar vein, John-Patrick Udo and Deborah Fels argue that closed captions should be incorporated into the production process rather than completed at the end of the post-production process; as they assert, "[W]hy is it deemed acceptable for a third party, such as a describer or captionist, to independently attempt to convey a director's vision or interpretation of a piece of content?" (217). I argue that, in contrast, when we composers create our own videos, we can design captions that embody our rhetorics. When we design captions, as Amy Lueck states in her research on conventionally-placed captions, we "make significant rhetorical decisions about how voice, identity, language(s), and meaning are represented on the screen." When *integrating* captions, video creators likewise make design choices—such as changes in caption placement or color—to embody our rhetorics on screen in ways that shape viewers' interpretation of our message.

Going beyond closed-captioned popular media, researchers in various fields have been developing software programs and tools that create kinetic and dynamic captions—that is, captions that change in size, shape, and placement on screen. For instance, some have manipulated visual text to reflect rising pitch or loudness or modified text to convey emotions (Fels, Lee, Branje, and Hornburg; Fels, Polana, Harvey, Degan, and Silverman; Forlizzi, Lee, and Hudson; among others). These progressive studies can be limited by technology, as Lee, Fels, and Udo observed when they developed a tool that allowed them to create graphic captions for files associated with emotion variations. As they note, it is difficult to determine how best to convey emotions through appropriate graphics since expressing emotions becomes more of interpretation than translation (Lee, Fels, and Udo 5). On the other hand, Andy Brown, Rhia Jones, and Mike Crabb found that dynamic subtitles that were incorporated into the frame—as opposed to at the bottom of the screen—made it easier for users to follow the action, improved users' sense of involvement with their video content, and improved usability of the video content (107). While researchers' findings vary, they show the potential for redesigning captions to embody messages.

I distinguish integral captions from kinetic and dynamic captions because integral captions are ingrained into the video composer's creative process (instead of added after the fact or by a third party) and do not necessarily change in size or shape. Yet, my argument for integrating captions does not mean to suggest that standard captions are inferior or that creating integral captions is the easy answer. Any discussion of integral captions must acknowledge that integrative design strategies would not be appropriate for all contexts. For instance, the standard placement of captions at the bottom of the screen tells viewers where to expect to read captions, and this allows viewers to keep up with fast-paced dialogue at high reading speeds. In these cases, reading speed is important—although reading captions at the bottom of the screen may draw viewers' eyes away from the action within the meaningful space of the screen.[3]

Due to the complexity of captioning, designers of integral captions need to keep aesthetic, rhetorical, and accessible design in consideration. As Theo van Leeuwen observes when discussing a program for kinetic typography: "The software designer has decided what moods will exist and how they are expressed . . . The question has to be asked: What can you do . . . and what can you not do?" (23). We composers should challenge what we think we cannot do and consider how audiences access our messages. We should ask: Who is interpreting our multimodal composition—and how can integral captions recreate the embodiment of the performers on screen? Alphabetic text can become multidimensional aesthetic and rhetorical performances through which audiences access composers' embodied rhetorics.

Embodied Rhetorics

Integral captions are designed to interact with other modes, embody a signer's or speaker's emphasis, and enable the viewer to experience meaning in its multiple forms. If the captions are designed effectively, the viewer can access the embodied rhetorics of the video. Because of this integral designer-caption-viewer connection, understanding embodied rhetorics is essential.

To appreciate embodied rhetorics, let's begin with *embodiment*, a term which captures how our bodies influence the way we interpret the world. In Anne Wysocki's words, "[W]ithout our bodies—our sensing abilities—we do not have a world; we have the world we do because we have our particular senses and experiences" (3). We interact with the world through text, visuals, sound, and other modes of communication. Similarly, I use *rhetoric* to refer to how individuals interpret meaning through different and multiple modes in interaction. I agree with Andrea Lunsford, Kirt Wilson, and Rosa Eberly's suggestion that rhetoric may be the "primary means through which humans overcome their physical separation to create communities, affiliations, and networks of collective meaning" (xxi). For that reason, I consciously use *rhetorics* in plural form to draw attention to the multiple ways we make meaning (and in the spirit of cultural *rhetorics* scholars, including Del Hierro, Levy, and Price). Integral captions and subtitles—as the embodiment of multimodality—connect bodies and modes of meaning. My study of integral captions is informed by my Deaf identity and culture—and the importance of embodied experiences is central in disability studies scholarship. James Wilson and Cynthia Lewiecki-Wilson's introduction to *Embodied Rhetorics* presents an "embodied rhetoric of difference" and argues that we need strategies for using language to include and empower different individuals (18). In the same line of argument, Jay Dolmage asserts that rhetoric is embodied and that "disability shapes our available means of persuasion. Embodied difference can actually be read as the very possibility of meaning" (*Disability* 289). I argue that integral captions are a multimodal (and multilingual) means of creating visual access to embodied rhetorics, or how we all interact with each other in different ways through bodily modes.

I am inspired by disability studies scholars who foreground the value of different experiences and perspectives (Dolmage; Yergeau et al., among others). My identity as a rhetoric scholar and member of Deaf culture encourages me to push Deafness to the center—and captions to the center of the screen—so that we can transform the design of words. I join Brenda Brueggemann in considering how experiencing the world through a "disability enables insight—critical, experiential, cognitive, and sensory" ("Enabling" 321). In 1995, Brueggemann wrote: "I believe that growing awareness of Deaf culture and its visuospatial language, ASL, will provide fertile ground for studies in rhetoric, literacy, and culture" because studying Deaf culture and ASL can inform composition scholars about issues of power, pedagogy, and language use ("Coming Out" 411). More recently, in 2009, she called for a rhetorical approach to ASL literature that enables us to attend to ASL's meaning-making potential, the role of the audience, and the importance of performance—all features of a rhetorical situation (*Deaf Subjects* 39). I endorse the rhetorical benefits of studying ASL and I use this article to argue that Deafness enables an insight into multimodal literacy practices, particularly through integrating captions.

Deafness as insight can transform caption studies, which leads me to cultural rhetorics scholars Victor Del Hierro, Daisy Levy, and Margaret Price's request that readers disrupt the marginalization of those not perceived to be at the center of a discipline because "centers and margins are fluid." As they write, we can engage in relations with different identities and cultures within the same space because "no(body) actually lives in a margin. As allies, as we start to occupy similar space, we have to learn to think about what spaces privilege whom, and why." I ask readers to now think about the video spaces that we privilege and the benefits of moving captions beyond the bottom margin of the screen to create access to a holistic message. I will return to the fluidity of space when discussing Deaf Space, but first I want to discuss how integral captions and embodied rhetorics share a space with multimodal literacies.

Designing Multimodal Literacies

My advocacy for designing integral captions synchronizes with scholarship on developing multiple literacies, or rhetorical strategies for communicating through multiple modes. The *interplay* of modes is fundamental in multimodal composition pedagogies (Halbritter; Kress and van Leeuwen; Wysocki; among others)—and I argue that this interplay is lost when we add captions after the video production process. After all, removing these add-ons would not change the meaning or message of the video that has already been produced. In contrast, incorporating captions into the design process becomes an act of engaging in the non-linear processes of new media composing that has been identified by Bump Halbritter and others.

Engaging in the multimodal literacy practice of designing integral captions enables composers to consider how we embody our rhetorics. This multimodal approach to captions reflects Kristie Fleckenstein's embodied literacy of imageword in which we make meaning through the relations between words and images. She reminds us of the "material dimension of writing-reading, to meaning's reliance on our physical participation in the world" because literacy is formed "within the context of bodies" (Fleckenstein 46; 47). Multimodal composition occurs through the body in interaction with space—akin to designing a space for integral captions that embody rhetorics.

Designing integral captions as a multimodal text can create visual access to embodied rhetorics that might not be possible in other forms. After all, by allowing for different modes to complement each other, multimodality opens "up what counts as valued communication" and welcomes "varied channels of expression" (Hull and Nelson 253). Tracey Bowen and Carl Whithaus remind us that as the screen transforms composition, the change from alphabetic literacy to multimodal literacies "affords a diverse range of graphic representations beyond which case, conventions, and rules of usage applied to words are no longer plausible" (6). Multimodal captions—which embody three-dimensional movement—transform the possibilities of textual representation.

As informed by the multiliteracies pedagogical approach, composers need to develop rhetorical and design skills for communicating effectively through multiple modes, media, and cultural and linguistic diversity (New London Group; Cope and Kalantzis; Kress and van Leeuwen). Design is a fundamental component of multimodal literacies because composers actively (re)design strategies for expressing themselves to different audiences and develop new strategies for communication. The potential for redesign is apparent in Jason Palmeri's history of multimodal pedagogies, which views multimodal composition as a means through which we can recognize embodied differences in communicating and accessing composition. As he states, when composition instructors ask students to use multiple "forms of composing to critically rehear and resee the world, we might increase the likelihood that they will come to recognize and attempt to transform the unjust hierarchies of race, class, gender, sexuality, and disability" (Palmeri 159). In response, I suggest that those who integrate captions into the design process recognize the limitations of conventional modes, critically resee the world on screen, and transform access.

Integral captions—as multimodal and embodied forms—enable Deaf and hearing viewers to access meaning in its fullest embodiment and to experience shared space. In specific terms, access is the process of designing a space for different bodies (Brewer, Selfe, and Yergeau). Dolmage is prominent in advocating for the participatory design of space ("Mapping Composition"). And when individuals are involved in the design of the spaces they use, they engage in what Yergeau calls "an act of embodiment and reclamation" ("Multimodality in Motion"). The next section discusses how Deaf people have embodied and reclaimed multimodal communication through the accessible design of (Deaf) space.

I caution that designing a space for captions requires making decisions about how modes interact to embody multimodal meaning. In the same spirit, my research consciously argues for *visual* access—not universal access—in awareness that captions are not accessible to those who cannot see. Each time we improve access, we may still be excluding others, but we need to always consider the needs of our audiences. For that reason, I encourage future projects to explore other strategies that improve access through captions and subtitles.

Embodied Rhetorics and Deaf Space

The integration of captions leads us to the value of embodied rhetorics in Deaf culture and the design of Deaf Space in videos. These concepts emphasize the rhetorical effectiveness of integral captions as opposed to other forms of captions. This section will frame Deaf Space as a multimodal literacy practice that benefits Deaf and hearing video designers. As an anchor to this section, I provide an overview of a video that designs Deaf Space for subtitles—*Gallaudet: The Film*—and conclude with five criteria for identifying the function of integral captions. The principles of Deaf culture and Deaf Space reflect the important connections between rhetoric, access, embodiment, and multimodality; hearing composers can emulate these principles to strengthen embodied rhetorics in captions.

Embodied rhetorics and multimodal communication might be at its most salient when experiencing a signed conversation between two or more members of Deaf culture—whether Deaf or hearing. Essentially, ASL is an embodied language created through the movement and interpretation of coordinated gestures and facial expressions. This visual-spatial communication shapes the Deaf cultural values placed on maintaining eye contact and connections between bodies (Bahan). It seems natural, then, that members of a culture who communicate through an embodied language would develop a strong physical sense of our shared presence and spaces. The embodied rhetorics of Deaf culture and ASL are, then, deaf rhetorics.

Embodied rhetorics and deaf rhetorics guide my approach to identifying integral captions in hearing and Deaf contexts. When members of Deaf culture communicate through the screen, signers place themselves strategically within the camera frame so that viewers can maintain continual eye contact with bodies and signs. In *Gallaudet:*

The Film, for instance, signers, bodies, and subtitles interweave in three-dimensional harmony within the frame to make embodied rhetorics and multimodal meaning accessible.

Designing for embodied communication is a Deaf Gain, or a benefit, for deaf and hearing members of society. Deaf Gain, a popular theory originated by Deaf Studies scholars H-Dirksen Bauman and Joseph Murray, frames deafness not as a hearing *loss*, but as a *gain* for deaf and hearing individuals. Deaf Gain and Deaf Studies scholars insist that hearing "individuals would be enriched by becom[ing] a bit more Deaf . . . more acutely aware of the nuances of communication, more engaged with eye contact and tactile relations . . . and if nothing else, more appreciative of human diversity" (Bauman and Murray, "Deaf Studies" 222). Attending to the embodied nature of communication could contribute to how individuals form connections—such as through integrating captions that enable viewers to maintain eye contact with the meaningful space of the screen.

The phrase, "space of the screen," brings me to the concept of Deaf Space. Deaf Space began as an architectural practice that intentionally draws from Deaf experiences and designs buildings and other physical spaces for embodied and visual-spatial communication (H. Bauman 379). Deaf Space is space created by and for deaf individuals who navigate through the world through physical, visual, and spatial means. For instance, Figure 2 shows a wide walkway that has been designed so that two individuals can walk side-by-side without needing to move around obstacles or miss each other's signs.

Wide walkways, curved corners, and other Deaf Space design practices enable individuals to stay connected with each other as they travel through spaces. The collaborative and active design of Deaf Space is an actively participatory process that benefits embodied communication. This participatory design can benefit deaf and hearing individuals, which leads Hansel Bauman to discuss Deaf Space as a specific application of Deaf Gain. He insists that instead of adapting buildings to meet the needs of deaf people, we can move to "creating an aesthetic and meaning that emerge out of the ways deaf people inhabit and construct their spaces" (378). I argue further that the embodied design of space can be reflected in video space, such as in the design of the integral subtitles in *Gallaudet: The Film*.

Deaf and hearing composers can adopt the principles of Deaf Space as a multimodal literacy practice in which we actively explore strategies for integrating accessible embodied communication. Composers can design a (Deaf) space for captioning that embodies how Deaf and hearing individuals communicate through the interaction of modes, and that becomes a (Deaf) Gain for video editing processes. Take David Armstrong and his statement that the "investigation of Deaf Gain has the potential to influence the productive use of the new communication technologies . . . [and the] capacity to communicate using the visual medium" (88). Integrating captions is a creative and sensory gain that benefits the connections we make amongst modes and bodies.

Figure 2: Two men are walking along an outside pathway and signing to each other. "Space to sign" appears in large white font next to the men. ("How Architecture Changes" 2:06).

Embodying Rhetorics through Integral Subtitles

To show the effectiveness of embodying rhetorics through integral captions and subtitles, I will briefly analyze one scene from *Gallaudet: The Film*. This eight-minute film was created by members of the community of Gallaudet University, the nation's only liberal arts university for the deaf, including producer Dirksen Bauman and director of photography and editor Wayne Betts Jr. The camera guides viewers fluidly through scene after scene—from a sign language performance to an overview of the grounds of Gallaudet University to an architectural conference on designing Deaf Space and other scenes. In lieu of audio and music, this silent film interweaves fluid subtitles to enrich visual access to embodied and deaf rhetorics. Since the predominant language on screen is ASL, I write that English *subtitles* provide access to the signed language.

I see the integral subtitles in this film as a response to Bauman and Murray's observation that "no research has been conducted to this point about the potential innovations that would emerge from Deaf filmmakers" and that "such exploration is clearly an important trajectory for Deaf Studies to explore the potential of Deaf-gain" in film language ("Deaf Studies" 218). As Rhea Kennedy reports, film producer Dirksen Bauman and director Ryan Commerson envisioned this film as "a small harbinger of a greater renaissance to come in deaf media production that . . . 'promotes Gallaudet and frames deaf people and their signed languages as positive aspects of human diversity.'" The subtitles embody the movement and value of ASL and Deaf culture so that hearing and Deaf audiences experience deaf rhetorics in action.

Now, I will discuss one scene in the film that reveals the effectiveness of integral subtitles in embodying multimodal rhetorics. This critical classroom scene encapsulates the cultural values of Deaf Space, eye contact, visual flow, and connections. The instructor and students are seated in a circle around the room—an accessible design that is standard in Deaf pedagogical spaces so that all individuals can see each other—and are engaging in a signed discussion as integral subtitles appear in the spaces around their bodies to guide viewers not only through their signs but through the connections between instructor, students, and viewers.

The instructor begins with the key question, "Is the concept of 'beauty' universal across cultures?" Each word appears in the space next to his face and upper body in tandem with his signs. Most of the words are in white font while the term "beauty" appears in yellow font to stand out against the other words and to emphasis the concept to be discussed: beauty. As shown in Figure 3 and Figure 4, the subtitles stand still next to the instructor's upper body while the camera rotates around his body and travels through the subtitles. In the same fluid movement, the camera turns behind the instructor's body to show the instructor's view of the students; at this moment, the subtitles are shown in reverse text as if the viewer were looking at the students through the back of the words. The intentional placement of the subtitles aesthetically and rhetorically establishes the question that will remain on everyone's mind during discussion.

The rhetoric and aesthetic design of subtitles continues with the first student to respond. She is seated and the subtitles appear in front of her in alignment with her signs, which makes the textual display of information as visible as the signed statement. She discusses the contrasting standards of beauty across time; while most of the words are in white font, the different time eras appear in yellow font to reinforce the difference between the standards of the past and the present. As she signs each new word, the accompanying text appears near her signs. After she completes a statement, the original text remains on screen while she signs new words and then accompanying subtitles replace the words already on screen one by one. Her signs *and* the subtitles coordinate to embody her message—that the standards of the past transform into the standards of today. The responses of the other individuals appear fluidly near their signing spaces as the camera moves around the room.

This classroom scene is a pivotal moment that shows how *Gallaudet: The Film* encapsulates embodied rhetorics through subtitles that are designed as rhetorical and aesthetic elements of the film. The significance of this particular scene is explained by Deaf filmmaker Wayne Betts Jr. in a signed TEDx Talk. After sharing this scene with the audience, he explains:

Figure 3: An instructor is signing in a classroom as subtitles appear next to him on the right side of the screen. The incomplete subtitles read "Is the concept of 'beauty' universal across." The sentence is in white font but the word "beauty" appears in yellow font for emphasis (*Gallaudet: The Film* 5:50).

Figure 4: Here, the camera frames the same instructor from the side to show his profile. The completed subtitles, "Is the concept of 'beauty' universal across cultures" appear at an angle (*Gallaudet: The Film* 5:54).

> Another thing. Notice the captions? They weren't fixed to the bottom of the screen. [*Shakes head.*] That feels the same as cuts and breaks. My eyes fall down to the bottom. No! I want to see and stay up here with the actor's eyes. [*He then recreates the panoramic movement of his captions while smiling.*] My eyes are following the action and I can still feel the flow. I feel connected to what's going on. [*He nods and gently moves his connected hands to show the harmonic connection.*] That's my world. That's it.

Betts's statement—and the embodied gestures that I describe in brackets—emphasizes the importance for viewers to visually access meaning and embodies the value of fluidly connecting viewers with the rhetorics on screen.

The five functions of integral subtitles become evident at this point. The subtitles are organically integrated into the *space* of *Gallaudet: The Film* and they provide *visual access* to the meaningful space of the screen—such as when they are interweaved near signs and facial expressions. Viewers are able to experience the *embodied rhetorics* of the performers on screen. *Multimodal and multilingual communication*—particularly American Sign Language and textual English—as well as the *rhetorical* message and the deaf *aesthetics* of the film are made possible through the subtitles. These elements are important functions of integral subtitles that distinguish them from subtitles that are not integrated into a video's message.

I will now describe the five criteria for distinguishing the function of integral captions and subtitles so that composers can apply these principles to other compositions.

Five Criteria for Identifying Integral Captions

At this point, the following question may be asked: *How do we determine which videos effectively integrate captions within the space of the screen and how do we understand what function these integral captions perform within the video?* To answer that question, I present the criteria that I developed for identifying integral captions and subtitles:

1. Space has been reasonably designed or prepared for captions in the pre-production, filming, and post-production process.

Composers incorporate captions throughout the video production and editing process. The video designers prepare for captions to be on screen when drafting the script; they might set aside a space around the performers in the camera frame for the captions to appear in post-production; and during the editing process, they integrate captions into the video. Space is reasonably designed for captions throughout this process.

I use the qualifying term *reasonably* to recognize that even when composers might intend for captions to be integrated into the space of the screen, they might not necessarily define that exact arrangement in advance. They might not tell performers where exactly the captions will appear and they might not decide until the editing process where the captions may appear. This is part of the rhetorical and aesthetic process of deciding the most accessible design.

2. The captions provide visual access to the meaningful content of the video.

The captions are placed in meaningful areas of the screen (though they may appear at the bottom of the screen when necessary). For instance, designers of an instructional video might integrate captions that move with the physical instructions to guide viewers' eyes through the step-by-step instructions.

3. The captions complement viewers' and performers' embodied rhetorics, or meaning that is produced through the body within specific cultural contexts.

For instance, the captions may be placed near speakers' or signers' faces and upper bodies to coordinate with the performers' meaningful facial expressions and body language.

4. Multimodal (including multilingual) communication and the interconnection of modes and language in constructing meaning occurs with/through the contribution of captions.

For instance, when a language that is foreign to viewers is spoken on screen, subtitles might appear around the performers' faces to support the interactive construction of meaning. Through this design, viewers may be able to see characters' expressions concurrently with the subtitles and understand the multimodal and multilingual message.

5. The captions enhance the rhetorical and aesthetic qualities of the video.

The captions strengthen the designer's rhetorical message for audiences while improving the aesthetic composition. For instance, designers of an instructional video for an organization would need to select the aesthetic layout and typography that best reflects or embodies the organizational environment (its rhetorics) and meets users' expectations.

These five principles combine in identifying captions that are *integral* to the meaning of their compositions. As Sigrid Norris explains, an analysis of multimodal compositions is only effective when modes are "intricately interwoven," "not easily separable," "interlinked and often interdependent" (102). Integral captions intricately coordinate with other modes of meaning in a video, enabling audiences to analyze the holistic embodiment of multimodal meaning.

Accessing Integral Captions and the Five Criteria

The value of Deaf Space and embodied rhetorics is a Deaf Gain for instructors and scholars who redesign access to academic spaces so that hearing and d/Deaf audiences can interpret the embodied rhetorics of multimodal compositions. To support this endeavor, I conclude with strategies for accessing rhetoric, embodiment, and multimodality through integral captions as a multimodal literacy practice. These strategies are inspired by the five criteria of space, visual access, embodied rhetorics, multimodal/lingual communication, and the rhetorical and aesthetic qualities of a video.

First, I encourage scholars and instructors to assess the affordances and accessibility of caption styles in the programs available to them before choosing the appropriate video editing software for their rhetorical situation. I call on scholars to research different designs and placements of captions and subtitles in different video contexts. I encourage multilingual scholars to explore how they can integrate captions that connect languages and cultures, such as by interweaving Spanish and English text. Finally, I emphasize that integral captions are not accessible to those who cannot see, so we must consider approaches such as incorporating audio descriptions of the movements on screen to improve the accessibility of videos.

The possibilities for designing captions are constrained by certain limitations, particularly since the process of embedding alphabetic text into videos is time-consuming and videos may need to be captioned quickly. Professional captioners who transcribe popular media and other time-sensitive projects need to create conventional captions quickly. Consequently, the opportunity for transforming video editing practices exists in academic and personal contexts in which composers—instructors and students alike—can integrate captions that embody the multiple, different, and accessible ways that we interact with each other.

Through the five essential principles of integral captions, we can assess how we translate information across languages, cultures, and modes. We challenge the limitations of technologies and conventions in order to unite text with visual-spatial-gestural-aural compositions. We integrate captions into the center of the screen and insist on the instability of modes, margins, and embodiments.

Notes

1. The capitalized Deaf is used to refer to those who identify as members of Deaf culture. The lowercase deaf is used to refer to the physical state of being deaf.

2. I thank RR reviewers Julie Jung and Sean Zdenek for their constructive feedback and suggestions as well as editor Elise Verzosa Hurley for her support.

3. For a study on how viewers can focus on faces and saccade between subtitles and faces, see Perego et al.

WORKS CITED

Armstrong, David. "Deaf Gain in Evolutionary Perspective." *Deaf Gain: Raising the Stakes for Human Diversity*. Eds. H. Dirksen L. Bauman and Joseph M. Murray. Minneapolis: U of Minneapolis P, 2015. 77–94.

Bahan, Benjamin. "Upon the Formation of a Visual Variety of the Human Race." *Open Your Eyes: Deaf Studies Talking*. Ed. H-Dirksen L. Bauman. Minneapolis: U of Minnesota P, 2007. 83–99.

Bauman, Hansel. "DeafSpace: An Architecture toward a More Livable and Sustainable World." *Deaf Gain: Raising the Stakes for Human Diversity*. Eds. H-Dirksen L. Bauman and Joseph M. Murray. Minneapolis: U of Minneapolis P, 2015. 375–401.

Bauman, H-Dirksen L., and Joseph M. Murray. "Deaf Studies in the 21st Century: 'Deaf-gain' and the Future of Human Diversity." *The Oxford Handbook of Deaf Studies, Language, and Education*. Eds. Marc Marschark and Patricia Elizabeth Spencer. New York: Oxford UP, 2010. 210–25.

—."Deaf Gain: An Introduction." *Deaf Gain: Raising the Stakes for Human Diversity*. Eds. H-Dirksen L. Bauman and Joseph M. Murray. Minneapolis: U of Minneapolis P, 2015. xv–xlii.

Brewer, Elizabeth, Cynthia L. Selfe, and Melanie Yergeau. "Creating a Culture of Access in Composition Studies." *Composition Studies* 42.2 (2014): 151–54.

Bowen, Tracey, and Carl Whithaus. *Multimodal Literacies and Emerging Genres*. Pittsburgh: U of Pittsburgh P, 2013. Brown, Andy, Rhia Jones, and Mike Crabb. "Dynamic Subtitles: The User Experience." *Proceedings of the ACM International Conference on Interactive Experiences for TV and Online Video*. Eds. David Geerts, Lieven De Marez, and Caroline Pauwels. Association for Computing Machinery, 2015.

Brueggemann, Brenda J. "The Coming Out of Deaf Culture and American Sign Language: An Exploration into Visual Rhetoric and Literacy." *Rhetoric Review* 13.2 (1995): 409–20.

—. *Deaf Subjects: Between Identities and Places*. New York: New York UP, 2009.

—. "An Enabling Pedagogy." *Disability Studies: Enabling the Humanities*. Eds. Sharon Snyder, Brenda Brueggemann, and Rosemarie Garland-Thomson. New York: The Modern Language Association of America, 2002. 317–36.

Butler, Janine. "Where Access Meets Multimodality: The Case of ASL Music Videos." *Kairos* 21.1 (2016): Web.

Cope, Bill, and Mary Kalantzis, eds. *Multiliteracies: Literacy Learning and the Design of Social Futures*. New York: Routledge, 1999.

Del Hierro, Victor, Daisy Levy, and Margaret Price. "We are Here: Negotiating Difference and Alliance in Spaces of Cultural Rhetorics." *Enculturation* 21 (2016): Web.

Dolmage, Jay. *Disability Rhetoric*. Syracuse: Syracuse UP, 2014.
—."Mapping Composition: Inviting Disability in the Front Door." *Disability and the Teaching of Writing*. Eds. Cynthia Lewiecki–Wilson and Brenda Jo Brueggemann. Boston: Bedford/St. Martin's, 2008. 14–27.
Fels, Deborah I., Daniel G. Lee, Carmen Branje, and Matthew Hornburg. "Emotive Captioning and Access to Television." *AMCIS* 2005 *Proceedings*. Association for Information Systems, 2005.
Fels, Deborah I., Lorelle Polano, Terry Harvey, Singh S. Degan, and Charles Silverman. "Towards Emotive Captioning for Interactive Television." *Proceedings of HCI International* 2001. 2001.
Fleckenstein, Kristie. *Embodied Literacies: Imageword and a Process of Teaching*. Carbondale, IL: Southern Illinois UP, 2003.
Forlizzi, Jodi, Johnny Lee, and Scott E. Hudson. "The Kinedit System: Affective Messages Using Dynamic Texts." Proceedings of the SIGCHI Conference on Human Factors in Computing Systems. Eds. Gilbert Cockton and Panu Korhonen. Association for Computing Machinery, 2003.
Gallaudet: The Film. Dir. Ryan Commerson. Gallaudet U, 2010.
Halbritter, Bump. *Mics, Cameras, Symbolic Action: Audio–Visual Rhetoric for Writing Teachers*. Anderson, SC: Parlor P, 2012.
"How Architecture Changes for the Deaf." *YouTube*, uploaded by Vox, 2 March 2016. Web.
Hull, Glynda A., and Mark Evan Nelson. "Locating the Semiotic Power of Multimodality." *Written Communication* 22.2 (2006): 224–61.
Jackerson, Justin. "Why ASL?" *ASLized! Journal of American Sign Language and Literature* 1(2011): Web.
Kennedy, Rhea Yablon. "Community Converges at Gallaudet Renaissance Event." *On the Green* [Washington, DC] 8 April 2010. Web.
Knoblauch, A. Abby. "Bodies of Knowledge: Definitions, Delineations, and Implications of Embodied Writing in the Academy." *Composition Studies* 40.2 (2012): 50–65.
Kress, Gunther, and Theo van Leeuwen. *Multimodal Discourse: The Modes and Media of Contemporary Communication*. New York: Oxford UP, 2001.
Lee, Daniel G., Deborah I. Fels, and John P. Udo. "Emotive Captioning." *Computers in Entertainment: CIE–Interactive TV* 5.2 (2007): 1–15.
Lueck, Amy. "Writing a Translingual Script: Closed Captions in the English Multilingual Hearing Classroom." *Kairos* 17.3 (2013). Web.
Lunsford, Andrea, Kirt H. Wilson, and Rosa A. Eberly, eds. *The SAGE Handbook of Rhetorical Studies*. Thousand Oaks, CA: Sage, 2008.
New London Group. "A Pedagogy of Multiliteracies: Designing Social Futures." *Harvard Education Review* 66.1 (1996): 60–92.
Norris, Sigrid. "Multimodal Discourse Analysis: A Conceptual Framework." *Discourse and Technology: Multimodal Discourse Analysis*. Eds.

Philip LeVine and Ron Scollon. Washington, DC: Georgetown UP, 2004. 101–15.

Palmeri, Jason. *Remixing Composition: A History of Multimodal Writing Pedagogy.* Carbondale, IL: Southern Illinois UP, 2012.

Perego, Elisa, et al. "The Cognitive Effectiveness of Subtitle Processing." *Media Psychology* 13 (2010): 243–72. "TEDx Islay—Wayne Betts Jr.—Deaf Lens." *YouTube*, uploaded by TEDx Talks, 22 June 2010. Web.

Udo, John-Patrick, and Deborah I. Fels. "The Rogue Poster-Children of Universal Design: Closed Captioning and Audio Description." *Journal of Engineering Design* 21.2–3 (2010): 207–21.

Van Leeuwen, Theo. "About Images and Multimodality: A Personal Account." *Interactions, Images, and Texts: A Reader in Multimodality.* Eds. Sigrid Norris and Carmen Daniela Maier. Boston: de Gruyter Mouton, 2014. 19–23.

Wilson, James C., and Cynthia Lewiecki-Wilson. "Disability, Rhetoric, and the Body." *Embodied Rhetorics: Disability in Language and Culture.* Eds. James C. Wilson and Cynthia Lewiecki-Wilson. Carbondale, IL: Southern Illinois UP, 2001. 1–25.

Wysocki, Anne Frances. "Opening New Media to Writing: Openings and Justifications." *Writing New Media: Theory and Applications for Expanding the Teaching of Composition.* Eds. Anne Frances Wysocki, Johndan Johnson–Eilola, Cynthia L., and Geoffrey Sirc. Logan, UT: Utah State UP. Selfe, 2004. 1–42.

Yergeau, Melanie, et al. "Multimodality in Motion: Disability and Kairotic Spaces." *Kairos* 18.1 (2013). Web. Zdenek, Sean. *Reading Sounds: Closed-Captioned Media and Popular Culture.* Chicago: U of Chicago P, 2015.

SUPPLEMENTAL MATERIAL

Part I: Reflection on the Origins of the Article

The seeds for "Integral Captions and Subtitles" began to emerge six years before the publication of this article in *Rhetoric Review*. As a graduate student in rhetoric and composition, I quickly gravitated towards digital and visual rhetoric in my scholarship. When studying multimodal compositions, I often connected what I read and discussed in my courses with how Deaf performers, musicians, and video creators evoke the physical sensation of feeling sound through body movements that vibrate in live performances and on screen—including through dynamic visual text that dances around the screen in ASL music videos. At the same time, accessibility and multimodality became a core component of my composition pedagogy.

My appreciation for innovative videos that enable audiences to see and feel sound through different modes took form as I reviewed scholarship on multimodal composition. Scholars eagerly identified the benefits of helping composition students learn through the recursive process of layering sound and visuals in videos. Captions were also being mentioned more often in texts on video composition, which reinforced my dedication to the forward-thinking field of writing studies. Yet, the same texts that celebrated the affordances of multimodal composition often reminded video creators to include captions at the *end* of their video editing process to make their completed videos accessible.

I was intrigued by the contrast between the interactive quality of multimodal composition processes and the representation of captions as add-ons. To me, captions were salient examples of modes that could be manipulated to move with the vibrations of sound, bodies, and other meaningful elements. When reflecting on this contradiction, I interrogated my own captioning practices and realized that I had treated captions as static lines of words to be added to the bottom of the screen. Now, I realized the importance of challenging the conventions and my own practices.

To understand how captions could influence our multimodal composing processes, I began to explore the affordances and limitations of video editing programs and recorded myself looking at, gesturing towards, and moving with visual text around me. I experimented with the amount of space around my body and the color, speed, and number of words that appeared on screen at any given time. I taught rhetorical analysis and design of captions to students in my composition courses and scrutinized a wide range of videos to determine the potential for transforming captions into interactive modes of meaning. Filtering out the vast number of inadequate examples—including the many videos on social media with open captions that do not provide access to the full composite's meaning—only strengthened the exemplars that remained, including *Gallaudet: The Film*.

By analyzing and comparing caption designs across different media, I concluded that the creators of these videos made these captions *integral* to the meaning of their multimodal message and I developed five principles that define the unique functions of integral captions. The threads of analysis, design, and pedagogy came together in my dissertation on integral captions and subtitles, which later evolved into this article in *Rhetoric Review*.

Part II: Description of Research Methods, Findings, and/or Pedagogical Impact

When developing my analysis of integral captions and subtitles, a major driving force was my insistence on foregrounding captions as multimodal components that composition students can work with as they develop and strengthen rhetorical skills for communicating in accessible and multiple modes. While captions are primarily indispensable devices for making language accessible to audiences, I encourage scholars and students to recognize the nexus of linguistic, visual, and spatial modes of communication in captions. Specifically, instructors and students can create integral captions by honoring the five principles detailed in this article: 1) space; 2) visual access; 3) embodied rhetorics; 4) multimodal/multilingual communication; and 5) rhetorical and aesthetic qualities of videos. At the same time, I envision scholars and instructors expanding the applications of these five principles in the classroom.

These five principles operate just as productively in face-to-face interactions, physical spaces, and other academic spaces. As a prominent example, we can apply these five principles in real-time teaching spaces and determine how instructors facilitate communication with students in classroom settings. We can assess the degree to which instructors design *spaces* for different forms of communication with students; we can evaluate how instructors provide *visual and other forms of access* so that students are able to connect with each other and the learning material; we can review how instructors convey meaning to students through their *embodied rhetorics*; we can accentuate the potential of *multimodal and multilingual communication* amongst class participants; and finally, we can determine how students and instructors accentuate the *rhetorical and aesthetic qualities* of their compositions.

The five principles can serve as an analytical tool through which we can assess how instructors design our spaces for communicating and composing in multiple forms with students with different language practices and abilities. This analytical tool can also be applied to situations such as face-to-face discussion between two participants. In a consulting session between an instructor and student, for instance, an observer could assess how the two participants coordinate through space, access, embodied rhetorics, multimodal/lingual communication, and rhetoric/aesthetics. The instructor could use that assessment to modify or improve her communication practices for future students.

Finally, these principles can become an instrument for students to utilize in case studies and other course projects. An instructor could ask students to analyze a given composition or context through the five principles. Students would be equipped with five specific strategies for understanding how a composition or context enables—or prevents—communication through embodied and multimodal/multilingual rhetorics. In addition to analyzing given contexts, students can use the five criteria as a guiding framework through which they design compositions that embody their identities in accessible ways. As an example, students might use the five principles to inform their rhetorical analysis of audio description in media and then work on projects in which they conscientiously design a space for making verbal description of visuals accessible.

By analyzing and designing accessible spaces for embodied rhetorics and multimodal communication, students and instructors recognize the multitude of ways through which we challenge conventions, transform technologies, and access visual and sonic words.

Part III: Discussion Questions

1. Any discussion of integral captions must acknowledge that certain design strategies would not be appropriate for all contexts. The placement of traditional captions at the bottom of the screen enables viewers to know where to direct their gaze and read at high speeds. While keeping the advantages of traditional captions in mind, consider your own and your students' expectations for the design and conventions of videos with audio. What features or uses of videos are entrenched in our online lives, viewing habits, and classroom experiences? How might we reflect on what defines a video and how that definition might be reshaped? For instance, when watching popular media with foreign languages spoken on screen, why are subtitles often placed at the bottom of the screen and how might someone recreate the program with integral subtitles that effectively convey the multilingual message?

2. A limitation of "Integral Captions and Subtitles" is the focus on visual access to the exclusion of other forms of access. The decision to choose *visual* access was the result of careful deliberation and acknowledgement of the limitations of ensuring access for all individuals at all times. At the same time, integrating captions does not automatically equate visual access because we must ensure that we select the correct design for integral captions (including the correct color, size, placement, and other features). How do the limitations of integral captions inform our field's understanding of access as a process? How might we teach our students and ourselves strategies for developing an appropriate visual design for captions in each project and how might we recognize the most suitable design for delivering a complete multimodal message to our audience(s)? What are some possible avenues for improving visual, aural, and other modes of access to videos, podcasts, and other media in our professional and pedagogical practices?

3. The analysis of media suggests that integral captions and subtitles might be most natural and productive in multilingual and multicultural spaces, as illustrated in intermingling of signed and written communication in *Gallaudet: The Film*. Integral captions can be the multimodal bridge across which creators and viewers access communication—but if that is the case, then what are the implications for videos in which English or another language is the primary language of communication? Correspondingly, what are the implications for multilingual videos? For instance, how might native Spanish speakers and their audiences benefit from integrating subtitles in multiple languages in their video compositions?

COLLEGE COMPOSITION AND COMMUNICATION

CCC is on the Web at http://cccc.ncte.org/cccc/ccc

College Composition and Communication publishes research and scholarship in rhetoric and composition studies that supports college teachers in reflecting on and improving their practices in teaching writing and that reflects the most current scholarship and theory in the field. The field of composition studies draws on research and theories from a broad range of humanistic disciplines—English studies, rhetoric, cultural studies, LGBT studies, gender studies, critical theory, education, technology studies, race studies, communication, philosophy of language, anthropology, sociology, and others—and from within composition and rhetoric studies, where a number of subfields have also developed, such as technical communication, computers and composition, writing across the curriculum, research practices, and the history of these fields.

Writing in Social Worlds: An Argument for Researching Composing Processes[1]

Advancing an argument for resuscitating our field's interest in composing processes, Pamela Takayoshi offers a thorough review of scholarship from the heyday of process research and finds that there is plenty of unfinished business to attend to in this area. "Much of the composing process scholarship," Takayoshi writes, "concluded with questions the current research left unanswered and calls for further research." Then, focusing on the composing processes of a contemporary writer who is deeply reliant on digital technologies, Takayoshi delineates specifically what these paths for "further research" might be.

---

1. *College Composition and Communication*, vol. 69, no. 4 © 2018 by the National Council of Teachers of English. All rights reserved.

Writing in Social Worlds: An Argument for Researching Composing Processes

Pamela Takayoshi

> *Empirical research on composing processes is virtually absent in our field. What do contemporary writers actually do when they compose? I argue that we need a return to research on composing processes, as writers are every day weaving together the social and cognitive through writing. One writer's composing process think-aloud suggests how some writers today weave together cognitive and cultural processes of meaning making in ways unimagined at the time of the last composing process research.*

Since the March 1950 inaugural issue of *College Composition and Communication*, the central question grounding composition studies has been about how writing is produced, taught, and learned.[1] This central focus on writing abides across time, space, and paradigm shifts. Composition studies is grounded in an object of study that is both profoundly significant and invisibly mundane in human experience. Although the uniquely human activity of writing is present in nearly every cultural practice people undertake, from formal educational settings to workplaces to social worlds, no other discipline or field of study has paid such close, systematic attention to the actual act of composing written texts. Over time, our field has collectively explored the ways writing is best taught and learned, what writers do when they compose, how the broader cultural context shapes written discourse and the people who produce it, and the many ways written literacy is socially situated and always dependent on context for its function, meaning, and practice.

Yet, for a discipline whose key term is *composition* (whether we call ourselves *composition* studies or rhetoric and *composition*), it is odd that over the past two decades we have so completely neglected to examine in any systematic or fine-grained way composition as a process. Our disciplinary focus has pulled back to draw a larger picture than the originating focus on the college writing classroom alone, as Jacqueline Rhodes and Jonathan Alexander note: "Many compositionists now see the teaching of writing as tied profoundly and intimately to inviting students to understand how naming is an ideological act; how narrating experience can both reinforce and challenge the dominant order; how language use both buys into and potentially exceeds normative understanding; and how learning to write can both serve the existing order and help us reimagine it" (483–84). Likewise, inquiry in composition research has largely centered around research questions focused on the ideological, cultural contexts for writing (questions about literacy, power, normativity) and objects of study larger than individual writers (ideologically inscribed subject positions, social groups, and literacy as a social practice). This broad scholarly view on composition examines *the literate contexts* of writing rather than the *composing processes* of individual writers embedded within those contexts. Very few researchers today focus their attention on the writing processes writers use in navigating culture and text.

As early as 1976, articles in *College Composition and Communication* examined in a data-based way just what it is that writers do when they write.[2] However, as I show in this article, by 1995, composing process research had virtually disappeared from the pages of the field's flagship journals (*College Composition and Communication* and *Research in the Teaching of English*). It is my contention that as a field, we prematurely turned away from composing process research just as we were establishing "an adequate understanding of the term composition" (Cooper and Odell 74). This premature turning away has not prepared us for understanding in any depth what writers twenty years later do when they compose with technologies, multiple audiences, contexts, and purposes that were unimaginable at the height of composing process research in composition studies. Deborah Brandt and Katie Clinton note that "communication revolutions of the late 20th and early 21st centuries have blasted concepts of place and space and proliferated social interactions and involvements that were nearly impossible in the past" (257). A lot has changed in the world of writing since composing process research last captivated our field, and disciplinarily, we have yet to account for the effects of those changes on what people do when they write and the role writing plays in acts of meaning making across the human landscape.

This article makes two inextricably linked arguments: (1) as a field, we have turned away from the data-based study of what people do when they write at a time when (2) contemporary writers' composing processes explicitly weave together culture, the individual, and literacy in ways that are inadequately explained by the composing process research that does exist. Thus, the article is organized in two related parts: In the first half, I trace the evolution and extinction of research on composing processes as it is represented in the pages of *CCC*. Central to the demise of composing process research were critiques that composing process research took too little account of the sociality of writing and that the dominant methods of composing process research were impoverished. I believe, however, that in 2018, these two critiques are more difficult to sustain. First, composing process researchers today cannot responsibly ignore the sociality of writing processes—writers are composing on internetworked computers, and they are always on, always connected. The sociality of writing is visible and present almost every time a writer writes. Secondly, data collection technologies unavailable in the 1980s such as screencasting, eye tracking, and keystroke recordings provide contemporary researchers with unprecedented, detailed recordings of composing processes coupled with the writer's vocalized thoughts. In the second half of the article, I share one contemporary writer's composing process, which provides a window into the sociality of her writing processes. This writer's screencast suggests some of the ways writers today weave together cognitive and cultural processes of meaning making in ways unimagined at the time of the last composing process research. I believe that looking at the micro level of detail of what writers do when they compose is necessary in a world where writers are negotiating their place in the larger culture through their written language.

Reclaiming Composing Process Research

In October 1978, Martha King described a group of researchers who met to examine the state of inquiry on the composing process at the 1976 Convention of the National Council of Teachers of English:

> From the outset, many of those present expressed concern about the lack of a coherent theoretical framework within which research on composing was being done or might be done. . . . The group's concerns centered mainly on two inter-

> related perspectives: the composing process and the context of writing. Much of the research on composition in the past has failed to scrutinize writing at "the point of utterance," that is, has not studied what composing actually involves. [Additionally,] writing takes place in an environment that shapes the purpose, function, writer-audience relationships, and modes of discourse; to a large extent the context determines whether or not writing will occur. . . . Although some participants had more interest in one aspect than the other, highest priority was given to studying the composing process. Impressive work is already underway in this area, and moreover, investigations of process will necessarily involve contextual factors. (193)

In the years that followed, specifically from 1976 through 1995, composition studies cohered as a field, researchers developed more detailed understandings of composition "at the point of utterance," and the field moved toward a "coherent theoretical framework" within which composing research might be done. In 1980, Stephen Witte reflected that composing process research "has functioned as an open-ended heuristic, pointing contemporary researchers in directions previously unknown, generating important questions that fifteen years ago could not even have been asked, much less answered" ("Toward" 74). Referring to Charles R. Cooper and Lee Odell's 1978 exhortation that "What we have needed for decades and what we must have soon is a period of vigorous research on written discourse and the composing process," Witte notes, "This 'period of vigorous research' spanning now a decade and a half may be the mark of a discipline seeking to redefine itself " ("Toward" 74). The important questions being generated and described by King, Cooper and Odell, and Witte largely centered around *how* writers work and think. At the time, research aimed at describing and testing out speculative theories of composing through the examination of actual practices.

Tracing the presence of empirical research on composing processes published in *CCC* ("the official journal" of CCCC) and *RTE* ("the flagship research journal" of NCTE) reveals a diversity of research questions, methodological designs, contexts, and participants in writing research focused on the moment of utterance. It also reveals that by 1995, composing process research had almost completely disappeared from the field's official journals. In order to reveal these trends in the field, I reviewed the contents of every issue of *CCC* and *RTE* and identified articles that provided data-based answers to the research question, "What do writers do when they compose?" Beginning in 2015, I moved backward in time through the journals, identifying articles that focus on what writers actually do in the moment of composing (as distinct from, for example, articles that report on broader uses of literacy or classroom instruction).[3]

As Figures 1 and 2 demonstrate, empirical research on composing processes first appeared in the journals in 1976 (*CCC*) and 1978 (*RTE*), and by 1995, research on composing processes had virtually died out. In the twenty years between 1995 and 2015, *CCC* published no empirical research articles on composing processes while *RTE* published seven. Within the time frame of when empirical research articles appeared (1976 to 1995), several features are worth noting in order to understand the history of composing process research in the field:

- In *CCC*, 40 articles reported empirical research on composing processes.
- In *RTE*, 66 articles were published during the same time period.
- For *CCC*, the peak year of composing process research was 1983, with 10 out of 42 articles published that year focused on composing process research.
- For *RTE*, the peak year of composing process research was 1984, with 6 out of 17 total articles published focused on composing process research. In 1991, composing process research again rose to the forefront in *RTE*, with 6 out of 16 articles published that year focused on composing process research.

Against this quantitative rendering of the landscape, and given the limitations of space, in this section I focus on the articles published in *CCC* to provide a descriptive picture of the composing process research movement. A descriptive review of *RTE* articles provides further evidence rather than countering this descriptive picture, and likewise, reviewing composing process research that appeared in monographs, edited collections, and other academic journals during the time period reviewed provides further evidence for the robust yet impermanent vitality of the composing process moment (Bereiter and Scardamalia; Cooper and Odell; Emig; Flower, "Writer-Based"; Flower and Hayes, "Problem-Solving," "Identifying," "Images"; Gregg and Steinberg; Hayes and Flower; Humes).

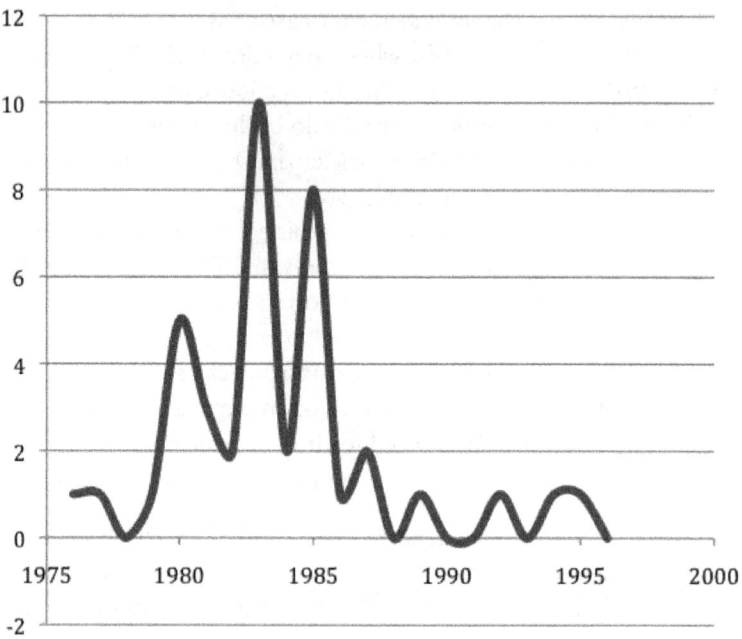

Figure 1. Number of empirical studies of composing process published in *College Composition and Communication* by year (1975–2000)

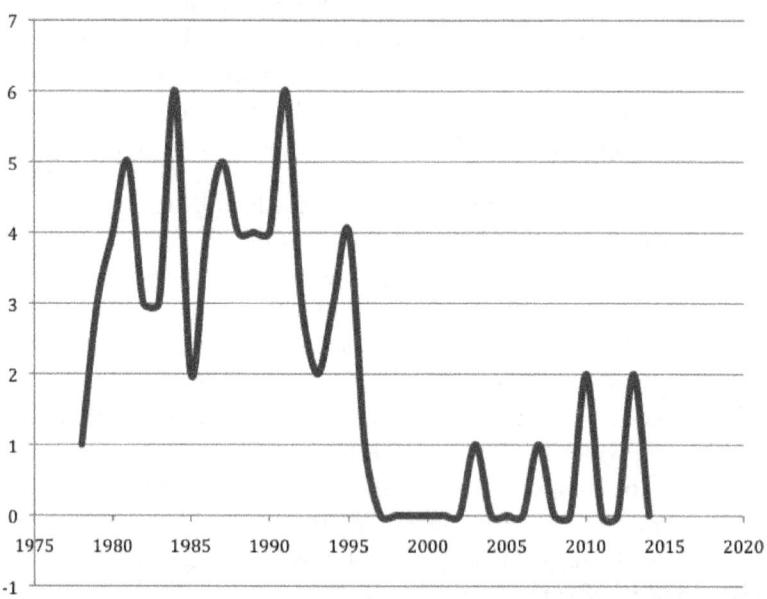

Figure 2. Number of empirical studies of composing process published in *Research in the Teaching of English* by year (1978–2015).

Propelled by a desire to help students become more effective writers, composing process researchers published in *CCC* asked questions that led to detailed descriptions of what writers actually do when they compose (Bean; Blau; Crowley; Flower, "Cognition"; Flower and Hayes, "Cognitive"; Perl; Pianko; Rodrigues; Witte, "Pre-Text"), with some studies focusing on specific moments and components in the composing process:

- revision (Collier; Flower et al.; Harris; Sommers, "Revision"; Witte, "Topical")
- audience and social context (Berkenkotter, "Student"; Faigley and Hansen; Flynn; Nelson; Skubikowski and Elder)
- personality type and sense of authority (Daiute; McCarthy et al.; Penrose and Geisler)
- self evaluation (Beach; Rubin)
- writer's block (Clark and Wiedenhaupt; Rose)

The field endeavored to understand expertise in writing by studying professional writers (Berkenkotter, "Decisions"; Catano; Miller; Murray; Peterson; Schwartz) and experienced writers in comparison with "novice" writers (Aldrich; Berkenkotter, "Understanding"; Boice; Case; Faigley and Witte; Flower and Hayes, "Cognition"; Jensen and DiTiberio; Knoblauch; Selzer; Sommers, "Revision"). Researchers explored questions about writers' behaviors by focusing on individual writers in situated contexts (Aldrich; Berkenkotter, "Understanding"; Boice; Case; Faigley and Witte; Flower and Hayes, "Identifying"; Jensen and DiTiberio; Knoblauch; Selzer; Sommers, "Revision"). In these articles, writing teachers turn to empirical methods to understand what actually happens in the messiness of composing. They ask a range of questions centered around writers in the moment of composing: What do [college students, engineers, middle management, professional writers, poets, novelists, academics] do when they write? What basic patterns occur during composing? What is the nature of [pre-text, revision, audience, problem solving, decision making, invention, reading] in writers' composing processes? How do experienced writers and student writers differ in their processes? What role do computers play in composing processes? In what ways do cognition and context work together when people write?

Researchers interested in answering these questions turned to a variety of data collection methods: interviews, think-aloud protocols, process diaries, surveys, analysis of multiple drafts, observations, timed writing, and (thought, process, or time) logs. Researchers gave participants prompts for composing essays, required types of essays (expressive, explanatory, persuasive), asked for a particular number of revisions, compared writing at the beginning and end of a semester, and had raters score the quality of written products. Many of these research studies relied on think-aloud protocols as the most appropriate data collection method for revealing in part the writer's thinking as he or she composed (Berkenkotter, "Decisions," "Understanding," and "Student"; Collier; Flower; Flower and Hayes, "Cognition" and "Cognitive"; Murray; Penrose and Geisler; Perl; Rubin; Sommers, "Revision"; Witte, "Pre-Text").

CCC is representative of the field as a whole working under the belief that "[t]he accumulation and analysis of answers to such questions [about composing processes] may eventually lead to significant advances in both theory and pedagogy: a deeper awareness of how and why writers behave as they do, and a better understanding of how to develop those behaviors advantageously in the classroom" (Knoblauch 159). However, as composing process research was accumulating an aggregated understanding of how writers behave, a shift was brewing. Lynn Quitman Troyka sensed the coming change in her review of CCCC program proposals, a change she explicitly attributed to a response to methods:

> One of the most unmistakable trends revealed by the 1980 program proposals is the move toward rigorous research. Research proposals were offered in many areas and with an admirable mix of models that ranged from the experimental to the descriptive, from case studies to longitudinal studies, and from data derived in naturalistic settings to data obtained in more controlled environments. As a result, the 1980 program included an unprecedented 16 sessions on research in writing. Along with this increased attention to research, a reaction urging caution seems to be developing, in that some proposers asked to discuss what they see as dangers inherent in an overemphasis on scientific method or an uncritical acceptance of research methods or results. (229–30)

Troyka presciently sees in the developing response to composition studies' "rigorous research" a reaction to methods (both the scientific method and an uncritical acceptance of methods) and foreshadows a significant shift in epistemological approaches and methods for research. John Trimbur describes this "social turn" of the 1980s as "a post-process, post-cognitivist theory and pedagogy that represent literacy as an ideological arena and composing as a cultural activity by which writers position and reposition themselves in relation to their own and others' subjectivities, discourses, practices, and institutions" (109). As Troyka and Trimbur suggest, the social turn in the field was an epistemological but also, significantly, a methodological turn *away from* particular research questions, methodological approaches, and objects of study. In particular, three interconnected contentions were central to the demise of composing process research: critics charged that composing process researchers were attempting to construct A (singular, homogenous) Theory of Writing, relying on empirical data that was impoverished and suspect and on analysis that took too little account of the sociality of writing.

Social turn critics charged composing process researchers with attempting to create a universal model of composing that focused on the individual writer in isolation without adequately accounting for the influence of social and cultural context. Patricia Bizzell, for example, breaks the field into two camps:

> One theoretical camp sees writing as primarily inner-directed, and so is more interested in the structure of language—learning and thinking processes in their earliest state, prior to social influence. The other main theoretical camp sees writing as primarily outer-directed, and so is more interested in the social processes whereby language-learning and thinking capacities are shaped and used in particular communities. ("Cognition" 388) [4]

Bizzell's influential critique suggests that composing process research (the inner-directed camp) is homogenous and resolved. Instead, in 1982, when Bizzell was writing, I believe composing process research was a diverse body of scholarship at the beginning of a much bigger project than was ever accomplished. In that initial phase, individual writers were a methodological entry point for revealing—*as had never before been revealed in any discipline*—what actually happened when writers composed. Social science research on a phenomenon as complex as writing processes has to proceed in stages, with smaller pieces of the complex whole accumulating into an understanding that honors the complexity of the phenomenon. Within that framework, the inner-directed processes of writing might have been the *beginning* of a broader research agenda rather than a *conclusion* that writing is inner-directed. Much of the composing process scholarship concluded with questions the current research left unanswered and calls for further research.

Instead, in the wake of the social turn, the field turned away from these unanswered questions and a shared commitment to the cumulative understanding of research (which implicitly recognizes the partiality of any research). Seeing empirical research as inadequate, Bizzell calls for a completely different kind of research: one that is "literary-critical in method" rather than "social science oriented" (*Academic* 8). The disciplinary turn toward literary-critical methods for research was accompanied by a critique of composing process research methods (particularly think-aloud protocols) as suspect, limited, and impoverished. Marilyn Cooper and Michael Holzman, for example, dismiss think-aloud protocols outright (regardless of their appropriateness to particular research questions) as "an unsound methodology" (284). They contend, "Protocols, far from being [as Flower and Hayes say] 'extraordinarily rich in data,' are exceedingly impoverished sources of information on what writers are thinking about" (286). As with any method, though, think-aloud protocols might best be understood as resulting in data that lies somewhere between extraordinarily rich and exceedingly impoverished. Think-aloud protocols provide *partial* data appropriate for answering *specific* questions; the value in the method lies not in some essential value of the method itself but in what the method reveals in answer to an inquiry. Peter Smagorinsky points out, "Ironically, [Cooper and Holzman] criticize protocol analysis for its gaps, when protocols have far fewer gaps than data collected through any other method" (469). After reviewing claims and criticisms about protocol analysis in a variety of fields, Smagorinsky concludes, "To discount protocol analysis as a method is to ignore the many contributions it has already made to our understanding of written communication, and to dismiss the knowledge it is bound to uncover about composing in the future" (476).[5] Indeed, although numerous studies in *CCC* alone were examining questions involving the impact of a writer's context on his or her composing (Berkenkotter, "Student"; Clark and Wiedenhaupt; Faigley and Hansen; Nelson; Penrose and

Geisler; Skubikowski and Elder), the field's social turn derailed the trajectory toward insight into how culture, society, and other people impacted the inner workings of writing process.

The branch of theory that calls itself "post-process composition studies" (Kent) proposes what would seem to be a movement interested in connecting itself with the composing process research I have reviewed here, but I agree with Lee-Ann M. Kastman Breuch that

> the broader implications of post-process theory have very little to do with process. Furthermore, I suggest that the only importance process has to post-process theory is in the form of an illustration—and a poor one at that. That is, "process" as it is cast by post-process scholarship is the scapegoat in an argument to forward postmodern and anti-foundationalist perspectives that are critical to post-process theory. (120)

Indeed, the post-process movement seems to be a continuation of historical critiques that composing process research is an attempt to "theorize various aspects of composing [in order] to construct a model of the composing process, thereby constructing a Theory of Writing, a series of generalizations about writing that supposedly hold true all or most of the time" (Olson 8). The post-process movement continues working within the binary Bizzell established so many years ago between empirical and literary and against more nuanced arguments that recognize "it is possible and, more importantly, necessary for composition studies to have an agenda for inquiry comprised of theory and empirical research in a mutually informing relationship" (Sanchez 1). I believe we need to dismantle the assumptions of post-process theories that assert that empirical researchers believe data-based studies capture the essence of reality (we don't), that composing process researchers are attempting to build a singular theory of writing process (we aren't), and that theoretical understandings of writing are sufficient because data-based research can never be complete (it isn't, and they aren't). Instead, to be explicit, I am arguing that writing is a complex meaning-making, symbol-using, socially situated activity. Writing in contemporary lives is explicitly an interrelationship between culture and individual cognition. Data-based scholarship is not any more committed to creating a homogenous, monolithic Theory of Writing than post-process scholarship; rather than seeing data as a pure representation of some truth, ethically motivated and theoretically informed researchers understand data as a building block toward knowledge—a partial representation of some aspect of an experience that is suggestive of the ways some people experience some things in the world. For empirical researchers, this partial yet significant window into lived experience—from the perspective of the people engaging in it—is a crucial part of knowledge building. Like Paul Prior, I believe "[t]here is a wide gap between an everyday representation of writing, as in 'I wrote a paper last night,' and the image of writing that a think-aloud protocol makes available, and filling that gap remains a critical project for writing research" (180), and like Raul Sanchez, I imagine that a return to composing process research might result in a richer understanding of writing in which "empiricism [is seen] as simultaneously a producer and recipient of theoretical insight" (238) and "as an unavoidable part of theoretical inquiry, not as an obstacle to it" (239). As a discipline, we will benefit from multiple methods of understanding, including both theoretical and data-based scholarship, although the latter has been virtually absent in our field since the social turn toward theory.

The ending of composing process research in our flagship journals coincided with the beginning of an explosion of digitally mediated writing in daily life, a time when writing is changing in dramatic ways and, in particular, becoming increasingly social. Writing is networked, digital, mediated, and multimodal; writing technologies include pens on paper, word-processing programs, page design programs, email, real-time chatting, social media, and mobile phones; writers write in academic, social, civic, and workplace settings in a range of formal and informal ways; and writers write publicly and privately for known and unknown individual, multiple, or massive audiences. And yet, in the last nineteen years, there have been no articles published in our flagship journals which examine composing processes using these tools in these contexts. This lack of attention to composing processes related to the ubiquitous technologies of contemporary life is connected to the lack of disciplinary attention to computer technologies more generally. Since at least 1983, when Cynthia Selfe and Kate Kiefer founded *Computers and Composition,* there has been a body of scholarship examining the materiality of writing, particularly in the ways computer technologies enable, mediate, and change writing processes and practices. However, this subdiscipline—with its own journals, annual conference, numerous edited collections, single-authored books, and documented history (Hawisher et al.)—has been largely peripheral to the pages of the flagship journals. As Patricia Sullivan and James Porter rightly lamented in 1997, "Computers and composition researchers examine the effects of computer technologies on writing, and hardly anybody else bothers to do so" (93). Ten years later, James E. Porter put it even more strongly: "The field of Rhetoric/Composition has yet to acknowledge, truly acknowledge, that changes and developments in writing tools have changed writing, literacy, and communication practices in fundamental ways—that, given how writing happens in the 21st century, *all* composition research needs to be computers and writing research" (xii). Writing in the twenty-first century is almost always mediated through technologies that did not exist prior to 1995; understanding what writers do when they actually compose is crucial to understanding how writing happens in the twenty-first century.

For contemporary researchers interested in understanding composing processes in these data-based ways, the critiques that derailed the composing process research of the 1980s are difficult to sustain in at least two ways: First, researchers today cannot responsibly ignore the sociality of writing processes—writers are composing on internet-worked computers, tablets, and mobile phones, and they are almost always connected. The sociality of writing is visible and present almost every time a writer writes. Second, data collection technologies unavailable in the 1980s such as screencasting, eye tracking, and key stroke recording document every detail in a writer's composing process (down to the level of the individual character as it appears on the screen) against which to measure the writer's expressed thoughts. Rhetoric and composition as a discipline also has a more sophisticated and nuanced understanding of research epistemologies, methodologies, and methods, with a body of recent scholarship articulating that while there are many ways to research writing, all methods have affordances and constraints (Nickoson and Sheridan; Powell and Takayoshi; Royster and Kirsch). Informed by the last two decades of composition scholarship on the social situatedness of literacy, researchers investigating what writers do are well prepared to understand the intertwined cognitive and cultural complexities of writing as a social practice. New research technologies provide an unprecedented window onto the sociality of writing processes and can suggest some of the ways writers today weave together cognitive and cultural processes of meaning making in ways unimagined at the time of the last composing process research. *How do writers write in digital contexts? How do writers negoti-*

ate "*the social processes whereby language-learning and thinking capacities are shaped and used in particular communities*" (Bizzell, "Cognition" 388, emphasis added)? Contemporary social networking sites present social constructionists and writing researchers with a rich environment for uncovering the deeply intertwined social processes and composing processes of writers. The following case study reveals the inextricable nature of individual and culture in contemporary composing processes and the writer's continual negotiation of that relationship in the production of written language.

ONE WRITER'S SOCIALLY SITUATED COMPOSING

Lakshmi, a twenty-something Indian American college undergraduate, was a participant in a larger study of eight Facebook users' literate practices.[6] As such, she recorded a fifty-minute screencast video of her computer screen accompanied by think-aloud audio as she engaged in a range of literate practices anchored by Facebook. In her think-aloud narration, Lakshmi describes what she's doing and the decisions she's making as she's reading and writing, and a retrospective interview conducted shortly after the think-aloud provided further insight into Lakshmi's composing processes.

Lakshmi's process of composing the largely short form, interactive, interpersonal writing of Facebook is characterized by the backward and forward truncation of drafting-revising-editing exhibited by all of the participants in the larger study. I have elaborated on these features of their composing processes elsewhere (Takayoshi, "Methodological" and "ShortForm"), suggesting that this process of composing is quite different from the one upon which composing process theories rest. Before turning my attention in this article to the negotiations of culture and individual composing process that take place at the site of the local utterance, however, it's important to understand that the sociality of the writing process is mediated through this recursive, truncated, character-focused way of composing.

The central feature of Lakshmi's composing process is that she unremittingly revises as she produces text. The following, for example, is Lakshmi's process of composing the status post *I'm glad you thought this was funny, in hindsight I did too, and yes it goes without saying that you would certainly be disappointed if I accidentally blinded myself. :D.*

She writes: I'm glad you thought this was funny, in hindsight I did too, and tha

deletes ,and tha

writes :D

She inserts her cursor between *too* and *:D*

writes and yes th

deletes th

writes it goes without saying that you would be disappointed if I accd

deletes d

and writes identally blinded myself.

She inserts her cursor between *would* and *be* and writes certainly.

In composing this short piece of writing, Lakshmi creates, deletes, revises, and edits as she writes, reads, evaluates, and decides to change the unfolding written statement. Notably, like the other writers in the larger study, she does not produce a draft of the whole statement that she rereads. Instead, Lakshmi assesses the appropriateness for her meaning of *each individual alphabetic character* as it appears on the screen. The process of composing this statement is a movement forward as each character appears on the screen, and it is a movement backward as she deletes and replaces those characters and also as she moves backward into the text to insert her cursor and add text.

In the context of a composing process that is attentive to each individual alphanumeric, symbolic character, Lakshmi is also attentive to larger composing matters, most especially to the larger cultural context in which her writing participates. This attention is stimulated by the intrusion of the cultural context into the writing environment and her continual awareness of her audience at the receiving end of her writing. The real and immediate presence of the audience and larger culture could not have been imagined by composing process researchers in a pre-Internet writing environment. Yet, these features are characteristic of contemporary writing—as Lakshmi's think-aloud shows, the access computers provide to multiple audiences and multiple purposes as well as to multiple writing platforms requires an almost constant negotiation of multiple writing tasks, registers, genres, and audiences on the part of the writer. As researchers like Stacey Pigg and Amber Buck have likewise demonstrated, contemporary writers are often negotiating multiple writing purposes through multiple active platforms (email browser, word-processing program, other social networking sites, various websites, music programs, or chat programs). Writers do not compose in isolation from communities of other people unless they consciously turn off their computer's network connection or perhaps opt to constrain their social connections through "productivity programs" that lock them out of the Internet for set amounts of time.

One of the most significant consequences of the always networked nature of writing is the constant disruption of one's writing process by the social networks in which the writer produces text. Indeed, one of the most notable features of writing among all the Facebook writers was that *any time* a notification alerted the participants that something had been updated, they stopped what they were doing and responded immediately. As Lakshmi explained, "Just seeing the red notification is like 'Oh, I just have to deal with this *right now*.'" In fact, Lakshmi's think-aloud screencast begins with the Facebook notifications link. She noted, "First, I'm going to check my notifications because there might be something important," and she clicks the notifications link eleven times in the first eleven minutes of her screencast. Her reliance on the notifications link is situated within a larger drive to see what's new in her newsfeed: in her 3,600-word think-aloud, Lakshmi uses the word *see* one hundred times and *check* twenty-three times, as in "Let's see what else is going on" and "I'll check my home feed again." In addition to her active conscious searching for new activity in her social world, Lakshmi is notified by an alert when something new happens. In the forty minutes Lakshmi spent on Facebook, she received twelve notifications. Although not actually a composing feature, the constant presence of and high value placed on notifications make them into a key element involved in this literate practice for Lakshmi. The seven times Lakshmi responds most quickly (from 2 to 6 seconds response time), she is somewhat aimlessly surfing Facebook. She's moving up and down in her newsfeed or chatting through the Facebook chat feature with her cousin, Aman, aware that her cousin is also writing and reading the conversation as it unfolds in real time. Yet, even when Lakshmi is more fully engaged in complicated task (editing her profile picture, figuring out how to solve a technical problem, searching for a mentioned image), her response time to alert notifications is at maximum 75 seconds (the next longest response times are 32, 30, 16, and 14 seconds).

Lakshmi's constant attentiveness and responsiveness to notifications suggests that as a writer she is highly attuned to the social world in which she composes. But even more significantly, Lakshmi has adapted attentiveness and responsiveness as seamless features of her composing process. While Lakshmi is very quick to respond (all responses occur in under 75 seconds), she is also very quick to return directly to whatever literate activity—reading or writing—was interrupted by attending to the notification. Lakshmi's screencast suggests, in fact, that she is able to address intrusions from her social world in a focused way. This sense of focused distraction is contrary to commonsense depictions of the always on, always connected nature of contemporary literate practice—a feeling that the distractions are intrusive, disruptive, and counterproductive for writers. Instead, Lakshmi's focused distraction suggests that while we currently have little pedagogical theory about how to address the culture of distraction, writers like Lakshmi are developing effective responses on their own and recognizing notifications as a connective tissue of the writing process.

The notifications are clearly a driving force in Lakshmi's experience in this writing space. The notifications—both those she actively searches out and accompanied by an audio alert—are reminders of the social world in which she exists, writes, and communicates. The notifications are the identifiable moment when the social insists on being foregrounded by the individual in her writing—the social world is, of course, always present when writers write (we never write in a social vacuum even when we're writing for ourselves), and sometimes it is more foregrounded than at others. The notifications are the constant rupture of the social, and the writer's immediate responsiveness reveals the high priority placed on writing as a social act as well as the insistence that the writer remain highly alert to the social implications of her writing.

In her retrospective interview, Lakshmi talks about her response to notifications as an issue of ethos. Describing how she responds immediately to notifications, she says, "I just want to check to make sure that I don't like unintentionally ignore someone or something. I like to make sure I'm attentive enough to actually have a conversation. I don't want [my friends] to feel like, 'oh, you're off in like your own world, doing great things and like not paying any attention to us anymore.' I want to come across as non-intimidating basically I don't want to come across as being like all snooty or whatever." Being "attentive" to her audience, in other words, is a deeply meaningful part of her composing process. It contributes to her ethos as a caring, non-intimidating, accessible person. Whereas an outsider might see her responsiveness to notifications as being disruptive rather than attentive, Lakshmi understands her responsiveness to notifications as an indication of her attentiveness. The potential distraction of notifications has been folded into Lakshmi's composing process as an important matter of ethos.

Lakshmi's screencast reveals (a) that her writing process is interrupted and fragmented by mediation and (b) that both mediation and her reaction to it are social concerns. The notifications, edits, and re-writings are responses to the increased sociality of writing in digital environments and to composing processes that are increasingly situated within a larger composing actthatis multilayered. Literally, Lakshmi's writing environment is multilayered in that there are multiple windows open and layered onto one another at various times (Facebook, email client, university records window, blog), but also conceptually, Lakshmi's writing is multilayered as she is at the same time negotiating multiple writing tasks, writing sites, and audiences. One constant layer of Lakshmi's writing on Facebook during her think-aloud session was multiple real-time chat conversations in which her considerations of her audience constantly shape her emerging text, as shown in the following transcription of her process composing in a private, one-to-one chat with her cousin:

> She writes That's right Mom told you
>
> deletes you
>
> writes me you have
>
> deletes ve
>
> writes ve a baby! Congratulations
>
> deletes Congratulations
>
> writes belated congratulations. and it's gra
>
> deletes a

> writes <u>eat that Shiv is familiar with Londo n</u>
>
> deletes the space between *o* and *n*
>
> writes <u>and can</u>
>
> deletes <u>can</u>
>
> writes <u>can show you around</u>
>
> deletes <u>can show you around</u>
>
> writes <u>help you get comfortable. What is the weather like this season?</u>

It takes Lakshmi 283 key strokes in order to compose her final 184-character message (*That's right Mom told me youhave a baby. belated congratulations, and it's great that Shiv is familiar with London and help you get comfortable. What is the weather like this season?*). As her think-aloud reveals, this editing and rewriting process is driven by expectations of her audience's response. As she changes *congratulations* to *belated congratulations,* she comments, "'Belated congratulations' I should say because I think he's close to a year old." And after writing *can show you around,* she wonders aloud, "Do I want to say that? [rereading:] 'show you around . . .' Errr, no, I'm going to say 'and help you get comfortable.'" Two minutes later, when Lakshmi searches her cousin's photo album for baby pictures, she worries aloud, "I hope I didn't say your son because it's a daughter," and returns to her comment to reread it, saying with a sigh of relief, "No, I said 'you have a baby.'"

Lakshmi's composing process is in these many ways determined by what Lester Faigley and Stephen Witte described as "situational variables" that influence composing processes:

> are probably the following: the reason why the text is being written, the format, the medium, the genre, the writer's familiarity with the writing task, the writer's familiarity with the subject, the writer's familiarity with the audience, the projected level of formality, and the length of the task and the projected text. So important are these variables that writing skill mightbe defined in part as the ability to respond to them. (410–11)

In Lakshmi's writing process, these situational variables all drive what ends up being the final utterance; her writing process is in large part driven by her ability to respond to these muling, though, we can see in detail how this writer skillfully weaves culture and written text. Through data-based studies focusing on the level of the composing process, the local concerns (forming the individual words and utterances) as well as the higher-order concerns (negotiating interruptions and multiple audiences) are partially revealed in a way that can begin to answer some questions left unanswered by the composing process research of the late 1980s.

Contemporary writers' writing processes are embedded in a network of social, familial, work, academic, and cultural contexts. A reorientation toward process research can reveal for the field in unprecedented ways the very things for which process research of the 1980s was faulted—the ways composing processes take up and are shaped by the social contexts in which they are functioning. As Lakshmi's case suggests, contemporary writers are intensely aware of the social contexts, audiences, and competing genres that shape their composing processes. In Lakshmi's case, we have a window into the contours of the composing process as a decision-making and recursive process of accounting for and responding to the social context's influence on the composing process and the composition itself. Literacy is always practiced within social contexts, and the shaping forces of that context—the literate object of writing, as well as the writer's position, purpose, audience, and cultural factors—are likewise being shaped within the act of composing. Thus, by capturing the composing moment, we can see that just as literacy is itself in constant motion, so too are the contextual elements that give rise to literacy in any given social interaction. The composing moment allows us to explain and anchor the differences that appear across contexts in terms of how people write, use, and think about composing. Given vast changes in composing contexts and the increased sociality of writing since 1990, a return to composing process research can finally answer the critiques made of previous composing process research. Lakshmi's case reveals that a new orientation toward process can account for writing processes in their social context—unlike 1980s process researchers (who studied writers with pen and paper, and writing processes in physical isolation from their social context), contemporary process researchers can (and must) address head-on the sociality of composing processes. In other words, informed by the last twenty years of literacy studies scholarship and writing technologies, a return to composing process is, in fact, an examination of sociality.

Conclusion

Deborah Brandt notes that "it is worth remembering that almost every major understanding we have about writing processes, writing development, and written language, for that matter, derives mostly from research conducted in the bygone era of traditional print" (212). Our field has paid woefully little attention to theorizing in a data-based way the differences between the bygone era of traditional print and a world in which people are always connected, always writing and reading. It's as important to document this moment in writing as it is to begin asking questions about the composing process. In the introduction to their wide-ranging collection on digital writing research methods, Heidi A. McKee and Danielle Nicole DeVoss argue that "[d]igital technologies and the people who use those technologies have changed the processes, products, and contexts for writing and the teaching of writing in dramatic ways—and at this cultural, historical, and intellectual moment, it is imperative that our research approaches, our methodologies, and our ethical understandings for researching adequately and appropriately address these changes in communication technologies" (11). I agree with them that in order to teach better we need to have a better research-based understanding of what successful writing is and what experienced and inexperienced writers do when they write. What happens to composing in a world where writers are using multiple tools to complete multiple tasks at the same time? How do nonstop interruptions affect the writer's thought process—and how is it that writers like Lakshmi have developed such smoothly functioning processes for dealing with interruptions? How can writing instruction contribute to writers' effortless negotiation of the multiplicity of writing demands?

The beginning of an empirical accumulation of knowledge about composing processes research was undone by critics in the early 1990s. Those critiques—that composing process researchers were attempting to construct a capital T Theory of writing, that the data was inherently flawed and impoverished, and that there was too little attention to the sociality of writing—are understandable coming from those critics' epistemological and methodological tradition (a tradition, remember, that Bizzell described as *literary-critical*). Informed by the last twenty years of composition and literacy studies scholarship, however, as a discipline we might understand research as a process of accumulation in which empirical research is an attempt to build an accumulated body of scholarship detailing what (experienced, student, workplace, and academic) writers do in multiple locations rather than attempting to create a homogenous one-size-fits-all Theory of writing. Such an understanding recognizes that all data is partial but that *some* data of actual writers is better than *no* data of actual processes because it is through multiple forms of understanding that a field of study builds complex understandings of complex phenomena.

In one of the last pieces published on composing process research in *CCC*, Linda Flower turned her attention to an empirical investigation of context and culture in composing. Describing her motivation in researching writing processes, Flower wrote that she wanted a method for revealing the complexity of writing processes that had up to that point gone unnoticed, or "a vision of the writing process that can . . . talk about the experience of writing by being adequately fine-grained and situated in that experience. I want a framework that acknowledges the pressure and the potential the social context can provide, at the same time it explains how writers negotiate that context, create their own goals and develop a sense of themselves as problem-solvers, speakers, or Subjects who create meaning and affect other people through their writing" ("Cognition" 284). The framework Flower describes—one that *explains how writers create meaning and affect other people through their writing*—is as necessary today as it was for process movement researchers. Such an understanding is crucial for understanding the ways people are composing with contemporary technologies—how people write within the changing contexts of technologies, environments, and contexts for writing across contemporary life experience. My review of the field's scholarship—as represented in the two main official journals of NCTE—suggest that our existing knowledge about *how writing is produced* is grounded in a historical moment and cultural context that looks very different than the one in which writers compose today. While the field has examined writing's functions and purposes in academic and non-academic lives, the ways teachers interact with writers in their processes of learning, and the writer himself or herself as a nexus of multiple ideological identities within a range of cultural contexts, very little research over the last twenty-five years has taken a writer's *composing process* as the central object of study. If teachers of writing are to effectively help writers learn to be effective and productive in contemporary academic and non-academic contexts, then we need to know what composing demands writers must negotiate and how they can make their meanings understood in these complexly layered writing environments.

Stepping back to gain a broader vision of what writing entails has allowed us to understand the broader context of literacy as a socially situated practice. We have come to see—in some detail—how

> literacy skills [are] not just a set of techniques to be easily and quickly acquired but [are] part of a complex ideology, a set of specific practices constructed within a specific infrastructure and able to be learnt and assimilated only in relation to that ideology and infrastructure: the acquisition of literacy is, in fact, a socialisation process rather than a technical process. (Street 180)

I believe there will be much to learn by moving closer to the actual moment of composing as an object of study, informed by the knowledge we have now about literacy (particularly writing) as a set of specific practices constructed within a specific framework. Research conducted at the moment of composing might reveal—as Lakshmi's think-aloud suggests—the complexity of literacy as a socialization process. Returning our disciplinary and methodological attention to the moment of composing can not only begin to flesh out the specific ways writers negotiate social worlds through text, but it can also provide a microcosmic view of important disciplinary questions: How are people using writing in their lives to compose and make meaning? How are contemporary technologies supporting and constraining the meaning-making practices literacy makes possible for people?

Notes

1. In his "Editorial Comment," editor Charles W. Roberts wrote, "Such a publication as the new Conference on College Composition and Communication has in mind might do a great deal of good and be of service for a long time" (13). He might be quite pleased to find that time has proven his prediction correct.

2. Additionally, articles published in the journal prior to 1976 speculated theoretically about what writers do when they compose, laying the

groundwork for composing process research (de Beaugrande; Graves; Odell; Rohman; Shaughnessy; Sommers, "Need").

3. The research for this article was completed in 2015. However, the trends identified continued into the 2016 and 2017 issues of the two journals.

4. Notably, like many of the social turn critics, Bizzell focuses on Flower and Hayes's research and the model they uniquely construct as representative of composing process research. This is problematic because Flower and Hayes have a different agenda than most of the composing process researchers: they wanted to use their data to create *a model of* composing processes while the majority of composing process research aimed to provide a crucial but initial descriptive understanding.

5. Relevant but not central to my argument here, Cooper and Holzman believe that "the way in which protocols are elicited raises serious questions about their validity—questions not limited to the protocol method, but applicable to all research concerning human thought and behavior" (290). It is arguments like these that Smagorinsky has in mind when he points out, "To claim that protocols are unnatural and therefore misleading because the conditions (promptings from a researcher, the 'unnatural' setting, the time limit) affect performance would seem a dismissal of all experimental research" (469). The slippage from critique to dismissal of research and its methods couldn't be clearer.

6. The larger study asks, "In a multi-literate, multimodal world of communication, what do writing processes look like? What do writers do when they write?" Research team members Ashlee Brand, Matt Fink, Uma Krishnan, Phil Sloane, Melinda Stephan, Chelsea Swick, Yvonne Teems, Cynthia Vigliotti, and I collected data, transcribed it, and organized video data.

Works Cited

Aldrich, Pearl G. "Adult Writers: Some Reasons for Ineffective Writing on the Job." *College Composition and Communication*, vol. 33, no. 3, 1982, pp. 284–87.

Beach, Richard. "Self-Evaluation Strategies of Extensive Revisers and Non-revisers." *College Composition and Communication*, vol. 27, no. 2, 1976, pp. 160–64.

Bean, John C. "Computerized Word-Processing as an Aid to Revision." *College Composition and Communication*, vol. 34, no. 2, 1983, pp. 146–48.

Bereiter, Carl, and Marlene Scardamalia. *The Psychology of Written Composition*. Lawrence Erlbaum Associates, 1987.

Berkenkotter, Carol. "Decisions and Revisions: The Planning Strategies of a Publishing Writer." *College Composition and Communication*, vol. 34, no. 2, 1983, pp. 156–69.

—. "Student Writers and Their Sense of Authority over Texts." *College Composition and Communication,* vol. 35, no. 3, 1984, pp. 312–19.

—. "Understanding a Writer's Awareness of Audience." *College Composition and Communication,* vol. 32, no. 4, 1981, pp. 388–99.

Bizzell, Patricia. *Academic Discourse and Critical Consciousness.* U of Pittsburgh P, 1992.

—. "Cognition, Convention, and Certainty: What We Need to Know about Writing." *Cross-Talk in Comp Theory: A Reader,* edited by Victor Villanueva. 2nd ed., NCTE, 2003, pp. 387–412.

Blau, Sheridan. "Invisible Writing: Investigating Cognitive Processes in Composition." *College Composition and Communication,* vol. 34, no. 3, 1983, pp. 297–312.

Boice, Robert. "The Neglected Third Factor in Writing: Productivity." *College Composition and Communication,* vol. 36, no. 4, 1985, pp. 472–80.

Brandt, Deborah. "Struggles for Perspective: A Commentary on 'One Story of Many to Be Told': Following Empirical Studies of College and Adult Writing through 100 Years of NCTE Journals." *Research in the Teaching of English,* vol. 46, no. 2, 2011, pp. 210–14.

Brandt, Deborah, and Katie Clinton. Afterword. *Travel Notes from the New Literacy Studies: Instances of Practice,* edited by Kate Pahl and Jennifer Rowsell, Multilingual Matters, 2006, pp. 254–58.

Breuch, Lee-Ann M. Kastman. "Post Process 'Pedagogy': A Philosophical Exercise." *JAC,* vol. 22, no. 1, 2002, pp. 119–50.

Buck, Amber. "Physically Present and Digitally Active: Locating Ecologies of Writing on Social Networks." *Literacy in Practice: Writing in Working, Private, and Public Lives,* edited by Patrick Thomas and Pamela Takayoshi, Routledge, 2016, pp. 86–102.

Case, Donald. "Processing Professorial Words: Personal Computers and the Writing Habits of University." *College Composition and Communication,* vol. 36, no. 3, 1985, pp. 317–22.

Catano, James. "Computer-Based Writing: Navigating the Fluid Text." *College Composition and Communication,* vol. 36, no. 3, 1985, pp. 309–16.

Clark, Beverly Lyon, and Sonja Wiedenhaupt. "On Blocking and Unblocking Sonja: A Case Study in Two Voices." *College Composition and Communication,* vol. 43, no. 1, 1992, pp. 55–74.

Collier, Richard M. "The Word Processor and Revision Strategies." *College Composition and Communication,* vol. 34, no. 2, 1983, pp. 149–55.

Cooper, Charles R., and Lee Odell. *Research on Composing: Points of Departure.* National Council of Teachers of English, 1978.

Cooper, Marilyn, and Michael Holzman. "A Cognitive Process Theory of Writing." *College Composition and Communication,* vol. 32, no. 4, 1981, pp. 365–87.

Daiute, Colette A. "The Computer as Stylus and Audience." *College Composition and Communication,* vol. 34, no. 2, 1983, pp. 134–45.

de Beaugrande, Robert. "Moving from Product toward Process." *College Composition and Communication,* vol. 30, no. 4, 1979, pp. 357–63.

Emig, Janet. *The Composing Processes of Twelfth Graders.* National Council of Teachers of English, 1971. NCTE Research Report no. 13.

Faigley, Lester, and Kristine Hansen. "Learning to Write in the Social Sciences." *College Composition and Communication,* vol. 36, no. 2, 1985, pp. 140–49.

Faigley, Lester, and Stephen Witte. "Analyzing Revision." *College Composition and Communication,* vol. 32, no. 4, 1981, pp. 400–14.

Flower, Linda. "Cognition, Context, and Theory Building." *College Composition and Communication,* vol. 40, no. 3, 1989, pp. 282–311.

—. "Writer-Based Prose: A Cognitive Basis for Problems in Writing." *College English,* vol. 41, no. 1, 1979, pp. 19–37.

Flower, Linda, and John R. Hayes. "The Cognition of Discovery: Defining a Rhetorical Problem." *College Composition and Communication,* vol. 31, no. 1, 1980, pp. 21–32.

"Talking about Protocols." *College Composition and Communication,* vol. 34, no. 3, 1983, pp. 284–93.

Crowley, Sharon. "Components of the Composing Process." *College Composition and Communication,* vol. 28, no. 2, 1977, pp. 166–69.

—. "Identifying the Organization Writing Processes." *Cognitive Processes in Writing,* edited by Lee W. Gregg and Edwin R. Steinberg. Routledge, 1980, pp. 3–30.

—. "Images, Plans, and Prose: The Representation of Meaning in Writing." *Written Communication,* vol. 1, no. 1, 1984, pp. 120–60.

—. "Problem-Solving Strategies and the Writing Process." *College English,* vol. 39, no. 4, 1977, pp. 449–61.

Flower, Linda, et al. "Detection, Diagnosis, and the Strategies of Revision." *College Composition and Communication,* vol. 37, no. 1, 1986, pp. 16–55.

Flynn, Elizabeth A. "Composing Responses to Literary Texts: A Process Approach." *College Composition and Communication,* vol. 34, no. 3, 1983, pp. 342–48.

Graves, Richard L. "Levels of Skill in the Composing Process." *College Composition and Communication,* vol. 29, no. 3, 1978, pp. 227–32.

Gregg, Lee W., and Edwin R. Steinberg, editors. *Cognitive Processes in Writing.* Routledge, 1980.

Harris, Jeanette. "Student Writers and Word Processing: A Preliminary Evaluation." *College Composition and Communication,* vol. 36, no. 3, 1985, pp. 323–30.

Hawisher, Gail, et al.. *Computers and the Teaching of Writing in American Higher Education, 1979–1994: A History.* Ablex, 1995.

Hayes, John, and Linda Flower. "Writing Research and the Writer." *American Psychologist,* vol. 41, no. 10, 1986, pp. 1106–13.

Humes, Ann. "Research on the Composing Process." *Review of Educational Research,* vol. 53, no. 2, 1983, pp. 201–16.

Jensen, George H., and John K. DiTiberio. "Personality and Individual Writing Processes." *College Composition and Communication,* vol. 35, no. 3, 1984, pp. 285–300.

Kent, Thomas, editor. *Post-Process Theory: Beyond the Writing-Process Paradigm.* Southern Illinois UP, 1999.

King, Martha. "Research in Composition: A Need for Theory." *Research in the Teaching of English,* vol. 12, no. 3, 1978, pp. 193–202.

Knoblauch, C. H. "Intentionality in the Writing Process: A Case Study." *College Composition and Communication,* vol. 31, no. 2, 1980, pp. 153–59.

McCarthy, Patricia, et al. "Self-Efficacy and Writing: A Different View of Self-Evaluation." *College Composition and Communication,* vol. 36, no. 4, 1985, pp. 465–71.

McKee, Heidi A., and Danielle Nicole DeVoss, editors. *Digital Writing Research: Technologies, Methodologies and Ethical Issues.* Hampton Press, 2007.

Miller, Susan. "How Writers Evaluate Their Own Writing." *College Composition and Communication,* vol. 33, no. 2, 1982, pp. 176–83.

Murray, Donald M. "Response of a Laboratory Rat—or, Being Protocoled." *College Composition and Communication,* vol. 34, no. 2, 1983, pp. 169–72.

Nelson, Jennie. "Reading Classrooms as Text: Exploring Student Writers' Interpretive Practices." *College Composition and Communication,* vol. 46, no. 3, 1995, pp. 411–29.

Nickoson, Lee, and Mary P. Sheridan, editors. *Writing Studies Research in Practice: Methods and Methodologies.* Southern Illinois UP, 2012.

Odell, Lee. "The Process of Writing and the Process of Learning." *College Composition and Communication,* vol. 31, no. 1, 1980, pp. 42–50.

Olson, Gary A. "Toward a Post-Process Composition: Abandoning the Rhetoric of Assertion." *Post-Process Theory: Beyond the Writing-Process Paradigm,* edited by Thomas Kent, Southern Illinois UP, 1999, pp. 7–15.

Penrose, Ann M. and Cheryl Geisler. "Reading and Writing without Authority." *College Composition and Communication,* vol. 45, no. 4, 1994, pp. 505–20.

Perl, Sondra. "Understanding Composing." *College Composition and Communication,* vol. 31, no. 4, Dec. 1980, pp. 363–69.

Peterson, Linda. "Repetition and Metaphor in the Early Stages of Composing." *College Composition and Communication,* vol. 36, no. 4, 1985, pp. 429–43.

Pianko, Sharon. "Reflection: A Critical Component of the Composing Process." *College Composition and Communication,* vol. 30, no. 3, 1979, pp. 275–78.

Pigg, Stacey. "Researching Social Media Literacies as Emergent Practice: Changes in Twitter Use after Year Two of a Longitudinal Case Study." *Literacy in Practice: Writing in Working, Private, and Public Lives,* edited by Patrick Thomas and Pamela Takayoshi, Routledge, 2016, pp. 17–31.

Porter, James E. Foreword. *Digital Writing Research: Technologies, Methodologies and Ethical Issues,* edited by Heidi McKee and Danielle DeVoss, Hampton P, 2007, xii–ix.

Powell, Katrina, and Pamela Takayoshi, editors. *Practicing Research in Writing Studies: Reflexive and Ethically Responsible Research.* Hampton P, 2012.

Prior, Paul. "Tracing Process: How Texts Come into Being." *What Writing Does and How It Does It: An Introduction to Analyzing Texts and Textual Practices,* edited by Charles Bazerman and Paul Prior, Lawrence Erlbaum Associates, 2004, pp. 167–200.

Rhodes, Jacqueline, and Jonathan Alexander. "Reimagining the Social Turn: New Work from the Field." *College English,* vol. 76, no. 6, 2014, pp. 481–87.

Roberts, Charles W. "Editorial Comment." *College Composition and Communication,* vol. 1, no. 1, 1950, p. 13.

Rodrigues, Dawn. "Computers and Basic Writers." *College Composition and Communication,* vol. 36, no. 3, 1985, pp. 336–39.

Rohman, Gordon. "Pre-Writing: The Stage of Discovery in the Writing Process." *College Composition and Communication,* vol. 16, no. 2, 1965, pp. 106–12.

Rose, Mike. "Rigid Rules, Inflexible Plans, and the Stifling of Language: A Cognitivist Analysis of Writer's Block." *College Composition and Communication,* vol. 31, no. 4, 1980, pp. 389–401.

Royster, Jacqueline Jones, and Gesa Kirsch. *Feminist Rhetorical Practices: New Horizons for Rhetoric, Composition Studies, and Literacy Studies.* Southern Illinois UP, 2012.

Rubin, Lois. "Exploration of the Writing Experience: A Way to Improve Composing." *College Composition and Communication,* vol. 34, no. 3, 1983, pp. 349–55.

Sanchez, Raul. *The Function of Theory in Composition Studies.* State U of New York P, 2006.

Schwartz, Mimi. "Two Journeys through the Writing Process." *College Composition and Communication,* vol. 34, no. 2, 1983, pp. 188–201.

Selzer, Jack. "The Composing Processes of an Engineer." *College Composition and Communication,* vol. 34, no. 2, 1983, pp. 178–87.

Shaughnessy, Mina. "Some Needed Research on Writing." *College Composition and Communication,* vol. 28, no. 4, 1977, pp. 317–20.

Skubikowski, Kathleen, and John Elder. "Word Processing in a Community of Writers." *College Composition and Communication,* vol. 38, no. 2, 1987, pp. 198–201.

Smagorinsky, Peter. "The Reliability and Validity of Protocol Analysis." *Written Communication,* vol. 6, no. 4, 1989, pp. 463–79.

Sommers, Nancy. "The Need for Theory in Composition Research." *College Composition and Communication,* vol. 30, no. 1, 1979, pp. 46–49.

——. "Revision Strategies of Student Writers and Experienced Adult Writers." *College Composition and Communication,* vol. 31, no. 4, 1980, pp. 378–88.

Street, Brian. *Literacy in Theory and Practice.* Cambridge UP, 1984.

Sullivan, Patricia, and James Porter. *Opening Spaces: Writing Technologies and Critical Research Practices.* Ablex, 1997.

Takayoshi, Pamela. "Methodological Challenges to Researching Composing Processes in a New Literacy Context." *Literacy in Composition Studies,* vol. 4, no. 1, March 2016, pp. 1–23.

——. "Short-Form Writing: Studying Process in the Context of Contemporary Composing Technologies." *Computers and Composition: An International Journal for Teachers of Writing,* vol. 37, 2015, pp. 1–13.

Trimbur, John. "Taking the Social Turn: Teaching Writing Post-Process." *College Composition and Communication,* vol. 45, no. 1, 1994, pp. 108–18.

Troyka, Lynn Quitman. "The Pulse of the Profession." *College Composition and Communication,* vol. 31, no. 2, 1980, 227–31.

Witte, Stephen. "Pre-Text and Composing." *College Composition and Communication,* vol. 38, no. 4, 1987, pp. 397–425.

——. "Topical Structure and Revision: An Exploratory Study." *College Composition and Communication,* vol. 34, no. 3, 1983, pp. 313–41.

——. "Toward a Model for Research in Written Composition." *Research in the Teaching of English,* vol. 14, no. 1, 1980, pp. 73–81.

SUPPLEMENTAL MATERIAL

Part I: Reflection on the Origins of the Article

Like any piece of writing, this article is the meeting point of numerous experiences I've had: as a writing student, as a graduate student in the 1990s studying the still au courant composing process research, as a new writing teacher using that research to shape my pedagogical theories, and as a qualitative researcher influenced by literacy studies research.

My high school English and College Writing classes were informed by the then newly emerging process pedagogies: students wrote multiple drafts, received responses from peers and teachers, and grades were delayed until the final products were submitted (and in my College Writing classes, those were submitted in a portfolio of final works). So my pedagogical experience prepared me in some ways for the research on composing processes I did so many years later in this piece. I've just always understood writing as a process, and as a profoundly human meaning making activity, and I've always been interested in that moment of utterance—what happens when thought takes shape as written word on the page or screen. When I got to graduate school in the early 1990s, I was enthralled with the composing process research of the previous decade because it helped me think about and unpack this activity I was so immersed in as a writer and as a teacher. The research helped me shape my pedagogical practices. So this project began there—with an interest in how people really use writing to make meaning in their lives.

Then the semester this research began, I was teaching a Research Design graduate course, and I wanted us to work as a collaborative research team on a real research project, so students could experience—rather than just read about—the ebbs and flows of conducting human subjects research. Together, we designed a study which collected screencast videos and retrospective interviews of college-aged writers using Facebook. These screencasts are remarkably rich sources of data—they raised many interesting questions students in the course took on about, for example, invention, audience, revision, and ethos. I was struck by how all of those more specifically focused questions, though, raised a much more basic one: what do people _do_ when they write? Any work on writing processes that focused on this deceptively simple question had been done in a time when the material world of writing was dramatically different; the tools and environments in which contemporary writers compose are dramatically different in kind than those of writers in the 1980s, when most of the composing process research in the field was done. As writing technologies scholars have shown us over those forty years, the materiality of writing plays an important role in the shaping of thought into text, so I thought these huge changes—in the culture, in the writing tools, in the ubiquitous uses of writing—had to have implications for the ways writers used writing.

Part II: Description of Research Methods, Findings, and/or Pedagogical Impact

I believe that one of the reasons our field turned away from composing process research—in addition to what I write about in the article—was a negative turning away from empirical research as a whole. There was such a backlash to writing process research—and I think our richer, deeper disciplinary understanding of empirical research allows us to see the mistakes in some of that. Critics accused composing process research of setting out to build an autonomous model of writing process (this was never a stated goal in the literature), of believing think aloud protocols could provide a transparent window onto a writer's thinking (no good qualitative researcher would ever believe any method could do this—but qualitative researchers do believe some data is better than no data), of studying a writer's work in isolation of the contextual forces of culture. I believe the latter especially was an unfair reading of composing process research—in part because attention to culture is present across the composing process research but also because it feels to me like a willfully selective charge against one's colleagues in the field. No writing teacher, researcher, or writer would ever thoughtfully assert this, would they? So for me, a big part of this project was a methodological one—to return to composing process research with a better understanding of research methods which might allow us to respond to and move on productively from those critiques and fears of methodological ways of knowing. A human phenomenon as complex and evolving as writing processes benefits from an imbrication of understandings coming from multiple perspectives and diverse methodological approaches.

One practical way this study has shaped my teaching: I have taught two sections of first year writing in which students studied their own composing processes throughout the semester. Students read about composing processes, learned to screencast themselves composing, worked on those screencasts on research teams led by graduate students in a Writing Technologies seminar & wrote analyses of their writing process as a final paper in the course. They have found the work fun and engaging, according to their reflective responses throughout the course, and I think they've learned a good deal about themselves and about the nature of writing.

Part III: Discussion Questions

1. 1. What further research questions does the data on Lakshmi's process raise for you?

2. 2. Are the literate processes of meaning making and the composing processes of meaning making incommensurate as research focuses?

3. 3. What are the affordances and constraints of think aloud screencasts as a methodological approach to understanding what writers do when they compose?

4. 4. What does your own composing process reveal about literacy and meaning making? About the social situatedness of writing?

REFLECTIONS

Reflections is on the Web at https://reflectionsjournal.net/

Reflections, a peer reviewed journal, provides a forum for scholarship on public rhetoric, civic writing, service-learning, and community literacy. Originally founded as a venue for teachers, researchers, students and community partners to share research and discuss the theoretical, political and ethical implications of community-based writing and writing instruction, *Reflections* publishes a lively collection of scholarship on public rhetoric and civic writing, occasional essays and stories both from and about community writing and literacy projects, interviews with leading workers in the field, and reviews of current scholarship touching on these issues and topics.

Research as Care: A Shared Ownership Approach to Rhetorical Research in Trauma Communities[1]

Maria Novotny and John Gagnon theorize the ethics of research, an area in which they encountered a lack of resources as doctoral students working on their dissertation studies. In "Research as Care: A Shared Ownership Approach to Rhetorical Research in Trauma Communities," the authors describe how their ethnographic, trauma-related research raised critical questions about their responsibility to participants in their studies, leading them to propose a methodological toolkit based on indigenous and feminist perspectives centered on the concept of "shared ownership." Citing Linda Tuhiwai Smith, they argue that "…research as care transforms research from a mere recounting of stories and rhetorical analysis into a process that might otherwise be described as an 'activity of hope'" In this article, they make a significant contribution on the ethics of research that fills a gap in the literature and will be of great interest to graduate instructors, students, and ethnographic researchers in general.

---

1. *Reflections*, vol. 18, no. 1 © 2018 by New City Community Press.

Research as Care: A Shared Ownership Approach to Rhetorical Research in Trauma Communities

Maria Novotny and John T. Gagnon

In this article, we tell stories from our own research experiences to demonstrate the need for a set of methodological tools within Rhet/Comp that is more fully responsive to the ethical challenges of working with traumatized communities. Drawing on feminist and indigenous approaches, we propose a methodological toolkit for trauma-related research to reduce participant risk. In so doing, we situate shared ownership within a research as care framework and suggest five pillars for conducting trauma-related rhetorical research: (1) mediating academic use, (2) responsivity to re-living trauma, (3) recognizing participant motivations, (4) collaborative meaning-making, and (5) accounting for identity evolution. In sharing our stories about our research and the complications involved in negotiating researcher-participant dynamics in traumatized communities, we hope to help other researchers more effectively navigate similar territory in their own work.

In Spring 2017, we—two newly minted PhDs in Rhetoric & Writing—were invited by our faculty mentor to talk with graduate students about our respective experiences conducting community-based ethnographic research using oral history approaches. Maria's focus community was comprised of women dealing with infertility and reproductive loss; for John, the community was comprised of women who had been sex trafficked. Both projects explored participants' lived experiences and storytelling around traumatic events. While telling stories about conducting research within these communities, we noticed overlap in our thoughts about the ethical management of trauma-related research and our shared challenges. As we responded to questions from students, it became clear that we were both theorizing concerns about the lack of methodological resources on the ethics of rhetorical research within such communities. In what follows, we develop a set of methodological tools responsive to the ethical challenges of working with traumatized communities.

The concerns raised by our own experiences navigating research, and the questions graduate students posed after our panel, made us realize the need for methodological tools for trauma-related research. In particular, we saw a need to reduce participant risk and the risks of writing about their stories within the framework of institutional expectations. Drawing on feminist and indigenous approaches, we propose a methodological toolkit that we refer to as *research as care*. This phrasing suggests that our research not only cares for the stories we are told when collecting participant narratives, but that care is extended to recognition of embodiment (i.e., taken *onto* bodies). We care for the embodied being of our participants by operating through a series of reciprocal and fluid premises centered on the notion of *shared ownership*. These premises also act as a series of ethical checkpoints, aiming to care for participant stories by enacting methods that reinforce relationality between researcher and participant. More so, these premises take into account those unpredicted scenarios of negotiation that occur in trauma-related research.

THE NEED FOR A METHODOLOGICAL TOOLKIT

A review of literature demonstrates that currently no scholarship within rhetoric and composition specifically addresses *how* to work and do research within traumatized communities. While the discipline has, indeed, taken up and been concerned with experiences of trauma, calling for scholars to "bear witness to how rape scripts remembrance and forgetting" across two documentary films (Hesford 1999, 215) or address composition course design in response to the trauma of "Indian removal and U.S.-Indian relations in general" (Cole 2011,122), little methodological work has been conducted. While Lynne Lewis Gaillet (2012) raised archival research concerns in attending to "trauma, Asian diasporas, and the social dynamics of Asian culture" (43), the *how* of working with traumatized communities remains absent.

Instead, writing to heal from experiences of trauma has dominated our disciplinary scope, ranging from the need to advance pedagogical theories based on conflict, dissensus, and engagement "with discourses on healing, shelter, and trauma" (West 2000, 52), to Laura Micciche's (2001) suggestion to build "theories of emotion in composition studies [so as to] help teachers respond to students who may be damaged in ways that inhibit their ability to learn" (140). More recently, Cathryn Molloy (2016) evaluated the "efficacy of claims that writing personal narratives can heal individual pain" (134). On a broader scale, Gloria Anzaldua (1987), Jacqueline Jones Royster (1996), and Victor Villanueva (1993) have also made clear the traumatic violence of policed language. All of these authors crucially remind us that understanding trauma is important to rhetorically analyzing text and film, conducting archival research, and enacting thoughtful pedagogy, yet none articulate a methodological approach to *doing research* with traumatized communities or individuals.

From our research projects working with traumatized communities, we see a real methodological need to discuss *how to* care for these populations involved in the research process. While existing scholarship prepares us to guide students in using writing as a practice to reflect on and heal from traumatic experiences, little-to-no scholarship exists on rhetorical methods to prepare rhetorical researchers to work with and learn from individuals who have encountered trauma.

FEMINIST AND INDIGENOUS PERSPECTIVES

Our research orientation derives from our training in a program with faculty known for their work in cultural rhetorics and public rhetorics. These two areas influenced the scope of our dissertation projects and our goals for working within traumatized communities. Drawing from our own personal experiences and motivations to revise narratives impacting these communities, we see our work as community-based activist scholarship. That is, we see our scholarship as not *only* listening to and representing marginalized voices and scenes of meaning-making, but as deconstructing current systems that fail communities so as to offer methods and possibilities to create more just, supportive systems. As Stuart Blythe (2012) suggests, the practice of reciprocity is paramount when working with communities to conduct disciplinary research (275). As such, we both attempt to build communities of practice and study their stories for activist purposes. Like Andrea Riley-Mukavetz (2014), who called for researchers to "speak with and alongside" (122) our participants, we work as scholar-allies and view our research practices and findings as outcomes that can promote a better sense of care for communities. This is the ultimate goal of *research as care*.

Our toolkit draws on two cultural rhetorics pillars: feminist and indigenous perspectives. While these theoretical frameworks inform working within traumatized communities, they are not focused solely on them. We engage in an effort to constellate these theoretical frames in a way that shapes our methodological toolkit specifically for doing this type of research. These approaches woven together remind us that: (1) research is embodied, acting on all bodies involved in research, the researcher/s and the participant/s; (2) stories are sacred and must be honored as such once transcribed, analyzed, and revised into "academic" scholarship; and (3) scholarship can serve as a model of alliance with those communities it represents. Such perspectives complement community literacy studies, which also seeks to create and utilize rhetorical scholarship to create social change.

Like community literacy scholars, we listen to silenced communities and work in relation with them so as to make their voices and needs heard. The need to account for embodied stories that comprise communities can be realized through attention to relationality. As Powell et al. (2014) put it, there is a tendency in rhetoric studies "to fetishize texts, to turn everything into a text that can be read, and to sometimes objectify those texts in a way that disconnects them from their relationship to humans and to place/space" (Act 1, Scene 2). We draw on their concern about fetishizing texts, including stories, to establish a methodological need to connect with the people we write about and the motivations for writing about these stories. While these theoretical pillars inform our approach, it is in the actual *doing* of research that the application of these theories gets messy—especially when working with those who have endured trauma. In sharing our stories and reflections about our research and the complications involved in such negotiations—by airing the messiness, fluidity, and moments of disorientation we experienced in attempting to do so—we honor our participants by shifting the lens to focus on what we learned *from* working with them. Such reflection is our way of continuing to be accountable to our research participants. By taking ownership of our own missteps, and offering up our learnings from them, we hope to help other researchers more effectively navigate similar territory in their own work.

Research Stories

We lead with two stories about our respective research projects to root our discussion in actual research experiences and to set the stage for our discussion on why we believe *research as care* is so pivotal to doing research with participants who have experienced trauma. In what follows, we share vignettes that convey the spectrum of experiences we later address in our discussion. John's story demonstrates the actual and perceived tensions that emerge in real time while conducting interviews and across the writing process. Maria's story shows the complex evolution of working with people and obtaining consent across the entirety of a research project.

John: Developing Relations

Prior to enrolling at Michigan State University for doctoral studies, I worked in federal law enforcement handling issues around human trafficking. It was a topic that I had been steeped in, and it made sense for me to reorient that work to an academic setting because of the potential for community engagement and activism. For me, engagement with the issue required direct involvement, and I sought out opportunities to build relations with local area organizations involved in developing public awareness and providing survivor support services, as well as legal representatives and law enforcement. The epicenter of engagement for me—because it brought all of those elements together—was the Michigan Human Trafficking Task Force. I spent the first couple of years attending meetings and developing friendships. During that time, I built a solid working relationship with the organization's director and I reached out to her when it came time to initiate my project.

She helped me identify and initiate communications with potential research participants who self-identified as survivors of human trafficking and who had been involved with the organization in some way. My recruitment process was careful, slow, and methodical, spanning many months and encompassing a series of conversations with potential participants. It was during this time that I met Deb, who became one of my research participants. It took three months from the time I met her until the time she committed to enrolling in the study. That time was spent having multiple off-the record conversations through email, phone, and in-person. I did my best to address her questions, provide clarifications about the scope of the project, and— most importantly—tell her my own story. Deb, as someone whose trauma spanned decades and who suffered criminalization even as someone who had been trafficked, was deeply suspicious about working with me because of my law enforcement background. She needed to know more about how I had gone from the work of enforcing to the work of researching. This reticence reflected, I think, a concern on her part about my motivations. It was also something I was wholly unprepared for: her questions forced me to think about my own journey and why I had made the decisions I had. I realized, early on, that for me to truly develop a relationship with her, I would need to be wholly transparent. Telling my own story, which sometimes included telling the stories that I had "taken" in an interrogation setting, was emotionally fraught for me, but necessary to build trust. It was only when I was openly able to acknowledge the tensions in my own life and past as a law enforcement agent that she became willing to open up to me.

Gaining Consent

One of the first things I learned about Deb was that she possessed an incredible ability to communicate and that she seemed to enjoy talking the most about what her experiences had taught her. She knew we would likely cover some tough topics and painful moments from her past and, as such, her primary request was that the project should *not* focus on her trauma but on the transformation that occurred in her life following those experiences. In her view, her participation was linked to an ongoing part of her evolving sense of comfort in telling her story to help others, something that she had been doing in various ways for the past few years but was still difficult. We agreed that the project, especially the write-up, would not focus on her traumatic experiences, but rather on her transformative moments. That was an important, perhaps essential, point to gaining consent to move forward to the interview stage.

The Interview

I'm in a conference room in the Learning Resource Center, sitting across from Deb, and we're engaged in some small talk while I work on setting everything up for our second interview. I am purposely not wearing a tie—they make me uncomfortable—instead opting for a cheery sweater vest that I hope presents a friendly and open appearance. I'm also wearing glasses, an overt attempt to look the part of the academic while also knowing that they help me appear a bit less rigid. The room is comfortable, with soft seats, mood lighting, and paintings on the wall. Deb comments, "I like these paintings—they're nice." I agree. I have with me the tools of my trade—a laptop, a recording device, some legal documentation. We're almost ready to get started, when Deb poses a question: "So, can you tell me again what you're trying to do with this?" She goes on to tell me that, after our last interview "something came over me a little bit. I was a little uncomfortable." I feel a shimmer of anxiety. *Uh-oh,* I think, *she's having second thoughts.* And then I catch myself. . . . So what if she is? That's her right. These are her stories, not mine. I'm *not* just here to take her story and leave. I realize that she needs reassurance, but I'm also at a loss because no one has taught me how to handle this particular scenario. I talk again about my own story, how I became interested in how human trafficking narratives are framed, and that I am here to listen and to learn from someone who has lived through the experience. I reiterate the important elements of the process, the protections, and the consent form. "Deb," I say, "you can withdraw from this study if you want." She looks at me: "No, no. It sounds very interesting. I want to do this. I've got a lot to say." And she reaches out for the consent form and signs her name.

Every now and then she drops in an F-bomb, wondering if she can use that language—"isn't this being recorded?" she asks, and laughs. She reflects on her experiences and tells me about survival and healing. She talks about what it means to not be believed, to not be listened to, to not be heard. And she shares with me the discomfort she still struggles with when it comes to her feelings, how every day remains a constant negotiation between past and present, between shame and pride, between pain and hope. She tells me what it means to be a mother and what it means to be a business owner. She also tells me about trauma, about being used, about life on the streets. She tells me about how others used her body for their own profit. We linger here on this, on the word "use." I ask her about it, how she feels about telling her story, and what she thinks about how *it* will be used. "Each time you talk," she tells me, "you have to go back to that place. It's painful. It's uncomfortable." I ask about this discomfort. She responds, "I don't know. I guess you never know, what you say, how people will take it and use it or anything." This acknowledgement leads to a continual evaluation and reevaluation of what is being said and, more importantly, a questioning of how what is being said will be used by me and by others.

Relationality and Co-Participation

Our interview sessions were scheduled closely together, and after the first sessions Deb made it clear that she needed to pause, reflect, and recuperate. She simply needed more time to go through the process between interviews. That was a hard adjustment for me, as I was dealing with timelines, but I recognized that the adjustment was crucial if I was to maintain her participation. After our interview sessions were finally completed, I stayed in touch with Deb, making sure she received copies of the interview transcripts and initial chapter write-ups. She never requested any changes to the transcripts, observing that if she said it, she meant it.

The chapter write-ups were a slightly different story. Some of my initial writing had been constructed from a pre-designed outline, something I had in mind at the prospectus stage. Deb felt that it focused too heavily on my own preconceptions about what I had been hoping to do with the project—and she told me so, bluntly. So, I asked her what *she* thought her story was really all about and how she thought it could be better represented. That led to some generative conversations that resulted in some major changes to the writing, including: (1) the inclusion of participant-selected standalone excerpts that stood as vignettes between chapters to give participants space within the dissertation to fully express their own voices and to highlight what they felt were the important parts of their stories; (2) trashing the outline, going back to re-listening to the interviews and rereading the transcripts, and building the dissertation from the bottom-up, rather than trying to fit participant stories into my preconceived ideas; and (3) adding in bits and pieces of my own story to be more transparent about my own motivations, concerns, and the inherent tensions involved in someone with my background and identity doing this type of work.

Confusion and Unease

It took a few months to make the necessary changes. I remember waking up one morning and checking my email, finding a message from Deb asking me what was going on with the project—why hadn't I been in touch? I immediately responded, apologizing for the delay and explaining what I was attempting to do. "It'll be another month or so,

Deb," I wrote, "But you'll have a new draft to review soon." I could sense that she was growing impatient with the process and I realized that I needed to do a better job of keeping her in the loop. The next iteration was well-received, though she rightfully complained about how long it had taken. Her subsequent line of questioning was simple and straightforward: what was I going to do with this now that it was complete, how was I going to use it? She also wondered whether *she* could use it. The questions echoed those posed earlier, both during recruitment and the interviews. Even at this stage, the unease at how her stories might be used and circulated represented a primary concern. She particularly balked at the notion that I might tell parts of her story while on the job market, reminding me that her participation was linked to the idea that our work was activist in nature. I realized, well after the research itself had been completed, that I had done an inadequate job of addressing her confusion and unease, leaving her feeling vulnerable and, perhaps, without a sense of control over the application of her own story. This recognition made me aware of my own unease and left me wondering what else I should have done.

Maria: Developing Relations

I first met Meg in May of 2015. The two of us connected at a national infertility advocacy event, where I was interviewing individuals for an infertility oral history project. Interested in telling her story, Meg agreed to participate, and I learned about the years of diagnostic tests and a multitude of failed treatments she underwent to try and become pregnant. As her interview concluded, she shared how she and her partner were at a turning point. Nothing had worked to date, and they needed to decide if they would continue with one more round of treatment or embrace living "childfree."

As she shared her story, I found myself connecting to Meg personally and shared with her my own personal struggle to embrace living childfree. Connecting over these shared experiences, we decided to stay in touch and began exchanging notes over email and social media. We became friends who confided in each other about the personal troubles of living with infertility. During this time, I was also in the process of designing my dissertation study, which focused on rhetorical representations of infertility. Meg's story frequently came to mind as I created my dissertation prospectus—specifically, with respect to how her story countered typical representations of infertility. Curious if she would be willing to share how she negotiates her infertility identity against these more dominant infertility narratives, I emailed her asking if she would be willing to participate in my dissertation. She did not agree to participate right away.

Gaining Consent

Prior to agreeing, Meg requested that we have a brief a phone call. She told me that she did want to participate but wanted to know more about the project at large. On the phone, I explained how this was a project I was personally motivated by: I wanted to make the everyday challenges of being infertile more visible. It was with this larger goal, I told her, that I wanted to learn how others were engaging in forms of resistance by offering representations of infertility that countered typical infertility narratives. Her story, I believed, illustrated how counter-narratives of infertility frequently are not given as much attention, as they confront more standardized, culturally accepted views.

Sharing this over the phone, Meg explained that she wanted to participate but that we needed to be careful with who learned of her story and how it was told. Her openness to discuss her infertility was relatively new, and her decision to discuss her struggle to get pregnant was previously not well-received by some family members. Nonetheless, she said, she wanted to help. After all, we were friends. And she felt compelled to participate as she knew this work—and her story—may make space for other infertility narratives to more easily exist. I thanked her and assured her that throughout the research process I would try to ensure she felt protected. Feeling assured, we set a date for the dissertation interview.

The Interview

A few weeks later, Meg and I met on Skype and began our interview. During the two hours we talked, she recounted her diagnosis with infertility, when treatment failed, when friendships failed because of insensitivity to Meg's infertility, and how she used art as a method to make sense of an infertility narrative that seemed to counter those that emphasized "success." Before ending the call, I informed her that I would be sending the interview out for transcription and would then give her a copy of the transcript to correct or alter anything that she might feel was inaccurate. Later, I asked her to review the chapter of my dissertation that contained portions of her story, so as to involve her in the knowledge-making and consent process of the dissertation.

Relationality and Co-Participation

Weeks passed, but I eventually received Meg's transcript and sent it to her for review. After her initial review, she sent me a revised transcript clarifying portions of her story and clarifying moments during the interview that, upon reading now, she opted to slightly change. I thanked her for taking the time to review and informed her that I would be using the amended version of the transcript for my analysis.

After analyzing my transcriptions, I sent Meg an outlined "data" chapter containing a portion of her story. In the email, I asked her to review the information revealed, making sure she was okay with disclosing particular health information. A few days passed, and I heard from Meg. She informed me that since our interview, she and her partner had undergone additional testing, revealing that male factor health conditions were now being considered the primary cause of infertility. This differed from the information shared in our Skype interview. Then, it was understood that female factors were the primary cause. Wanting her story to act as a counter to the many dominant infertility narratives that perpetuate assumptions that infertility is primarily a female issue, Meg made it clear that her story should highlight this male factor as the primary cause of their infertility. With his diagnosis revealed, I wrote back saying I would make this change and revise portions of her narrative to better represent the new information.

Confusion and Unease about Dissertation Circulation and Use

Months pass, and my dissertation is on hold. It is late summer, and I am preparing my dossier for the academic job market. Reviewing my materials, it occurs to me that my participants may want to understand how their stories will be shared in academic job materials and situated as having importance to the discipline of rhetoric and composition. Explaining how infertility connects to the field of rhetoric and composition was always a bit challenging for participants to wrap their heads around. Wanting to clarify this further, I email drafts of my dossier documents to each participant, informing them that these materials explain the importance of their participation to the discipline.

A day later I receive an email from Meg. She is deeply concerned and emphatically upset that I am sharing her story in my job market materials. She writes that she had no idea that her story would be used in this manner and feels betrayed. I write back panicky and extremely apologetic for eliciting such concern and anger. Taken aback by her response, I realize how participants may have no idea how their stories become circulated and shared on the job market. Frustrated at my inability to foresee such a disconnect, I send another email reminding Meg of our initial phone call, when I shared how participation in the project would ultimately include her story appearing in my dissertation. I then go on to outline the role of the dissertation in relation to the academic job market, explaining the need to demonstrate tenure-worthy scholarship via a dissertation, how her story is my "data," and when interviewing for jobs hiring committees want to understand the potential implications of my research. Given this, an abbreviated version of her story must be included in these materials. Pushing the "send" button, I cross my fingers hoping this explanation will relieve her concern.

A few hours later a reply from Meg arrives. Anxious, I hesitantly open and read the email. She writes that she did not fully understand the consequences of her participation. She notes that I should have done more to inform her of where and with whom her story would be circulated and that not doing so leaves her feeling as if I have betrayed our friendship. I am crushed. I feel like I have failed all of my methodological training.

Over the next few days, we exchange more emails. It is clear that if she could go back in time she would have never participated. She explains that over the past months, since being interviewed, she and her partner have decided to live childfree. Given this recent decision, she explains the difficulty of participating in the project. In particular, she tells me that her participation in this project is a continual disruption to her ability to find closure with infertility. Her email ends explaining to me that if we did not have a personal connection, she would have opted to pull out entirely. Instead, she tells me she wants to honor our friendship and agrees to let me use her story with a pseudonym. I write and extend my sincere thanks.

Research As Care: A Framework Reimagining Academic Use

Reviewing our two stories, we see a recurring theme of stories and their "uses." In particular, we call attention to how stories are used and situated in traditional academic research. By this, we mean that the way in which academic scholars talk about and write about issues like trauma is often rooted in otherness/othering. As a result, much of the language used, particularly when referring to those who have lived through traumatic experiences—is language of *use*. This, for Deb and Meg, was the lynchpin in the decision whether to continue their involvement. It is this language of use in the research paradigm that is so problematic.

While our research stories demonstrate how our participants struggled to understand the use of their stories, our stories also clarify our failure as researchers to better prepare and predict moments in which we had to provide further explanation of use. In response to those unpredicted moments, we tried to find a path of balance: one that responded both to our accountability to participants as well as to the institution of academia. In this, we attempted to flesh out our responsibility to participant stories while also trying to acknowledge and adhere to institutional expectations. In retrospect, we believe these need not be necessarily mutually exclusive. Instead of *use*, we opt to acknowledge agency, emotion, humanity and re-imagine the "use" of trauma-related research within a *research as care* framework that meets the needs of participants and the needs of researchers while navigating institutional requirements.

Research as Care

As we conceive of it, the idea of research as care responds to concerns about "use" by embracing the idea of *shared ownership*. In *Research is Ceremony,* Shawn Wilson (2008), a Cree author and researcher, describes the role of researchers as that of mediators:

> We are mediators in a growing relationship between the community and whatever it is that is being researched. And how we go about doing our work in that role is where we uphold relational accountability. We are accountable to ourselves, the community, our environment or cosmos as a whole, and also

> to the idea or topics that we are researching. We have all of these relationships that we need to uphold. (106)

Mediation necessarily implies collaboration and relationship, close listening, and responsivity. The notion of shared ownership derives from the idea of researcher as mediator because the acceptance of knowledge as relational requires—in response to concerns about vulnerability and potential harm—a more deeply considered and enacted collaboration between researcher and participants. Therefore, the idea of researcher as mediator fundamentally shifts the paradigm from the traditional conception of research to *take/use,* to research as *creative collaboration* or co-creation.

Andrea Riley-Mukavetz (2014) situates Wilson's discussion of mediation within the context of academic discourse generally and the discipline of rhetoric and composition specifically. Recalling how the stories of her dissertation participants continue to impact her, she calls for practicing "there-ness," a concept that underlines the centrality of both participant and researcher in the co-construction of knowledge. There-ness makes "visible the complexity of being the arms of the institution while working with and across cultures" (121) and hence is collaborative and responsible to the stories of participants. We draw on Riley-Mukavetz's concept of "there-ness" as it practices *care* for participants by theorizing *with* participants the meanings of their experiences for greater intercultural knowledge. In our respective research projects, we both tried to follow a framework of *there-ness*, yet still struggled with the practical question of how to enact it. While some of this difficulty likely stems from the sensitivity of our participants' stories, it also demonstrates the need for a clear methodological toolkit that incorporates concepts like mediation, there-ness, and shared ownership within a framework for researching trauma.

In what follows, we situate shared ownership within a research as care framework and offer five pillars to address tensions of the academic use of participant stories through the lens of relationality.

Pillars of Shared Ownership

I. Mediating Academic "Use"

Despite the increased visibility of feminist and indigenous approaches "toward more reciprocal, collaborative, mutually beneficial research methods," the reality is that community-based ethnographic research in rhetoric and composition—situated in and mediated by institutional expectations and the limited/limiting forms of academic writing—remains fraught with tension regarding not only how research is conducted, but *used* (Royster and Kirsch 2012, 34). Stuart Blythe (2012) offers a series of best practices to push back against approaches we believe are inappropriately justified as academic use. In his model, "researchers must attend to the needs and agenda of participants. Purposes, questions, methods, and results should be developed collaboratively, rather than by the researcher alone" (275). Blythe's comments underscore the exigency for relationality—as Wilson and Riley-Mukavetz view it—to inform and guide community-oriented research. His methods apply to moments of negotiation, with participants playing a clear role in defining outcomes in relation to research-based publications. In Blythe's view, researchers should "publish article-length works not so much to report results of research—those improvements or changes that many readers may expect—but to comment on issues related to research and social problems" (283). In this model of relationality, activist and community-engaged research almost always has *two* deliverables, one that is community-oriented and one that is academic-focused. This perspective is important, given the tendencies of academic publishing on participant stories and how publishing the stories of participants work to benefit the scholar and not always the community member. Lynne Davis's (2004) work reiterates such tensions, stating "telling stories is not innocent. Often, researchers reap not negative sanctions but professional rewards in the form of prizes, titles, promotions, accreditation as being an 'expert,' and other accolades" (17). Davis's work reminds us that while researchers may have good intentions in the sharing of stories, there is increased need and work to be done on behalf of participants to ensure that by going public with their stories. To be clear, as scholars working in communities, it is our responsibility to ensure that more good than harm is occurring when collecting, circulating, and publishing participant stories.

Building on the perspectives of these scholars, we contend that working with trauma requires an approach that explicitly pushes back at traditional expectations of academic use by deploying the lens of relationality to the researcher's methodological toolkit to open up use as a site of both negotiation and re-imagination. Relationality requires us, as researchers, to view ourselves not as "being *in* relationship with other people;" rather, "we *are* the relationships we hold and are a part of" (Wilson 2008, 80). In other words, because we *are* relationships rather than *in* relationships, we operate from a position that is less interested in *taking for use* (a violence that would harm both participant and researcher) than in finding the locus of what ultimately benefits the relationship itself. This moves the researcher beyond the definitional framework of the institution or academic field and situates research *as* relationship, thereby positioning both researcher and participant to open up "use" as a site of negotiation and re-imagination, collaborating, and theorizing in tandem to create meaning while also pushing back against traditional conceptions of academic use.

Our participants questioned how their stories would be used; even the consent forms they signed made explicit reference to the fact that their stories would be used at conferences, in publications, and elsewhere. By viewing research *as* relationship, any "use" must necessarily be negotiated within the context of the "beingness" and benefit to the relationship. Rather than solely considering how the project adds value to institutional knowledge, this approach to research instead focuses its inquiry on negotiating what it means to create and use knowledge within the relationship and, only then/after, on what it means to decide to extend that beyond the boundaries of the relationship. This negotiation, and the effort to situate the research as care, either happens or does not happen at the initiation of the research project in relation to a traumatized participant, i.e., the moment of "first contact" for recruitment. Whether it happens or not sets the tone for both how research is understood by participants *and* how it is conducted by the researcher(s).

Such a paradigm, viewing research *as* relational rather than researcher-participant *in* relationship, requires a re-imagination of what it means both to *do* and *use* research. This re-imagination, in turn, requires a stance of active mediation—in particular, mediating with respect to our own (i.e., the researcher's) understanding of the academic research process itself. Under the traditional model, a research project requires specific questions that need resolution. It expects the researcher to predict not only the nature of researcher-participant relationships before they're ever initiated, but also the ways in which participants will respond to or engage with research questions. In other words, academics are trained to predict the outcome of research; we assert that predicting *how to care* for participants should be paramount.

II. Responsivity to Re-Living Trauma

The stance of research as relationship necessarily makes space to halt the research process at moments when "re-living" trauma becomes too much. In respecting the relationship and in sharing ownership over the production of materials that result from that relationship, such an approach honors the idea that these stories are not lived in the past; rather they live on and in the body. Johnson et al. (2015) remind us that stories are embodied, and because of this, adjustments need to be made for moments when the body becomes overwhelmed or fatigued or enters into a state of pain.

Thinking about embodiment reinforces the need to recognize the materiality of lived experiences. This necessitates focusing less on "words" and more on the underlying embodied humanity that is involved in storytelling, both our own and that of our participants. Language represents and yet never wholly captures embodiment, materiality, or event, so words cannot be the only focus when it comes to researching trauma. Yet, we cannot escape language: it arguably constructs a sense of reality. And we cannot escape embodiment; it is through the body that we construct language. Therefore, the practice of listening to bodies in the moment of storytelling becomes central because if the bodies are where the stories reside (*on* and *in*), then the bodies are also where the research and the there-ness of relationship manifests.

To re-live trauma is to be bombarded by a series of micro and macro decisions. For example, as an embodied aspect of identity, re-lived trauma must be claimed or the traumatized individual must "come out." In our respective projects, few, if any, visible markers signified participant bodies as traumatized. Thus, when an individual who has lived through trauma is in an interview, they must, in that moment, quickly evaluate how best to respond to questions and convey their story. The response may vary depending upon interviewer, the scene/location of the interview, and other factors, such as the mood of the participant or the even the fatigue of retelling and re-living past traumatic experiences.

Our participants, at various times, felt the need to pause, withdraw, question the process, and express their discomfort. In John's project, Deb explicitly asked for more time between interviews, realizing the discomfort they caused as well as the need for recuperation from the fatigue of telling stories about her trauma. This put the research timeline at risk, yet was essential to continuing the research at all. In Maria's project,

Meg made clear her misunderstanding of how, when, and where her story would be used. Her lack of familiarity with the academic research process led, unfortunately and unexpectedly, to additional stress. Centering on research as relationship requires responsivity to these needs for the sake of the bodies involved. This responsivity engages with Krista Ratcliffe's (1999) rhetorical listening, listening for pauses, and the articulation of concern. For example, in both of our research stories, our participants gave either pause (as in John's story) or spoke to us about concerns they had with sharing their story and making it public (as in Maria's story). Listening to the pauses as well as reflectively taking into account participants' anxiety about potential harm and risk is responsive to care, especially when working with individuals who have experienced trauma. Listening for these moments requires the cessation of research activities, pulling back to re-negotiate the needs of the bodies in relation. Simply put, the mediatory role of the researcher affords moments—whether brief or extended—to stop the process and check in with participants to determine, first, what their needs are and, second, whether the desire exists to continue the research relationship.

Julie Lindquist's (2012) "Time to Grow Them: Practicing Slow Research in a Fast Field" serves as a useful resource for rethinking our relationships when working with participants in trauma communities. Allowing participants time to think through their involvement and potential co-construction of the scholarship, as Lindquist notes, "is a long uneven process, and it develops within the context of carefully cultivated relationships of trust between researchers and participants" (649). The expectation for research is demonstrated *progress*. However, in working with trauma, progress is not always so clear cut and not always in the best interests of the participants, the researchers, or the project itself. The ways in which time-centric concerns can take over a project are serious matters. Those who have experienced trauma, physical or psychological, simply don't recount full stories in a perfect linear format. Reorienting scholarship towards models that embrace the slowing of the research process may allow for increased responsivity and care. While academia operates on institutional timelines (i.e., timeline to tenure, timeline for promotion), research as care asks scholars to make critical cases in promotional review materials about a slower-paced timeline as a purposeful and ethical methodology that engages in care for the greater community.

While the normative research model is deeply attentive to timelines, responsivity to the risks inherent to participants re-living trauma requires an orientation that revalues time-centric research milestones. The notion of time, particularly as it relates to academic research, poses significant risks for research done in/around trauma. Indeed, in both of our projects we faced clear deadlines, grappled with the fear of "time running out," and at various moments had to negotiate time in ways that unfairly burdened our participants. Even more importantly, rushing the process while participants needed to pause because of the pain and negotiation of re-living trauma presented unacceptable risks.

In the re-living of those moments, people who have experienced trauma sometimes need to stop, think, reflect, heal, and move on. Their stories exist in space, on/in bodies, and in memory; therefore, in the re-living of trauma, the trauma exists not so much at a point in time in the linear past but rather in an embodied space of experience and memory. Therefore, they have to negotiate competing temporal logics to organize events—the space of lived experience, the space of remembered experience within/on the body, and the unraveling of sequential time in the re-living of the trauma through telling. Consequently, we contend that trauma-related research requires patience and an orientation that is not only willing, but committed to rethinking the timeline.

III. Recognizing Participant Motivations

Research as care extends beyond bodies to consider the motivations of participants for agreeing to tell their stories in an academic research context. Sharing a story—any story, let alone one centered on lived trauma—is an inherently vulnerable act. In thinking about care, we believe it is essential to put the researcher's orienting lines into conversation with participants' orienting lines, guiding how listening, interpretation, response, and co-creation are enacted. Each of these intersections creates a complex constellating story matrix. Weaving together stories allows us to make new meanings by seeing our experiences and world in new ways. When we refer to putting orienting lines into conversation those of our participants, what we mean is that *shared ownership* necessarily must account for and be responsive to the multiplicity of participant motivations for sharing their stories, for making themselves vulnerable. In agreeing to participate in such research projects, participants don't necessarily need to tell their stories; they are under no obligation. And, frankly, they often have more to lose than gain by such sharing.

Across our respective projects, we learned that some participants simply want their voices to be heard, some want to extend a helping hand to others, some just want to express themselves out-loud, some seek to effectuate broader change or increase awareness about an issue, and others are curious about what academic research *is* and find personal value in being involved in it. By recognizing our connecting lines—the ways in which our stories connect with theirs and the ways in which trauma-related research creates spaces of increased vulnerability and potential harm—the idea of shared ownership enacts a stance of flexibility and caring in response to participant values and motivations.

With respect to the idea of shared ownership within this framework, researchers should meet participant expectations in the writing, conveyance, and "use" of their stories. It isn't *just* about listening to their reasons; it is about applying their wishes to the project as a whole. Take Meg's story. Meg wanted to share her story in Maria's project for a variety of reasons. One, Maria and Meg had a friendship rooted in shared experiences of infertility. The two had formed a personal bond and because of their shared experiences, they noted an area of further study, infertility counter-narratives. Yet, as the research process evolved and Meg received additional information regarding her infertility, Meg felt it important to disclose particulars about her story (i.e., her husband being the main factor of IF) that added to the larger focus and aim of Maria's research project. New negotiations had to take place and further complicated the control Meg felt over her own story.

Understanding how participant motivations can be developed out of friendships and shift throughout the research process, in part, situates the relevancy of Blythe's call for a practice of reciprocity by looking to participants to play a clear role in defining research outcomes. While he advocates the creation of two research deliverables (one for the academy, one for the participant community), the reality is often more fluid and complex, requiring negotiation. Some participants may welcome the invitation to co-create or to collaboratively make theory, while others may not tell stories for those reasons. The subsequent move of co-creation and collaborative making can often be "too much" for any of a number of reasons. So, a negotiation has to occur in such instances in how stories are represented when a participant does not want to participate beyond the telling.

IV. Collaborative Meaning-Making

In those instances when participant motivation *aligns* with co-creation, we recommend consistently approaching the project from a perspective of commitment to making meaning collaboratively. Granted, it is far easier to conduct an interview, transcribe it, code and interpret the "data," and then write *about* it. From our vantage point, this *"use"* fits well within the traditional model of academic research conduct that we're attempting to push against. Instead, we believe that each participant "creates frameworks in their language and on their terms" (Riley-Mukavetz 2014, 79). There must be an ongoing conversation involved about meaning and interpretation. Riley-Mukavetz represents, in our opinion, the best example of collaborative meaning-making within the rhetoric and composition field. Her orientation to and descriptions of collaboration are important ones, and her work serves as a foundation to our own thinking about collaborative meaning-making in the context of conducting research within traumatized communities. The application of this approach centers on the idea of theorizing and constructing ideas together, constellating stories—theirs and ours. Such emphasis helps us see the ways in which participants actively tell stories not only to theorize their own experiences, but also to theorize the world(s) they inhabit, particularly how they exist and are transformed by the act of storytelling.

Collaborative meaning-making isn't just about the questions asked—or not asked—in an interview session; it is also about the ways in which the researcher writes the experience, inviting participant perspectives, ideas and input, and offering spaces for participant voices in the project write-up. This requires ongoing conversation with participants well after the "data" collection phase is completed. These considerations serve as the orienting lines for the research project as it moves from conceptualization to interviews to analysis to write-up to dissemination. In enacting shared ownership, the researcher creates spaces for participants to voice their needs and requests—what, for example, do they view as important? What do they see as unimportant? What do they think should be excluded? How do they want their stories shared? For research to have any integrity, participants should wield substantial influence over what is emphasized and de-emphasized.

Take John's work with Deb, for example. Early on in the project she mentioned that "a lot of the time when I do tell my story, it's the bad stuff that everyone focuses on. But I like to talk about the recovery part of it. Only because that's the most important part." It would have been easy for John to focus his work on the horrors that Deb had been through—and she did share those stories with him, sometimes in quite explicit detail. But her comment—that she wished there would be less focus on the trauma and more focus on her personal transformation—provided a foundation for collaborative meaning-making across the project, guiding the decision-making process for what to emphasize, what to include, and, crucially, what to exclude from the write up. For Deb, her lived experiences of trauma and exploitation were not what she wanted the project to be about, asking that those details be left out in favor of a focus on healing, transformation, and her own community work. In considering this, John purposefully excluded the experiences of her trafficking experiences from any write-ups stemming from the interviews, re-orienting to engage in a shared process that aligned with participant expectations.

V. Accounting for Identity Evolution

Conducting research around trauma is hard work. Re-living trauma as stories are told is even harder. And, so, when doing this type of research, it is important to account for the fact that it involves individual transformation for both the participants and the researcher. Sharing stories, reading through transcripts, negotiating use, collaborative co-creation—each of these manifests in individuals in different ways. Some grow weary with fatigue; others find the process invigorating. In John's project, Deb vacillated between fatigue and invigoration, asking for pauses in the research process and, afterwards, negotiating the meaning of her involvement by taking a more proactive stance in her own work in supporting and mentoring others who had been through similar traumatic experiences. Throughout Maria's project, Meg was in the process of coming to terms with her infertility. When she was first interviewed, Meg very much identified as infertile. Yet, as time passed and the reality sank in that pregnancy would not occur, Meg began to remove herself from the infertile community so as to embrace living childfree. We learn from our stories that the researcher must account for the shaping of identities throughout our interactions. Stated another way, it requires a stance of recognition that participation in research not only shapes the identity of the participant but also that of the researcher.

Throughout both of our projects, the identity evolution, level of engagement, and embodied impacts for participants varied. We experienced polarizing extremes of participant response. Some participants felt empowered by their participation, leveraging their involvement into their own individualized approaches to activism and advocacy. On the other end of the spectrum, some participants felt profound emotional fatigue, and simply let the process conclude without further engagement, in some instances severing the conversation at the project's conclusion. In between these extremes, participants found themselves at various times conflicted about their scope of involvement, leading them to push back and interrogate research approaches and motivations. No two people respond to trauma in precisely the same way, and responses to re-living that trauma through research can and do vary to the extreme. As researchers doing this work, we have to remain attentive to the individual needs of participants whose traumatic experiences and emotional responses are unpredictable and different. And because these are individuals who have endured trauma, we have to be willing to accept their individual reactions without questioning and provide support where we can, always furthering their wishes and respecting their position even if we might not fully understand.

This sort of individualized engagement across the spectrum of emotional ebb and flow and identity evolution also plays out for the researcher. As we listened to the stories our participants told, we slowly began to understand how they interacted, intersected, and constellated with our own. In some sense, too, they become part of our own becoming as researchers and as humans, not in the sense of academic ownership, but rather shared experience and shared ownership. The telling and the listening are events that fold into our own stories in sometimes very personal ways. There is some discomfort in this recognition because in first coming to this work, we both desired to keep our lives separate from the stories of our participants. We both internally struggled with our own acquired and preconceived notions, the institutional expectations, and our dis/re-oriented understandings of story and self.

Conclusion

Our research projects inevitably concluded with defenses and "final" manuscripts forwarded to our graduate school for approval. Our lives and our work transitioned as we moved to different cities, started positions as faculty, and engaged in our individual processes of orienting to new contexts. But the fatigue associated with researching trauma and participant negotiation lingered. The space we each took after completing our dissertations was crucial in helping us think through where we had succeeded and where we had failed. More importantly, it allowed us to begin considering more deeply, without the limitations of time, what research as care might actually look like in rhetoric and composition. Given the complexity of trying to enact shared ownership in working with trauma participants, we hoped to begin developing a guiding framework while leveraging our own experiences to encourage conversation around the questions of what this type of research *is* and what it should or shouldn't be like. As we write this essay, reflecting back, we realize that what we're really talking about is a *state of mind*—an orientation to research—that informs *practice* as well as a set of practices.

A methodological toolkit that centers on shared ownership is necessarily fluid and flexing. It is messy at times and straightforward at others. But, by being adaptable, it allows for researchers to address the unpredictable, and thus acts as a more reflective and embodied act of "care." We believe research as care transforms research from a mere recounting of stories and rhetorical analysis into a process that might otherwise be described as an "activity of hope" (Tuhiwai Smith 2013, 203). The individuals who agree to participate in this type of research—and the worlds they inhabit—are *real*, sometimes overlapping, and sometimes divergent. There is an impulse merely to read their words and to think about the implications of the experiences that they describe. But it is important to remember that while *we think*, they continue to *live and deal with their lives*.

A *research as care* framework re-imagines this orientation and instead emphasizes researcher-participant interaction, relationship-building, role-definition, and participant agenda/needs from the moment of "first contact." Re-imagining the research process and the methodological toolkit in this way shifts the lens from "answering tailored questions" or "getting desired results" to one that focuses on ethics, on initiating and sustaining moments of quality interaction with individual participants and participant communities, and that educates participants on the purposes and goals of academic theory, research, and jargon. This methodology also represents a better practice in searching for new meaning and knowledge. Rather than attempting to predict how participants will engage with the project, this orientation instead asks and honors—from first contact through the entirety of the project—how participants prefer to engage, provide input, and negotiate terms of use.

Stressing the nature of research as care from the beginning encourages the researcher to more carefully account for the ways in which he/she might enact a practice of care for participants while opening up opportunities for participants to articulate their needs, agenda, and stance of collaborative co-creation in relation to the project findings. The research as care approach, to a large extent, mitigates unpredicted moments of tension later in the process, while also re-situating the ownership of research as *shared*. By moving away from the predictive research model and towards a research as care model, the project necessarily becomes one of shared ownership, rooted both in researcher and participant negotiation, while mediating the traditional framework of academic use.

Notes

1. Our experiences were drawn from our recently completed dissertation projects.
2. As researchers embedded within these marginalized communities, we seek to work alongside them as allies making their stories more visible to necessary stakeholders.
3. We draw on Maureen Johnson et al.'s (2015) discussion of embodiment as feminist rhetoric to inform this claim.
4. Clark and Powell (2008) serve to guide our indigenous framework, particularly on the sacredness of stories. As researchers working with stories as data, we draw on indigenous scholarship to recognize the original purposes of these stories. In other words, such stories are normally not told for academic purposes but told for reasons that support needs in their communities.
5. We use Konrad's (2018) call to reimagine the effects of accessibility on labor as a model of how rhetorical scholarship can be operationalized in order to improve public lives.
6. We purposefully share stories about unpredicted interactions with our participants to highlight and frame the ways in which those disorienting learning moments led us to rethink/re-theorize the notion of "use."

7. In response to potential critiques about the language of "ownership," we are merely reflecting and responding to the realities of academic research. The economic system of academia necessarily means that research is owned; we cannot change this. But we can reorient our work towards an approach that values and makes visible steps toward shared ownership.

8. Sara Ahmed's (2006) *Queer Phenomenology: Orientations, Objects, Others* is a particularly helpful resource in thinking about orientation to research and orientating research with participants. In her introduction to that book, Ahmed writes "orientation is a matter of how we reside in space" (1). If so, then we might consider research activity to require us to carefully think about how we and our participants inhabit/reside in the research space.

9. We came to these projects based on our respective individual experiences, our lives intersecting with the communities we worked with. Working around trauma can and does take its toll on the researchers. While it is beyond the scope of this essay to engage in a protracted discussion on secondary trauma and the ways in which working around trauma individually impacted us, we do acknowledge such questions as important, even essential.

References

Ahmed, Sara. 2006. *Queer phenomenology: Orientations, objects, others*. Durham, NC: Duke University Press.

Anzaldúa, Gloria. 1987. *Borderlands: La Frontera*. Vol. 3. San Francisco: Aunt Lute.

Blythe, Stuart. 2012. "Composing Activist Research." In *Practicing Research in Writing Studies: Reflexive and Ethically Responsible Research*, edited by Katrina Powell & Pamela Takayoshi, 275-292. New York: Hampton Press.

Clark, D. Anthony Tyeeme, and Malea Powell. 2008. "Resisting Exile in the" Land of the Free": Indigenous Groundwork at Colonial Intersections." *The American Indian Quarterly* 32, no.1: 1-15.

Cole, Daniel. 2011. "Writing Removal and Resistance: Native American Rhetoric in the Composition Classroom." *College Composition and Communication* 63, no. 1: 122-144.

Davis, Lynne. 2004. "Risky Stories: Speaking and Writing in Colonial Spaces." *Native Studies Review* 15, no. 1: 1-20.

Gaillet, Lynée Lewis. 2012. "(Per) Forming Archival Research Methodologies." *College Composition and Communication* 64, no. 1: 35-58.

Hesford, Wendy S. 1999. "Reading Rape Stories: Material Rhetoric and the Trauma of Representation." *College English* 62, no. 2: 192-221.

Johnson, Maureen, et al. 2015. "Embodiment: Embodying Feminist Rhetorics." *Peitho* 18: 39-44.

Konrad, Annika. 2018. "Reimagining Work: Normative Commonplaces and Their Effects on Accessibility in Workplaces." *Business and Professional Communication Quarterly* 81, no. 1:123-141.

Lindquist, Julie. 2012. "Time to Grow Them: Practicing Slow Research in a Fast Field." *JAC* 32, no. 3-4: 645-666.

Micciche, Laura R. 2001. "Writing Through Trauma: The Emotional Dimensions of Teaching Writing." *Composition Studies* 29, no. 1: 131-141.

Molloy, Cathryn. 2016. "Multimodal Composing as Healing: Toward a New Model for Writing as Healing Courses." *Composition Studies* 44, no. 2: 134.

Mukavetz, Andrea M. Riley. 2014. "Towards a Cultural Rhetorics Methodology: Making Research Matter with Multi-Generational Women from the Little Traverse Bay Band." *Rhetoric, Professional Communication, and Globalization* 5, no. 1: 108-125.

Powell, Malea, et al. 2014. "Our Story Begins Here: Constellating Cultural Rhetorics." *Enculturation:A Journal of Rhetoric, Writing, and Culture* 18: 46.

Ratcliffe, Krista. 1999. "Rhetorical Listening: A Trope for Interpretive Invention and a 'Code of Cross-Cultural Conduct'." *College Composition and Communication* 51, no. 2: 195-224.

Royster, Jacqueline Jones. 1996. "When the First Voice You Hear is Not Your Own." *College Composition and Communication* 47, no. 1: 29-40.

Royster, Jacqueline Jones, and Gesa E. Kirsch. 2012. *Feminist Rhetorical Practices: New Horizons for Rhetoric, Composition, and Literacy Studies.* Carbondale, IL: Southern Illinois University Press.

Smith, Linda Tuhiwai. 2013. *Decolonizing methodologies: Research and indigenous peoples.* Zed Books Ltd.

West, Thomas. 2000. "The Rhetoric of Therapy and the Politics of Anger: From the Safe House to a Praxis of Shelter." *Rhetoric Review* 19, no. 1-2: 42-58.

Wilson, Shawn. 2008. *Research is Ceremony: Indigenous Research Methods.* Fernwood Publishing Company.

Villanueva Jr, Victor. 1993. *Bootstraps: From an American Academic of Color.* Urbana, IL: National Council of Teachers of English.

SUPPLEMENTAL MATERIAL

Part I: Reflection on the Origins of the Article

As we explain in the introduction of our article, this piece emerged out of our joint participation as invited speakers to a Cultural Rhetorics graduate seminar at Michigan State University. The two of us had both recently defended our dissertations, and, as a result, had not seen each other in some time. The conversation that emerged from each of us speaking about our completed projects revealed (rather surprisingly to us) how similar our research experiences had been and yet that these strikingly similar experiences had not been shared until our conversation in that class.

Maria: I remember listening to John openly discuss his complicated interactions with his participants. As he described how he struggled with representing them and their stories, I suddenly began to feel a sense of relief. For months, I had been hiding and privately talking with only my dissertation director about how I felt as if I had failed my participant, Meg. I had spent the final months of graduate school recapturing what I could have changed, how I could have better cared for Meg and her story. But as I sat and listened to John openly talk about his similar struggles working with his participant, Deb, the feelings of guilt subsided. Instead, I began to question why I felt as if I needed to hide or disguise what occurred between Meg and I. We should talk openly about these moments of researcher-participant interaction, I thought to myself as students began the Q&A session of that Cultural Rhetorics class.

John: There certainly was relief for me, too, in hearing Maria's accounting of research. Our experiences had been strikingly similar and knowing that I wasn't alone was an important realization. My response to Maria's account was immediate and strong. I distinctly recall listening to Maria speak about "care" in research, which is something I'd been fixated on for the duration of my project. I sat there thinking: "we have to talk about this!" I felt it was important that we share our experiences in more detail with each other. I'm so glad we did… not only because those conversations eventually led to the development of this piece, but also because I think that in sharing we were both able to more fully process and work through some of the more difficult aspects of the impact of this kind of work on the researcher.

There was a fairly long time of individual processing following our conversation after the seminar at Michigan State. We didn't actually decide to write this piece until after we had each transitioned to different cities, started our first positions as tenure-track faculty, and were engaged in our own individual experiences of essentially building new lives. It was a challenging moment. We tried to make sense of the failures and successes of our research, individually and together, before we mutually decided to write this piece. Interestingly, one of the topics that eventually entered into our ongoing conversation during while writing was that the idea of "research as care" had pretty important implications for thinking about other things too, such as how junior faculty could think about care and support for one another, which had become an important part of our shared writing practice as we searched for ways to support one another in life and academe.

Part II: Description of Research Methods, Findings, and/or Pedagogical Impact

Since embarking on this project, the two of us have continued to stay in touch and have developed a series of ideas related to the practice of care in rhetorical research. Talking through the everyday issues we tackle whether in our classrooms or in our community work, shared ownership as a framework continues to be a useful and reliable tool assisting us as we navigate our scholarly identities.

John: Thinking about doing research with/in/around trauma communities, has made me think a lot more carefully about classrooms as community spaces that have to be handled with a similar level of care. The pillars we discuss in the piece can be repurposed towards a pedagogical approach. As I've started teaching graduate seminars of my own, I actually think a lot about what it means to address "use" in the class, to be responsive to the traumas that may be (are) embodied in that space, to recognize my students' varying/various motivations, to work towards collaborative meaning making and realize that the teacher/student identities evolve in ways interestingly similar to (yet also divergent from) researcher/participant identities. The bottom line, for me, is that my pedagogy changed dramatically after writing this piece; I spend a lot more time emphasizing trust, emotion, relatability and—yes—shared ownership of the class.

Maria: Like John, my pedagogy has been impacted by this work — particularly in the context of mentorship. I serve as a faculty mentor on many undergraduate student research projects and find myself needing to unpack for them the role and purpose of the IRB. For many of my students, the IRB is often overwhelming. For one, even the existence of the IRB is a new phenomenon and requires situating the history and intentions of an institutional review. Two, once students develop an understanding about the IRB, its power and oversight they find intimidating. As such, I have found myself needing to provide transparency about it. In doing so, I have realized that I have turned to much of what is shared in our article. Specifically, I find that student encounters with the IRB allow for a more considerate discussion about the design of their research project and frankness over which stakeholders may benefit from that work. Many of my undergraduate students come to my office thinking research is something objective and performed only for the benefit of the researcher. I apply the concept of shared ownership to these discussions and such application has broadened not only the design of studies but the objective — with many students creating public deliverables from their research projects to broaden the impact of their work. These encounters have made me reflect on the relationship between institutional policies, research, and scenes of learning at the undergraduate level. On the same note, these experiences have made me question the extent to which not only our undergraduate students but also community members understand the role of the IRB and the purpose of academic research. This article has left me to question, how may we make more transparent the relationship between our institutions and the research we engage in with the communities we study and partner with? Too often we teach research and IRB in academic settings, what would it mean to educate broader publics about the intentions and purpose of institutional oversights like the IRB?

Part III: Discussion Questions

1. Dissertation and thesis prospecti ask researchers to predict and situate their research based upon what findings may result and how those findings may add to disciplinary conversations. Yet often these very institutional practices fail to account for the learning that occurs in the doing of a large research project. How may we as future professors/mentors of these research projects make space for students to discuss the learning that occurs? How may we as researchers make the learning (even those failures) more transparent as part of the research process?

2. As the discipline embraces more community-engaged projects (see the CCCCs statement on community engagement), how are we preparing scholars in the discipline to anticipate the

needs of these communities? For example, in our article, we express concern over the lack of mental health training that we had when working with trauma communities. How may we build in institutional practices to ensure that we effectively care for the communities we work with?

3. What types of specific actions can we take to broad the impacts of our research findings? What steps might we need to take to do this for the purposes of directly supporting the communities we are researching? How may such actions reimagine the deliverables we create as humanists? In turn, how may actions that broaden the impact of research raise new considerations and possibilities for negotiation in relation to tenure and promotion?

WRITING ON THE EDGE

Writing on the Edge is on the Web at https://woejournal.ucdavis.edu/

Writing on the Edge is an interdisciplinary journal focusing on writing and the teaching of writing, aimed primarily at college-level composition teachers and others interested in writing and writing instruction. First published in 1989, *WOE* is currently entering its 29th year of continuous publication. It is edited and published at the University of California, Davis and appears two times a year—in spring and fall. In the tradition of its founding, we believe that new and varied forms of expression can yield fresh insights. We seek engaging, readable articles on writing and the teaching of writing, inviting scholars to approach their experience and research interests from new angles.The edges that interest us are less external and more internal--the spaces between genres, the boundaries that tell us we are reading this or that genre: a business letter or a personal essay, a personal statement or a short story. We recognize and celebrate the evolving landscape of writing studies, and seek to reflect that evolution. We want our articles to be enjoyable to read as well as stimulating for their contributions to pedagogical theory and practice.

Fieldwork with a Five-Year-Old: A Summative Report[1]

In this creative nonfiction essay, the author describes the process of doing international fieldwork as a single parent. The essay uses the format of a social scientific research report to highlight the parts of ethnographic fieldwork that exceed generic conventions.

---

1. *Writing on the Edge*, vol. 28, no. 2 © 2018 by UC Regents, Davis Campus. All rights reserved.

Fieldwork with a Five-Year-Old: A Summative Report

Kate Vieira

In this creative nonfiction essay, the author describes the process of doing international fieldwork as a single parent. The essay uses the format of a social scientific research report to highlight the parts of ethnographic fieldwork that exceed generic conventions.

Judge's Note: We're told that each of the tiny individual cells in our bodies carries the DNA directions for constructing our entire body. So in this essay, it's as though the prose of each sentence embodies the intricate consciousness that the whole essay is about—the complex thinking and feeling involved in living and working in Latvia (what's deeply foreign) and being mom to a five-year-old daughter (what's deeply intimate and domestic). I also enjoyed the counterpoint play with the genre of an official research report.

—Peter Elbow

Introduction

In the summer of 2014 I spent five weeks in the former Soviet and new European Union state of Latvia researching the writing of immigrants' families.[1] More specifically, but still rather generally, I was conducting an ethnographic study of how families who were separated across borders communicated with and therefore resurrected absent loved ones through the abstract symbol system otherwise known as writing. For example, frequently reported phrases tapped across cellular and Internet and sometimes postal networks included: "I miss you" and "me too." Also heart emojis.

One of the assumptions of this kind of research is that to understand writing, one must examine its context. By "context," I mean the

---

1. Winner of the Donald Murray Prize 2018

social, historical, and geographic conditions of its production. By "the social, historical, and geographic conditions of its production," I mean relationships, time, and space. By "relationships, time, and space," I mean I conducted this research a year out from my divorce, with my daughter in tow, on the memory-laden ground on which I met her father, with the tenure clock ticking like a small but sharp-toothed bomb just behind the spot where I used to feel my heart.

I also mean that I designated an exclusive email inbox to my ex (e.g., *ex-box*), where I received regular custody threats and which I checked every-other-daily between the hours of four p.m. and six p.m. so as to ruin neither my day nor my increasingly fragile nights of sleep.

Now that I have defined my terms, let me lay out the scholarly problem this essay seeks to solve: Writing is born on shifting terrain. Put another way, terrain shifts, birthing writing. Put more simply: Fissures. Then words.

What follows will demonstrate this thesis using the qualitative methodologies widely accepted as appropriate to keening. By "keening," I mean spending one's cash on a babysitter for nights out dancing on second-hand Ferramago's, red, because sometimes the only antidote to the emptiness in one's gut is to lose oneself in the sweat of another human being moving underneath the same flashing lights.[2] At other times, the antidote is writing.

Literature Review

Relevant Background Literature I: The Author

The author first encountered Latvia in 1999 during her service in the Peace Corps. The author's decision to join the Peace Corps instead of to attend graduate school was literary. Among the many books the author read during her senior year at UT Austin, two stood out: a practice test book for the literature GRE (*Which description of a tree was written by Emily Dickinson?*) and a slim volume of essays from returned

---

2. On "babysitting cash," see: "Student-loan Debt in Excess of $90,000: A Case Study of One Assistant Professor," *The Annual Review of Careers in the Humanities*; "The Failure of the Hague Convention: How Dead-Beat Dads Avoid Child Support with International Addresses," *Patriarchal Practices in a Globalized World*. Also see Appendix F, "Receipts from the author's high-end consignment store purchases, 2013–2014."

Peace Corps Volunteers (*a Mongolian yurt, a cup of frozen-over tea*).³ One of these books bled the life out of words. The other promised intrigue and adventure, and also a kind of character-building self-denial that the author found seductive.

Also: Leaving the country seemed like a good way to end the author's tormenting relationship with an economics major who told the author he loved her, but who would not introduce her to his parents (see *self-denial* above).

So that was the author at twenty-two—who for the purposes of peer review will remain anonymous, but who for the purposes of this study will reveal all.

Thus the United States government sent the author to counsel Latvians—a resourceful people who could make meals for five from foraged mushrooms and some yogurt cultures—in what her Peace Corps training manual described as "sustainable development." She was to "sustainably develop" the Latvians by teaching them English.

The author felt that this literature contained a gap.

Relevant Background Literature II: The Host Country

Latvia, for its part, was reeling from the crushing poverty that followed its recent independence. Words that come to mind are: hungry, disillusioned, shocked. Smells that come to mind are: stale, musty, but sometimes lilacs. The street sounds are the crack of knuckle to flesh, hoarse shouts of pain, and then silence against a Euro-techno backbeat. There were also inside sounds, including sweet nothings heaved up in Russian, singing, and/or sighs.

What the author means is that after teaching her English lesson, she would often stop at the bazaar for pastries stuffed with farmer's cheese. There she would see a line of track-suited men holding plastic bottles to fill with beer from a barrel. But sometimes there was no barrel. At those times, there were no men.

It sounds bleak, but the author liked it. The town was both brutal and big hearted, echoing certain of the author's early experiences in the economically depressed immigrant community of her childhood. She soon learned passable Russian. She soon felt at home.

She was so at home that by her second year (during and after such events as: giving an emotional birthday toast; laughing at a horserad-

---

3. Heller, Matthew. "Cold Mornings." *Peace Corps: The Great Adventure*. Washington D.C.: U.S. Peace Corps, 1997. pp 97–100.

ish/penis joke; and/or helping to chop cucumbers into perfect one-centimeter cubes), she was often paid what she took as a compliment of the highest order: "*Ty nash.*" Literally, "*You ours.*" Figuratively, "*You are one of us.*"

In the author's mind, being *theirs* brought her closer to her original blueprint—vaguely ethnic female person who reveled in fast conversation, an outrageous shade of lipstick, and kissing friends on the mouth, because if you love someone, why not? Being "theirs" was embracing life with abandon and integrity. By which I mean that during that first stay in Latvia in her twenties, the author drank homemade vodka, linked arms with comrades, sang Russian folk songs into the wind, and felt, no not felt, she *knew,* in the way ethnographers ensconced in the passionate earth of their field sites *know,* that she had discovered something so precious, so stubbornly *itself,* that it would later defy her efforts at translation.

The author loved the Latvians. The Latvians loved the author. But as warming as the phrase was to hear, "*You are one of us*" remained figurative and not literal, because there was not an empirically documented *us* of which she was actually a part.

Her gap gaped.

Relevant Background Literature III: The Man

As readers have seen, in 1999, Latvia was offering up from its ravaged earth rich gifts of love to the author. It followed that there was a man. With whom she fell into it. By "it," you know what the author means. Please don't make her say it.

An archival study of the author's early courtship with the man was conducted and revealed:

(a) notes penned in a mix of Latvian (Roman, Indo-European), Russian (Cyrillic, Slavic), and English (mostly Beatles lyrics) on thin napkins from the town's one pizza joint (as they passed the pen back and forth across the table, their fingers touched);

(b) an email to the author's best friend that described romantic walks under the shadow of the pulsing red Geiger counter in what used to be Lenin Square, in which the author (young, insensitive, forgive her please as I am trying to do) wrote, "We are so in love, we are glowing";

(c) a photograph of the author nestled into the man's shoulder, a plate of potato dumplings on a coffee table in front of them (her face radiated the superior satisfaction of the cat that got the cream; there was also perhaps joy, but that is difficult to make out from the vantage point of the author, so let the more qualified, limited statement stand: the girl's/woman's cheeks were flushed full of beautiful words).

In conclusion, when in 2001 the author waved goodbye from the bus window at the friends—no, by then they were family—who had come to see her off (*Olga, Ilona, Alla, Alexei, Oleg, Galina, Ja vas ljublu!*), she had sustainably developed. She had also met the person whom she would marry, with whom she would have the aforementioned child, and whom she would subsequently divorce.

That is, she thought the gap was filled, but it wasn't. That is why there are more words.

Theoretical Framework

The plan for the present research was developed: thirteen years after the author waved goodbye from the bus window (see above); twelve years after she took a day off of work from her post-Peace-Corps job as an elementary school teacher in Dallas, Texas to go to city hall and say those two words that she is currently finding it difficult to type; five years after she submitted to a scalpel and birthed a daughter; three years after the man attached to the face that she kissed that day she took off of work misplaced his ring and blamed her for it; one year after the author threw an official divorce party that she catered with expensive cheese and to which she wore consignment-store gold Guess heels and a smoking hot aquamarine spandex dress.[4] The author is just sayin'.

Popular accounts, including that of the author's therapist and dwindling circle of friends, have suggested various rationales for the project, including: a) to unnecessarily stoke nostalgia and b) to self destruct. As the author's mother put it, *it just never ends, does it?*

---

4. The dress was borrowed from her best friend's sister, but never returned. The author sometimes still slips it on for certain celebratory occasions, for example when Camila Cabello's Havana comes on the radio.

This article, however, holds tight to the premise that these popular accounts are bunk. In fact, this article's knuckles are white from gripping this premise. The purpose of this project, as stated in the introduction, was *fieldwork,* which will be examined here empirically, using the three theoretical frames described below.

Theoretical Frame One: Academic

By "academic theoretical frame," the author means that she alchemized scholarly energy and post-divorce despair in the cauldron of her university-issued laptop and sent the result to various funding agencies (see *tenure clock/ticking bomb* above).

The grant looked something like this, summarized here for the sake of brevity and dramatized here for the sake of fun:

"Brains are being drained!" said the prime minister.

"It's a demographic disaster!" said the economists.

"What is to be done?" cried the teachers, those tireless stewards of the young.

"Never fear!" said the "I" that is the academic hero of all successful grant applications. "I will do some research!"

And then, trembling at her own intellectual audacity, she typed the research question:

Might left-behind family members have something to gain from loved ones' departures?

And then, sweating from the forehead but betraying only the slightest hint of desperation, she proposed a potential answer:

This project hypothesizes that left-behind family members are learning new digital writing skills to stay close when loved ones are far.

And then she threw caution to the wind:

Writing, this project will show, reconfigures family relationships across distance.

Writing, the author prayed but did not commit to words, *would heal.* She compiled letters thick with citations, pithy statements of urgent implications, and careful budget calculations. She uttered a ritual incantation and sprayed the screen with drops of blood squeezed from a fresh paper cut before she hit submit.

Theoretical Frame Two: The Children

She paid no less writerly attention to the email to her ex-husband requesting permission to take their daughter abroad. He allowed her (then prohibited, then allowed her again) five weeks—not nearly enough for full-on ethnographic research, but just enough for her to almost complete the thirty oral history interviews she had promised in her grant (see above).

For the purposes of the current study, we can call this the "work-life balance" theoretical frame. Then we can laugh the kind of laugh that goes on too long and begins to frighten the children.

Theoretical Frame Three: Cinematic

Theoretical Frame Three emerged only after a fourth round of increasingly tiresome data analysis.[5],[4] This recursive process led the author to name frame three, "the cinematic frame." "Cinematic" accounts for the author's quietly abusive internal movie director who seemed hellbent on propelling her into increasingly painful personal situations for no other good reason than to increase dramatic tension. He (such directors are always a *he*) then hurled her towards resolution, but not before rolling the credits, because if there isn't someone to credit, there isn't someone blame, and if there isn't someone to blame, words and meanings cease to correspond, which puts the author right back in those second-hand Ferramagos, mutely grinding up against a stranger (see above). Readers should note that the author had already worn her heels to stubs.

> *In 2014, newly divorced and accompanied by her five-year-old daughter, the author returned to the former Soviet country of Latvia, where 15 years earlier as a Peace Corps Volunteer, she met her (ex) husband. She planned the trip to carry out anthropological field research that would secure her position as a tenured professor. But really, unmoored from the immigrant community of her upbringing and wrecked from her divorce, she was crossing languages and cultures in search of home. With her ex threatening to sue for custody from abroad, her daughter and herself*

---

5. See Appendix C for money spent in therapy from 2011–2016; see Appendix D for a chart of which friends, by geographical location and length of friendship, tired of hearing his name; see also "Hindsight is 20-20" (*Quarterly Journal of Mid-Life Regrets*, forthcoming for readers under 40).

increasingly at odds, and time running out on her research, this moving film reveals how one woman unraveled the threads of her failed marriage, ultimately creating a home with the tools of the anthropologist: unearthing and writing the past.

In frame three, the author dreamed a cinematic dream, picturing fieldwork in a vibrant glow made radiant by the lengthy days of the Latvian summer and slightly uncomfortable by the mosquito-infested Soviet sympathetic region she and her daughter would be inhabiting. She would dig through the wreckage of her marriage, survey the aftermath, sort the evidence, and draw the conclusions that might help her sleep at night. And she would do it in Russian. As savvy readers have likely surmised, due to certain emotional traumas incurred in childhood (in perpetual press), she also hoped for a gold star. As the savviest of readers have also likely surmised, in this theoretical frame, the author looks like Julia Roberts in *Eat, Pray, Love.*

METHODOLOGY

It is recommended that researchers attempting to replicate the present study do not deviate from the methodology the author employed, presented here in the second-person-imperative. On this grammatical choice, please humor the author. As is perhaps already clear, she likes the illusion of control.

1. *Attain appropriate funding*: They could not refuse you. You witched them with your words.

2. *Gather materials:* Pack dietary supplements, a stuffed bunny, a laptop, and an inflatable booster seat. No one uses a booster seat in Latvia, but compile photographic evidence in case your ex decides to paint you as unfit in court.

3. *Arrive:* Hug old friends. Dust off the Russian you have been storing in the cellar underneath your diaphragm. Stutter it out. Begin to feel something like the person you used to be. Eat *borscht.* Watch your daughter spit hers into her hand.

4. *Interview someone:* Occupy your daughter with: a) the educationally valuable game of popping bubbles on your iPhone; b) a face-sized plate of chocolate pudding; and c) a bribe involving

knock-off Beanie-Boo stuffed animals, sold at the bazaar for four Euros each. When, despite your three-pronged plan, your daughter interrupts you in the middle of a particularly productive follow-up question to show you how many bubbles she has popped, remember the women's meditation class you took in the aftermath of your ex-husband's affairs. Breathe.

5. *Ensure validity:* Repeat Step Four twenty-seven times. Worry that you will never complete the thirty interviews you promised in your grant (see above).

6. *Account for historical context:* In a quiet hour or two or three, have your daughter help you cut up a piece of paper into irregularly shaped bits. On a smooth surface, push the bits together. Explain the Soviet Union. Pull the bits apart. Explain Independence. Push them in a different direction. Explain the European Union. Wonder at your five-year-old's fascination with the dissolution of previously stable governing bodies. Despite being an English professor, fail to grasp the obvious metaphor.

7. *Wait for insight:* During the all-night midsummer festival, open your mouth and sing the traditional Latvian song about the reed that sways but does not break. Then run barefoot over the freshly dewed grass, because it means luck and magic. Sleep briefly and wake in your friends' cozy *dacha* to find *blini* with fresh jam for breakfast. Hold your baby close. He can't get her here.

8. *Wrap up the study*: Take the train back to the capital. Look at your daughter's face. There is a lollipop in her mouth at a rakish angle, her eyes squint into the sun, and her backpack is akimbo. Run a hand over her curls, and watch her smile up at you, revealing a gap where a tooth used to be.

FINDINGS

In things almost come together. I hope you see what I mean.

Finding one:

My daughter's curly hair flying as we run, holding hands, to the shaky red tram on our way to an interview, where I occupy her with chocolates, and where she interrupts to perform for my interviewee her new ability to decode Cyrillic. "*Umnitsa,*" what a clever one, the interviewee responds.

Finding two:

The rageful face of my Latvian host mother, disgusted with my divorce (think of your daughter, not your career!) and with my reluctance to force feed my daughter soup (you'll cry when she's dead!), and the fear that bleeds me for a week, because my ersatz mother might be right on one or both counts and more than that I can't afford to lose more family, ersatz or not.

Finding three:

My stained red backpack, stuffed with digital recorders, consent forms, crayons, a child's graphic novel written from the perspective of a mystery-solving mouse, and staling bits of those farmer's cheese pastries.

Finding four:

My daughter won't stop vomiting, won't stop, how many times this hour, and I neglected to purchase travel health insurance, emphasis on neglect, negligence, not worthy of a child, too career-oriented, too scatter-brained, should have stayed married, stayed in the US, stayed in my place, stayed in the kitchen, stayed under a rock, I'll cry when she's dead. And then a friend makes a house call, makes her voice soft, gifts us her stethoscope, and my daughter stops vomiting. *I might like to be a doctor,* my daughter tells us, eyes brown, clear, blessedly bright. *Or a dancer.*

Finding five:

In the standing-room only but silent tram, because Latvians don't speak much or loudly on trams, my daughter's high clear American voice, "But Mommy, what was the Soviet Union? But what *was* it?" And I explain again, despite the judging or curious eyes of our fellow passengers, at whom I stare back, steely. And then a carefully dressed elderly lady, gem green hat, ventures "*Vy anglichani?*" *Are you English? My daughter is there.* And I think of unions and disunions. I do not think of reunions. I am an empirical researcher, after all, and not some kind of methodological floozy who gets her kicks from flirting with fantasy.

Finding six:

I am longer "*nash.*" I have come apart. Have imperfectly reassembled. Though my younger self continues to peek out at me from behind corners. Open-faced. Game. Fresh.

Finding seven:

My ex-box blinks red, he wants her, would take her, has the right, and I think my chest will burst forth from my throat in a rain of holy fire, and my head is clanging loud,

Finding eight:

but then some time later it becomes quiet and still. He has vanished to Austria, or perhaps to Spain, but maybe to Brazil, and it turns out he doesn't want her/me/us after all, turns out the pronouns do not agree, not with the appropriate verb, nor with each other, which leaves us a family of two plus a phantom limb in the shape of a man my daughter calls dad, a figure so ghostly that Dane County Child Support would later suspect I fabricated him,

Finding nine:

and maybe I did. While in Latvia, my daughter and I often walk past the courtyard where my ex and I first kissed, but I let the landmark stand without annotation. Except sometimes I grunt. Nothing more.

Limitations of Study

Nine findings are too many, and I ask readers' forgiveness for this unruly number. Intractable, recalcitrant, ornery, my findings refused to be cowed by the hostile adjectives I was compelled to use to describe them. They balked at my efforts to wrangle them into a single comprehensive theory, a theory that appeared fleetingly in my dreams, bright and shiny and neat as a marble, but which in the end eluded the daytime clarity of print.

I wish it were otherwise, but no unifying concept was developed. There were crystals, but no crystallization. By which I mean the light refracted, but did not reflect.

To this day, my findings continue to run amok, although occasionally I manage to lure one or two in from the fort they are making in the backyard with the promise of cookies and milk, which sometimes allows me to take a satisfying swipe with a tissue at a crusty nose before they wriggle from my grasp and, God love them, tumble back out into the wild, leaving my countertops smudged with the grease from their fingers.

Discussion

My daughter and I stroll the banks of the Daugava river, picking flowers and skipping stones, the same banks my ex-husband and I strolled fifteen years earlier, the same river that leads out to the Baltic sea, out into the West, where so many Latvians, once locked into the Soviet Union, have fled, leaving family members behind.

They gaze towards their homes, the contents of which have shifted.

This shifting—it makes me wax geologic, as in tectonic plates, as in earthquakes, or perhaps less abruptly but no less dramatically, as in continental drift.

Conclusion

Did writing suture the traumatized terrain? This was my question and here is your answer.

One time, long ago, before the author's ex became deadbeat (accent on "beat," beat on the beat, for he lives still, just absently, not to be confused with *beets,* see *borscht* above, and not to be confused with *bleat,* which are the noises he sometimes makes from afar), the author's daughter was at his house. The author and her daughter were Skyping. The daughter asked to do a puzzle. So the author coached her through the screen. *The edges first,* the author said. *You want to have a frame.* The daughter looked down, and as she did her downy eyelashes curled up, and as they did the author moved to wipe a lock of hair from the daughter's face, and as she did the author was shocked to knock her knuckles not against glowing warm flesh but instead against glowing cold pane.

In that moment, the daughter existed only in pixels.

Another time, just yesterday in fact, the daughter existed in sticky hands, sweaty scalp, that breathless flush from the outside, and her life and blood and body were in the orbit of the author's own.

They circled each other, these two earthly bodies, generating heat, creating their cosmos. The author taught the daughter the word "matriarchy" along with other words, including the precise anatomical terms for all her parts. The author and her daughter laughed but were also quite serious, for their lives were not footnotes to forget.

In conclusion, this study has examined the keening associated with the fraying of family ties. This study has concluded that yes, keening. This study has concluded.

Implications

But there is more. The more is this: The distant or close hum of the fieldworkers, the mothers, knitting their stories together. Click click tap. Click click tap. Ity tap.

Supplemental Material

Part I: Reflection on the Origins of the Article

This piece grew out of an attempt to create a coherent narrative from a profoundly chaotic moment in my life when I was pursuing tenure, recovering from a divorce, trying to raise my child without doing too much lasting damage, and conducting international fieldwork. I started writing bits and pieces of this article therapeutically. I shared parts of it with my writing group and also workshopped parts of it in creative writing classes I attended. It was only after years of fiddling with it and a conversation with memoirist Gail Konop that I came to embrace the format of a social scientific research report. That tight structure freed me. It was a container for the personal contradictions and wild energy that characterized that time period in my life.

Part II: Description of Research Methods, Findings, and/or Pedagogical Impact

This essay describes the same fieldwork I conducted for my forthcoming academic book (*Writing for Love and Money: How Migration Drives Literacy Learning in Transnational Families,* Oxford University Press), but from a narrative perspective. My methodological goal was to move beyond the "positionality statement" in qualitative research, to address what Ralph Cintrón calls the "autobiographical questions" that animate fieldwork, and which anthropologists such as Ruth Behar, Alma Gottlieb, and others have discussed. In essence, the question animating both the academic book and this excerpt of my memoir was the same: *What happens when families separate?* And the answer was the same, too! *Writing.* But how I got there was different. Instead of constructing a narrative from participants' experiences as I did in the academic book, in this essay I was trying (and as I hope the essay shows failing) to construct a narrative of my own. I wanted to lay bare the parts of academic life that exceed the boundaries of generic conventions, and to perform the pain and humor in trying to make them fit.

Part III: Discussion Questions

1. How is genre both constricting and liberating in this piece?

2. If you had to define fieldwork based on this piece, how would you define it? What kinds of knowledge construction and/or artistic production and/or community engagement does your definition make possible and/or foreclose?

3. What autobiographical questions animate your teaching and/or research?

About the Authors

Elizabeth G. Allan is associate professor of Writing and Rhetoric at Oakland University, where she teaches ethnography, history of rhetoric, writing center studies, literacy studies, and first-year writing. Her research interests include rhetorical ethnography, multimodal rhetorics in design disciplines, writing pedagogy, assessment, and the scholarship of teaching and learning (SoTL).

Janine Butler is an Assistant Professor at the National Technical Institute for the Deaf, a college of Rochester Institute of Technology, where she teaches writing courses. Her writing has appeared in *Kairos*, *Composition Studies*, *Rhetoric Review*, and *Composition Forum*. She can be contacted at jmbdls@rit.edu.

Eileen Kogl Camfield has faculty appointments in the Writing Studies Program and the Center for Engaged Teaching and Learning at the University of California in Merced where she teaches courses in pedagogy and supports WiD/WAC through faculty development. Her research interests include writing self-efficacy development, student resilience, and mindful assessment.

Cati V. de los Ríos is an assistant professor in the School of Education at University of California, Davis. She was a public school teacher in Massachusetts and California and holds a PhD in English Education from Teachers College, Columbia University. Her research explores adolescent literacies, translanguaging, and youth community engagement.

John Gagnon is an Assistant Professor in the Department of English at the University of Hawaii at Mānoa. He is a cultural rhetorician interested in human rights and the rhetorical framing of human rights issues. He teaches courses in composition studies, rhetorical theory and history, and argumentation.

Romeo García is Assistant Professor of Writing and Rhetoric at the University of Utah. His research interests include critical theory, critical rhetoric, and de-colonial studies. García has published in the Writing Center Journal, Community Literacy Journal, and Journal of Hispanic Higher Education. He is the co-editor (with Damián Baca) of *Rhetorics Elsewhere and Otherwise: Contested Modernities, Decolonial Vision* published by Studies in Writing and Rhetoric.

Lara Killick is an Assistant Professor in the department of Kinesiology and Health Promotion at California Polytechnic University, Pomona where she teaches courses in the sociology of health promotion and sport. Her research interests include the efficacy of youth participatory action methodologies, social injustices in sport and health disparities.

Ruth Lewis is a Research Fellow at University of Glasgow where she is involved in social science studies aiming to improve health and well-being among young people and communities. Ruth was previously a Visiting Assistant Professor in the Sociology Department at University of the Pacific.

Maria Novotny is an Assistant Professor in the Department of English at the University of Wisconsin-Milwaukee. She is a feminist rhetorician interested in reproductive loss. As a community-engaged scholar, she co-directs The ART of Infertility. She teaches courses in technical communication, public rhetoric, and the health humanities.

Wendy Pfrenger is the Assistant Director of Pre-College Programs at the University of Mississippi. Her research has appeared in the *Journal of Basic Writing*, *Praxis: A Writing Center Journal*, and the collection *Making a Positive Impact in Rural Places: Change Agency in the Context of School-University-Community Collaboration*.

Allison (Alice) Ragland is a graduate teaching associate at The Ohio State University in the College of Education and Human Ecology. Her research interests include neoliberalism in urban education, Black radical thought, critical pedagogy, and Afro-pessimism.

Elaine Richardson is professor of literacy studies, Department of Teaching and Learning, in the College of Education and Human Ecology at The Ohio State University. Her research interests include the liberatory literacy, language, and discourse practices of people of the African Diaspora, most intimately those of Americans and Jamaicans of Black African descent.

David Riche is a Teaching Assistant Professor in the University Writing Program at the University of Denver. His teaching and scholarly interests center around rhetorical vulnerability, definitions of rhetoric, multimodal composition, and the study of tabletop games.

Christina Saidy is an associate professor of English at Arizona State University whose research focuses on writing and writing transitions with secondary students, teachers in professional development groups, and students entering college. Christina's work has appeared in journals such as *English Journal, College Composition and Communication, WPA,* and *TETYC.*

Kate Seltzer is an assistant professor of Bilingual/TESOL Education at Rowan University, where she teaches pre- and in-service teachers of bilingual students. She is the co-author of the recent book, *The Translanguaging Classroom: Leveraging Student Bilingualism for Learning* as well as several other journal articles and book chapters on translanguaging in schools.

Shari J. Stenberg is professor of English and Women's and Gender Studies at the University of Nebraska-Lincoln, where she teaches courses on writing, pedagogy and feminist rhetorics. Her most recent book is *Repurposing Composition: Feminist Interventions for a Neoliberal Age* (Utah State UP). Her writing has appeared in *CCC, College English, Composition Studies,* and *Pedagogy.*

Pamela Takayoshi is Professor of English at Kent State University. Her work includes several edited collections (the most recent one co-edited with Patrick Thomas: *Literacy in Practice: Writing in Public, Private, and Working Lives)* and articles in numerous scholarly journals.

Kate Vieira is associate professor and the Susan J. Cellmer Distinguished Chair in Literacy in the School of Education at the University of Wisconsin, Madison. She is the author of *American by Paper* (University of Minnesota Press, 2016) and *Writing for Love and Money* (Oxford University Press, forthcoming).

Anthony Warnke and Kirsten Higgins teach writing at Green River College in Auburn, Washington. At Green River, they have led equity-focused reforms of developmental English. Their work has appeared in, or is forthcoming from, *Teaching English in the Two-Year College, Basic Writing e-journal,* and several edited collections.

CPSIA information can be obtained
at www.ICGtesting.com
Printed in the USA
FFHW021931181019
55638517-61466FF

9 781643 170640